# Powers and Principles

# Powers and Principles

*International Leadership in a Shrinking World*

Edited by
Michael Schiffer and
David Shorr

LEXINGTON BOOKS

A division of
ROWMAN & LITTLEFIELD PUBLISHERS, INC.
Lanham • Boulder • New York • Toronto • Plymouth, UK

LEXINGTON BOOKS

A division of Rowman & Littlefield Publishers, Inc.
A wholly owned subsidiary of The Rowman & Littlefield Publishing Group, Inc.
4501 Forbes Boulevard, Suite 200
Lanham, MD 20706

Estover Road
Plymouth PL6 7PY
United Kingdom

British Library Cataloguing in Publication Information Available

**Library of Congress Cataloging-in-Publication Data**

Powers and principles : international leadership in a shrinking world / edited by Michael
Schiffer and David Shorr.
    p. cm.
  Includes index.
  Part of the Stanley Foundation's powers and principles project.
    ISBN 978-0-7391-3543-3 (cloth : alk. paper) — ISBN 978-0-7391-3544-0 (pbk. : alk.
paper) — ISBN 978-0-7391-3545-7 (electronic)
  1. United States—Foreign relations—21st century. 2. International relations. 3.
World politics—21st century. I. Schiffer, Michael, 1965– II. Shorr, David. III. Stanley
Foundation.
  JZ1480.P67 2009
  327.73—dc22                                                    2009003117

Printed in the United States of America


∞™ The paper used in this publication meets the minimum requirements of American
National Standard for Information Sciences—Permanence of Paper for Printed Library
Materials, ANSI/NISO Z39.48-1992.

# Contents

Acknowledgments     vii

Introduction     1

Part 1     Old Guard

A Stake in the System:
Redefining American Leadership     11
*Suzanne Nossel and David Shorr*
*Reaction by Nikolas Gvosdev*

Japan: Leading or Losing the Way Toward
Responsible Stakeholdership?     45
*Steven Clemons and Weston S. Konishi*
*Reaction by Masaru Tamamoto*

Rue de la Loi: The Global Ambition of the
European Project     73
*Ronald D. Asmus and Tod Lindberg*
*Reaction by Robert Cooper*

Part 2     Challengers

A Rising China's Rising Responsibilities     99
*Bates Gill and Michael Schiffer*
*Reaction by Wu Xinbo*

India: The Ultimate Test of
Free-Market Democracy 125
    *Barbara Crossette and George Perkovich*
*Reaction by C. Raja Mohan*

Russia's Place in an Unsettled Order:
Calculations in the Kremlin 165
    *Andrew Kuchins and Richard Weitz*
*Reaction by Dmitri Trenin*

Part 3    Bellwethers

Turkey's Identity and Strategy: A Game of
Three-Dimensional Chess 197
    *Zeyno Baran and Ian O. Lesser*
*Reaction by Hüseyin Bağci*

Brazil's Candidacy for Major Power Status 225
    *Paulo Roberto de Almeida and Miguel Diaz*
*Reaction by Georges D. Landau*

Part 4    Square Pegs

South Africa: From Beacon of Hope to
Rogue Democracy? 259
    *Pauline H. Baker and Princeton N. Lyman*
*Reaction by Khehla Shubane*

Refashioning Iran's International Role 295
    *Suzanne Maloney and Ray Takeyh*
*Reaction by Omid Memarian*

Laggards on Responsibility: The Oil Majors 321
    *Susan Ariel Aaronson and David Deese*
*Reaction by Edward C. Chow*

Index 349

About the Contributors 361

~

# Acknowledgments

We undertook this project in the belief that we had an interesting question—what paths could different international powers take toward model international citizenship—and that the question might elicit interesting ideas from capable analysts. It is quite gratifying when a hunch plays out, but we could hardly have hoped for a better set of expert participants. Our first thanks go to the thirty-one colleagues who joined us in this venture; we are extremely grateful for the time, effort, and insight that they contributed.

Any venture in which thirty-three writers draft, mutually review, and then revise material for publication is bound to be an organizational challenge. We were fortunate to have our colleague Veronica Tessler, who kept everything coordinated and on track to a successful conclusion.

The Stanley Foundation is the rare sort of place that you can hatch an ambitious idea during the drive to work one day and then see it come to fruition. We are deeply appreciative of the investment that the foundation made in this initiative and the help from colleagues to ensure its success—especially Michael Kraig and Jeff Martin, who read and commented on the draft chapters; Matt Martin, for helping David with arms control issues for his chapter; and Amy Bakke, who helped with design and production. For this resulting book, we thank Joseph Parry of Lexington Books for making its publication possible.

We also benefited from the input and feedback of a number of colleagues who took part in discussion sessions related to the project, including Colin Bradford, James Clad, Craig Cohen, Stuart Eizenstat, Robert Herman, Michael Kergin, Charles Kupchan, Ellen Laipson, Robert Litwak, James Mann, Terry Markin, Phillip Saunders, Kori Schake, James Schear, David Shambaugh, Richard Soloman, Bruce Stokes, and Jane Stromseth.

~

# Introduction

Ever since then–Deputy Secretary of State Robert Zoellick first urged Chinese leaders to make their nation a "responsible stakeholder" in the international system, the term has been bandied more than it has been unpacked. Given the context in which it was coined, it was bound to be viewed as a demand placed by an established power on an emerging one. Yet there is nothing inherent in the concept that presumes a global hegemon or an immutable set of values. Isn't it a good thing for a nation to help maintain a functioning international system? Shouldn't every member of the world community strive to be a responsible stakeholder?

Indeed, this is the first premise of the Stanley Foundation's Powers and Principles project: that the very idea of stakeholdership, and perhaps the shape of the international order itself, could be clarified by exploring what it demands of various nations. What would the international system look like if the duty of global stewardship were a shared one, with full participation by all the major powers? Would the norms and institutions that guide the community be notably different? What roles would upstanding members be expected—indeed, required—play? Would the system be perceived as less skewed toward a privileged few?

As an organization committed not only to a strong rules-based global order, but also to collective inquiry about how it can be built, the Stanley Foundation was ideally suited to draw specialists together to plumb this question. We sought colleagues to help put flesh on the conceptual bones of *responsible stakeholdership* by examining the issues that confront different global and regional powers in their stance toward international norms—a bottom-up perspective from the stakeholders themselves.

Contributing writers were asked to describe the paths that nine powerful nations, a regional union of twenty-seven states, and a multinational corporation could take as constructive stakeholders in a strengthened rules-based order. For each case, the writers discuss how their given country might, in the next decade, deal with the internal and external challenges posed by international norms pertaining to the global economy, domestic governance and society, and global and regional security.

## Lofty, but Not Too

Unlike most crystal-ball projects that think tanks conduct, we did not ask participants to rate the probability of their scenarios or filter them through any test beyond mere plausibility. This exercise was about a particular global future—an international community with broad support for norms—and how it might take shape. While interdependence and the necessity of international cooperation are increasingly recognized even by many of the most hard-nosed, *Powers and Principles* was focused on an admittedly lofty vision. It was vital, therefore, to go beyond the bromides of multilateralism to identify the specific actions and developments that would lead to a greater degree of international solidarity.

This delicate balance between high-minded aspirations for the world and measured judgment about interests and the related practicalities was both the animating tension of the project and the criterion for selection of its participants. Naturally, all of the writers were recruited for their deep knowledge of the country about which they would be writing. Beyond that, though, participants were required to accept the premise that the nations and leaders at the focus of their given country could plausibly steer policy and politics toward service to the greater global good.

A particular kind of optimism is presumed and woven through the chapters. The contributors to this volume were really "hired," though, to flesh out the optimistic future. The substance of these chapters had to be politically salient at two levels. If the project had looked at all international norms for all countries, it would have overshot the mark and offered scant insight into the workings of the rules-based order. So the first task of the writers was to determine which norms are (or belong) on the leadership agenda for their focus country—think of them as the unresolved business between the nation and the world community. This is a question of what issues stand or might arise between that country and membership in good standing in the international system.

Naturally, analysts taking part also had to consider the political salience of a nation's response to these unresolved normative questions. Again, this would have been a fairly dull, and inaccurate, enterprise if we had asked the writers for a uniform set of scenarios. Each country comes with its own characteristic geostrategic position, economy, society, history, and political system and culture. Those factors all weigh into leaders' calibration of their interests, international posture, and foreign policy; we asked thirty-three top specialists to explain precisely how.

Although inevitably we expect some readers of this volume to question why a certain country was included or another excluded, the cases included here were selected as powers that, in different ways and in different magnitudes, will all likely be critical for the emerging global order. The organizers of the initiative asked themselves which ten powers will determine the health and durability of the order. The choices were not obvious, but in the end we believe that China, the United States, the European Union, India, Japan, Russia, Turkey, Iran, Brazil, and South Africa represent a critical mass for the international community. If there is rough alignment among these ten, the community should be able to surmount the formidable challenges it faces—if not, we should worry about the future of the planet. There is bound to be criticism over the candidates that didn't make the cut, and we would agree that some of those candidates would be our eleventh, twelfth, or thirteenth choices. But we drew the line at ten, and these ten seemed the most compelling.

Actually, we didn't stop at ten. As the top-ten list was being prepared, the question was raised regarding how we could reflect the growing influence of nonstate actors in the international system. The idea of including a stand-in for nonstate actors was intriguing, particularly to look at how multinational corporations respond to international norms and the impact of their own operations. The oil and gas industry posed the most interesting, and widest, set of issues. While options were considered for particular energy companies, ultimately it seemed best to deal with the issues generically rather than for a specific case.

Before getting fully underway, the project held a session to focus on the criteria of responsible stakeholdership. Participating authors would naturally need substantive points of reference as touchstones for their analysis. Which leads back to the question: Whose rules-based order is it any way? Stakeholdership was never viewed as an all-or-nothing proposition. Indeed, the interplay between different types of norms—e.g., peace and security versus democracy and domestic governance—was one of the most interesting features of the inquiry. Yet the designers of the project felt compelled to acknowledge our Western (primarily American) liberal internationalist bias. Therefore we decided to pair each chapter with a shorter comment by an expert from the country itself.

The project organizers/editors confess to noteworthy ambivalence even within the Western liberal bias that we share. We believe that, in broad terms, the core principles of the liberal international order are fundamentally sound. Yet having focused in this and other work on the tectonic shifts taking place under our very feet, we are acutely aware of the need for a revision of the current order, particularly to give greater pride of authorship and ownership to emerging powers.

## The Problem of Categories

Because of this ambivalence, we stress that the ordering and grouping of this volume's chapters was self-conscious and should not be misunderstood. The chapters are grouped according to the relationship of their subject toward the existing (i.e., post–World War II) international order. This collection, and our own respective contributions to it, contains many value judgments of different kinds, but the grouping labels for the book sections are intended to be value-neutral.

The United States, European Union (and European Community previously), and Japan are all established global powers under the current order. Notwithstanding recent American unilateralism, they are all aligned with the liberal order and can only be considered status quo powers. The postwar order or post–Cold War order poses problems for China, India, and Russia—and vice versa. These key powers, two clearly on the upswing (at least as things stand in 2008) and one with a more complicated relationship to traditional measures of power, are neither fully vested stakeholders nor renegades. If one were forced to pick three countries on which future peace, prosperity, and stability hinge, it would certainly be these. If they become full-fledged responsible stakeholders the order would be immeasurably strengthened. But if they are to become full-fledged responsible stakeholders, they will have a say in the terms of stakeholdership. China, India, and Russia may or may not challenge the established major powers, but they will unquestionably be challengers to the international order.

As the authors of the Turkey and Brazil chapters demonstrate, these important emerging powers could contribute a great deal to a strengthened rules-based order. At the same time, both countries confront cross-pressures that will make their next decade anything but an assured glide path. Because they are grappling for the first time with the responsibilities of global power and influence, and their orientation is not yet set, they strike us as interesting bellwethers for the future health of the order.

The final category is a variety pack, and consciously so. The Republic of South Africa and the Islamic Republic of Iran have followed quite different paths of political and economic development. Each in its way, though, has a deep-seated and unresolved ambivalence toward the liberal order and the industrialized powers of the global north. And as our experts on corporate behavior explain, the very notion of a responsible stakeholder must be handled with great care when applied to private oil companies. Again, these categories are determined purely by the nature of the relationship between the given actor and the international system as a whole, and the categorization of these quite different entities as "square pegs" is based on the fact that they are not easily pigeonholed into other categories.

It should also be noted that the chapters and reactions were written and released on a rolling basis. Consequently, some of the chapters were finalized in mid-2008, while others were completed toward year's end. This meant that the different pieces straddled such pivotal events as the Russian invasion of Georgia, the global financial meltdown, wide swings in oil prices, and the U.S. presidential election (though we have updated all chapters to reflect that U.S. policy will be made by the Obama administration).

At root, each chapter is an assessment of what steps toward greater international common cause are politically possible (and impossible)—with a description of the associated pressures and incentives. The chapters point toward which new stances or orientations a nation would adopt as it places increasing priority on the norms of the international order. They examine how the national interest calculations of governments reflect not only the particular needs of their country, but a shared stake in the international common good. They identify potential sticking points or tensions between national perspectives and the order as it now stands. And, given the project's emphasis on a healthy world community, they look at the public goods of the global order, and how they might be generated or preserved.

## Issues and Challenges

By comparing the results for eleven key global players, we can identify the areas of convergence and divergence in the normative outlooks of powers that are bound to shape the emerging twenty-first-century international community. Think of the chapters, taken together, as a sort of mapping exercise offering a glimpse at the broad contours of a new global order still yet coming into focus. We can see how the key powers might approach the core challenges for a sustainable and enduring international community—their mixes of interests, perspectives, and approaches to the rule of law and legitimacy of the use of force, nonproliferation, and energy and climate change. Of course the first questions for any power's stance toward a rules-based order are its attitude regarding rules themselves and, given the role military force plays in international relations, its views on the use of force. The chapters show notable variation on these questions. According to Ronald D. Asmus and Tod Lindberg's view of the European Union, Europe's aspiration for a world of law—rights-regarding, liberal, and democratic—"extends well beyond the continent," with the European Union as a beacon and benchmark for the world. Yet Andrew Kuchins and Richard Weitz remark about Russia that "rather than 'norms' and 'public goods,' Russian leaders and political analysts frame Russia's terms of international cooperation as realpolitik bargains and 'trade-offs' of interests."

Likewise, the chapters offer different perspectives, ranging across the spectrum, on the legitimacy of the use of force to resolve territorial disputes. For some of the powers, views are clearly converging. Europe, for example, holds borders to be sacrosanct, although it is far more willing to consider the use of force in the context of peacekeeping and humanitarian assistance. And Bates Gill and Michael Schiffer note that China, which has been embroiled in territorial and sovereignty disputes with many of its neighbors and has used military force to push their claims on numerous occasions, can be seen in the last fifteen years to be "taking significant steps to resolve disputes peacefully, and to shelve others indefinitely." Convergence is far from complete, however, as the Kuchins-Weitz chapter highlights that "responsible stakeholdership would restrain Moscow from adding further provocation and ceasing threats to retaliate by supporting separatist aspirations in other breakaway regions, such as Abkhazia and South Ossetia in Georgia."

A second key marker of responsible stakeholdership that arose in many of the chapters relates to the norm of nuclear nonproliferation where, again, fissures can be seen in the different approaches of major powers—with domestic politics one of the key drivers. As Suzanne Nossel and David Shorr's chapter on the United States notes, "Restoring the norm of nonproliferation is still possible, but complacency and the passage of time combine to make it increasingly difficult. A fresh and bold U.S. approach to nuclear policy and disarmament could help stem the proliferation tide, and the United States has every interest in doing so."

In their chapter on India, Barbara Crossette and George Perkovich strike an even more cautionary note, pointing out that the "multiple Indian interests in nuclear testing . . . offer a case study of how values and international events" interact with Indian politics and interest groups—i.e., domestic pressures for further nuclear testing that raise serious questions about whether India can serve as a paragon of nonproliferation. Gill and Schiffer point toward an international political test of China's willingness to be an active participant rather than standing on the sidelines: "Potential future mileposts might include a continued reduction of its sensitive exports to such countries as Iran, Pakistan, and North Korea. China could exert greater pressure on Iran to fully comply with demands of the international community regarding its nuclear capabilities and intentions. China could also demonstrate greater concern over its long-standing ally, Pakistan, and the safety and security of that country's nuclear programs and materials."

Energy security and climate change is another substantive area where the chapters offer a window into the varied mix of needs, interests, and perspectives that will need to be satisfied in order for the institutions for global governance to tackle this challenge. As Kuchins and Weitz note, for example, "Russian efforts to dominate transport infrastructure of gas and oil from Russia and the former Soviet Union to European and Asian markets have also sparked outcries in Europe and the United States. Russia views efforts to develop alternative pipeline routes that bypass Russia as overtly hostile. Disputes between Russia and the West over the Baku-Tblisi-Ceyhan, and more recently plans for the Nabucco and Trans-Caspian pipelines, have been sharp."

And Nossel and Shorr judge that "to be seen to offer leadership befitting its global stature, the United States will need to take a number of steps. The heart of the matter is a trade-off between the need for urgent action and the desire for ambitious, binding, and comprehensive limits on greenhouse gases applicable to all nations, including the world's fast-growing developing economies, mostly notably China. The United States needs to approach global climate change negotiations with an open mind, accepting the prospect of limits that are enforceable for Western countries before they are made binding on the world's largest developing economies, such as China and India."

For Brazil, Paulo Roberto de Almeida and Miguel Diaz note a mixed picture: "There is pride of place that goes with having hosted the first world environment summit in Rio de Janeiro in 1992." On the other hand, Brazil remains "a major contributor to global warming"—the burning of the Amazon (about 70 percent of which lies in Brazilian territory) makes up about half of the world's annual greenhouse emissions from deforestation, which, in turn, contributes about 20 percent of world greenhouse emissions. Yet it can clearly also play a leadership role, given that "Brazil's energy matrix is the envy of the world—drawing 47 percent from renewable resources, such as sugar cane and hydroelectric plants, and ethanol now making up 40 percent of the fuel used by light vehicles."

With the "unipolar moment" now fading (if it ever existed), and the world moving on to an era of Post–Pax Americana, the oft-remarked diffusion of power is reshaping the global order in ways that we are barely beginning to understand. It is high time for an examination of how the influences of emerging and established powers might coexist, or even combine. Many of the core concerns of this volume—the role of interests, ideals, power balances, and norms in determining the actions of nations—are classically the province of international relations theory. Yet it struck us as more appropriate in a multipolar world to focus on how these issues appear from the vantage of different world capitals, especially the domestic determinants of foreign policy. In a way, the contributing authors' essential subject is the relationship between international politics and domestic politics. Indeed, one valued academic colleague of ours described this project as an exercise in "comparative foreign policy."

Whatever subdisciplinary label one uses, we hope that we have offered a persuasive case that the impulse to virtuous behavior, while hardly irresistible, is actually a potent international political force. As we see it, this impulse is a key source of hope for the state of the world that our daughters will inherit.

# PART 1

# OLD GUARD

# A Stake in the System: Redefining American Leadership

*Suzanne Nossel and David Shorr*
*With a Reaction by Nikolas Gvosdev*

## America's Burden of Proof

Restoring the U.S. role as a bulwark of the rules-based international order is essential for four reasons. First, it is necessary to reestablish U.S. global credibility and influence in the near term. Second, this role is vital to the United States' ability to advance its policy and security interests within that order over the medium and long terms. Third, U.S. reengagement is critical to the continued strength and evolution of the international order itself. Fourth, the vitality and relevance of the international order is—in turn—the most durable structural basis on which the United States can promote its interests and values globally.

Until recent years, the U.S. status as a responsible stakeholder in the global system went mostly without question. The United States played an essential role in designing and erecting the compacts and institutions on which the international order is based and subsequently became a leading player in nearly every one. The UN Charter, the major human rights treaties, the international financial institutions, and the global trading system would not exist in their current forms had it not been for U.S. engagement and guidance.

This is not to say Washington always played by the rules. The tradition of American exceptionalism—the notion that the U.S. global position is unique and merits special prerogatives—remained strong throughout the latter half of the twentieth century, frustrating allies and critics alike. Consequently, Washington drew international criticism for failing to sign key international treaties, fulfill payment obligations to multilateral institutions, or adhere consistently to the principles that it espoused for others.

The policies of the George W. Bush administration nonetheless represented a drastic turn in U.S. position in relation to the international order. During the first half of 2001 alone, the Bush administration adopted a new posture as the president defiantly "unsigned" the Rome Statute creating the International Criminal Court, refused to sign the Kyoto Protocol on climate change, and opposed the UN agreement to curb small arms. The administration stood in fleeting solidarity with others after the September 11 attacks to strike al-Qaeda's sanctuary in Afghanistan and unite the United Nations in a series of far-reaching global measures to counter terrorism. The lead-up to the Iraq war marked another turn in the dial to a stepped-up unilateralism. The American drumbeat for war was strong enough to drown out both Iraq's cooperation with the International Atomic Energy Agency (IAEA)—half-hearted though it was—as well as the paucity of international diplomatic support for an attack. When support in the United Nations for the invasion lagged, the United States attacked anyway. The administration's articulation of the new doctrine of preventive war meant that the Iraq invasion was not seen as an isolated act but rather as an imperious attempt to reshape international law.

When the search for Iraqi nuclear weapons came up dry and the war dragged on, opinion in the Middle East—and around the globe—hardened further. Revelations of human rights abuses against terrorist suspects in custody in Iraq and in U.S.-controlled facilities reinforced perceptions that Washington had exempted itself from the rules. The protracted extrajudicial detentions at Guantanamo Bay, the revelation of secret CIA black sites, and reports of suspects being turned over to foreign governments for torture further undermined U.S. credibility.

The net result is that U.S. popularity, credibility, and influence have declined sharply. Beyond that, the very premise of U.S. leadership has come into question. A July 2007 Pew Global Attitudes survey concluded that "global distrust of American leadership is reflected in increasing disapproval of the cornerstones of U.S. foreign policy." In thirty-two out of thirty-seven countries surveyed by Pew in 2002 and/or 2003 and then again in 2007, the proportion of people expressing approval for American ideas of democracy declined, often precipitously. Another compilation of 2006–2007 surveys of international public sentiment by WorldPublicOpinion.org and the Chicago Council on Global Affairs found that "publics around the world reject the idea that the United States should play the role of preeminent world leader. Most publics say the United States plays the role of world policeman more than it should, fails to take their country's interests into account and cannot be trusted to act responsibly."[1]

Even without this credibility crisis, the rise of new powers means that no matter what it does, the United States cannot simply assume its former mantle of relatively unchallenged authority. The unipolar moment has passed. The task for Obama will be to carve for the United States a place in the emerging world order that leaves behind the baggage of the last eight years and allows Washington to regain a strong hand in shaping the order in the decades to come.

In doing so, the United States will bear the burden of proof, needing to show through its actions that it is prepared to behave as a responsible stake-holder in the global system. This will require a stance toward norms and institutions that is guided not only by self-interest, but also by a commitment to the global order itself. Without that, the United States will continue to be weighed down by the millstone of international mistrust.

Americans perceive, even if they do not fully appreciate, the challenge that awaits. In the fall of 2007, three out of four Americans believed that the United States was less respected by other countries than it used to be and that this was "a major problem."[2] This concern is reflected, for example, in the following passage from Senator John McCain's March 2008 address to the Los Angeles World Affairs Council:

> The United States cannot lead by virtue of its power alone. We must be strong politically, economically, and militarily. But we must also lead by attracting others to our cause, by demonstrating once again the virtues of freedom and democracy, by defending the rules of international civilized society and by creating the new international institutions necessary to advance the peace and freedoms we cherish.

Today, the electorate expects leaders to craft policies that are not only tough but also smart about consequences and effectiveness. A bipartisan spectrum of foreign policy specialists, for instance, now supports recalibrating counterterrorism efforts to make them more cooperative, with a new cost-benefit calculus to keep from unnecessarily arousing resentment.[3]

That said, signs of shifting attitudes do not bespeak a thorough political transformation. The new internationalism will be tempered by traditional U.S. concerns and political realities. The United States will not go as far as some allies would like in embracing the international order—membership in the International Criminal Court and multifold increases in the share of U.S. gross domestic product (GDP) allocated to governmental foreign aid are unlikely to happen, at least right away.

Because so many elements of the international order bear the United States' clear and long-standing stamp, the U.S. disavowal of norms and institutions carries special weight. The U.S. refusal to participate in the International Criminal Court or the Kyoto Treaty are perceived not as the neutral distancing of a Switzerland or Norway but rather as the rebuff of a presumptive insider.

As the United States repairs the damage, it will not have free rein to be a skeptical observer or a leery critic. Because of U.S. economic and political influence, it must reposition itself near the center of global conflict resolution and institution-building initiatives to be seen as anything but a deliberate spoiler. In effect, then, when it comes to the international system, the United States must be for it or against it. Put that way, of course, the choice is obvious: being part of the system allows Washington to shape the rules, to utilize international mechanisms and organs to advance policy goals, and to legitimize American actions in a way that makes them easier and less costly to carry out. For all these reasons, the reestablishment of the U.S. position as a leading pillar of the rules-based international order is critical to the attainment of long-term U.S. policy and security objectives.

The reemergence of the United States as a custodian and shaper of the international system is also critical for the system itself. It is not that U.S. participation is a formal prerequisite for the emergence of effective international institutions and norms. The International Criminal Court and the international bans on landmines, small arms, and now cluster munitions illustrate that effective multilateral initiatives no longer depend singly on Washington. Even so, on the most pressing global issues (climate change, nonproliferation, the use of force, and global trade protocols), multilateral approaches without U.S. involvement are bound to fail. It is also fair to say that given U.S. economic and military strength, its relationship to particular norms and institutions—whether positive or negative—can influence the weight and strength of those standards and organs globally. U.S. nonparticipation offers an easy excuse to other would-be recalcitrants.

Just as the U.S. absence weakens international institutions, its presence strengthens them. U.S.-led, North Atlantic Treaty Organization (NATO)–sanctioned intervention to end the Bosnian war, to provide expedited relief and aid in response to the Asian tsunami, and to put in place the protocols that underlie the functioning of the global Internet are all examples of crucial multilateral initiatives that would not have happened without U.S. leadership. U.S. ingenuity and political, technological, and economic dynamism are national assets that, if properly harnessed, can contribute to the evolution of an international system that is more responsive and effective than it would be otherwise.

The U.S. status as a stakeholder will be judged across an array of dimensions including international politics and diplomacy, peace and security, and the global economy. In each arena, U.S. behavior will be judged in the near term on the basis of whether it signals a clear break from recent unilateralist policies and indicates a new willingness to bolster global norms. Over the longer term, the United States will need to be seen not just to resume its seat at the table but to take responsibility for fundamental global challenges, to work to reinforce international rules and institutions for a fast-changing world, and to exert its leadership in a way that induces others to contribute to order building.

## Diplomacy and the Maintenance of the International Order

In the diplomatic arena, the U.S. near-term challenge is to undo the damage of recent years and reestablish American credibility as a global actor. Until trust is restored, diplomatic overtures risk being met with ongoing suspicion of American hypocrisy and self-serving motives. Once initial steps have been taken to restore U.S. credibility, the long-term challenge of demonstrating responsible stakeholder status is threefold: 1) demonstrating clear leadership on issues that the United States is uniquely positioned to help resolve; 2) being seen to uphold the evolving international order through efforts to shape and strengthen international norms and institutions that benefit the United States, rising powers, other major powers, and the developing world alike; and 3) exerting its leadership in a manner that accommodates, rather than resists, the growing role of other global powers and of international institutions.

The initial steps to restore the United States' international credibility are by now fairly obvious.[4] At the top of the agenda is to restore the U.S. record on human rights and specifically the treatment of detainees. Key measures include passing legislation forbidding torture in interrogations, eliminating secret detentions and renditions, and closing Guantanamo Bay with a commitment to the trial or release of those imprisoned there. Without these threshold measures, U.S. credibility in the arenas of human rights and the rule of law will remain tattered. Beyond undoing the most egregious abuses of the Bush years, the Obama administration will need to identify some affirmative steps that signal a new willingness to uphold international norms and institutions. There is no single formula for this, but a set of visible gestures is needed. Two possibilities are running for a seat on the UN Human Rights Council and taking steps toward greater cooperation with, and ultimate accession to, the International Criminal Court. Both steps would signal a sharp break from the recent policies and mark a turn toward participation in the rules-based order. By demonstrating willingness to take part in forums that were designed and founded by others, the United States would send an important signal that its commitment to the international order is not limited to made-in-America concepts and structures. They would also entail confronting skeptical and entrenched domestic political constituencies.

The Human Rights Council is an obvious starting point. The council, established in 2006, is a successor to the disgraced UN Human Rights Commission, which had been notorious for its anti-Israel fixation and a fox-guarding-the-henhouse membership that included many of the world's most egregious violators of rights. Thus far, the council has not proven much better. It lacks definitive criteria for membership, its substantive agenda has continued the traditional anti-Israel bias, and its response to the worst human rights crises arising during its short lifetime has been close to nil.

Even so, the council has shown flashes of potential. Human rights groups have waged successful campaigns to prevent serious abusers like Belarus and Sri Lanka from being elected as members. The council has initiated a sweeping universal review process whereby every single UN member state will periodically have its human rights practices scrutinized, thereby ensuring that even powerful governments do not get a free pass. Joining the council would not require the United States to refrain from criticizing the body, but simply to devote a few years of honest effort to see whether it can be reshaped into a credible force. Merely moving from a posture of outright rejection to one of skeptical but constructive engagement will go a long way toward resetting perceptions of U.S. behavior.

**Middle East Peace**

The United States is widely seen as a pivotal player on a number of issues on the global agenda, which will serve as tests of its commitment to the health of the international order. Fairly or not, any lack of progress in these areas is laid at Washington's door. The Middle East peace process and the stabilization of weak and failing states are two of the most prominent issues. This is not to say the international community expects, or even wants, the United States to act alone in these areas. On the contrary, constructive U.S. leadership will empower directly affected parties and engage a broad range of international actors.

Because of its staunch support of Israel, closeness to some Arab leaders, and historic mediating role, the United States is viewed as a linchpin of any durable solution to the Israeli-Palestinian conflict. Although the causes of the current impasse are manifold, the Bush administration's lack of attention to peace efforts prior to 2007 has made it easy to blame the United States for abdicating leadership in an arena where no other nation-state or institution can fill the gap. Compounding the case are arguments, valid or not, that without a solution to the Israeli-Palestinian conflict, various ancillary disputes in the region—tensions involving Syria, Lebanon, Iran, and Iraq—will continue to fester. Progress toward peace will not magically resolve these other conflicts, but it would undermine an oft-cited excuse.

To the extent that the Israeli-Palestinian dispute serves as a drain on international politics more broadly—by virtue of being a source of long-term instability in a strategically and economically pivotal region—a strenuous effort by the United States to resolve the long-standing conflict is a prerequisite for an American claim to upstanding citizenship. Meeting this standard will take early and sustained high-level diplomatic engagement, including that of the president. It will also require U.S. willingness to take on the difficult job of convincing Israel, as it has in the past, to take the risky steps it needs to for the sake of peace.

At numerous levels, the Israeli-Palestinian conflict raises core issues for the rules-based order. The occupation, the settlements, and the status of terrorist groups that enjoy apparent political support pose a set of interlocked challenges. The longer the current stalemate drags on, the more likely the United States will be blamed for failing to break the impasse and allowing conditions in the Gaza Strip to continue to deteriorate. By showing some incremental pragmatism toward the challenge posed by Hamas's leadership, the United States can avoid being perceived as the main obstacle.

Over the long term, assuming that an intensified U.S. diplomatic effort helps achieve peace, it will be up to the United States to act as guardian of the agreement—ensuring that the needed political, security, and economic support is provided. Since one key incentive is increased economic opportunity for the Palestinians and the wider region, the United States will need to ensure that these benefits are realized.

### Terrorism and Weak and Failing States

A key measure of U.S. success in reasserting itself as an effective force in the international system will hinge upon its success in making the fight against terrorism a truly multilateral campaign. Insofar as it remains a centerpiece of U.S. national security policy, the fight against terror should be transformed into a campaign that strengthens, rather than detracts from, the vitality of the international system. This is consistent with U.S. interest in ensuring that counterterrorism efforts remain a broadly shared international priority in the years and decades to come. During the next few years, absent dramatic intervening events, combating global terrorism will become a permanent, yet less prominent, feature of the global security landscape. The long-term effectiveness of a steady-state U.S.-led effort to deter and interdict terrorist action will depend upon broad and consistent global cooperation. As other economic, political, and national security imperatives gain in relative priority, the United States will want the ability to sustain wide support for counterterror measures without having to exert heavy bilateral leverage on a state-by-state basis in order to elicit it.

To date, however, the United States has not succeeded in securing the adoption of an overarching international treaty on terrorism and has, for the most part, downplayed multilateral counterterrorism frameworks in favor of bilateral arrangements struck on Washington's terms. While effective in disrupting plotted attacks and impeding the ability of terrorist networks to communicate and plan, ad hoc bilateral approaches will not be effective over the long term in fully eliminating terrorist sanctuaries or building the capacity of states worldwide to combat terrorism within their own territories. Such approaches have already backfired in places like Pakistan, where the United States was regarded as having strong-armed its ally while failing to build a U.S.-Pakistani relationship that went beyond terrorism.

To avoid further backlash, counterterrorism efforts should be based on inclusive international participation in initiatives with intensive engagement by the United States along with recognized global legitimacy. U.S. willingness to enmesh the fight against terrorism in broad-based multilateral institutions, including the United Nations and regional and specialized bodies, is essential to the long-term sustainability of the fight and, by extension, to the level of international support it receives. Indeed, efforts are underway to intensify the United Nations' counterterrorism activities, drawing on its roles in norm-setting, technical support for the capacity of member state governments, and serving as the main forum for global dialogue.[5]

The related problem of weak and failing states is another challenge on the global agenda where U.S. leadership is seen as lacking, and where stronger performance will be central to the U.S. claim to stakeholderdom. The debacle in Iraq has exposed just how ill-prepared the United States is to help stabilize and rebuild a conflict-torn society. Weak and failed states are widely recognized as among the principal security challenges of the present era—owing to the grave humanitarian and human rights crises they can precipitate, their potential to spawn regional conflicts, and their susceptibility to violence and terrorism by predatory nonstate actors. These anarchic stresses are highly corrosive to the global system, and any effort to strengthen the international order must deal with them.

The world community will inevitably expect the world's strongest conventional military to play a role, regardless of whether or not the United States bears direct responsibility for a situation, as in Iraq and Afghanistan. When a major country teeters on the brink, eyes turn to Washington for expertise, strategic military capabilities, and equipment. Indeed, until a much stronger, more coherent multilateral capacity to bolster weak states is built, any indecisiveness on the part of the United States will be viewed as a dereliction of leadership. So while a U.S. contribution of ground troops may not always be appropriate, the United States will be a likely backstop to any kind of multilateral effort.

Military stability operations are only a part of the postconflict recovery and reconstruction process. Nation-rebuilding is just one of the international challenges for which the United States needs urgently to reform and revitalize its civilian agencies. Several dozen recent studies have been done or are underway looking at specific measures to strengthen this infrastructure by bolstering the foreign service and making aid efforts more coherent. Here again, the United States must show its willingness to strengthen not only the capacity of its own government to stabilize weak states but also the complementary international mechanisms. Identifying and pressing for strong, dynamic, and experienced leadership in key roles at the United Nations and its specialized agencies will be one key step. While it is crucial that the United States be able to work with the most influential global civil servants—the UN secretary-general and his key lieutenants, for example—the United States must not undermine the efficacy of these posts in the name of avoiding any challenge to U.S. points of view. The United States is, for instance, a member of the newly formed UN Peacebuilding Commission, a legacy of former UN Secretary-General Kofi Annan's 2005 UN reform campaign. Building that foundering body's ability to coordinate aid to postconflict missions and mobilize necessary resources could help prevent duplicated efforts, harness international contributions more effectively, and ensure that global partners match the United States' own offerings.

### International Law and Norms

The U.S. commitment to be a global stakeholder will also be judged by its respect for international institutions and treaties. While the United States was the key engineer of much of the world's current security and diplomatic architecture, it has long had an uneasy relationship to international organizations and norms—reserving the right to stand aloof from organs and agreements at will. Domestic politics and Congress have played a major role in dictating the U.S. posture toward its international obligations. The

United States has often had to ask the forbearance of other member states in tolerating, for example, refusal by Congress to fully and consistently fund the payment of U.S. dues to the United Nations and other international organizations. The same understanding is tacitly extended in relation to the U.S. unwillingness to fully assume certain treaty obligations; for example, its refusal to accede to the UN Convention on the Elimination of All Forms of Discrimination Against Women or the UN treaty banning the use of child soldiers—agreements ratified by nearly all of the nations of the world.

The days when U.S. leaders could fend off diplomatic pressure simply by blaming Congress are gone. With the rise of new powers, many democracies themselves, U.S. leaders should anticipate rising expectations that the United States will overcome domestic isolationist pressures rather than dodging international obligations that are a tough sell in Middle America. As a bipolar/unipolar world now becomes multipolar or even nonpolar, the international community's patience with the idiosyncrasies of its largest members will diminish. The international system would buckle under the weight of numerous capitals, each seeking to make its own rules or demanding exceptions when it suits them. The concern is not merely theoretical; after Congress passed laws barring full payment of UN dues and requesting a lower UN rate of assessment, the Japanese parliament followed suit.

That said, the domestic misgivings that stand in the way of wider U.S. participation in global institutions cannot be wished away. Over the coming years, U.S. leaders and diplomats will need to mount an intensive long-term effort to build support within the electorate and Congress for compliance with international norms. This will require a series of related steps: measures to bridge the divide between Congress and the world community through exchanges and dialogue, aggressive use of polling data to highlight and build upon the American people's generally positive attitudes toward international cooperation and compromise, and—at least in the beginning—political leadership to take stands likely to draw heat from vocal minorities.

## Institutions in an Age of Rising Powers

The U.S. stakeholder status will also hinge on its leadership in transforming international institutions to accommodate the rise of new powers. If the United States is seen as clinging to outmoded structures or forums, it will be accused of resisting the inevitable evolution of the international system. It will need to actively make room for new seats at the table or else face intense pressure from others trying to muscle their way in. To date, the United States has gingerly sidestepped such debates. On UN Security Council (UNSC) reform, it has neither facilitated nor blocked progress, leaving it up to those with the greatest interest in council enlargement to fight their own case. The United States will not be able to remain aloof forever, though.

If the riddle of UNSC enlargement proves difficult to solve in the next few years, the United States should pursue other ways to satisfy new powers' ambitions for greater participation in global decision-making. Advancing proposals to revamp and expand the Group of Eight to include a broader group of countries like China, India, and Brazil would be one way to demonstrate the U.S. commitment to ensuring that the international order remains up-to-date and relevant. Given the time-capsule quality of its membership, it is hard to imagine that the UNSC reform can be put off indefinitely. When the time finally comes to break the long-standing impasse, the United States could be in a position to help. The United States is the only current permanent member confronting neither pressures to step down nor direct rivals among the aspirants, which could give it a patina of neutrality and an ability to offer constructive proposals. The United States should remain on the lookout, amid shifting power dynamics and changes of the guard in key capitals, for a formula that stands a chance of winning the requisite support. The United States' relatively disinterested position may also mean that if UNSC reform continues to stall, blame will be increasingly laid in Washington, deservedly or not.

Meanwhile, the discussion in U.S. policy circles of forging a new concert or league of the world's democracies as a key decision-making body is a wasteful distraction at best and probably somewhat damaging to the U.S. image. To the extent that the United States is seen as "forum shopping" for a set of countries it hopes would be more conducive to American wishes, this sends exactly the wrong message. Increased consultation and collaboration among democracies at the United Nations and other global forums is a worthwhile pursuit. But the idea that the United States can remake the global security architecture by anointing a handpicked group of countries into decision-making roles is far-fetched and, if pursued, risks exacerbating the tensions wrought by eight years of U.S. policies that were judged as high-handed and self-interested. From a more practical vantage point, it is hard to imagine this proposal gaining support from those nations whose stamp of approval would be needed to give it any credibility—i.e., India, South Africa, and Brazil. Even if they did agree to participate, there is little to suggest that such countries would succeed in forging the consensus necessary for collective action.

Playing a constructive role as a stakeholder in leading multilateral institutions goes beyond paying attention to issues of membership and composition. On the question of structural and management reforms to multilateral institutions, the United States must hone a new approach that avoids denigrating or punishing the institutions themselves. The substance of U.S. criticisms and reservations toward international institutions is not without foundation, but repositioning the United States as a leader and mainstay of the international order will require new approaches to advancing the calls for accountability. Bland calls for the United States simply to "play by the rules" offer scant guidance for the challenge of advancing U.S. interests constructively without undercutting the institutions and norms in question. An important litmus test is whether the U.S. approach to advancing its views and positions is one that could be followed by a wider group of countries without a broadly corrosive effect on the institution itself. [6] In the case of withholding dues, it is clearly not the case; U.S. financial withholdings have placed a heavy strain on the UN financial system, and wider holdbacks would be paralyzing. By focusing on intensive diplomatic efforts to drive reform—building coalitions, engaging in extensive consultations, and pressing recalcitrants—the United States can drive institutional reform while still being seen as a responsible stakeholder.

Over the long term, stakeholderdom must entail openness and leadership in developing institutional and structural responses to global problems. Without such leadership, the United States will increasingly be viewed as an outlier and outsider—a force for international institutions to reckon with, rather than a pillar within them. With the notable exception of NATO, the Bush administration has tended to emphasize ad hoc coalitions and formulas—for example, its coalition for intervention in Iraq and its proposed nuclear deal with India—over reliance on standing institutions with rules, norms, and members that cannot be changed or ignored at will.

The evolution of the international system to cope with new problems will have to depend upon the ability to develop new organs and structures that respond to new security and policy challenges. U.S. leadership in designing and building such structures will be key. Areas requiring attention include efforts to forge a bargain on the transparency of sovereign wealth funds and leadership in helping to evolve the world trade and nonproliferation regimes to deal more effectively with the pressures bearing down on these norm sets. In participating in such efforts, the United States will have to fashion its role not just as that of a protector of American interests but also as a steward of the international order as a whole. This will require the United States to work as hard to forge compromise as to push narrower interests.

### Democracy and Human Rights
The international order can only be as strong and effective as its constituent member states are politically stable and vital. One of the major questions

facing Obama will be how to approach the global spread of democracy and human rights.

During the latter years of the twentieth century, the United States became the self-styled global standard for democracy and claimed to be the key patron and partner to countries in Eastern Europe and elsewhere that had undergone democratic transitions. Although U.S. support for democratization was always uneven and opportunistic, the perception that the United States was a friend to reformers and democratic dissidents reinforced its own legitimacy as a beneficent power. The promotion of democracy also helped to ensure that full membership in good standing in the international order was not merely about nations' control of territory, but also about the empowerment of peoples and the legitimacy of governments.

Tragically, the Iraq war gave U.S. democracy promotion efforts a bad name both at home and internationally. By invoking democratization and the remaking of the Middle East as a post facto rationale for waging the Iraq war, the Bush administration opened itself up to a torrent of criticism. The United States was pilloried both for trying to impose an American-style democracy in Iraq and for failing so utterly to achieve anything close to that.

To be seen as a responsible stakeholder, the United States must prove that it remains committed to extending the benefits of democracy and human rights globally but that it will avoid doing so through unilateralist or militaristic means. By helping strengthen multilateral instruments to promote democracy, expanding hands-on programs that build skills and infrastructure to create favorable conditions, and providing long-term support for new democracies beyond election assistance, the United States can show its commitment to the patient cultivation of democracy, with local roots, not just to the sentimental ideal.

## Security in the Global Order

The earliest and most prominent signal of the new administration's international posture will be its handling of the war in Iraq. To prove its bona fides as a responsible stakeholder, the United States must take a series of steps no matter what the pace of its drawdown. The first is to open up sustained and substantive dialogue with Iraq's neighbors as well as with a broader group of leading global powers that share a long-term interest in the region's stability. Such discussions must be open, unfettered, and undertaken on the basis that other countries' views will be taken seriously in the formation of U.S. policy.

Second, as it withdraws its troops, the United States must do all in its power to avoid leaving chaos in its wake. Given limited U.S. leverage over

Iraq's internal conflicts with more than one hundred twenty thousand troops on the ground, the United States will have even less sway over how things unfold after the withdrawal. Iraq's neighbors, however, do have leverage that can be multiplied if their governments can cooperate.[7] Such a strategy of working "from the outside in" would call on Iran, Syria, Turkey, Saudi Arabia, and others to discourage the Iraqi factions from escalating their conflict, refrain from feeding the fire with arms, and keep control of borders. A carefully planned and executed exit will include detailed consultations with the Iraqi government, collaboration with the United Nations, engagement of the Arab League (and of its individual members), measures to fortify and expand the work of local and international nongovernmental organizations that can play a stabilizing role, and firm commitments to continued aid and technical assistance—all with a view toward keeping Iraq from descending into a spoiling ground.

From the perspective of the broader challenges to the international community, an end to U.S. military involvement in Iraq may be greeted with relief internationally; among other things, the United States would finally be able to pay attention to problems that had been pushed to the margins by the all-consuming Iraq situation.

### Shedding Obsolete Nuclear Policies and Weapons

Stakeholders in the international system have no obligation more urgent than the duty to protect the earth from nuclear conflagration. The international norm prohibiting nations from acquiring nuclear arsenals is under severe stress, and the United States will be measured by its role in keeping it from total collapse. Beyond immediate challenges posed by newer or potential nuclear powers, some of the solid citizens of nuclear nonproliferation are beginning to doubt the wisdom of their own good behavior. As new nations obtain nuclear weapons, others will reexamine their own strategic calculations—is it wise to remain nonnuclear in a world with more nuclear powers? It is easy to imagine regional nuclear arms races in the Middle East and northeast Asia. Meanwhile, the insistence of long-time nuclear powers upon retaining their massive arsenals only compounds the problem. The more jealously this group guards its own swollen arsenals, the more they undercut the idea that these most destructive of weapons have no valid military role.

Bolstering the norm of nonproliferation is still possible, but complacency and the passage of time combine to make it increasingly difficult. A fresh and bold U.S. approach to nuclear policy and disarmament could help stem the proliferation tide, and the United States has every interest in doing so. Each of the de facto and potential nuclear powers—North Korea, Iran, India,

Pakistan, and Israel—presents a special case requiring a customized political and security response that, of necessity, will involve a key role for the United States. Indeed, in the case of India, the United States has been wrestling with a new posture in relation to India's status as a nuclear power. India's acquisition of nuclear weapons hardly reinforces the nonproliferation norm, so it presents a delicate challenge of setting terms that deal with reality while placing some responsibility on New Delhi.

The gist of the Nuclear Nonproliferation Treaty (NPT) was fairly straightforward. States that did not have nuclear weapons would foreswear them (article II). Nations already possessing nuclear arsenals would ultimately disarm (article VI). Finally, nonnuclear weapon states would receive help in harnessing nuclear technology for civilian purposes, with a rigid separation walling these activities off from military uses (articles IV and V). As the United States struggles to keep nonnuclear weapon states from gaining weapons—and the Cold War fades into the past—it faces increased pressure regarding its own unfulfilled commitment to disarm. The NPT itself was sufficiently vague regarding disarmament by the nuclear weapon states that the United States cannot be found in legal violation, but the perception is widespread that the United States—and other weapons-possessing states—have let down their end of the bargain.[8]

With roughly ten thousand warheads remaining in the U.S. nuclear arsenal, much of current U.S. nuclear policy and posture remains a holdover from the Cold War. Continued maintenance and buildup of the arsenal is driven by a vague notion that the United States continues to face threats, including the threat of new and uncontrollable nuclear powers. It is not, however, grounded in spelled-out credible scenarios for how current or future levels of nuclear armament might actually be used in practice. The disjuncture between an American stance based largely on inertia and a normative regime under severe pressure confronts the United States with a trade-off: breathing life into the nonproliferation norm will likely require affirmative U.S. steps toward keeping up the disarmament end of the NPT bargain.

U.S. efforts to prevent and curb the spread of nuclear weapons should focus not on how to supplant the NPT but how to revitalize it based on fulfillment of its terms by the original nuclear powers. The essence of nonproliferation, the spirit of the law, must be to strengthen the taboo against nuclear weapons, regardless of whose weapons they are. Given the destructive power of nuclear weapons, lingering health effects of radiation, and danger of escalation following the use even of tactical systems, the use of these weapons is bound to elicit a moral revulsion more than outweighing any military advantage achieved. Accepting that, for this reason, a preemptive U.S. nuclear strike is virtually inconceivable, a high-profile nuclear policy debate involving the president could shift the focus from asking how many weapons the United States could afford to cut to how many it needs for effective deterrence and retaliation. While a handful of holdouts in Congress might rail against letting down America's guard in a dangerous world, wider consensus would likely appreciate that the outsized arsenal poses a security problem, impedes nonproliferation objectives, and is not a security solution. A revision of U.S. doctrine to minimize the role of nuclear weapons would not only give the rest of the world modest reassurance about U.S. strategic intentions, but it could also pave the way for deep cuts in the size of nuclear forces globally.

There are early glimpses of emerging political consensus, notably in the collective effort of George Shultz, Henry Kissinger, Sam Nunn, and William Perry, to press for a reduction in the U.S. nuclear arsenal as part of a broader reciprocal global effort to limit and ultimately eliminate nuclear weapons. Such bold approaches could be politically counterbalanced at home through the continuation and strengthening of measures to block and disrupt the efforts of would-be proliferators—raising not only the moral and political barriers to proliferation but the practical ones as well.[9] Accordingly, cooperative threat reduction, continuation of President Bush's Proliferation Security Initiative, and nuclear intelligence should be integral to nuclear policy in the coming years.

One option raised by a recast role for U.S. nuclear forces would be to adopt a posture of nuclear no first use. Even more significant for the long-term strength of the nonproliferation norm, it could pave the way to cuts in the U.S. arsenal—and, by extension, in the forces of other nuclear powers—to a lesser deterrent force. These steps should be pursued as part of a multilateral framework—enabling the United States to maximize political support at home and multiply the impact of its own actions.

Because the United States and Russia hold the largest nuclear arsenals by far—together comprising 95 percent of all warheads in the world—reductions in their forces are the logical first step. Under the terms of the 2002 Moscow Treaty on Strategic Offensive Reductions, the two are slated to cut their deployed forces to 1,700–2,200 weapons by 2012. Two near-term steps could help make the Moscow Treaty a basis for further agreed mutual cuts: carrying forward the verification provisions of the Strategic Arms Reduction Treaty II (START) agreement and preserving the overall structure of the treaty past its 2012 deadline. Two leading experts on nuclear arms control have crafted a proposal to amend the Moscow Treaty to set a lower ceiling of reductions to one thousand weapons apiece.[10]

An important preparatory step toward reductions to minimal levels will be a few key areas of technical work to confirm that existing weapons are still in working order, to keep them in that condition, and to dismantle those being removed from the arsenal safely and verifiably. Research by the U.S. Department of Energy (DOE) should be accelerated regarding methods for verifying warhead safety and reliability through measures short of nuclear testing. This work is vital to pave the way for U.S. ratification of the Comprehensive Nuclear Test Ban Treaty, a necessary complement to the NPT. The test detonation of a nuclear weapon is the milestone that announces a country's arrival as a nuclear power. From a nonproliferation perspective, a nuclear test is an after-the-fact threshold, a trailing indicator. For future rounds of negotiated reductions, it will also be crucial to devise ways to enable intrusive arms control verification without compromising sensitive information about weapon design or operation. Such measures are essential to enabling the United States to scale back its nuclear posture comfortably and responsibly.

### Minimal Nuclear Deterrents

Because article VI of the NPT requires nuclear weapon states to progress toward eventual complete disarmament, even U.S.-Russian bilateral reductions to one thousand weapons would not constitute a once-and-for-all fulfillment of this obligation. However, such bilateral reductions could be a very important stepping stone toward sweeping reductions to truly low levels. Once the two biggest nuclear powers reach that level, their arsenals will no longer be vastly larger than any others, building pressure for all countries with nuclear weapons to join in reductions.[11]

The next logical step would be for Russia and the United States to negotiate reductions with the other original Cold War powers of China, France, and the United Kingdom. In keeping with the concept of an arsenal only large enough to deter existential threats, the numerical limits in such a five-way treaty would leave sufficient forces able to survive and retaliate against any plausible attack. One especially rigorous analysis of the options and strategic implications for deep nuclear reductions presents a scenario under which no nation has more than two hundred nuclear weapons.[12]

Because of the way nuclear arms control treaties traditionally work, more ambitious arms control agreements would require a major leap in transparency. The counting rules of previous arms control agreements have focused on delivery systems—basing the official tally of warheads on multiples of the numbers of delivery vehicles, regardless of the fate of the warhead itself. As disarmament proceeds to minimal levels, this loophole is simply too large. To begin with, Russia and the United States will have several times more nuclear weapons, albeit decommissioned and removed from their delivery systems, than permitted under the specified treaty—hardly in line with the intention of article VI. In order to get to low levels of nuclear warheads, the parties to the new agreements would need to verify that nuclear weapons had not only been decommissioned but also dismantled. This is the point of the technical work by experts in the DOE national laboratories: devising ways to permit verification without compromising sensitive information about weapon design or operation.

The next wider circle would aim to bring in the "de facto" nuclear weapon states that never signed the NPT (India, Pakistan, and Israel), whose nuclear arsenals are all, in a sense, "demand-driven" by their geostrategic situation. Each of these nations can point out serious security threats to which their weapons are a response—in fact, two of the countries point at each other. Regardless of whether a thaw between Pakistan and India lessens their reliance on nuclear weapons, the two nations have been persistent critics of the older nuclear powers for failing to live up to the disarmament obligations of the NPT. Deep cuts by the original "permanent five" would effectively call their bluff.

Luring Israel into an agreement on reducing its nuclear arsenal is even more complicated, given that it has spent decades demurring any public acknowledgment of its arsenal. Such an agreement is inconceivable absent a comprehensive settlement of the Israeli-Palestinian conflict but potentially realistic after such a settlement has proven its strength and durability over a period of years.

All of this leaves the question of cutting all nuclear arsenals to zero. Abolition would pose political, strategic, and technical complexities of a different order. However daunting these difficulties might be, it is possible they will be counterbalanced considerably by an overall reduction in tensions and military competition.

### Dealing with Iran

While it will take several years for the nuclear powers to fulfill their part of the nonproliferation bargain, certain urgent nonproliferation challenges cannot wait. For the United States the priority is clear. Iran is simultaneously at the top of the nonproliferation agenda, a critical frontline state neighboring both Iraq and Afghanistan, and a state sponsor of terrorists operating in and around Israel.

Not only does Iran pose a compelling set of strategic challenges for the United States, its position raises fundamental issues about the workings of the international order. Can a government that is repressive internally improve its global standing by adopting a less threatening outward military posture? What role should leading global powers play—collectively and individually—in holding other countries to international norms, including nonproliferation?

Recent experience offers a few critical lessons for how to responsibly handle nations at the threshold of obtaining nuclear arsenals. First of all, it is not effective for Washington merely to issue decrees and demands for the target regime to capitulate—especially when matters are clouded by a message that the real problem is the regime itself. As long as Iran's leaders perceive that nothing short of surrendering power will ease external pressures, their imperative to arm themselves against a perceived existential threat originating in the United States is reinforced.

From the U.S. side, given the stakes and time pressures, the best way to pursue U.S. nonproliferation, regional security, and counterterrorism interests with Iran is through direct and wide-ranging talks. The just-around-the-corner urgency of the Iranian nuclear threat was over-hyped, to be sure, but Iran clearly is indeed drawing closer to a nuclear weapon capability with each passing year. The November 2007 U.S. National Intelligence Estimate provides evidence of Iran's suspended military effort to develop a weapon and gives a sober assessment of the time horizon for a possible Iranian nuclear capability. The fact that Iran is several years away from a nuclear capability opens the diplomatic window of opportunity.

Reaching a diplomatic settlement will be difficult, since even a committed effort may fail. Yet if it drags on, with wasteful pauses, the certain result will be a nuclear-armed Iran, just as it was with North Korea. So while coordination with other powers and multilateral venues such as the UNSC and IAEA remains important, the United States must keep the focus on sustaining momentum and taking advantage of the narrowing window in which Iran's nuclear capacity remains nascent.

Key elements of such a bargaining process—built around a succession of reciprocal, contingent, trust-building measures—must include Tehran's cooperation with the IAEA on the monitoring of its purportedly civilian nuclear program: safeguards, inspections, seals, and other disclosures sought by the agency. This could build toward a set of tailored and intrusive monitoring measures by which the IAEA could verify the civilian nature of Iran's nuclear activities, cap the size of its enrichment facility, and strictly account for all fissile material. In response, the United States would gradually remove sanctions, beginning with the lifting of diplomatic constraints and ultimately helping Iran upgrade its oil and gas industries.

The exchange of nuclear nonproliferation and transparency for economic integration is a bargain that has been pursued—though not yet all the way to successful implementation—with North Korea, but differences weigh in favor of at least trying a similar approach with Iran. Unlike North Korea, Iran has not yet built nuclear weapons. It has a stronger interest in global economic integration and is in a stronger bargaining position in that it has a bona fide civilian nuclear program and thus a legitimate reason to pursue key aspects of nuclear development. The NPT not only permits but also encourages civilian nuclear power as long as a nonnuclear weapon state does not initiate a military program and keeps its activities transparent.

So in effect, Iran still has plausible deniability in claiming civilian purposes for its uranium enrichment program. That enrichment program, and its implied technical prowess, is now firmly staked as a point of Iranian national pride. Iran simply will not foreswear enrichment entirely. Ambassadors Thomas Pickering and William Luers and MIT's Jim Walsh, who have spent five years in private discussions with Iranians, share this conclusion.[13] Weighing in favor of an Iranian leadership interest in nonproliferation, however, that nation also has a dynamic political system and somewhat empowered populace—thereby raising the potential costs for any regime viewed domestically as a willing pariah that puts its appetite for nuclear weapons ahead of the economic needs of its people.

Beyond the nuclear issue, Iran's role in the region—the Persian Gulf as well as the Levant—will be integral to any comprehensive bilateral negotiation. Despite the heated election-year debate over whether to talk to Iran, the United States and Iran have actually been in dialogue over Iraq (and before that, over Afghanistan) for years. Such regional diplomacy will only grow in importance as the United States withdraws its forces from Iraq. Indeed, the rationale for withdrawal is based on an assessment that the military presence in reality gives the United States very little leverage over the ultimate outcome in Iraq.

Ultimately, a full rapprochement with Iran cannot be reached until Tehran's backing of Hezbollah and Hamas ends. The key to a normal bilateral U.S.-Iranian relationship will be Iran's acceptance of a sovereign and secure Israel—the test of which would be support for a two-state solution and a decisive cutoff of military support for Hezbollah and Hamas to help spur their transformation into purely political actors.

Until a comprehensive deal with Iran is concluded, the United States will reserve the option of military action in case Iran negates the diplomatic process through hostile or threatening actions. The credible threat of force is a vital complement to intensive bilateral diplomacy with an unpredictable and at times menacing counterpart. Without it, the process would no doubt go through periods of drift, at an unaffordable loss of time. It should be noted, though, that the U.S. unilateral removal of a nonnuclear Saddam Hussein and the aggressive saber-rattling toward Iran have left the impression that the use of force is not a threat, but a promise.

Once Iran demonstrated its willingness to submit to the nonproliferation regime and renounce terrorism, the tables would turn and the burden of proof of nonaggression would shift decisively. In other words, if Iran takes steps to reduce the threat it poses toward others, it is only fair that it should not remain on the receiving end of threats. For this reason negative security assurances from the United States—a U.S. promise not to use force against Iran except in response to an Iranian act of military aggression—will be a necessary element of eventual resumed diplomatic relations between the United States and Iran.

## The International Community and the Global Economy

As the world's largest economy and the home to pivotal financial markets, banks, and multinational corporations, the U.S. position of leadership rests in significant part on America's roles as an engine and a guardian of global prosperity. As the 2008 subprime mortgage crisis illustrated, despite the emergence of other international economic power centers, when the U.S. economy sneezes, the world still catches cold. Accordingly, U.S. actions and accountability in relation to the global economy will be key measures of whether not just Washington, but also New York, Chicago, and Silicon Valley have fulfilled their responsibilities as stakeholders in the global order.

Given that the world's leading financial center, New York, comes within its purview, the United States must approach its financial regulatory responsibilities with a global perspective. U.S. failure to anticipate and guard against the fallout from the meltdown of subprime mortgages was grossly negligent and is projected to cause $1 trillion in global economic damage. Complacency about low liquidity levels and willful ignorance about the precariousness of the exotic financial instruments that were used to repackage unsound mortgage debt made the credit crisis all but inevitable. It will not be a simple matter to craft regulations that will anticipate and manage risk without stifling growth and innovation, but the credit crunch has served notice to the United States and the world about the global reverberations of U.S. financial regulation. While it would be facile to offer a specific prescription, acting responsibly clearly requires taking steps to rectify these shortcomings.

### Globalization and Trade

Another critical test is trade. As a primary author of the global trade system, American leadership is vital as the global trade system comes under mounting diplomatic and political challenge. In terms of both upholding the current rules and, as important, reshaping them to fold in new stakeholders and address emerging challenges, the U.S. commitment and initiative are indispensable.

Clearly trade and globalization have stirred deep domestic political rifts. Despite the American public's apparent desire to restore alliances and re-build the U.S. global image, the populace harbors substantial ambivalence about free trade and its associated dislocations. During the 2008 election cycle, regardless of whether or not citizens' own personal circumstances were affected by trade, the North American Free Trade Agreement became short-hand for why many Americans feel economically insecure.

The idea that the United States should "put a brake" on free trade is both fanciful and self-destructive. To fulfill its responsibilities as a global stakeholder, the United States must categorically reject any notion that resurrecting trade barriers is a viable route to greater domestic prosperity or security. That said, there can be no durable consensus embracing free trade absent urgent measures to prevent and redress the unavoidable and serious dislocations stemming from fulsome U.S. participation in the global economy. Preventing these threats from throwing a political wrench into the workings of the trading system has emerged as a central element of the U.S. global economic leadership.

One important piece of the protective social safety net is already at the top of the American domestic political agenda: universal health insurance. Other key protections include bolstering unemployment insurance, trade adjustment assistance and retraining that actually leads to well-paying jobs, raising the minimum wage, the earned income tax credit, access to childcare, and the affordability of higher education.

The United States must also address the problem of individual trade agreements that are seen as directly undermining to American workers, to the global environment, and to global labor rights and norms. Integration of practical and finely tuned labor and environmental standards into trade agreements will pave the way for such accords to be approved.

Criticisms of the U.S. free trade embrace do not stop at the U.S. borders. The large numbers of people worldwide for whom the global economy seems more of a threat than an opportunity are increasingly asking why their nations should play by the rules. Zbigniew Brzezinski warned of a potential "counter-creed" to globalization, whereby mass sentiment coalesces into coherent, focused hostility toward globalization, and, by extension, the United States as the world's greatest economic power.[14] The antidote, he says, is for the United States to "treat glo-balization less as a gospel and more as an opportunity for the betterment of the human condition. . . . The pursuit of open markets should not be an end in itself, but a means of improving economic conditions worldwide."[15]

Preventing a global backlash from impeding continued U.S. economic growth through trade will require realization of the original promise of the Doha Round as an equalizer of the benefits of globalization, even if this cannot be achieved—in the near term—by reaching a new global trade agreement. The case for trade as a driver of development is severely undermined by the skewing of the benefits from the prior Uruguay Round toward developed nations and the sizable tariffs they still collect from less developed countries.

A strategy that treats trade talks purely as an opportunity to gain advantage for Western negotiating partners will produce an inherently brittle structure. Industrialized powers have sought the free flow of capital, high-skill services, and legally protected intellectual property, while keeping a tight clamp on agriculture and low-skill labor—an unsustainable position from the standpoint of norms. While no nation can be expected to put aside consideration of the near-term domestic economic impact of trade proposals, the United States must be seen to acknowledge the wider and longer-range implications of its trade positions on the global system.

The United States has demonstrated the capacity to lead in this area, adopting positions more constructive than those of the European Union. The United States is credited with low tariffs on agricultural products and, in relative terms, low agricultural subsidies for many commodities. Yet U.S. trade barriers on textiles and apparel and some of the remaining agricultural subsidies are criticized for squeezing the livelihoods of African citizens eager to join the world economy. Addressing this issue through a progressive reduction of these tariffs would yield tangible development gains and help remove a major source of global criticism against the United States. Continued and expanded leadership in this arena will reverberate: strengthening the global trading system, ensuring that its rifts and shortcomings are not blamed on the United States, and setting an example that promotes more constructive stances, among others.

Migration is another arena in which U.S. policy has wide ripple effects and one that will be closely followed by those watching and judging America's standing as a stakeholder. American economic success in a globalizing world will depend not merely on containing post–September 11 xenophobia against immigrants and visitors but on maintaining a steady stream of both. The tightening of visa restrictions has put the United States beyond reach for many talented foreigners seeking educational and economic opportunity. These promising would-be migrants are increasingly focusing their ambitions on other Western countries. The private sector and the science and technology lobbies have raised serious concerns about the potential costs to the economy of such restrictions. While such policies are proving self-defeating in practical ways, they are also undermining more than a century of global perceptions of the United States as an open frontier for opportunity seekers. This openness has been a prominent symbol of America's global leadership, building bridges between populations worldwide and diaspora groups in the United States and setting a standard for other Western countries. By backing away from this openness, the United States would undermine what is almost universally viewed as a fundamentally American value and historic contribution.

In a related but distinct category, the United States should also broaden its acceptance of refugees from global humanitarian crises and, specifically, Iraq; accepting refugees who by definition are not able to be in their own country is a responsibility according to international law and a global public good. If it is not seen to do its fair share, and particularly to take care of victims of crises that the United States has itself precipitated, the U.S. risks being seen as unwilling either to deal with the consequences of its own actions or to acknowledge its moral responsibility to others.

## The Challenge of Climate Change

There are few issues that crystallize the questions of responsible global citizenship as distinctly as the challenge of global climate change. The analogy to citizenship in a domestic polity is quite direct: polluters, those who refuse to clean up after themselves, and those who stand outside—and thereby undermine—the preservation of the environment for public benefit are obvious civic delinquents.

The debate over global climate change is not amenable to easy prescriptions and this chapter will not attempt to devise a blueprint for U.S. positions. It is clear, however, that its rejection of the 1997 Kyoto Protocol puts the United States in the position of having to make up for lost ground when it comes to credibility as a steward of the global environment.

To be seen to offer leadership befitting its global stature, the United States will need to take a number of steps. The heart of the matter is a trade-off between the need for urgent action and the desire for ambitious, binding, and comprehensive limits on greenhouse gases applicable to all nations, including the world's fast-growing developing economies, mostly notably China. The United States needs to approach global climate change negotiations with an open mind, accepting the prospect of limits that are enforceable for Western countries before they are made binding on the world's largest developing economies, such as China and India. The arguments against such an approach may be logical in principle but will in practice risk negating any prospect of a broad-ranging accord to prevent environmental catastrophe. By adopting a long-term perspective focused on the value of achieving universal binding limits in the medium term, the United States can adopt a posture that is constructive and that balances U.S. interests against the imperative of an agreement that applies to all major emitters. Abdication based on the already moribund principle of uniform binding targets will not be an option. Domestic and international opinions have both reached the point at which action on global warming is considered mandatory.

In contrast to just a few years ago, the impetus to tackle greenhouse gases has gelled domestically in the United States such that domestic and international political imperatives, if carefully managed, could converge. Legislative momentum for a cap-and-trade system of emissions allowances has increased. Pressure has mounted for higher fuel economy standards for vehicles. Spiraling fuel prices have transformed fuel efficiency from a matter of principle to an even more compelling matter for the pocketbook. Numerous state and municipal governments have taken initiative to enact more stringent standards. The private sector has shown its belief in the promise and political imperative of green technology with investments (both venture capitalists and large cap companies such as General Electric). More so than previously, the potential exists for political leaders to muster the domestic consensus necessary for action.

### Development Assistance

The U.S. role as a global citizen has long entailed concern for the disadvantaged of other nations. Just as leading citizens are measured by their charitable giving, wealthy countries are expected to do their fair share in terms of global development and humanitarian aid. The United States ranks too low as an aid donor among the world's wealthiest countries. Much of this aid is channeled to countries like Egypt that have particular political significance for the United States, rather than to countries where the need is greatest. Although the Bush administration promised innovation and increased generosity in the arena of development aid, the results were mixed. Over the last eight years, the United States has positioned itself as a global leader in the fight against HIV/AIDS and other global diseases, earning respect and goodwill that—more than any other policy—has provided a counterweight against the negative impact of the Bush years on global public perceptions. U.S. leadership in the recovery mission after the Asian tsunami in 2005 had a similar effect, buoying U.S. popularity in the region. Unfortunately, the much-heralded Millennium

Challenge Account, an effort to link development aid to good governance, has been underfunded and slow-moving, falling well short of its targets.

Responsibly addressing the impact of ethanol production and other factors on global food prices is another critical test. Calls for the United States to bolster aid to the World Food Programme and to liberalize policies that govern where U.S. food aid is sourced in order to bolster local production around the world should be heeded. In the longer term, U.S. development aid and multilateral assistance need to focus on promoting agriculture in the developing world, including support for new technologies to increase crop yields that have been in a decades-long decline. Efforts to raise the U.S. ranking and reputation as an aid donor will quell criticisms of the United States as ungenerous and will shape positive perceptions both among other leading donors and among recipient governments and their regions.

## As Others See Us

International politics shares some of the same verities as domestic politics. In both arenas, the perceptions, expectations, and interests of others matter a great deal, and no political actor can ignore them without paying a price in the loss of influence. The explicit codes of conduct that are spelled out in international law are a necessary but insufficient condition for a robust rules-based international order. Such an order rests not only on clear standards for what is right and wrong, but also on broadly shared faith in the order's fairness, equity, reciprocity, commonweal, and balance of interests.

A nation's material power can be measured in fairly simple terms. On the one hand, military and economic strength may be arduous to acquire, but relatively easy to gauge. Moral authority, on the other hand, is more subjective and has no indices equivalent to GDP or naval fleet tonnage. Yet the moral high ground is politically a very powerful place, and it cannot be unilaterally claimed or declared. In other words, legitimacy is in the collective eyes of the beholders.

Both because of the threat posed by the disintegration of global norms and because of the U.S. national interest in shaping the terms that govern the international system, the United States has compelling reasons to reposition itself as a leading force in refashioning the international order. This leaves the United States with a (hopefully creative) tension. At its best, a consensual global system can bolster community standards and marshal collective action to tackle problems. At the same time, it is also prone to lowest-common-denominator politics and inconclusive diplomatic drift. So at the moment the United States confronts a dire need to replenish credibility by deferring to international expectations, there will also be an ongoing need for the United States to remain the backbone of the world community, helping ensure that norms are upheld rather than watered down.

If the first step is to admit to the problem, the erosion of U.S. credibility has created a harsh reality. U.S. effectiveness as a global backbone is severely compromised by the decline in its international standing. That is why so many of the near-term recommendations above are essentially concessions—in the international political dynamic of legitimacy, the United States will only be able to press its concerns and win wider support once our stores of trust and goodwill have been restocked.

This is not to say that the United States would or should, after it regains legitimacy, revert to a posture of many demands and few concessions. The United States should neither indulge nor reflexively fend off what the rest of the world expects of it. Instead, the United States must sift through those expectations to determine not only their implications for U.S. interests, but also their consistency with international norms and resonance for other members of the world community.

Indeed, the United States may find a rigorous approach to legitimacy to be surprisingly beneficial. It could be quite invigorating to create legitimacy the old-fashioned way—by earning it, rather than presuming it as a national birthright. Among other things, this would require the United States to keep its diplomatic antennae extended and well tuned. It would entail greater awareness of international perceptions, more conscious choices on issues that affect the U.S. global image and, by extension, gaining increased control over that image.

As U.S. leaders embark on the project of rehabilitating U.S. legitimacy, it is vital that they not underestimate the task. Neither the inauguration of Barack Obama nor measures to mitigate the errors of his predecessor will bring the United States back into a constructive relationship to the rules-based international order. In fact, according to the approach outlined above, legitimacy is not a static end state to be achieved but an ongoing dynamic undertaking. This may be—under some traditions of American national pride—a less gratifying stance. Nevertheless, it squares better with how the world really works, is apt to be more effective, and is, in the end, in line with democratic traditions of renewal through continuous critical reassessment. As with so many such issues, it also upholds traditions of the republic's founders who at its inception called on our nation to pay "a decent respect to the opinions of mankind."

～

## Nikolas Gvosdev's Reaction

Suzanne Nossel and David Shorr have sketched out an ambitious plan for restoring the world's faith in the efficacy of American leadership of the community of nations. I find myself somewhat less sanguine about the prospects for success, under current conditions.

To begin, while the policies of the Bush administration, particularly in its execution of the Iraq war, exacerbated and accelerated a number of negative trends, there is no "reset button" to return to the status quo of 2000 or 1992. The ongoing diffusion of power, particularly in its economic and financial manifestations, to more and more states makes it difficult for the United States to reclaim the mantle of unquestioned leadership.

In the past, American primacy was derived in large part from the ability of the United States to generate an international system that guaranteed free and open lines of communication, provided for free trade, and promoted regional security. Today, however, there are rising concerns that the United States, to use the description of Flynt Leverett, is a "dysfunctional hegemon" whose policies are seen as damaging to the interests of other states.[16] It is correct that closing the detention facility at Guantanamo Bay, combined with an announcement of U.S. commitment to negotiations for a new climate change arrangement to replace Kyoto and steps to wind down the Iraq war, will improve the U.S. image and may even bring a short honeymoon period for the Obama administration. Over the long run, however, U.S. leadership will depend less on how it treats detainees or whether it is seen as an honest broker in the Arab-Israeli peace process and more on whether the international system it sustains can manage problems like the food and fuel crises and spread the burden of challenges like climate change between developed and developing countries.

I would also raise a cautionary point: It may not always be enough for the United States to take the lead in "solving" a problem if other states are uneasy about the associated methods and precedents. In theory, the Kosovo problem was "solved" in 2008 when the province declared independence and had its new status recognized by the United States and most of the countries of Europe. But the manner in which these things were done has thus far failed to bring greater stability to the Balkans; again the European Union (EU) exposed its inability to formulate a common position and reopened a divide between the developed "North and West" and the rising "South and East."

The debate itself is also shifting—from whether the United States should "obey the rules" to whether or not "the rules" as they stand promote or impede the interests of other countries. In theory, yes, there is agreement around the world that international cooperation enhances peace and prosperity, but operationalizing the rules, procedures, and institutions is far more contentious—even here in the United States.

It is not simply that there is ambivalence toward the international system among both the American people and their elites—but something approaching schizophrenia. For instance, the United States wants leaders in Sudan or Burma to be accountable to international institutions for their dereliction of duty vis-à-vis their own populations but argues that bodies like the International Criminal Court should not have jurisdiction over U.S. officials. U.S. politicians on both sides of the aisle trumpet the virtues of an association of the world's democracies, yet, when it comes to banning landmines and cluster bombs or controlling weapons exports, the United States finds itself aligned against almost all other democratic states and in the company of countries like Pakistan, India, Russia, and China. The United States complains that China and Russia's veto power in the UN Security Council inhibits that body from taking effective action, yet from 1986 to 2007, of the fifty-three vetoes cast, thirty-six were by the United States (and another eleven by Britain and France). By and large, Americans do support a more robust international order—but many make that support contingent on a system conforming to U.S. preferences or giving Washington near total freedom of action, particularly when it comes to the use of force—expectations that were unrealistic even at the height of the unipolar moment of the 1990s.

This domestic incoherence is complemented by a growing international divide between two distinct interpretations of what a "rules-based" international system should be. (I use the shorthand of "Beijing" and "Brussels" to refer to these two poles.[17]) "Brussels" reflects the view that strong, independent international institutions that can limit, bypass, and override the sovereignty of individual states are needed to enforce the rules and to ensure desired outcomes; the sovereign state is de-emphasized in favor of international bodies that look out for the welfare of individuals and serve as a check on national power. For proponents of the "Beijing approach," the international order operates on the basis of contractual obligations taken on by sovereign states; they are interpreted and enforced in the course of a state's bilateral and multilateral relationships. International politics, to quote Weber and his colleagues, is managed "through a neo-Westphalian synthesis comprised of hard-shell states who bargain with each other about the terms of their external relationships, but staunchly respect the rights of each to order its own society, politics and culture without external interference."[18] The challenge confronting the United States (and the European Union) is not simply that the "Beijing model" appeals to nondemocratic regimes but that many of the "Southern democracies" tilt more toward "Beijing" than "Brussels"—something made quite clear in 2008, when India, Brazil, and South Africa aligned themselves with China and Russia in response to Kosovo's unilateral declaration of independence and when Asian and African states rejected the links drawn by France and other Western states between the "responsibility to protect" and the catastrophic failure of the Rangoon regime to provide aid to the people of Burma in the aftermath of Cyclone Nargis. For a majority of the world's states, the role of a "rules-based" system is to serve the interests of states (and those states' rulers)—not citizens. This growing concern with sovereignty was on display in recent comments of Brazil's ambassador to the United States, Antonio de Aguiar Patriota, on efforts to protect the environment and increase energy supplies. Ambassador Patriota said Brazil welcomed "international cooperation" but stressed that "the necessary policies and measures to ensure the sustainable use of natural resources fall unquestionably under the sovereign jurisdictions of the countries" concerned.[19]

While America is largely in alignment with most of the goals and outcomes sought by proponents of the "Brussels model"—a more liberal, democratic, and transparent world order—it is suspicious about the transfer of sovereignty "Brussels" entails. "Beijing's" stress on nation-state prerogatives is more appealing—except that many of the partisans of the "Beijing approach" seem to want to use sovereignty to protect a whole host of odious regimes from international, especially U.S., pressure. This is the context for various "League of Democracies" proposals—attempts to create a world order where nondemocracies might be subject to "Brussels rules" (e.g., active intervention into their domestic affairs) but where democracies would play by "Beijing rules" in their relations with each other.[20] I agree with the criticisms Nossel and Shorr make, but think that this idea will continue to have a good deal of bipartisan resonance in Washington in the years ahead and will indeed complicate consensus-building efforts among the major powers, both democracies and nondemocracies, both of the developed "North and West" and the rising "South and East." Such proposals will also continue to inspire efforts to bypass the United Nations and search for "coalitions of the willing" in dealing with international problems—which will certainly not enhance the development of a global, rules-based system.

At the same time, it is also unrealistic to expect that expanding the membership of key global institutions (UN Security Council, Group of Eight, Organization for Economic Cooperation and Development, etc.) to encompass more states of the global "South and East" will solve the problem. Such countries will not automatically become more supportive of a U.S. or even of a broadly Western agenda simply out of gratitude for being able to join these exclusive clubs and have a seat at the table.

The practical way forward might be the formal retention of the postwar international order but with an ongoing process by which new understandings—some formal, some not—could be negotiated among the major powers, principally resulting from an ongoing dialogue among the United States, the European Union, and China, with the participation of other key actors like India and Russia. This process might then be able to set basic global standards and ensure the adherence of the major powers. Indeed, I predict that we will see a move away from comprehensive treaties and in favor of more limited agreements dealing with specific items—eschewing formal organizations in favor of ad hoc, issued-oriented partnerships.

This could end up being a much more ad hoc process than the authors might like. It would likely produce few enforceable rules in favor of "voluntary mandates" assumed by nation-states and regional organizations at the global level, and indeed a shift from "binding regulations" to "basic standards." In particular, it may require significant compromises on both norms and policies.[21] Minister Xie Feng, deputy chief of mission of the Chinese embassy in Washington, noted earlier this year that the People's Republic of China was not simply another stakeholder but one of the "constructive partners" of the United States in forging the global order. Acknowledging that Beijing and the United States "do not see eye to eye on everything," he expressed the hope "that the United States will meet us halfway" in crafting solutions.[22] Iran may prove to be a test case as to whether Washington is prepared to make such a compromise in return for obtaining the full support of a meaningful global coalition.[23]

One of the "basic standards" that would need to be negotiated would be the terms by which other states would again accept and accommodate U.S. leadership of the global system—in return for more explicit limits and constraints on the exercise of U.S. power around the world. For instance, I do not foresee meaningful progress on efforts to eliminate nuclear weapons even if the United States were to take much more decisive action, since there would always be a lingering suspicion that the United States' true objective is not to make the world safer but to remove any remaining impediments to U.S. military action by freeing its formidable conventional capabilities from the fear of retaliation.

Such a suspicion is entirely reasonable, given recent history. In the aftermath of the 1999 Kosovo war and the 2003 invasion of Iraq, it became clear that the lack of UNSC authorization was no ipso facto impediment to the United States launching a military intervention, even at the expense of a perceived lack of legitimacy. At the same time, the targeted Yugoslav and Iraqi regimes had no appreciable deterrent capabilities, while Iran and North Korea—perceived to be closer to crossing the nuclear threshold—have been engaged primarily through diplomatic means. The appeal of nuclear weapons will diminish not simply because the United States decides to live up to its NPT obligations, but only if other states become convinced that countries like the United States (or a future rising China) are severely constrained in their ability to use overwhelming conventional force.

U.S. leadership will also depend on the extent to which the United States is prepared to reassess its level of involvement in world affairs. On the one hand, on issues such as a peace settlement for the Middle East, the United States will need to be a major participant, as Nossel and Shorr note. On the other hand, several rising powers are now active embryonic intergovernmental organizations that did not exist ten years ago (the Shanghai Cooperation Organization, the India-Brazil-South Africa Dialogue Forum) but that are developing capabilities and marshalling resources that significantly amplify the role of these powers—perhaps even enabling them to bypass or ignore the United States. Should Washington try to thwart groups that offer no leadership role—or can the United States become more comfortable with a "concert of powers" approach (or Franklin D. Roosevelt's vision of the "world's policemen")?[24]

It is important but not sufficient for a leader to occupy the moral high ground. In shaping the post–World War II world, FDR and his team were inspired by principles but also pragmatic enough to make needed trade-offs—including those that directly contradicted some of those ideals—to ensure that other major powers signed on (the veto power of the permanent five members of the UN Security Council being one such example). It is not enough for the United States to "follow the rules"; the other stakeholders must also actively embrace the rules. The postwar European-American partnership (especially as reflected in the International Monetary Fund and The World Bank) had sufficient heft to set the agenda. Today, new dialogues—especially the Sino-American one—will be critical for reshaping the international order. What results from this may not be the ideal. The goal, however, should not be to set idealistic rules that no one, especially the United States, will follow, but instead to strengthen the habits of international cooperation. Such habits may not even be formally defined or codified—we may need to think of "rules" less in terms of law and more as guidelines.

We have been presented with an ambitious agenda, but it may serve us to have a more modest backup plan in place.

# Notes

1. Pew Global Attitudes Project, "Global Unease With Major Powers," June 2007; Chicago Council on Global Affairs and WorldPublicOpinion.org, "World Publics Reject U.S. Role as the World Leader," April 2007.

2. Public Opinion Strategies and Hart Research, "The New American Consensus on International Cooperation," slide 21.

3. "Revitalizing International Cooperation: A Bipartisan Agenda," The Stanley Foundation, November 2007.

4. Suzanne Nossel, "Going Legit," *Democracy: A Journal of Ideas* 3 (2007).

5. Eric Rosand, Alistair Millar, and Jason Ipe, "The UN Security Council's Counterterrorism Program: What Lies Ahead," International Peace Academy, October 2007; "Implementation of the UN Global Counterterrorism Strategy: 42nd Conference on the United Nations of the Next Decade," The Stanley Foundation, June 2007.

6. Don Kraus, "The UN: Pay As You Like It?" *The Globalist* (December 8, 2005).

7. Brian Katulis, Lawrence J. Korb, and Peter Juul, *Strategic Reset: Reclaiming Control of U.S. Security in the Middle East* (Washington, DC: Center for American Progress, 2007).

8. Steven E. Miller, "US Nuclear Policy and International Law: Does Washington Have a Compliance Problem?" prepared for the International Conference on Nuclear Technology and Sustainable Development, Center for Strategic Research, Tehran, Iran, 2005.

9. This new political common ground in the rising generation is also exemplified by Stephen E. Biegun and Jon B. Wolfsthal, "A Full-Court Press Against Nuclear Anarchy," *Bridging the Foreign Policy Divide*, ed. Derek Chollet, Tod Lindberg, and David Shorr (New York: Routledge, 2008), 86–102.

10. Sidney D. Drell and James E. Goodby, "What Are Nuclear Weapons For? Recommendations for Restructuring U.S. Strategic Nuclear Forces," Arms Control Association, Washington, DC, 2005.

11. The scheme given for reductions to minimal forces is based on David Holloway, "Further Reductions in Nuclear Forces: Paper Prepared for the Reykjavik II Conference" (2007), 22–28. Obtained from the author.

12. Ibid.

13. William Luers, Thomas Pickering, and Jim Walsh, "A Solution for the US-Iran Nuclear Standoff," *The New York Review of Books* (March 20, 2008).

14. Zbigniew Brzezinski, *The Choice: Global Domination or Global Leadership* (New York: Basic Books, 2004), 151–63.

15. Ibid., 161.

16. Flynt Leverett, "Black Is the New Green," *The National Interest* (January/February 2008): 44.

17. Harry Harding describes this as the division between "reformers"—mainly Western states, and the "conservatives"—led by Russia and China, with the former emphasizing responsive, autonomous international institutions and the latter defending state sovereignty; presentation at "The Rise of the Rest: How the Ascent of

Russia and China Affects Global Business and Security," Carnegie Council on Ethics and International Affairs, New York, July 1, 2008. Transcript available at www.policyinnovations.org/ideas/briefings/data/000066.

18. Naazneen Barma, Ely Ratner, and Steven Weber, "A World Without the West," *The National Interest*, no. 90 (July/August 2007): 25.

19. Statement released by the Embassy of Brazil, May 21, 2008, at www.brasilemb.org/index.php?option=com_content&task=view&id=348&Itemid=124.

20. Robert Kagan makes this quite clear when, in discussing international regulations, he writes, "they chiefly provide democratic nations the right to intervene in the affairs of nondemocratic nations"; "The End of the End of History," *The New Republic* (April 23, 2008).

21. This would not preclude regional organizations, of course, from proceeding with enacting more stringent rules or even transferring sovereignty from the nation-state to transnational bodies, a process much more advanced in Europe and in its first stages in South America, for instance.

22. "Roundtable with Minister Xie Feng," The Nixon Center, Washington, DC, May 6, 2008.

23. No country in the world has expressed support for Iran obtaining nuclear weapons. There are significant disagreements, though, over whether and how Iran should have access to a nuclear fuel cycle, possible linkages between talks on the nuclear program and Iran's position on Israel and its support for rejectionist Palestinian groups, and possible negative security assurances. This tangle of issues does not bode well for the emergence of a new international consensus.

24. For instance, there has always been a certain ambivalence about a prominent diplomatic role for the European Union in dealing with Iran's nuclear program. Another example of American suspicion toward multilateral initiatives not "made in the United States" was apparent in the Bush administration's tepid comments on President Nicolas Sarkozy's July 2008 "Union of the Mediterranean" summit; Daily Press Briefing, July 14, 2008, at www.state.gov/r/pa/prs/dpb/2008/july/106986.htm.

~

# Japan: Leading or Losing the Way Toward Responsible Stakeholdership?

*Steven Clemons and Weston S. Konishi*
*With a Reaction by Masaru Tamamoto*

The call from then–U.S. Deputy Secretary of State Robert Zoellick urging China to become a "responsible stakeholder" in the international system inevitably reverberated to China's fellow northeast Asian power, Japan, and the Japanese sense of national self and place in the world. The discussion of China as a responsible stakeholdership also offered a template through which other nations, including Japan, are viewing their evolving identities—as well as those of their allies and foes in a plastic, pliable moment in world affairs. In the years since the end of the Cold War, the economic and national security equilibriums to which the world had generally become accustomed have been dramatically undermined, as American leadership of the international system has come into serious doubt, leaving Japan to reassess its proper role and strategic posture.

Indeed, the future role of the United States is a key variable of international security, politics, and economics, especially for Japan's strategic calculus. Therefore, in discussing Japan's future role as a global stakeholder and the evolution of its national identity, it should be noted that Japan's key national security and foreign policy choices have been substantially—though not entirely—determined by America's preferences and direction.

A number of tectonic plates already seem to be shifting: potentially dramatic new power vacuums and instabilities in the international system, continued reliance on global institutions based on anachronistic rather than contemporary power realities, and the likelihood that the United States will attempt to collaborate with Japan and other powers on the drafting of a new global social contract. Consequently, the issue of the nature of "responsible stakeholding" in the next international system is an open question.

## The Japanese Style of International Leadership and Foreign Policy

As for Japan, it has, in almost every respect, been a major responsible stakeholder in the world from the end of World War II up until, at least, the Iraq war of March 2003.[1] Since the end of World War II, Japan has embraced democratic reforms, proven its commitment to international peace, become an engine of economic growth, upheld global norms and institutions, and established itself as an indispensable contributor to a range of international initiatives. In addition, Japan has proven to be a valuable strategic ally of the United States and a reliable partner in the U.S.-led international system. All of these steps have helped Japan achieve its goal of rejoining the international community as a responsible and respectable nation after World War II.

Yet despite all that Japan has achieved in the postwar period, it often strikes a low profile in the international arena—content to follow rather than lead most global initiatives and take a minimalist approach to foreign policymaking in general. Much of this stems from a domestic allergy to international military adventures that was integral to Japan's postwar political culture. This societal antipathy to military power projection was codified, with American help, in Japan's postwar "peace constitution"—which significantly restricts Japanese participation in all but the most narrowly prescribed international security roles. Tokyo has also largely kept its diplomacy squarely within the bounds of the international order and the regional and global status quo—a status quo, it is important to note, in which the United States virtually guaranteed Japan's security and promoted its economic well-being.

Instead, Japan has been most comfortable exerting its influence as the world's second largest economy (though Japan's self-defense forces do represent a formidable military capability, the price tag of which makes it the world's second most expensive). But this strategy of focusing on economic points of leverage leaves Japan vulnerable to charges of "free riding" to protect its security interests—with "dollar diplomacy" as a convenient pretext to avoid the hazards of security operations. Japan was sharply criticized for this approach during the first Gulf War, when Tokyo helped finance allied operations but refused to send its own troops to aid in the liberation of Kuwait. Even today, Tokyo shows a proclivity for throwing money at global problems rather than sending its people to get involved at the ground level; this pattern only reinforces the perception that Japan is a less than fully active member of the international community.

Seen from another angle, by opting out of the enforcement of a rules-based order, Japan has chosen to be a different kind of great power whose economic strength instead requires greater concern and stewardship for non-military international institutions. This gives it a natural interest in many of the agencies and organs of the United Nations (sans the UN Security Council), including the UN High Commission on Refugees, UNESCO, the International Atomic Energy Agency, the World Health Organization, and the UN University. Japan also played dominant, sculpting roles in global economic institutions such the World Trade Organization, the International Monetary Fund, and the World Bank. In fact, if military dominance is fading in importance as a source of influence, Japan may be the first nation to demonstrate what a twenty-first-century normal "global stakeholder" might look like. Japan's record in exerting this form of influence and leadership over the last several decades showed that it could derive national sovereignty and power from its commitment to and stewardship of international institutions that it had no role in conceiving.

Japan had interests like any other nation, but it has largely refrained from engaging in global military matters, instead pursuing its interests through international economic and political institutions, and in effect promoting global interdependence as a public good and a way to diversify its security portfolio away from exclusive dependence on the United States. Japan thus emerged as a hybrid nation—one that combined both a normal, utility-maximizing, interest-driven nation with one that also looked to the international collective for security and strength. Japanese leaders have regularly made the argument that nations can attain security by embedding themselves, their interests, and ambitions in structures of interdependence that generated more public goods than the sum of its independent parts—and from which the costs of defection would be enormous. In many ways, then, Japan already established itself as the epitome of a "responsible stakeholder" nation before the term was even coined.

Regrettably, Japan's deep-rooted insecurities and fear of being different from other states has prompted it to abandon some stakeholder norms and habits. What Japan's national debate over becoming a "normal nation" failed to recognize is that Japan had already become a twenty-first-century "normal nation"—one that had shed the anachronistic trappings of normality to become a global stakeholder. When former Prime Minister Junichiro Koizumi, who had helped stoke the embers of a revived hawkish nationalism in Japan, abandoned a UN-centered diplomacy by sending Japanese self-defense forces to support America's March 2003 military action against Iraq, Japan opted for twentieth-century state normality and forfeited its position at the vanguard of a twenty-first-century redefinition of what a normal state would do.

For Japan, therefore, the question is not whether it will become a responsible stakeholder in the future, for it has already achieved that status. Rather, the issue is whether Japan can in the next decade re-engineer the terms of its global engagement and maintain active leadership in supporting the global common good—and whether it can do so in a way that helps stabilize and add to global welfare even as the United States slips from its dominant global position. To accomplish this, Japan will need to overcome various domestic impediments—including constitutional restrictions on collective security as well as a reluctance to commit human, rather than financial, resources to on-the-ground operations that promote international peace and stability. Indeed, contemporary global challenges call for a more active Japan that will extend its postwar achievements to further broaden and deepen its role in supporting international norms and institutions.

## Japanese National Identity: Implications for Stakeholdership

Today, Japanese intellectuals and policymakers are engaged in an ongoing debate about their nation's identity in the world and the nature of its power.[2] In many respects, this debate will set the contours and parameters of Japan's involvement as a responsible stakeholder in global affairs. Throughout most of the Cold War period, Japanese saw their nation as a "peaceful economic state" that was content to rely on the United States as its security guarantor, an arrangement that was codified by the 1946 peace constitution and the 1951 U.S.-Japan security treaty. But now many younger Japanese especially call for a more assertive international role and greater strategic independence from the United States. Some argue for Japan to become a "normal" nation, with a revision of article 9 of the peace constitution and augmented defense capabilities commensurate with its economic strength. Still others suggest that Japan should remain essentially as it is—an economic power with limited military capabilities.

The parameters that frame this debate are telling. On one hand, the debate tends to discount the merits of Japan's postwar experiment of balancing a close security arrangement with the United States and strong commitment to the international institutions that are a key feature of global stakeholding. On the other hand, the proposed changes indicate relatively modest power ambitions.[3] Even mainstream advocates of "normal" nation status do not argue for Japan to become a major military power beyond the bounds of the U.S.-Japan alliance. In general, the most compelling proposals for amending article 9 are aimed at legitimizing the nation's armed forces rather than scrapping the nation's constitutional ban on armed conflict as a means of resolving international disputes. On the contrary, "normal" nation proponents want to loosen Japan's stringent restrictions on the right of collective self-defense in order to participate more liberally in international peacekeeping operations and certain contingencies within the context of the U.S.-Japan alliance.

In fact, it is worth asking whether a fully "normalized" Japan—operating more autonomously from the United States and with an ostensibly more robust defense posture—would ultimately make it *more* of a stakeholder. But that depends on what is meant by *normal*. Presumably, a "normal" Japan would have a larger standing military, greater and more lethal power projection capabilities, and perhaps some form of nuclear deterrent. Such an extensive buildup would significantly raise anxieties throughout Asia, particularly in China, and likely lead to an arms race that could destabilize the region. Indeed, an incipient form of that arms race may already be underway. Therefore, in many ways, Japan might claim responsible stakeholder status simply by refraining from "going normal" to the fullest extent, and thereby avoiding a significant disruption of the regional status quo.

This appears to be the conclusion of a majority of mainstream policymakers and intellectuals in Japan. Indeed, if a consensus on the exact nature of Japan's postwar security identity has not yet emerged, there does seem to be widespread support for the nation to maintain its basic postwar role as an economic power committed to world peace, but also do more to contribute to collective security operations. Moreover, despite attempts by Prime Ministers Junichiro Koizumi, Shinzo Abe, and now Taro Aso to move Japan away from embedded internationalism to a more traditional national interest economic and security mercantilism, Japan is not apt to be a very differently styled power ten years from now than it is today. In other words, Japan will likely remain a stunted military and economic power for the foreseeable future and will, consequently, not become a significant norm-setting leader in the realm of international security. Instead, Japan will likely continue to be active in *supporting* international security norms, and occasionally take the lead within its established comfort zone—for instance, promoting environmental standards, nuclear nonproliferation, and international economic development.

Yet even absent a fundamental change in the nature of Japanese power, there are numerous areas in which it can play a more active role as a leading nation in the global community. The following sections outline a set of measures, across several issue areas, in which Japan can maximize its international contributions and enhance its status as a responsible stakeholder over the next ten years.

## Overcoming Domestic Impediments

A responsible stakeholder is, by definition, a nation with its own house in order, ready to contribute to the international common good above and beyond its own parochial national interests. Postwar Japan has certainly lived up to that basic benchmark. But the prospect for Japan to raise its stakeholdership to another level is clouded by at least four major looming domestic challenges. These include: 1) weak domestic political leadership; 2) underperforming economic growth; 3) a rapidly aging society; 4) and the potential rise of a virulent form of nationalism. Overcoming these obstacles, we believe, will be the threshold test of whether Japan is capable of shouldering greater international responsibilities.

### Political Reform
Japan's current state of political inertia hardly bodes well for the nation's ability to confront future challenges and assume a greater international role. Since July 2007, the Japanese Diet (parliament) has been divided between the ruling coalition-controlled Lower House and the opposition parties' control of the Upper House. The "split Diet" has all but paralyzed the legislative process, leaving critical bills and policies in a state of gridlock. Add to this the precarious state of the ruling coalition and uninspired leadership across the political spectrum, and it is hard to see a political basis for strategic policymaking. Most troubling of all is the fact that lawmakers have studiously (if cynically) avoided considering legislation to address the nation's looming challenges—from macro-economic reform to boost economic performance to a revamped security policy to enhance Japan's strategic standing in the world community.

While a prescription for Japan's political problems is beyond the scope of this chapter, at a bare minimum, wholesale political reform will be a precondition for Japan to enhance its international responsibilities. One tangible benchmark would be a potential realignment of parties that manages to unify the split Diet (possibly as early as the 2009 Lower House elections and as late as the next Upper House elections in 2013). Another potential outcome of these elections could be a more fundamental political and ideological realignment if the ruling Liberal Democratic Party (LDP) suffers a dramatic defeat. Ideally, the political environment resulting from reform or realignment will be one conducive to visionary and dynamic policymaking with a new generation of leaders willing to tackle the nation's core challenges.

### Economic Strength

Among the challenges confronting Japan are erratic economic performance and a rapidly aging society. As a self-styled "economic power," Japan's ability to be an international leader depends on a robust and competitive domestic economy. Even before the announcement of its current recession, Japan's projected GDP growth of 1.5 percent per annum seemed unacceptably low for such an advanced and prosperous economy.[4] Japan faces numerous other economic difficulties, including (but not limited to) an ossifying and highly protected agriculture sector, an underperforming service industry, low domestic consumption and ballooning public debt approaching 200 percent of the GDP—and all against the backdrop now of a global economic crisis. Reversing these trends with bold economic reforms will be an important sign of whether Japan is capable of maintaining its economic prowess over the long run.

Furthermore, given the recent collapse of credit and lending in the international system and the dawning appreciation for the fragility of the entire international financial order, most believe that a wholly new global financial arrangement is required. Japan should and will be expected to play a leadership role in helping to design a revised global financial architecture. But merely joining global policymakers at the commanding heights will not be sufficient to constitute robust "stakeholding" in this arena. Japan must also work to reorient its domestic economic patterns toward a more sustainable balance between production and consumption. The U.S. has been the world's consumer of last resort, and, given America's economic meltdown and years of expected malaise, the global economic order will need substantial upticks in consumption in the world's other leading economies—particularly Japan and China, but also Europe.

### Demographic Challenges

Mounting demographic challenges also hamper Japan's economic prospects. Beginning in 2005, the country's population began contracting, and it is estimated that by 2055, 40 percent of the nation's population will be over the age of sixty-five. This trend presents a significant hindrance as Japan tries to put itself on an economically vibrant and productive trajectory for the long term. To reiterate, this is a problem that demands bold measures—which current leadership is evading. Whether Tokyo ultimately implements much-needed policies such as immigration reform and improved conditions for women in the workforce will signal the nation's readiness to tackle the looming demographic crisis before it is too late.

## The Potential Rise of Nationalism

The challenge of Japanese nationalism is not to keep it entirely in check, but to channel it constructively. Here, Japan must walk a fine line. In the postwar period, repressing patriotic sentiment was an important way of breaking from Japan's militarist past and proving to the world community that it was once again a respectable nation. However, a younger generation of Japanese now yearns to shed this postwar guilt and contrition and become a more confident and assertive society, both domestically and internationally. If pursued prudently and constructively, this kind of "healthy nationalism" could actually instill a new sense of purpose that might help propel Japan toward more dynamic international leadership.

On the other hand, if Japanese nationalism were to take a more negative form, then the ramifications for regional and global affairs could be calamitous. At the very least, a powerful nationalist movement could lead to a more insular Japan that might redirect resources and attention inward, rather than outward toward the global common good; Japan's right-wing, for instance, has long opposed economic aid to China and the Koreas, which only highlights the political vulnerability of broader international aid efforts. At worst, a more virulent, hawkish form of nationalism might rekindle traditional militarist sentiments, potentially raising tensions with regional neighbors to dangerous levels. Indeed, a belligerently nationalistic Japan would present a major challenge to global peace and stability—a stark contrast with its current role, cultivated over the decades, as a respected pillar of the international community.

Nor are internal political pressures the only factor that could spur resurgent nationalism. America's decline as a global hegemon, combined with heightened competition among great powers, could cause serious instability in the global system. If the United States is not able to provide the security upon which Japan has depended for over sixty years, it could easily revert to aggressive nationalist impulses and behaviors—particularly with regard to China. Some of these tendencies can already be seen in Japan's reluctance to subordinate a desire to square accounts with North Korea over its abduction of Japanese citizens to the arguably more consequential challenge of North Korea's nuclear weapons program.

There are no signs yet that Japan is on a path toward again becoming a belligerently nationalistic power. Much will depend on how Japanese leaders supplant the postwar mind-set with a new sense of national pride and purpose. Over the next five to ten years, a younger cohort of Japanese leaders will rise to positions of power and influence, replacing the generation of leaders who came of age in the postwar period. This younger generation knows that it wants Japan to be more "assertive," but the nature of this new assertiveness remains vague. Japanese leaders can help allay fears of rising nationalism by more clearly elucidating their vision.

## Diplomatic Priorities

If Japan is to enhance its responsibility and leadership in the international community, it must take advantage of opportunities to maximize its contributions to the global common good. We have identified a number of key potential diplomatic priorities for Japan as a rising stakeholder.

### Resolving Historical Memory Issues

The greatest shortcoming of Japanese foreign policy in the postwar period has been the failure to fundamentally settle historical grievances with its mainland neighbors, Korea and China. Not all the blame rests on Japan for this predicament; Seoul and Beijing have often played the history card for domestic political purposes. Yet Tokyo has also willfully stirred historical controversy in ways that have ultimately harmed its diplomatic interests. Controversial visits to Yasukuni Shrine by Japanese prime ministers, textbooks that whitewash Japan's aggression during the war, and insensitive remarks by high officials have all complicated Japan's efforts to put the past behind and focus on future relations with neighboring nations.

In order to do so, Japan need not flagellate itself for past grievances, but it must avoid needlessly provoking disputes that only inflame tempers on the Asian mainland. A national effort to promote tolerance in much the way that German public schools have fostered healthy inquiry about the past and the present—shielded from nationalist-driven retribution—would constitute major progress and reassurance for regional neighbors concerned about Japan's historical memory problem.

Regrettably, one of the by-products (or moral hazards) of America's prominent military presence in the Asian Pacific is that politicians in the Koreas, Japan, and China recklessly exploit historical grievances safe in the knowledge that the American military serves as a buffer against any consequent flare-up or escalation. If the U.S. military presence declines, however, this habitual sparring over war memory may not subside and could in fact trigger serious collisions between Japan and its neighbors—or at least lead to high costs economically or diplomatically.

Reaching some degree of closure on history would also help boost trust among Japan's neighbors and create greater diplomatic space for Japan to pursue a more active international role, from UN peacekeeping operations to helping to maintain regional stability. Indeed, closing the book on the history problem—but actually "opening" the book on Japanese historical behavior and other issues in its domestic arena—will be a key indicator of Japan's ability to manifest "responsible stakeholder behavior" in this arena and forge a more engaged and effective regional leadership role for itself over the coming years.

### Establishing Foreign Policy Principles

As Japan extends its international involvement and becomes a more asser-tive player, it should articulate a clear set of core principles that underpin its foreign policy. In the past, Japan's declared diplomatic posture tended to focus on foreign policy means rather than ends—for instance, an emphasis on multilateralism rather than a normative disposition on, say, democracy or human rights. As noted sociologist Chie Nakane once put it, "Japan is not moral or immoral. Japan is amoral." In the future, though, Japan should bolster its credibility as a leading promoter of global norms and institutions with arguments for why these are important.

To the extent that Japan has embarked on such an initiative, some of the content is disconcerting to the authors of this chapter. In November 2006, the government of then Prime Minister Shinzo Abe announced a fourth pil-lar of Japanese diplomacy: the promotion of universal values such as freedom, democracy, human rights, the rule of law, and free market economies.[5] This policy course may trace back to an alignment with Washington and the values-driven militancy of a then-ascendant neoconservative movement in American politics, but it clearly represented a departure from Japan's tradi-tional economically based foreign policy. Such an emphasis also moves Japan away from its long-standing use of intergovernmental institutions to embed and enwrap—and thereby make interdependent—all major nations, regard-less of their commitment to democratic norms.

Since the 2007 collapse of the Abe cabinet, Japan's experiment with values diplomacy has been sporadic. Prime Minister Yasuo Fukuda, whose term was short-lived after succeeding the more hawkish Shinzo Abe, at-tempted but failed to reorient Japan toward international structures, an ethic of interdependence, and less demonization of nondemocratic states such as China and Iran. However, current Prime Minister Taro Aso, an early advocate of the emphasis on values, may yet revive a "values diplo-macy program."

Yet regardless of such changes in governmental leadership a more consistently implemented "values diplomacy" could boost Japan's role in supporting a norms-based international system—particularly in encouraging the growth of democracy in developing states. Values diplomacy offers a basis for cooperation with like-minded nations, from Europe to Australia, to uphold democratic principles and promote global stability. Japan's leadership in this area would likely differ somewhat from a Western approach, perhaps taking a less interventionist and more patient approach. In that respect, Japanese leadership could be quite constructive in promoting democracy, particularly among nations wary of outside "interference" in domestic affairs.

## Participating in Collective Self-Defense

The most severe constraint on Japan's international role has been its strict adherence to the pacifist principles embodied in article 9 of its postwar constitution. As a consistent policy, Japanese leaders have interpreted article 9 as forbidding their country from *exercising* the right of collective self-defense. This, in turn, has prevented Japan from entering into a reciprocal security treaty with the United States and from full participation in international security activities, including many UN-sanctioned peacekeeping operations (PKO). In recent years, Japanese policymakers have begun discussing ways to revise article 9 while still preserving a principled rejection of war as a legitimate means of international statecraft.

Given the political gridlock in the Diet, however, this debate has proceeded slowly. Even so, it is reasonable to expect Japanese lawmakers to grapple with the issue in the next several years and reach some conclusion about revising article 9—perhaps opening the way for enhanced Japanese participation in collective self-defense. Indeed, progress on this front will mark a significant milestone in Japan's broader efforts to become a more active contributor to international peace and stability. Conversely, the most constructive revision of article 9 would be framed within a resumed embrace of international institutions like the United Nations in matters of sanctioning war and promoting peace, rather than the expedient, realpolitik approach Prime Minister Koizumi took when he sidestepped the UN in support of the U.S. military invasion of Iraq.

## Attaining Permanent UNSC Status

Japan has long sought a permanent seat on the UN Security Council (UNSC) to boost its international prestige and leverage in the global community and overcome any remaining stigma from World War II. Tokyo stakes its claim on a number of arguments such as its postwar record as a leading proponent of global norms and its significant financial and human contributions to the United Nations. Yet Tokyo's strategy of attaining a permanent UNSC seat through broader UN reform has repeatedly failed, in part due to resistance from China. Even the United States, which rhetorically supports Japan's ascension to the UN Security Council, has not backed up its declared position with a real diplomatic push.

On its face, Japan's case for a permanent UNSC seat is quite compelling. It is the world's second largest economy, with a proven commitment to world peace and a nonmilitarist foreign policy that embodies the spirit of the UN Charter. The prospect of its membership on the UN Security Council can only be seen as positive for the body. But it is unclear if Japanese policymakers as yet view a permanent UNSC seat as political payment for services rendered or as an opportunity for Japan to play an even greater role in promoting international peace and security. It is telling, for instance, that the current domestic debate on the subject rarely acknowledges the point that a permanent seat on the UN Security Council would likely require some loosening of collective security restrictions. Clearly Japan's membership on the council would be of greater benefit to the world if the nation is prepared to use its enhanced status as a springboard for more active participation in such areas as UNPKO.

### Maintaining Official Development Assistance Levels

Among Japan's most prominent contributions to the global common good has been its significant official development assistance (ODA), which earned it the rank of top global donor from 1991 to 2001. In the past, Japan's ODA was driven by several factors. First, much of Japan's ODA was directed toward nations that were its victims in World War II. In all but name, this aid was a form of war reparations that Japan turned to its own commercial ends. So, while nations in Southeast Asia received large-scale aid from Japan, these funds were tied to Japanese industrial contracts and served a second purpose of helping fuel Japan's manufacturing industry expansion. Thirdly, because of complex quid pro quo arrangements in the U.S.-Japan security and economic relationship, Japanese ODA was often used as a proxy of American national security priorities. Finally, Japan saw ODA as strategic leverage over debtor nations like China—an approach that ultimately proved ineffective in the evolving post–Cold War security environment.

Today, Japanese policy is no longer driven by these considerations. And as a result, ODA has declined. Japan's ranking as an ODA donor has now slipped to fifth place, with aid constituting just 0.17 percent of gross national income. This trend is set to continue, since Tokyo's fiscal plans call for further aid cuts through 2011.

Meanwhile, even as Japanese aid levels decline, the global need for development assistance is rising—particularly in Africa, where foreign aid is critical for economic development, and social and political stability. In this regard, Japan's leadership in promoting aid to Africa through the Tokyo International Conference on African Development (TICAD) has been a welcome contribution. But here again, Japan could fall prey to its previous habit of using ODA as a strategic tool if its aid program serves primarily as a competition with China over the resource-rich African continent. Ultimately, Japan's success as a major ODA donor will be measured by striking a healthier balance between the pursuit of its interests and a more genuine commitment to improving the economic welfare of recipient nations. That, along with consistent increases in its ODA budget, will be a significant indicator of Japan's commitment to the global common good.

## Coping with the Rise of China

While the rise of China's power and influence presents challenges for the entire global community, the strategic impact of this rise is of paramount concern for Japanese policymakers, given Japan's geographic proximity to China and the delicate balance of power between the two countries. Currently, Tokyo's approach toward China mirrors that of the United States—with geopolitical hedging via the U.S.-Japan alliance and economic engagement through massive bilateral trade flows, direct investment, and cooperation in economic and trade forums such as APEC and ASEAN + 3. Indeed, a key test of Japan's future leadership will be how it balances these hedging and engagement strategies while helping usher China toward deeper integration into the international community. Tokyo can best accomplish this by resolving differences with Beijing such as historical disagreements and disputed oil resources in the East China Sea and fostering opportunities for expanded Chinese diplomatic involvement in multilateral institutions.

Fortunately, the recent short tenure of Japanese Prime Minister Yasuo Fukuda included a warming in China-Japan relations. In fact, one of the first "visuals" after Fukuda succeeded the more hawkish and generally China-suspicious Shinzo Abe was a "baseball catch" in full baseball uniform between Chinese Premier Wen Jiabao and Prime Minister Fukuda. Some thought that this "pitcher's mound diplomacy" was orchestrated as a conscious counterpoint to a similar moment between President George W. Bush and then–Prime Minister Junichiro Koizumi at Camp David—and the associated joint spurning of UN-based global security management in favor of a realpolitik

U.S.-Japan arrangement in the second Gulf War. Fukuda was signaling that China could be a key partner of Japan and that a zero-sum game between the two Asian giants could be avoided in favor of mutual interdependence.

It is unclear whether Japan's leadership will choose the more untethered course of realpolitik with regard to China or pursue something closer to Fukuda's posture of engagement with China and promotion of security and prosperity through institutionalized interdependence. The recent rapprochement, nevertheless, points toward a clear, practical agenda of shared concerns from climate change to international economic development. The extent to which the two countries continue this bilateral cooperation on regional and global initiatives—as well as avoiding potential conflicts with Beijing that lead to destabilizing outcomes—will be a key indicator of their commitment to concurrently become responsible powers in the global community.

## International Security

Although some experts see Japan on a path toward becoming a "normal" nation in the security realm, the constraints of its postwar constitution and its reliance on the U.S. security guarantee will continue to place limitations on Japan's international security role. Further, because of Japan's modest aspirations as a military power, it will likely be more of a follower than a leader when it comes to most global security issues. That said, there are many areas where Japan can boost its contribution to global peace and stability—from strengthening the U.S.-Japan alliance to improving its PKO contributions and building on its respected record in nonproliferation, arms control, and the goal of a nuclear-free world.

### U.S.-Japan Alliance

The U.S.-Japan alliance is the cornerstone of Japan's foreign and defense policies. As the bilateral security treaty approaches its fiftieth anniversary, the alliance appears to be fundamentally healthy. Nevertheless, there is plenty of room for Tokyo to take greater leadership in addressing the alliance's near and long-term challenges. The most immediate concern, particularly from Washington's perspective, is continued Japanese contributions to help deal with violent Islamist extremism around the world. Japan's commitment to Maritime Self-Defense Force refueling missions in the Indian Ocean has been an integral element of America's force projection in the Middle East. Initially approved by the Diet in 2001, under the so-called anti-terror special measures law, the refueling missions have provided prosaic yet valuable support for U.S. and coalition-led anti-terror operations in Afghanistan. The missions were briefly interrupted in 2007, when the Fukuda cabinet was unable to pass legislation to extend them, but were resumed at the beginning of 2008. Since the anti-terror law must be approved annually, these missions are likewise in jeopardy each year of being suspended or even terminated. The United States has repeatedly signaled that the refueling missions are a valuable contribution to the anti-terror effort and their termination would be taken as a serious blow to the bilateral alliance.

The legacy of the Iraq war, it should be noted, casts the U.S.-Japan alliance in a new light. The repercussions of the Bush administration's decision to invade Iraq without UNSC approval cannot be overemphasized. In effect, they opened a serious fracture in the global order. Prior to the Iraq war, Japan's support of U.S. foreign policy gave a good indication of what Japan was doing to help promote the global good—as American and global goods were largely convergent. The war, however, has cast doubt on whether American national security policy is in fact contributing to international public goods. And thus, while Japan has been supporting America's military program in the Middle East and Iraq, Japan's activities do not constitute "responsible stakeholder" behavior.

A second near-term challenge confronting the bilateral alliance is the implementation of force realignment plans reached by Japan and the United States in 2005. The purpose of these plans is to "transform" the U.S.-Japan alliance to meet future security threats while reducing the "footprint" of the U.S. military presence in the Japanese archipelago, particularly in Okinawa.

Among the steps mandated by the joint agreements are the redeployment of some eight thousand U.S. Marines from Okinawa to Guam and the relocation of the Futenma U.S. Marine airbase from downtown Naha, Okinawa, to a less densely populated area on the island. Yet local resistance to the measures has stalled progress on the realignment process, leading to renewed strains between Tokyo and Washington. Over the next few years, it will be critical for Tokyo to make progress in implementing the realignment plans to keep the strategic transformation of the bilateral alliance on track.

Over the long-term, however, the single greatest constraint on Japan's role in the bilateral alliance will remain its constitutional restrictions on the right of collective self-defense. While the SDF deployments to the Indian Ocean in 2001 and Iraq in 2003 were major steps, they also represent a plateau for what Japan can do under existing constitutional parameters. Meanwhile, U.S. expectations of Japan continue to rise in areas such as joint missile defense, the protection of U.S. forces in combat, and developing the bilateral alliance into one with truly global reach. If Japan is to meet such expectations—as well as its own aspirations for a greater role in international security affairs—then loosening its constitutional restrictions will be an important step.

## Peacekeeping Operations

Perhaps the most disappointing aspect of Japan's commitment to international security has been its anemic contributions of troops to UN peacekeeping operations over the years. It is true that Japan's significant financial contributions to UNPKO are critical to their ongoing operations. Nevertheless, Japan has deployed its own PKO personnel only sparingly since its first mission to Cambodia in 1992—despite the Ministry of Defense's stated goal of making peacekeeping operations a main pillar of SDF activity.[6] Currently, Japan has just thirty-five personnel deployed abroad in UN peacekeeping operations, making it eighty-second among the world's troop contributors. Much of the problem traces back to the sclerotic and ad hoc legislative process for approving Japanese PKO deployments.

Another persistent legislative obstacle is the parliament's tortuously esoteric debate on the use of arms each time an overseas SDF deployment is considered. A proposed "general law" (ippan-hou) includes measures to streamline legislative approval of overseas troop deployments, but its passage has been shelved as part of the overall gridlock in the Diet. Passage of this general law within the next several years, followed by a more robust PKO profile in trouble spots like the Sudan, would represent great strides forward.

## Humanitarian Relief

One area in which Japan has been a major international leader is in its contributions to humanitarian relief efforts. Humanitarian relief operations fit neatly into Japan's self-image as a "civilian power"—dedicated to nonmilitary means of promoting the global common good. These activities also give Japan an opportunity to send SDF personnel to operations that stir less controversy than typical combat conditions. In recent years, the two most prominent such operations were Tokyo's dispatch of six hundred SDF troops for postwar reconstruction efforts in southern Iraq and Japan's prompt provision of humanitarian aid in the wake of the 2004 tsunami disaster.

Since these activities seem to fit Japan so naturally, Tokyo could easily take an even greater role in strengthening and institutionalizing such operations. For instance, Japan could take the lead in formalizing a quadrilateral humanitarian relief mechanism (among the United States, India, and Australia) to prepare for potential future natural disasters. Japan could also incorporate China and South Korea into such a mechanism as a regional confidence-building measure.

## Regional Security

Fostering a stable regional security environment is a top priority of Japanese foreign policy, and also a key test of the nation's international role more broadly. In terms of its past record, Japan's involvement in regional security issues has evolved considerably. Throughout the Cold War, Japan took an essentially passive approach toward regional security, signaling its neighbors through its subdued military posture that it was no longer a threat. Since the end of the Cold War, however, Tokyo has taken a more active role in regional security as it has steered its way in the evolving regional security environment. Tokyo has, for instance, widened its role in the U.S.-Japan alliance to include rear-area support for contingencies in "areas surrounding Japan" and looked to regional security institutions such as the ASEAN Regional Forum (ARF) to enhance confidence-building and strategic transparency in Asia. Japan has also tried to help resolve the North Korea crisis through the Six-Party Talks and, most recently, established new strategic ties with Australia and India as a hedge against rising Chinese influence. Given that its limited "hard power" assets restrict its ability to take the lead in regional security initiatives, Japanese support for multilateral confidence-building and cooperation among Asian powers may be the best avenue through which Japan can promote regional stability.

## Regional Prosperity

At another level, Japan's long-standing emphasis on economic statecraft as opposed to classic security and power projection puts it in a strong position to contribute to regional financial stability—as important, if not more so, than hatching new regional security frameworks. Japan's so-called Miyazawa plan during in the 1997–1998 East Asian financial crisis helped prevent a regional collapse of credit and financing by creating instruments to fill the gap left by the pullback of American and European financial institutions.

The crisis destroyed Asian confidence in the neoliberal "Washington consensus" and the International Monetary Fund's involvement in the economic affairs of states in the region. As leaders around the world drew their own lessons from the crisis, it triggered the trend toward amassing huge currency reserves, not only in China but also by many nations.

Japan's stewardship of regional economic health indeed reinforces its claim as a global stakeholder. As an unintended consequence, however, the actions Japan took then also displaced the United States and Europe from their dominance of the global financial order—leaving the question of what order has replaced it. Indeed, Japan has been largely absent in the discussions about what to do to restore solvency to the global economic order after the credit collapse of 2008. Japan has been primarily focused on its own economic problems and the health of its own domestic equities, a focus not necessarily consistent with responsible stakeholding behavior.[7]

## North Korea

The most immediate security concern facing Japan is the ongoing nuclear crisis with North Korea. Japan has joined the United States, China, South Korea, and Russia in engaging Pyongyang in an attempt to resolve the crisis. Yet Japan's involvement in the Six-Party Talks has been criticized on the grounds of its preoccupation with the issue of Japanese abducted by the North Korean regime. With its resistance to deal-making with North Korea as long as the abductee issue remains unresolved, Japan has at times seemed sidelined in the ongoing Six-Party process (such as when it was the only nation to decline participation in recent installments of heavy fuel oil to North Korea). Recently, though, there appears to be greater political space for Tokyo to take a more flexible approach toward Pyongyang. A softening of Japan's hard-line position, as well as enhanced support for a united diplomatic front, will signal its appreciation of the high stakes for regional security and stability. Further, should a major breakthrough lead to the denuclearization of North Korea, Japan's willingness to normalize diplomatic relations with the regime will be an important element of any comprehensive resolution to the crisis.

Yet in terms of Japan's longer-term prospects as a responsible global stakeholder, its recent behavior on North Korea can only be seen as worrisome. Notwithstanding the inevitable emotionalism that the abductee issue represents in Japan as well as the very real trauma in the lives of the affected families, the larger global concern of keeping weapons of mass destruction out of terrorist, nonstate hands, and also halting any further expansion of North Korea's nuclear warhead production, is beyond doubt. These are the greater global goods for which, owing to its own myopia, Japan has given less than full support. At some point, Japan will have to calculate whether policies that play to hard-line domestic sentiments should really take precedence over the global security agenda at more serious and consequential levels. To some degree, the first step down this slippery demagogic slope was Koizumi's abandonment of principled Japanese support and promotion of international institutions that enmesh and constrain state behavior.

## Nuclear Nonproliferation

As the only nation to have suffered a mass casualty nuclear attack, Japan takes special pride in being among the most dedicated proponents of nonproliferation—a role for which it has earned much respect in the global community. Japan's commitment to nonproliferation is expressed by its long-held three nonnuclear principles: not to possess, produce, or permit nuclear weapons into Japan. In addition, Japan is a strong supporter of the Nuclear Nonproliferation Treaty (NPT) as well as the Comprehensive Nuclear-Test-Ban Treaty (CTBT), and has actively worked to support and enforce both of these arms control regimes. More recently, Tokyo joined the U.S.-led Proliferation Security Initiative (PSI) to control the transfer of illicit nuclear materials and arms on the high seas. In the future, Japan can maintain the respect it enjoys as a nonnuclear state by continuing to uphold its nonnuclear principles, particularly its pledge not to develop nuclear weapons.

But Tokyo is occasionally caught in a dilemma when the United States, its senior ally, works to undermine nonproliferation regimes, by backing out of the CTBT or striking ad hoc nuclear agreements with NPT outlier India. Armed with the credibility and influence of a close ally, Japan could burnish its bona fides as a globally responsible stakeholder by being a more forceful critic of Washington to spur the United States to uphold globally accepted nonproliferation norms.

Finally, Japan can take a more active role in the enforcement of norms. Despite its membership in PSI, for instance, Japan has refrained from getting involved in interdiction activities due to its strict constitutional limitations on collective self-defense. Particularly in this context, those restrictions are ripe for reinterpretation.

On the other hand, much less well known than Japan's image as a vigorous supporter of nuclear nonproliferation is the threat posed by its civilian nuclear power industry. Japan has imported more weapons grade plutonium than any other nation in the world and has created a system of networked nuclear power production based on nuclear fuel reprocessing. An MIT study—funded by the Japanese government and then subject to a government attempt to suppress it—concluded that the only rational interpretation of Japan's dependence on the type of plutonium it imports is a drive for the capacity to build nuclear weapons.[8] Henry Kissinger has said that Japan is a nuclear weapons nation in all but name and could assemble and deploy warheads in very short order. Japan has protested this interpretation of its nuclear power industry, but other nations, particularly Iran, have found in the Japanese example an ideal model for declared civilian intentions. As additional states declare that they want Japan's nuclear energy capacity and profile, a key test of Japan's "responsible stakeholder" status will be its eventual willingness to forfeit a do-mestic plutonium reserve in favor of international reprocessing arrangements suitable for Iran and others pledging to remain nonweapon states. If Japan remains an outlier on such issues, it only contributes to further international problems rather than helping seek international remedies.

## The International Arms Trade

The global trade in small arms and larger systems is another area in which Japan took a principled stance through self-restraint—imposing a ban on the export of arms to other countries. Japan has also recently played an important role in supporting disarmament efforts in Afghanistan. While Japan remains committed to ground-level postconflict disarmament and de-mobilization efforts, such as in Afghanistan and Cambodia, it has begun to soften its principles on export of major systems and high-technology in order to accommodate joint missile defense cooperation with the United States. Although Tokyo is likely to face increased pressure from Washington to further relax these restrictions over time, Japan should proceed cautiously in reevaluating its arms export policies. In addition to regional sensitivities that might be triggered by Japan's potential arms sales, it would be an unwelcome development if Japan emerged as a new major supplier of arms in the global market. Japan's restraint in this regard will be an important indication of its true commitment to international arms control.

## Economics

Before the global economic adage was applied to China, Japan was regularly accused of overproducing, exporting, and underconsuming—thereby con-tributing to a huge fault line in the global economic order, with the United States, conversely, underproducing and overconsuming. In both cases, the world eventually became too comfortable with and dependent on a glutton-ous United States as the primary engine driving global growth.

Those patterns of behavior have come to a dramatic halt with the global credit meltdown of the fall of 2008, confronting, initially, President George W. Bush and then President Barack Obama and other world leaders with the challenge of re-engineering the world's financial architecture. But in terms of "responsible stakeholding," one of the most important things Japan could do, for its own sake and the world's, is to wean itself from export-led growth and instead build more sustainable domestic consumption. Given the United States' diminished ability to play the role of consumption powerhouse, global economic vitality will depend upon the willingness and capacity of China, India, and Japan to unleash the domestic demand latent in their economies.

This process, in turn, could be facilitated by a revitalized multilateral trade regime, under the World Trade Organization (WTO) and other institutions, that promotes greater penetration of foreign goods and services into these key markets. If Japan and leading economies other than the United States move down this route, it would be a truly impressive display of global economic stewardship, not to mention responsible stakeholdership.

On another front, Japan is clearly one of the technology leaders in the world, and the next major challenge to the global economy is to transition to a new international energy regime less dependent on fossil fuels and without unacceptable environmental costs. Private sector and government investment will drive this new technological imperative, but the real test of leadership will not just be development but global dispersal, particularly in developing states like China, India, and many smaller states for which it is even more difficult to adopt technologies other than fossil fuel and coal consumption. Japan can be a key leader in both the development of technology and its deployment.

**Environment**
Ever since the initial success of the Kyoto Protocol in securing a (short-lived) international commitment to reduce greenhouse gas emissions, Japan's citizens and government have been agitators for the United States and other important global economies and large-scale firms to undertake new commitments. Japanese industry—particularly in the energy development, deployment, management sectors as well as automakers, construction firms, and utilities—has embraced the "environmental imperative," taking a cue from the government's emphasis on environmental sustainability as a national priority and an element of foreign policy. Japanese auto manufacturers lead the world in fuel efficiency and in the production of hybrid vehicles that use alternative energy sources. Japanese science has made a major push to investigate and explore practical renewable energy alternatives, an area in which the United States and Europe lag significantly behind.

Other aspects of Japanese policy and industry, however, are not so exemplary. Japan has resisted measures to promote the health of global fisheries and the oceanic ecosystem—partly tracing back to its previous resistance to dolphin-friendly net systems and its continued sparring with other nations over its whaling practices. Within its own borders, Japan has practiced active strip-mining and a few years ago built a dam in Japan's last free-flowing river, the Nagaragawa, feeding a perception that the country has become a nation of concrete everywhere (even the river beds) and steel. As many perceive it, manmade environmental management has almost entirely supplanted any real "nature" in Japan.

Thus, on the environmental front, Japan's record as a globally responsible stakeholder over the decade may be mixed. If Japan discovers and develops a highly flexible, non–fossil fuel energy source, this may be the global energy home run the world needs, thereby potentially dwarfing the negative factors outlined above. But to date, Japan has yet to earn an impeccable reputation as a model stakeholder on the environmental front.

One further test of Japan's leadership in the environmental realm will be its willingness to take the lead in pushing a norm-setting environmental agenda for the international community, much as it did under the Kyoto Protocol. Given the rejection of the Kyoto agreement by such key nations as the United States and China, Tokyo is understandably reluctant to go out on a limb again in forging a post–Kyoto Protocol set of emissions standards. But Japan is uniquely positioned to take a much-needed leadership role in the environment and climate change arena—and one that is a natural fit for a self-described "civilian power." Japan's appetite for prodding and cajoling the international community toward higher climate change standards will be a significant indication of its leadership and commitment in this crucial sector of global management.

## Will Japan Lead by Example?

To a significant degree, Japan set the mold for a new kind of global steward-ship and responsible stakeholding in the international system—long before it became popular to think in these terms. Japan did this in a time when protection by America as its biggest security and economic guarantor insulated it from many concerns and thus may have given it greater latitude to experiment with its national identity and commitment to global institutions than other nations.

Before the Iraq war of 2003 and the Koizumi government's controversial decision to support the U.S. invasion of Iraq without United Nations approval, Japan attempted to weave its national interests into multiple multilateral frameworks. While the United States was the primary architect of the post–World War II international institutions, Japan in many ways became more passionate about improving the efficacy and role of international institutions than the United States was. Even so, Japan felt compelled by the turbulent international environment after the September 11 attacks, for realpolitik reasons, to loosen its strong embrace of the international order and align with its key security guarantor regardless of principle. Hawkish nationalism and a return of right-wing rhetoric became more evident in Japan, and a somewhat milder version of neoconservative values were incorporated into Japan's foreign policy.

We may now be entering a stage in Japan's evolving national identity in which the heretofore careful balance between parochial national priorities and the provision of important global public goods could tilt toward Japan becoming just an ordinary nation driven by calculations of interest, undercutting or erasing its image as an exemplary stakeholder. Alternatively, Japan could realize that the world—in particular the United States, chief patron of the global order and Japan for many decades—is at a pivotal moment where everything needs to be rethought and reconsidered. In this spirit, Japan could take another look at the unique model it helped pioneer and can promulgate a new form of a "normal nation" in a twenty-first-century context. Japan could help other nations adopt the habits of harmonizing national interest with global interdependence. It could lead the way toward new, revitalized, and less anachronistic international institutions—and in doing so, Japan could reestablish a global equilibrium to compensate for the power voids left by receding American influence.

## Masaru Tamamoto's Reaction

It is premature. There is no precedent. And, if you need another reason, there is not yet a consensus among other countries. Japanese life follows a highly bureaucratic ethic, averting judgment and postponing action. It is hard to imagine how such an attitude produced the self-evidently dynamic achievements of modern Japan. And there is a certain smallness about the way the Japanese think.

Now Clemons and Konishi ask whether "[a]lternatively, Japan could realize that the world—in particular the United States, chief patron of the global order and Japan for many decades—is at a pivotal moment where everything needs to be rethought and reconsidered." The answer: it is premature. Japan remains passive.

Initiative and leadership are not Japan's strong suit. Still this does not detract from Japan's ability to play a constructive role in an international community with broad respect and support for norms. As the authors aptly and significantly point out, Japan has already set the standard of a responsible stakeholder nation. And even more, Japan "may be the first nation to have demonstrated what a twenty-first-century normal global stakeholder might look like." Yet there is scant consciousness among the Japanese of their country as a standard-bearer.

The Japanese have been obsessed with their national identity since the advent of the modern era in the mid-nineteenth century. "Who are the Japanese?" asks and answers Shuichi Kato, a prominent social critic: the Japanese are a people who endlessly and fruitlessly ask who they are. In a recent survey conducted by Pacific Forum, an American think tank, Japanese foreign policy- and opinion-makers were asked to name key elements of Japan's national identity. Tellingly, the respondents could not even begin to answer, so the question had to be rephrased: How do you think other countries see Japan? For Japan and the Japanese, the self is largely determined by what others make of it.

Herein lies the difficulty in guiding Japanese foreign policy by a clear set of principles. A country can only present to the outside world whatever values and ideas by which it lives, and any talk of principles in everyday Japanese life is frowned upon at best, for such talk exposes differences and is viewed as an invitation to conflict. Clemons and Konishi call on Japan to spell out the core principles and values that underpin its foreign policy as it becomes a more assertive player on the international stage. This is a reasonable request, and oft heard. Still, Japan's murky international posture may actually have been essential to its demonstration of what a twenty-first-century global stakeholder looks like. As squishy as it may sound, the post-1945 Japanese foreign policy principle has been to establish friendly relations with as many countries as the situation permits (within the parameters of the American-led world that Japan has willingly acknowledged).

## The Nature of Leadership

Perhaps even more than the authors recognize, modern Japan has exerted its leadership in a quite different style than typical major powers. An argument can be made that Japan deserves credit for the growing prosperity of many ASEAN countries and China today. It is not that Japan influenced these countries in ways normally understood. It was the other Asian leaders who saw in Japan a better way. Lee Kuan Yew in Singapore and Mahathir Mohamad in Malaysia decided to "Look East," where the primary task of government was economic growth and equitable distribution of wealth. Looking back to the 1970s, as the Vietnam War came to a conclusion, there was nothing inevitable about how then-impoverished and violent Southeast Asia would become what it is today. And then there was China's Deng Xiaoping, who drew from Japan's example the possibility of creating great wealth under centralized government as he embarked his country on the path of "market socialism." Japan thus led through its attractiveness as a model. Japanese foreign aid and investment were indeed instrumental in East

Asian economic development but, in essence, it was others who accorded Japan soft power.

Soft power is a murky "Made in the USA" concept. It sounds nicer than hard power. But it is murky because the rest of the world interprets soft power as simply another way of assertion and coercion—a way to exert one's will less unpleasantly. The point, of course, is to boost soft power to make the use of hard power less necessary. But when soft power proves ineffectual, does a country walk away or resort to hard power? Japan, with its indistinct identity and principles, walks away. Japan is thus the soft power par excellence. In a way, Japan can afford to walk away because America stays and does the global troubleshooting. Recently, Japan has begun to take a more principled stand, including a move toward flexing hard power, note Clemons and Konishi, and the authors find many elements of this shift disconcerting.

## What Does America Want?

The authors worry that, having set the standard for responsible stakeholdership, Japan "may be becoming just an ordinary nation driven by calculations of interest." I read this as a fear that Japan is becoming more like America since the Iraq war of 2003—more precisely, like the America of George W. Bush, whose administration deemed relations with Japan the best ever. But now America's embrace of Barack Obama points to the rejection of the ways of Bush. And this cheerfully opens the possibility of America's transformation into a more norm-respecting, multilateralist, stakeholder nation in an interdependent world—more like Japan and in line with the vision of this collection. Ultimately, the extent to which Japan can remain a demonstration of twenty-first-century stakeholdership depends on how America evolves.

The singularly powerful hold America has over Japan is in large measure a consequence of Japan's geopolitical location. Japan is a country that would be much more comfortable being in Europe, with a good fit. Japan in northeast Asia is so dependent on the American security guarantee that the U.S.-Japan security treaty effectively trumps the highest law of the land. Over the decades, the Liberal Democratic Party–dominated government, unable to garner parliamentary and public support for constitutional amendment, has simply enfeebled the constitution's pacific spirit and letter through a series of acrobatic reinterpretations. Now it has come to the point where government leaders can openly dismiss without consequence a High Court ruling that the military mission in Iraq is unconstitutional. While a norm-based international order is desirable, shaky is that order when its members are in the habit of violating their own rule of law.

A fair chunk of the Clemons and Konishi chapter is devoted to a discussion of the military security role Japan might play, which is in tune with the debate in Japan today. The tone of this debate was originally set by the Bush administration effort to turn Japan into the "Britain of Asia." However, there is a deeper question that ought to be considered before analyzing the details of Japan's military capability. How did Japan's principle of eschewing the use of force as an instrument of foreign policy contribute to the making of Japan as a stakeholder demonstration nation? The connection is direct and organic. Japan became what it is today exactly because it resisted becoming obsessed with military security issues. To pose a counterfactual, Japan after 1945 could have gone the way of South Korea, acting as a front line state in the Cold War. Such a Japan would have been highly militarized—and consequently authoritarian and illiberal, also far from a desirable world model. Indeed, this "path not taken" was historically likely and normal. Then, is it not better today to make Japan's neighbors more like Japan? As Clemons and Konishi themselves conclude, "Japan could take another look at the unique model it helped pioneer and can promulgate a new form of a 'normal nation' in a twenty-first-century context."

The threat and use of force is sometimes necessary, though its necessity has been greatly exaggerated, especially since September 11. In a multilateral and interdependent world, force ought not to be the prerogative of national armies, but an instrument of an internationally constituted body that is anchored by broadly agreed upon norms. For instance, while the prevention of nuclear weapon proliferation is unarguably important, as things stand, the Proliferation Security Initiative to control the transfer of illicit nuclear materials and arms on the high sea is an act of war and against international law. The American-led initiative barely escapes the odium of unilateralism by selectively co-opting Australia, Japan, and a few others. Here, again, Japan is necessarily in an ambiguous state. It is a member of the initiative but demurs from involving itself in the act of interdiction.

If indeed Japan is the very model of a twenty-first-century stakeholder country, its hazy foreign policy strategy can be clarified and its stakeholder principles articulated only if enabled by a shift in Washington's posture. During the Bush era, Japan had a choice thrust upon it—between the spirit of its internationalist constitution or the nineteenth-century world-as-anarchy assumption behind the U.S.-Japan security treaty. Bush's America stressed the latter, and Japan began to comply. This line was drawn when China was portrayed principally as a rival and threat, before the notion of China as stakeholder took root, hence the policy of Japan as the Britain of Asia.

Obama's America can do things differently. There are two major thrusts to the post-1945 American global design—one of economic interdependence and integration (represented by the IMF and GATT/WTO), the other of political division and conflict (represented by NATO and other military alliances). This moment is America's opportunity to reaffirm that the integration thrust was always meant, ultimately, to obviate any need for the divisive thrust. To a great extent, Japan as stakeholder is a result of its emphasis of the global integration thrust. And here we find a further irony. It is the very success of America's integration thrust that has lessened the efficacy of military power generally but, quizzically, makes many American policymakers ask: If we are the greatest military power, why can't we lead?

## A Region in Balance

The critical reason why Japan cannot become more independent of America and assert itself more is the nebulous unease felt by the Japanese about rising China. Even the optimistic scenario poses a problem. While it is rarely acknowledged in Japanese public discourse, China's successful transition to a middle-class society over the next several decades would leave Japan's relative position equivalent to that of Canada with respect to America. This ought not be a real concern, for Chinese success in this sense can be had only with thorough integration in global capitalism. In that circumstance, per capita income and equitable distribution of wealth will matter more than gross domestic product, and individual well-being more than aggregate national power. Everyday international relations will be conducted at so many different levels that the role of the state as primary agent will be greatly diminished. And the degree of interdependence will be such that borders will become increasingly porous—more like Europe where smaller Netherlands feels no security threat from bigger Germany.

Still, today in Japan, there remains a deep-rooted feeling that it is acceptable to be a subordinate of America but certainly not of China. Put another way, Japan must remain subordinate to America to fend off Chinese dominance. Which is precisely the reason that President Bush's push to strengthen the U.S.-Japan security alliance found resonance in Japanese policy circles. So a desirable turn in American East Asian policy would be to encourage Japan to further extend its stakeholder characteristics as captured by Clemons and Konishi, which in turn will help smooth China's sure-to-be-rocky-road to a middle-class society, and ultimately make East Asia and the world more like Europe. The goal, then, is to create a condition in which the issue of Japan having to choose between American and Chinese hegemonies disappears altogether.

This will require America to remain the pillar of the East Asian security architecture for some time to come, because balance of power still underlies regional thinking, and because the security architecture is already there. This security framework should aim to provide assurance to all concerned that they are safe from each other (including from America) while pursuing the Europeanization of Asia, a world of open borders, for the ultimate purpose of rendering such security architecture unnecessary. Let Asia "free ride" into the twenty-first century. The world is at a historic pivot point to rethink and reconsider, to imagine the kind of unprecedented vision and leadership necessary for the construction of a world without enemies, of a twenty-first-century global consensus. The moment is truly ripe.

# Notes

1. Note that the authors take somewhat different positions on the degree to which Japan's support for the U.S. invasion of Iraq diminishes its record as a "responsible stakeholder."

2. See Richard J. Samuels, *Securing Japan: Tokyo's Grand Strategy and the Future of Asia* (Ithaca, NY: Cornell University Press, 2007).

3. Andrew L. Oros makes a persuasive argument that Japan's security identity is not undergoing as dramatic a change as some suggest. See Andrew L. Oros, *Normalizing Japan: Politics, Identity and the Evolution of Security Practice* (Stanford, CA: Stanford University, 2008).

4. *Economic Survey of Japan 2008.* Organization for Economic Cooperation and Development.

5. www.mofa.go.jp/announce/fm/aso/speech0611.html.

6. See *Japan's National Defense Program Guidelines for FY 2005 and After.*

7. The authors again differ in their net assessment of Japan's international good citizenship. Tokyo's support for U.S. policies in the Middle East might not outweigh the other positive contributions that Japan continues to make.

8. Eugene Skolnikoff, Robert Art, and Tatsujiro Suzuki, "International Responses to Japanese Plutonium Programs," *MIT CIS Working Paper*, No. 2614 C/95-5, August 1995.

~

# Rue de la Loi: The Global Ambition of the European Project

*Ronald D. Asmus and Tod Lindberg*
*With a Reaction by Robert Cooper*

The creation of the European Union (EU)—or what is often known as the "European project"—is a remarkable and ongoing experiment. It is the example par excellence of norm-building at home and, increasingly, the projection of those norms abroad. At its heart, European integration was and remains a Wilsonian project designed to ban the possibility of conflict through the application of the rule of law and norm-building on a transnational scale. The enforcement of such norms is the core of the European Union's power. With its aim originally limited to making another war in Europe impossible—and above all in mending the relationship between France and Germany—the European Union today has graduated to a much broader vision of both unifying the European continent and becoming a model and inspiration for a global order based on the rule of law and international norms.

Like the United States, the European Union does not (and, by virtue of its essential character, cannot) have any kind of national or ethnic identity. It is an amalgamation of national identities, and one of its purposes is, over time, to transcend those identities. Thus, the only basis for a common European identity and action has to be rooted in values and norms. One of the many ongoing debates within the European Union has focused on what those values and norms should be. The answer to that question goes to the heart of the European project and European power in the twenty-first century.

The European Union, even more than the United States or any other state or contemporary actor, is a neo-Wilsonian experiment in the making. It is an attempt to ban and transcend international conflict through the rule of law and norm-building. It is symbolic that the key European institutions dedicated to upholding the rule of law are located on the Rue de la Loi in Brussels. Like the United States, the European Union today has universalist aspirations. It does not want to transform just Europe. It thinks and expects its norms and governing model to be applied at its periphery and then beyond. It hopes to inspire other regional integration efforts and to create the building blocks for a new norm-based international order.

## The Road to Brussels

The path of European unification following the ruin of World War II was and remains one of the most original political achievements of the twentieth and twenty-first centuries. We will not dwell on the history here, but even a review of the story's broad contours illustrates the magnitude of the accomplishment.

The American security guarantee for Western Europe through the NATO alliance provided not only protection from the external threat of the Soviet Union, but also an opportunity for Western Europe's war-weary nations to venture cooperation that did not come naturally in a charged postwar environment in which each state had to assess its external security not only in relation to a menacing revisionist superpower to the east but also in competition with one another. Today we often forget how central European unification was to America's early postwar vision, how Atlanticist the founders of the European unification movement were, and how crucial the American security umbrella was from the outset.

First steps at cooperation, such as toward the creation of the coal and steel community, were often taken warily and with more than a dose of realpolitik. Against a backdrop of seeming perpetual geopolitical rivalry and conflict, it took great courage for a country to tie its fate to a former enemy. There was, in general, no assumption of shared values and common aims among the parties. On the contrary, the founders of the European project were acting out of what they considered an existential need. One frank objective of French policy in the postwar period was to ensure that Germany would never again be able to reassert itself as a continental power. West Germany's early postwar leaders understood that abandoning sovereignty in the classical sense was the only path to political rehabilitation following the disaster of the Third Reich. The states of Western Europe (and the United States and Canada) were allies, but they were not (yet) friends. Thus, European integration was both visionary and mundane—a mix of architecture and plumbing.

The pioneers of European integration were wise enough not to deny or dismiss this wariness, but rather to work with and through it, often in protracted negotiations. These sometimes tedious discussions, however, eventually yielded agreement on norms and rules of the game for a growing set of key European issues on which the participants expected mutual benefit. A painstaking approach sometimes produces the most robust result achievable, as differences down to the smallest detail each get an airing and a resolution. The goal was in a sense self-emasculation but also projection: countries wanted to neutralize each other's potential to wreak havoc while also creating the capacity to act jointly. By abandoning its national sovereignty for a collective capacity, a state could in theory gain in collective leverage and influence. This required overcoming suspicions and clashes of interest by agreeing to binding norms that would guide such a collective will.

To the extent that the project of European integration has been put in jeopardy from time to time, such situations have usually stemmed from impatience born of enthusiasm. The vision of an ever-closer union has been a seductive one, and enthusiasts of a common Europe can be forgiven for their wish to hasten it. But the creation of something essentially new under the sun—a group of nation-states that had long been locked in violent struggle creating a common marketplace, a transnational juridical union, and, increasingly, political competence and a common foreign policy as a result of pooled sovereignty—is a task of such complexity and innovation as to beggar the imagination. If Europeans today take their union for granted, as some do, especially the young, that is testimony to the success of those visionaries who painstakingly dedicated their careers to the task of persuading Europeans that there is simply no other way—that the past was prologue not to an endless cycle of war, devastation, reconstruction, and war again, but to the moment at which it became possible to change course once and for all.

To observers both inside and out, European integration has often seemed to move at a glacial pace. EU officials often seem preoccupied with process and regularly on the verge of a crisis. But when results and agreements are reached, they have generally proven quite durable. In addition, the process of negotiating has itself had a "socializing" effect, drawing European leaders more firmly together in agreement on the process by which to resolve disagreement—at the negotiating table, and never again by military means.

## Europe's Achievement and the Challenge of Extending It

Europeans often say that their top priority is a world of law. There is much truth and self-knowledge in this observation. But in some sense it actually makes too little of the European achievement and aspiration. It risks ignoring what comes before law: namely, a willingness to be bound by law. It also risks ignoring the importance of the process by which law is set: namely, agreement through negotiation. Finally, it risks ignoring the process by which law is given force: namely, its ratification by competent national governments according to their own democratic constitutional procedures. The *acquis communautaire* did not come from the heavens or from tradition or from a great wise man or a committee of philosopher-kings, but from a self-conscious deliberative process. Europeans can rightly take pride in the totality of this process.

Initially, the European aspiration for a world of law was focused on Europe. Today it extends well beyond the continent. Indeed, one might say that the European aspiration today is to extend the European view of law (if not European law as such) globally. The aim here is both idealistic and practical. It is idealistic in the obvious sense that it envisions an entire world willing to be bound by law, willing to decide upon what the law should be in a deliberative process of negotiation, and willing to give the law force through ratification by national governments. Implicit in the European respect for such norm-setting documents as the Universal Declaration of Human Rights and the UN Charter is an aspiration for every national government to be rights-regarding, liberal, and democratic in character—though there is a cautious element to this aspiration that stands in contrast to the stereotypically American view. From a European perspective, the movement of a country from rights-restricting to rights-regarding, from illiberal to liberal, from authoritarian to democratic, ought to be internally driven rather externally imposed, and peaceful rather than convulsive and violent. It ought to be, precisely, European with regard to process as well as substantive outcome. One might well question whether the ideal world of law can ever be brought into being on a global scale—the more so if one adds the preference for its arrival by European means only.

But this in turn points toward the practical challenge of the European aspiration. It is that, in a world not yet governed wholly by law, the European Union itself must stand as a beacon of law and a benchmark for the assessment of progress toward such a world. Absent such a beacon and benchmark, as Europeans (and not only Europeans) rightly fear, the world may lose sight of the law and return to anarchy on a global scale. In this respect, a key element of the European project is to remind those not yet acting in accordance with a European view of law that there is a better way. Europe will remind others by example, by exhortation, and by withholding approval of or sanctioning acts that Europeans deem lawless.

A leading theorist of the European project, Robert Cooper has memorably described the situation: Europe has become "postmodern" in having overcome the state-on-state violent conflict characteristic of the modern world of sovereign state power. Yet Europe's postmodern condition does not exist in splendid isolation. The essential fact is that the postmodern European project must coexist with a world that is, in many important respects, determinedly "modern" in the Westphalian sense of sovereign nation-states clashing violently over national interests—and in many cases stubbornly "premodern," with weak or failed states that are unable to govern their own territory and leave themselves vulnerable to a struggle for supremacy among substate actors.

In this age of technology and the Internet, the authority of states is also being challenged by such networked transnational dangers as al-Qaeda. The expectation is that more of the same, if not worse, will follow in its wake, perhaps culminating in an unaccountable nongovernmental terrorist organization obtaining nuclear, chemical, and biological weapons. Such a hypermodern, and hyperdangerous, conjunction poses a threat to the whole global order.

The European preference for the European way of law has tried, not surprisingly, to assert itself upon the "modern" world, as well as upon the premodern and hypermodern worlds. This is true not least with regard to the United States, with which the European Union has had a sometimes complicated relationship. As noted above, the United States was one of the early key supporters of the European project, but American support has ebbed and flowed over the years, as the European Union has, in return, redefined its views of American power and its role in the world. The United States remains a distinctly modern state in the sense described here, but one with universalist aspirations of its own. America's own commitment to and debate over how to pursue international norms has itself been a factor shaping EU attitudes. Among the many causes of EU hostility toward the Bush administration, for example, has been the perception that Washington was walking away from its own historical commitment to norm-building, thereby abandoning a mutual commitment to one of the European Union's fundamental goals.

This fueled the recurring debate over whether the European Union should view itself as a counterweight in a multipolar world. But this aspiration has not materialized, at least not in the sense of the emergence of European power of a kind that gives pause for reasons of *force majeure* to the exercise of U.S. power. One reason for this is that the pursuit and exercise of such power on the European side would run counter to the very essence of the European project itself, the creation of a world (or at least a part of the world) in which law, not force, prevails. Another is that the other power centers in such a multipolar world may have even less of a commitment to norm-building than the United States does, EU frustration with U.S. policy notwithstanding. From an EU perspective, the United States remains at times a flawed partner, but one that is indispensable nonetheless.

So the European Union still needs the United States, not least of all because of the security umbrella the United States provides through NATO, which at some level remains a precondition for European integration. And given the size and power of the United States, cooperation with Washington is almost always needed to get things done—on issues ranging from climate change to Iran's nuclear ambitions. Sophisticated Europeans understand that the most effective way to "balance" the United States is through engagement, dialogue, and persuasion. To begin with, the United States is temperamentally inclined to pay attention to European views, on the grounds that the United States and Europe's shared values far outweigh their differences, and that these values form the potential basis of common action toward common ends. Although the op-ed pages of European newspapers are dominated by criticism of the United States, the most telling criticism is grounded in an awareness that Europe's "postmodern" identity and project benefits from a powerful United States that remains unabashedly willing to engage the modern, premodern, and hypermodern worlds on their own terms, rather than the more highly aspirational terms of postmodern Europe. The forward-looking European task with regard to the United States is to keep nudging American power in the direction of law.

## Lofty Aspirations, Messy Realities

As for European engagement with the rest of the modern world, when the aspiration has been the recruitment of the modern world *tout court* to a postmodern, law-based future, the result has not infrequently disappointed Europeans. Many of the interlocutors with which Europe has engaged—from Slobodan Milosevic in the former Yugoslavia of the 1990s to Mahmoud Ahmadinejad in today's Iran—have proven stubbornly resistant to the enticements dangled, preferring instead courses of action that seem based on a decidedly different view of the world and how it should work. The world of power is one with which Europeans must engage, but the terms of the engagement are not necessarily the same as the terms on which Europeans engage with each other (or with the United States). The experience of Central and Eastern Europe, in which newly independent or newly free states quickly looked westward for their destiny in response to Euro-Atlantic openness to them, was on one hand a spectacular success, but on the other a potentially misleading indicator about the eagerness of potential members to join a club whose rules they had no say in devising. It is not simply a matter of reaching out to and engaging with others by offering them European or Euro-Atlantic terms. Such an offer can be refused.

On security issues, many in Europe voice a preference for the arts of peacekeeping and postconflict reconstruction—and indeed, such tasks fit neatly into the European model of rules-based integration. It is no accident therefore that public opinion polls find European publics more skeptical than the American public toward the use of armed force for combat, but more supportive than Americans of using the military for peacekeeping and reconstruction missions. To the extent such missions contribute high value to a world that will continue to have a need for peacekeeping and reconstruction for the foreseeable future, they are welcome—indeed, essential. Unfortunately, peacekeeping and reconstruction alone do not meet the security demands of today's world in all their modern, premodern, and hypermodern configurations.

Afghanistan is the starkest illustration of this point. In contrast to Iraq, the war in Afghanistan is one Europeans deemed from the outset to be necessary and just. They committed themselves to it through NATO, perhaps with a premature view of an Afghanistan that would mainly need peacekeeping and reconstruction following the U.S. military intervention to oust the former regime in Kabul, rather than combat forces ready to engage a resurgent Taliban. Yet a stubborn enemy and an ongoing war is what we have in Afghanistan. It is made all the more complex by the ability of insurgents to find safe haven across the border in northwest Pakistan, beyond the reach of the Pakistani government—problematic as it, too, continues to be. Afghanistan has been more than Europeans thought they were getting themselves into—proof that the tendency of hope to underpin policy decisions is ubiquitous. The question then becomes whether Europeans are willing to engage themselves fully in the law-deprived modern and premodern world of power and force, or whether they will recoil and seek instead to isolate themselves from it.

Much depends on the answer to this question. The European Union, unlike many other states considered in this collection, is an astonishing success and a highly constructive member of the international community. But that can change if Europeans seek an early exit from the modern, premodern, and hypermodern worlds on grounds that engagement with the latter can only corrupt and endanger the European aspiration for a world of law. On the contrary, the European commitment to a world of law can only be effectual to the extent that Europeans are willing to engage in a world where geopolitical competition still exists, seeking to mute and transform it over time. This is the challenge of the next generation of European statesmen and thinkers: keeping the model alive as an aspiration and a beacon to which those of goodwill may repair, while doing the hard work of engaging with the world as it is in the belief that it can be made better.

## Domestic Challenges

The European Union's world of law, though in certain respects a work in progress, is in others strikingly complete. The *acquis communautaire* certainly remain open to modification and adaptation as circumstances change, but they are not likely ever to be subject to a wholesale repudiation—or if they ever were repudiated, that could only signal the emergence of a European Union that had somehow shifted its aims from a world of law to something radically different. The *acquis* are intended to have an element of permanence—not in the manner of divine law, but as the fruit of reasonable deliberation. To pick an element of EU law at its most controversial throughout much of the modern world (particularly the United States), the absolute European ban on the death penalty is unlikely ever to be reversed—or again, any reversal would not spring from a mere reconsideration by deliberative process, but rather from the transformation of the European Union into something very different from the European Union of today.

There are, of course, elements of the law of the European Union that might be improved upon. Likewise, as with all law, it is easy to point to elements that are arbitrary: decisions that could have gone another way without obvious harm, such as whether to drive on the left side of the road or the right. European papers are also full of examples of EU regulatory or legal overreach, regulating the size of vegetables or outlawing deep-rooted local cultural or culinary traditions. Subsidiarity often works better in theory than in practice. The conclusion does not follow, however, that, because some portion of law is fluid or arbitrary, all law is fluid and arbitrary. The law of the European Union is, by and large, good law—and it should easily be able to stand the test of time.

### Keeping Perspective

A few caveats must be noted, however, regarding the limits of law. A world of law, such as the European Union itself represents and aspires to more broadly, is not a world of law solely any more than any other political and social order is ever solely a question of the law that governs it. Any attempt to codify legally all aspects of life would be inherently despotic or totalitarian. European publics would regard any state or transnational initiative mandating how many children parents can have, for example, to be dictatorial.

Likewise, the law is not well equipped to give people guidance on how much or which of life's many desirable things should be enough for any and all of them. Here, the law rules in many things as permissible and rules out others as off-limits—and it provides a framework for the fair pursuit of what is permitted as well as punishment for illicit pursuits. But a broad range of choice remains for individuals or families.

Third, the law is at best an incomplete source for self-definition. The question of identity usually draws more from genealogy, place, and decisions about what ultimately is good to pursue than about compliance with a legal code that claims jurisdiction over oneself.

And so it is no criticism of the EU aspiration for a world of law, nor of its achievement in bringing about such a world in Europe, to note that there are a number of places the law doesn't go because it can't easily or properly go. Notwithstanding the success of the European Union in tackling the subjects that are properly matters for the law, significant challenges for Europe remain on social concerns that are not readily susceptible to a legal resolution. Foremost among these challenges are European demographic trends, the impact of prosperity, and the question of European identity.

It is important to keep these challenges in perspective. Russia and China confront far more alarming demographic trends than Europe does. In most parts of the world, the problems associated with prosperity are a distant aspiration, not the here and now. And the question of identity and what it means to find fulfillment as a whole person is universal, and in many places more up for grabs than in Europe. Most countries would gladly trade the challenges looming over their own horizons for the challenges facing Europe.

Nevertheless, the aspirations of Europe are quite high, and Europeans deserve the respect of an honest assessment of the difficulties their project faces both internally and externally. They are challenges well understood by Europeans themselves.

## Demographics

While there are important regional differences, European birthrates have fallen well below replacement levels, with potentially dramatic consequences. The effects of even a generation or two of birthrates running 50 percent below replacement would likely be transformative. As successful as Europe has been in integrating Europeans, the ability to absorb and successfully integrate non-European immigrants has been far less stellar.

Some see low birthrates as a product of a crisis of civilizational morale in Europe and an existential threat to the region as we know it. Although it seems to us that these problems are prone to overstatement—and have certainly been seized upon by some Americans (and even some Europeans) who are basically hostile to the European project as proof of its "failure"—the issue is real.

As European birthrates have fallen, the population has aged. Fortunately, European prosperity makes the care of an aging population a manageable task, although a heat wave that recently claimed the lives of thousands of elderly Parisians ought to serve as a reminder that the affordability of health care does not automatically result in adequate levels of care.

The more striking demographic question is whether Europeans will look to additional immigration to make up for population decline, and if so, where the immigrants will come from and what effect their arrival in large numbers would have on European society. For the foreseeable future, there is an "eastern option" for immigration on a scale that would compensate for declining populations due to subreplacement birthrates. Yet these countries to the east of the European Union's current borders suffer from their own ticking demographic time bomb. Even the influx of "East Europeans" has the potential to cause social disruption and is already, to a considerable degree, a source of anxiety on the part of host populations. The notorious specter of the "Polish plumbers" arriving en masse and willing to work for less than the French or German plumber charges was on many minds as the European Union enlarged.

Devising and implementing a legal regime for immigration is one of the most challenging problems any state faces, as the United States knows well—especially when the receiving state offers opportunities out of proportion to those available in the source countries. Add the social dimension and cultural dimension, including the question of identity (to which we will shortly turn), and the magnitude of the challenge becomes all the greater. Then there is, so to speak, the southern element of immigration, for the clearest complementary match for the European Union's labor shortfall is the surplus in Turkey, northern Africa, and the broader Middle East. Already, the European Union is home to many Muslim immigrants, in proportions that vary from country to country. If European birthrates are in general below replacement, the birthrates of Muslims in Europe are much higher. The population characteristics of Europe are therefore, to varying degrees, already shifting significantly.

This fact, too, is one that critics have seized on in alarmist fashion, aided in certain respects by the sometimes expressed aspiration of radical clerics for the eventual adoption of *sharia* in Europe and even a European caliphate. Although such statements provide fodder for outraged polemics and lamentations of a world that is passing, in reality, the more perfervid visions on offer would require nothing less than a revolution in Europe.

But because Muslims represent a large and growing share of the European population, it is not unreasonable to ask what effect Islam will have on Europe—and what effect Europe will have on Islam. If it is true that Europeans (particularly at the level of the European Union) have become largely post-Christian in orientation, abandoning churches and turning to secular sources as the ground of human rights and democracy, it also seems true that Muslims are not so ready to abandon the mosque.

Obviously, European governments and many European Muslims themselves will not tolerate radical efforts to subvert the European project or to undermine European governments. But the measures taken to counter such influences will always be controversial, and in some cases be in tension with European aspirations with regard to the rule of law—the European project being largely silent on the question of covert counterintelligence and counterterrorism policy.

One key question will be the extent to which a "European Islam" emerges, one that is in basic accord and sympathy with the European project while being regarded as religiously legitimate within the faith. It seems to us that such a possibility is within reach, though it will require careful nurturing across a range of policy choices and issues of identity. It is probably not an accident that the most controversial and interesting debates on these issues today rage in countries like the Netherlands and Denmark—countries long seen as among the most tolerant and liberal in Europe. The fundamental issue that has arisen is whether the essence of a liberal norm-building society is to guarantee the freedom of the individuals to lives they want—even or especially if they choose to live in an illiberal manner—or whether the state must guarantee the basic liberal order by encouraging if not inculcating those values. This, too, is a test of norm-building. Finding a calibrated and sustainable balance here is key.

**Prosperity**

The European Union is an economic powerhouse, currently enjoying per capita incomes at all-time highs. The prosperous states of Western Europe have also developed elaborate social welfare protections. By most accounts, Europeans are largely satisfied with the social stability that has resulted. The newer members of the European Union are in many cases providing an additional entrepreneurial spark to the EU economy as they seek to catch up with their wealthier fellow members.

One remaining question, however, is whether opportunities for personal advancement are sufficient to fill latent demand. This is a matter that applies at all levels. Is it possible for immigrants to get ahead? Will Europe offer the highly motivated and well educated of the next generation adequate outlets for their entrepreneurial energy, or will such people seek their fortunes elsewhere, perhaps by emigrating to the United States? While the United States has certainly benefited from this brain drain, Europeans need to find ways of nurturing and keeping such local talent.

Rigidities in European labor markets and other disincentives to job creation have not just economic consequences, but also social repercussions. The matter of identity comes in once again—the extent to which upward mobility cultivates a sense of belonging. If Europe is to continue to prosper, it must keep from growing complacent in the face of prosperity. The preservation of the many desirable features of the European social model must be made compatible with the provision of sufficient opportunity for individuals.

### Identity

Even a brief consideration of the demographic and economic challenges of the European Union leads quickly, as we have seen, to the question of European identity—perhaps the paramount internal challenge that faces the European Union. One component of this challenge is to acknowledge that postmodern Europe is no longer the crucible of world history that it was for centuries. The Napoleonic era is long past, as is the Hitler era. In fact, one could argue that the European Union's essential success in eliminating the possibility of armed conflict among its members guaranteed that international attention and concern would focus elsewhere, to the benefit of Europe and the wider world. The European Union's vision of a world of law, no less noble in its way than the long-gone courts of kings, should prove to be a more than adequate substitute for a more modern "political" role in the world. European identity in this respect seems secure.

But the problem of what it means to be European remains acute for many of the populations of Europe. This is true among certain national populations dubious about the value added by the European Union to their lives. It is certainly true for the many groups for which their national governments provide little source of identity. It is a truism that one can come to the United States and become fully American almost at once, whereas one may move to Germany or Denmark and three generations later, one's descendants will still not be considered German or Danish. This would be true even for an

American of Danish ancestry moving to Denmark. It is all the more true for those who come from very different ethnic backgrounds.

A key test of the internal success of the European Union and the European project broadly construed will be the extent to which the problem of minorities' sense of marginalization in the states in which they live can be assuaged by a common and inclusive "European" identity that encompasses them and satisfies their need for belonging. Some hoped that such a sense of "Europeanness" would quickly follow on the arrival of a European flag in Brussels and national capitals. Among elites, there is indeed an increasing sense of Europeanness. But such elites were not suffering an identity deficit to begin with; that they can now be proud Europeans is an added bonus on top of national, international, and transnational lives that were already quite rich. Such a sense of Europeanness, though, has not quickly "trickled down" to those most in need of it. It now seems clear that such transnational European identity will not emerge automatically from the success of the European project. On the contrary, for those who currently feel themselves to be the most excluded, it will almost certainly require deliberate social construction.

Last but certainly not least, there is the European Union's ongoing and seemingly perpetual struggle for legitimacy in the eyes of its own citizens. At one level, this is the ongoing attempt to define power relationships between the EU institutions and member states in a new and unprecedented political animal. But there are also deeper questions that are closely linked to the main subject of the present chapter: from where does the European Union derive the legitimacy to pursue its norm-building aspirations? It is probably fair to say that the European Union is, in essence, far more neo-Wilsonian in its aspirations than many of its member states. And one does not have to spend much time in Brussels to understand that individual member states with short-term national agendas use their national powers and vetoes to seek advantages at fundamental odds with the European Union's transformative aims and the conditionality the European Union supposedly demands.

There is clearly a spectrum of views and degrees of national commitment to many of these goals. In recent years, this debate has been cast in terms of new versus old members of the European Union—with the new members from Central and Eastern Europe presumably more committed to making democratic transformation a higher priority in EU policies, for example. But the lineup and political fault lines on these issues and norm-building more generally are often much more complex and nuanced. The Nordics, for example, are probably the most committed to such transformation, as are other "old" Western European EU members like the Netherlands. Some Central and Eastern European members are clearly strongly committed to democratic norms, but others have quickly accommodated themselves to European traditions of realpolitik or joined in the prevalent internal EU log rolling.

Forging a consistent policy attempting to transform Europe's periphery and the world, while contending with divided national views among member states and managing the gap between elite and public views, is not easy. Nowhere are these tensions more apparent or acute than in Turkey, itself a candidate for EU membership. The European Union today is committed to transforming Turkey and anchoring Ankara to the West. Indeed, there are few EU policies that, if successful, could match its far-reaching and positive ramifications for many of the European Union's internal challenges discussed in this section—let alone the geopolitical advantages for Europe, the Middle East, and beyond. It is also a major test of the European Union's neo-Wilsonian and transformative ambitions.

Yet it is precisely the case of Turkey that highlights the European Union's greatest weaknesses: the internal rivalries and the divide among different member states and the gap between what the EU elite wants and what public opinion will support. The debate over Turkish membership in the European Union is not just about religion or money. It is also about political power and who will run the European Union in the future. It is about what kind of European Union will exist in ten or twenty years, domestically and internationally. It is about managing a political split within Europe on this issue between right and left as well as between north and south. And it is about the legitimacy of an EU elite that sees itself as a vanguard pursuing a noble goal—a goal that is all about norm-building—about which segments of its publics are increasingly skeptical if not opposed. While European publics are generally very supportive of a common foreign policy, this does not mean they give their leaders a blank check when it comes to tough issues.

## External Challenges

Europe confronts considerable internal challenges in its effort to remain true to its vision of a world of law. The external hurdles to the European Union's playing an analogous role globally are also serious. They can be grouped into several categories.

The first is the European Union's ability to pursue a consistent and effective policy that lives up to its own ethos and values. If the European Union is the world's first Wilsonian experiment at home, to what extent can it pursue effective Wilsonianism in its foreign policy? How compatible are internal policies to sustain and expand peace on the European continent with harder-edged external policies in a more hostile world? Can the Kantian EU experiment survive in a Hobbesian world? Can the European Union both recognize the nature and requirements of this more Hobbesian world, while sustaining transformational policies to make it more Kantian?

Related to this conceptual dilemma is the practical question of external effectiveness. The European Union's ability to act strategically in some areas is real; in others, quite limited. It was created as an instrument to render war within Europe impossible, not to pursue global strategy. It is trying to evolve into a political entity that pools sovereignty and strives for a common foreign and security policy that could eventually embrace common defense (at some ill-defined future point). The European Union works reasonably well in those areas where the questions of will and organization have been worked through and resolved, and not in those where they have not. Effective policies coexist with ineffective ones. In areas like competition or trade policy, for instance, the European Union can bring the most powerful American corporations to their knees and play on par with the United States in global talks.

In many ways, the power of the European Union is rooted in the transformative possibility of the rule of law. It lies in a firm set of rules for doing business in and with Europe that compels other countries to go along as the price of admission. That is how the European Union acts as an economic or trade superpower. In his 2005 book *Why Europe Will Run the Twenty-First Century*, Mark Leonard argued that the European Union would shape the international normative rules of the game more than anyone else—and thus shape the future world order in spite of its lack of any meaningful hard power. The European Union's power, he argued, was its ability to draw countries into its orbit, embed them in its legal and economic framework, and change them from the inside out. U.S. military power might be able to change regimes, but the European Union can transform societies.

But is that kind of power by itself enough? And can the European Union apply it to the hard cases? The same European Union that can deal with Microsoft has thus far been unable to deal with Gazprom—largely because it cannot agree on how to apply regulations and competition law effectively to the realm of energy security. It is better at economics than politics and better at soft- than hard-power issues. On the former, it tends to have both the will and the mechanisms, whereas on the latter it does not. The same institution that can regulate American corporate giants can often barely manage to deploy a handful of civilian or military experts on foreign policy missions because of a lack of political will, disagreement among member states, or the inadequacy of its related machinery.

The European Union's great external success has been its ability to transform its neighbors in Central and Eastern Europe through enlargement. When it comes to EU policies with the declared aim of promoting democratic transformation in the southern Mediterranean, we again see that the European Union's own lack of cohesion and consistency has depleted the leverage it has, in theory, amassed through considerable amounts of aid to the region. The same is often true even for countries that, themselves, may aspire to join the European Union and transform themselves, such as Ukraine or Georgia, but where the European Union is divided and has doubts as to whether it wants them. When it comes to the hard diplomatic cases, such as the efforts of the EU-3 (the United Kingdom, France, and Germany) to engage Iran to convince it to change its behavior, the limits of the norm-based approach become apparent. And when it comes to the use of hard power, the European Union's ability to act is, of course, even more limited.

The European Union's new Africa strategy—which calls for extensive assistance to African states and the African Union to help build capacity—represents an ambitious and potentially important foray even further abroad. There is, in principle, strong potential for conditional transformative diplomacy. Here, the European Union must ensure it is getting the results desired for the assistance on offer. Such EU initiatives need sufficient local support so as to constitute genuine partnerships rather than external impositions. That is the best route to effective implementation and sustainability. At the same time, the European Union must make sure that its policies and conditionality are sufficiently firm so that partner African governments and institutions undertake necessary reforms. This is a formidable challenge for policymakers and diplomats alike.

The question of the adequacy of soft power becomes even more pertinent if one believes that we are entering a phase of history characterized by more rather than less geopolitical competition—an era less conducive to this historical experiment in Wilsonianism. How many true allies does the European Union have when it comes to its longer-term norm-setting aspirations? Is the United States an ally in this quest? The European Union is both dependent on, and ambivalent about, the American role. Historically, the European Union would probably never have been ventured, or have succeeded, without strong American support in the 1950s. It could not have thrived throughout the Cold War without the U.S. security umbrella provided through NATO. It could not have enlarged in the 1990s without NATO taking the lead in enlarging first and then defusing concerns about security guarantees.

Here again, we find the European Union both dependent on and ambivalent about a country like the United States that it considers both an opportunity and a challenge. Dependency can breed different feelings. Many have believed that the American role and presence constrains rather than fosters European integration. Others have sought to define a new European identity in contradistinction to or as a counterweight to—as opposed to a partnership with—the United States. American attitudes have also fluctuated. There are undoubtedly many factors that went into the breakdown of transatlantic cooperation after the election of George W. Bush and the rise of a new wave of anti-Americanism in Europe. But one key factor that alienated Europe's elites was their perception that, with the unilateralism of the first Bush term, Washington had ceased to be a partner and indeed threatened to undercut the European Union in its essentially Wilsonian project.

A third reason to raise the question of the adequacy of soft power is that, in addition to ambivalent allies, there are the real adversaries. The real threat to the European Union's vision is not the United States but Russia. European leaders nervously recognize that the world is becoming a more dangerous place. The dream of a Kantian peace led by the European Union and extending to the global scene has faded as sober Europeans eye the specter of nationalism, geopolitics, and rising powers on their borders. Nowhere is this clearer than in the case of the apparent Russian attempt to rewrite many of the heretofore accepted norms upon which European security since the end of the Cold War was supposed to be built. As Ivan Krastev has written in *The American Interest*, the real clash of civilizations today is between a postmodern Wilsonian Europe that has eschewed power politics and is seeking to extend its vision of how the world should be run, and Putin's premodern illiberal notion of sovereign democracy, complete with aggression across international borders. In its "A Power Audit of EU-Russia Relations," the European Council on Foreign Relations—a think tank set up specifically to advocate and lobby for the European Union's notion of a new world order—noted that Moscow is not only pursuing a policy of divide and conquer among the European Union's member states, but also is "setting itself up as an ideological alternative to the EU, with a different approach to sovereignty, power and world order."

Nowhere is this challenge clearer than on Europe's border—in those countries referred to as wider (or, jokingly, wilder) Europe, where the European Union's reformational and Moscow's counterreformational impulses collide. And it is no accident that these are precisely the areas where the European Union and Russia today are at loggerheads as both sides try to set, or rather reset, the rules of the game in the countries between Brussels and

Moscow. Looking further afield, however, one must look far and wide before one finds major powers that share the European Union's worldview. Neither China nor India today appears to be in the European Union's camp when it comes to such issues of world order. So with whom, how, and with what is the European Union realistically going to pursue its vision?

## The Indispensable Stakeholder

The European project is an ambitious undertaking. While recognizing its flaws and weaknesses, one must neither lose sight of the magnitude of the European Union's achievement, nor of its potential. For any effort to bring about a more norm-based international order, the European Union's authority, power, and success are key ingredients. Anyone who aspires to live in a world governed more by norms than by raw political power in pursuit of advantage should be a friend of the European project.

The European Union has considerable resources at its disposal to pursue its neo-Wilsonian vision. The European Union is a rich and, in its way, a powerful actor with substantial room to maneuver that few nations in the modern world enjoy. Already a responsible stakeholder in the international community, the European Union has much to contribute in helping others become fully responsible stakeholders. The world toward which the European Union points lays plausible claim to the title of "best of all possible worlds"—one in which norms are generally accepted and universally upheld; disputes between states are subject to peaceful resolution through a voluntary, deliberative process; and ample space remains for people to pursue the ends they desire so long as those ends are compatible with the law.

Yet the European Union remains an incomplete institution. Its members are still struggling over the question of its basic architecture, and there have been setbacks aplenty along the way, some of which are a product of the gaps between the aspirations of law and the underlying social order. Perhaps more important, the EU aspiration for a world of law does not neatly overlap the world in which we seem destined to live for some time to come. Norms are, in the long run, self-perpetuating—having been undergirded by broad agreement about what they are and how to live in accordance with them. But in the shorter term, they can slip into platitudes in the absence of the power to enforce and defend them against indifference or active opposition. The European Union remains deeply ambivalent about power in a way that may yet jeopardize the European project as a whole.

Though the European Union has not adequately addressed these internal and external challenges, surely it is in the interest of the United States for the European project to succeed. Indeed, the failure of the European Union would have devastating consequences for the emergence of a norm-based world order. One would have to start again almost from the beginning. More likely, at least for a time, the world and the powerful countries remaining in it would revel in their freedom from the sort of accountability a norm-based order brings—with grave consequences for human rights, political participation, deliberative processes, and material prosperity.

Whether the European project succeeds is up to Europeans themselves. They conceived it; they have brought it along this far; only they can see it through. But many outsiders are coming to appreciate how great a stake they, too, have in the outcome.

〜

## Robert Cooper's Reaction

Perhaps it takes Americans to understand Europe, just as it took Americans to invent it. Without the policies of Marshall and Truman, there would have been no European Union. NATO created the security conditions for a co-operative Europe, but before that the Marshall Plan had begun to create the political conditions. It was the method as much as the money that mattered; this was money used in the most intelligent and political fashion that a state has ever imagined (strangely, those who followed Marshall and launched aid programs throughout the Third World forgot this and imagined instead that it was possible to transform countries by economic intervention alone).

As just one instance of his foresight, George Kennan wrote in an early strategy paper that the European recovery program "should be designed to encourage and contribute to some form of regional association." And indeed this was what it did: the Europeans were obliged to work collectively to develop the initial proposals for the program; the results included institutions such as the European Payments Union and the Organization for Economic Cooperation and Development, together with reductions in trade barriers among European countries. These were not so much forerunners of the European Union as a part of the environment that made it possible. Jean Monnet himself had extensive contacts with the authors of the Marshall Plan.

Asmus and Lindberg are as sympathetic toward the European Union as any European could wish, both in their appreciation of its achievements and their awareness of the obstacles. If they err at all, it is in overoptimism—but that is a useful American offset to chronic Euro-pessimism.

Perhaps one has to be American to imagine a European ambition to transform the world. It is true that there are ambitious Europeans who believe that
Europe can—even must—contribute to a better, more secure world. And
there are idealist Europeans who commit themselves to the cause of justice or
of ending poverty. But these worthy sentiments do not have the same force
as the ruthless self-confidence that once sent Europeans abroad to build empires, or the patriotism that drove Japan to prove itself the equal of the West,
or that now drives China to return to its rightful place among nations. Nor
do these calm European passions compare with the mobilization that gripped
America after September 11. This kind of popular fervor is visible neither
when Europe's citizens contemplate the achievement of the European Union
itself (toward which most of them are indifferent), nor when they look outside their borders. There is little to be seen of a desire to spread civilization
or democracy, or even to protect their way of life—which most do not view
as under threat, unless it is from immigration or high prices.

Fear and greed, the driving forces of mankind, are not much in evidence.
The greed for glory died with the empires. It had turned out to be the taw-
dry glory of the stage set—flashy from a distance, false close up. Fear has
gone because of the success of Europe itself. When you have lived through
a thousand years of invading armies, the sudden arrival of regional harmony
undermines the position of those concerned about threats as they fight the
battle for budgets. What is the point of the Belgian army today? It is not to
defend Belgium, since no one is going to attack it. Rather it is to demonstrate
a sufficient commitment to "the West" that friends and allies—above all, the
United States—will be there if Belgium should ever need help. Conceived
on a national level, there are not many threats to European countries: if we
are going to be serious about defense we have now to think on a larger scale,
either European or Atlantic. There is no reason why we should not have
both. In foreign policy, postwar Europe has grown up with both an Atlantic
and a European identity. Pluralism and the ability to operate in different
formations according to political circumstances is a Western strength.

But that is not the whole story. It may be that popular fervor is in scarce
supply, but Europe was always partly a project of elites, and elites have their
own kind of evangelism. Asmus and Lindberg are right to see the spread of
law as the essence of the European project. The European Union is above
all a community of law—a framework of rules and norms to resolve conflict
and avoid violence among nations. And law outside Europe? How else can
peaceful countries join in a civil order except through a system of rules?

A community of law must also be a community of compromise. Laws are
made by agreement, and the unwritten rule that underpins the European

Union is the commandment "thou shalt negotiate." It is not good enough to block something and rely on a veto right; if there is a common will to move forward, you must offer an alternative way. And thou shalt negotiate in a cooperative spirit and be ready to compromise. For this to work, there must be the sense of a common enterprise and a spirit both of solidarity and of give and take.

### President Wilson's European Heirs

We are indeed a Wilsonian project: not just that European countries are national states liberated from empire (either as its masters or its victims), but also as a community of democracies. The European Union has always been much firmer on this criterion than NATO, partly for the reason that a reliable administration of the rule of law is a functional necessity for any country to be acceptable as a member. The European Union is also the realization of the third part of the Wilsonian package, the idea of an organization of states who would maintain security among themselves by negotiation and by the fact—oft repeated by the league's advocates—that public opinion would never allow them to go to war with each other. Finally the European Union enjoys what the league never had: the benevolent support of the United States.

We underestimate the extent to which we already live in a rule-governed world. If you make a journey by plane, you are within the security and safety rules that govern international aviation; you are flying in a machine that has received an international airworthiness certificate, and its every component must meet some internationally accepted industrial standard. While in the air, your safety will be in the hands of an international system of air traffic controllers. This experience of living within a state-run international system is replicated, unnoticed, in a thousand ways every day.

The spread of these rules is the spread of civilization. But it comes about by negotiation, not by conquest. The idea of a world of rules is hardly something that inspires vision or ambition. But it is bothersome when others do not follow the same rules as you do, whether this is in accounting standards or airport security; and this imperative of cost inclines us to seek common rules. In Europe the habit of cooperation and negotiation has led to a naive expectation of what can be done by persuasion and goodwill. So we persist in believing in negotiation when more rational actors might give up. But then, what great work was ever accomplished without some element of irrationality?

Ultimately, though, these qualities of patience and bureaucratic persistence may be quite valuable. The problems of tomorrow—proliferation, terrorism, and global warming—will be surmounted only through cooperative efforts of north and south. This will need a new environment of collegiality, a willing-ness to listen and to compromise, a new style of leadership even. Perhaps a group of countries not driven primarily by ambition for glory, nations with habits and techniques of compromise honed over long dull years of working together, may indeed have something to contribute.

## How Will Europe Compete?

Among the many interesting questions Asmus and Lindberg pose, two stand out as critical for Europe's future. The first is whether we are moving into an era of growing geopolitical competition. If they are right—and these are not the only commentators to predict this—what form will the competition take? In an era of heightened military competition, Europe will not be a ma-jor force, and certainly not a winner. But then nobody will be a winner. So far, post–Cold War military interventions have not brought great success for the interveners—the best have been in the cause of peace, as in the Balkans, or in reply to another's bid for glory, as in the Gulf War of 1991. And they have been in marginal areas. It is hard to imagine direct military competition between great powers bringing anything but ruin. Stupidity is, however, al-ways an option—and a future of tension, threat, and proxy wars thus remains a possibility. If so, the European Union will be ill-equipped, and NATO will again become the primary locus of international politics in Europe.

But there is another possibility. Questions of law and regulation could be-come the main competitive arena. That sounds dull, but the great struggles of history have always been about who would rule whom, and how. Asmus and Lindberg's point that the European Union has so far proved better at dealing with Microsoft than Gazprom illustrates how far Europe still has to go in this area. Even so, this is terrain where Europe could—indeed, must—succeed.

If this emerges as the battleground, the decisive question will be where China positions itself. Of the so-called BRICs (Brazil, Russia, India, and China), the dynamic factor is China. It is China that has brought the raw material boom to Brazil and Russia, and has spurred India into competition. A decision by China that a rule-governed world is in its interest would do more to make such a world possible than any other development. This ques-tion is thus more important for us and for our future than whether and when China adopts democracy—though in the end democracy is probably the best way of ensuring the rule of law domestically. Europe may therefore be right and even perhaps more hard-headed than the United States in emphasizing the rule of law rather than democracy. Yet this too is in keeping with the European preference for technical rather than political concepts. Asmus and Lindberg say that neither China nor India seems to be in the European Union's camp on issues of world order. It is too early, though, to make such a judgment. It is at least encouraging that China, for good reason, has taken to the World Trade Organization like the proverbial duck to water. Besides, there is another world out there—the Association of Southeast Asian Nations, the African Union, and the countries of Latin America—all of which would like to follow the European route.

The European approach of endless negotiation and technical solutions for political problems, however, can work only where the basic geopolitical questions are resolved. That is why no amount of aid or talk has so far been able to bring decisive progress in areas such as Palestine or North Africa where bad political relations prevent normal trade and other exchanges. The spread of law must be complemented and facilitated by an effort to solve political problems and to spread a culture of compromise. The genius of the Marshall Plan was that its economic and political dimensions were mutually reinforcing.

### A Matter of Identity

The second question that the authors raise, also decisive for Europe and even more difficult to answer, is that of identity. For Europe's internal development, the ability to integrate immigrant populations will be critical. Different European states are struggling with this question in different ways and according to their own traditions. It is vital that one of them finds an answer as convincing as that of the United States so that the rest can copy. Is it possible that the European Union could somehow offer help, providing a wider identity for new arrivals, rather as the empire became a source of British identity for Scots who still felt foreign in England? It is a nice idea, but the reality is that identity in Europe is primarily national.

The purpose of the European Union is not to replace the nation-state, but to enable it to function better. It does not seek to replace national identity either (nor could it succeed if it tried). We must not expect, therefore, that European action in the world will be based on a widespread identification with a project viewed essentially as European. But perhaps, even if a popular European identity is neither possible nor desirable, we may be able to create a sense of common purpose among those dealing directly with foreign affairs. That is one of the big potential benefits from the European External Action Service proposed in the Lisbon Treaty—not a competitor for the national services, but a network joining them in a common enterprise.

All of this makes the European Union different from the United States. No intelligent person would dream of the European Union as a competitor.

Where we have had success—always a rarity in foreign policy—it has been together, as in the Balkans. The European Union does not want to return to a world of great power competition; it was created precisely to bring this to an end. If the United States is the indispensable nation, Europe's ambition is to be its indispensable partner.

PART 2

# CHALLENGERS

# A Rising China's
# Rising Responsibilities
*Bates Gill and Michael Schiffer*
*With a Reaction by Wu Xinbo*

## How Will China Fit In?

By 2050, if present trends continue, the People's Republic of China (China, or PRC) will have the largest gross domestic product (GDP) in the world, will be the globe's largest emitter of carbon, will have the world's largest standing military, and will have the world's second-largest population.

It is inconceivable, in other words, to imagine the future global order without allowing for the central role that China will have in it—for better or for worse—as well as the major influence China will have in shaping that order. Whatever the new patterns and processes are that will determine the international order of the twenty-first century, they will emanate, in many respects, from China. Although some have yet to recognize it, the question of whether China will be an integral part of the international community has long since been settled: it certainly is. But an open question remains regarding how China will use its position as a rising global power that is deeply woven into the fabric of international regimes on security and economic and political affairs.

For more than thirty-five years the United States has sought to foster a relationship with Beijing aimed at bringing China into that order. Richard Nixon's historic visit and the Shanghai Communiqué put in place a framework for U.S.-PRC accommodation that has led over time to China's steady, though sometimes fitful, integration into the existing international system. Remarkably, it was just ten years ago that *Foreign Affairs* published an article seriously asking "Does China Matter?" Today, China matters so much that professional strategists place the enormous and unprecedented challenges and opportunities it presents at the top of the agenda for the United States and others in the international system. Just as China is "part of the problem" on big issues affecting world order—economic competition, free and fair trade, climate change, dealing with odious national leaderships, promotion of justice and good governance—more optimistically, China will also be a "part of the solution" to resolve the long-term challenges of our time—maintaining stability among great powers, sustaining global economic growth, combating terrorism, stemming dangerous weapons proliferation, and addressing new transnational threats of infectious disease, environmental degradation, international crime, and failing states.

Hence it was in September 2005 that U.S. Deputy Secretary of State Robert Zoellick spoke of how it is in both American and Chinese interests that China become a "responsible stakeholder" in the international system. Explicit in this construct is the idea that because China has so richly benefited from its steady integration into the global order over the past three decades, it therefore has a self-interested "stake" in strengthening and sustaining that order.

Although the intrinsic logic of that argument may appear self-evident to many in the United States, it is not necessarily so to the Chinese. Viewed from a Chinese perspective and a longer historical horizon, over the past 150 years, China's version of history is replete with abuse and exploitation at the hands of the outside world: from the occupations and forced concessions of colonial powers in the late Qing and its abandonment by the League of Nations in the face of Japanese aggression to the invasion and brutalities of the Imperial Japanese Army, to ill-fated alliance with the Soviet Union, and to the U.S. Cold War containment policies. From this history, many Chinese reasonably may conclude that the international community is not exactly filled with responsible stakeholders and that China can be only deeply skeptical of the concept at best. Who defines "responsible"? A stake in whose "order"?

It is interesting, in that context, to review the evolution in the past decade of the Chinese lexicon for China's orientation in global affairs from *heping jueqi*—peaceful rise—replaced by *heping fazhan*—peaceful development—to the currently operative *hexie shijie*—"harmonious world."[1] Although all three imply a certain degree of buy-in to the international order, there are subtle yet significant differences—suggesting shifting Chinese conceptions of both China's role in the world generally as well as its posture specifically toward rules of the game that preceded its rise. Just as there is evidence of Chinese policies in line with U.S. views about "responsible stakeholdership," so too there is evidence that China is seeking to play by its own set of rules, and it is increasingly capable of doing so.

This conundrum—that China is both a beneficiary of the neoliberal world order and, owing to the benefits it has accrued, increasingly capable of diverging from it—makes it particularly opportune to ask how it is we might know when China is indeed a "responsible stakeholder"?

## Fundamental Assumptions and Understandings

Six strategic understandings should frame the question of China's prospects of becoming a responsible stakeholder. First, efforts to lure China more deeply into the community of nations must be conducted with utmost sensitivity to China's self-perception as a unique player in the international system. Given China's ages-old civilization, historical contributions to mankind's development, former imperial glories, and a strong cultural identity, the Chinese leadership and its people share a sense of their country's unique character and "differentness" from the dominant political West. This is not necessarily an insurmountable obstacle to integrating China, but any attempts to do so must take into consideration the country's self-image.

Second, a necessary precondition for the United States and others to preserve a working relationship with Beijing is for them to acknowledge and work with the current one-party Chinese political system. It is critical to note that this does not mean turning a blind eye toward specific practices of the Chinese government that violate norms or conscience. Nor does this mean governments and others outside China should refrain from criticizing perceived defects and shortcomings of the Chinese system. Rather, this approach proceeds from the realistic understanding that any hopes for genuine international partnership can begin only with the international community's expressed willingness to accept as a given the internal political arrangements of the other players in the system.

A third precondition is likely to be a clear international acceptance of China's territorial unity and integrity. Again, this does not imply that the international community must shy away from such issues as the peaceful resolution of the Taiwan issue or meaningful autonomy for Tibet. Rather, in recognition of China's historical sensitivities, the "One China" policy should be applied consistently.

A fourth precondition is for the international community to be prepared to match China's sheer magnitude as a nation—its economic strength, population size, territorial breadth, and ethno-cultural heft—with a commensurate seat at the table in the high councils of international politics. The Chinese might call this regaining the country's "rightful" place as a major power in a more multi-polar world. At the same time, though, such adjustments imply an increase in Chinese weight and influence relative to the United States—and all the associated unease that can result for Americans.

Fifth, China is more likely to work constructively with the international community as long as relations with other key powers, especially the United States, do not deteriorate. A lingering sense of grievance remains just below the surface in China—one that is quick to react negatively to slights and destructively in the face of open hostility. The point is not to indulge a China that exploits its (often too easily) wounded pride, but to have a realistic recognition that any blatant attempts to coerce or issue ultimatums to China will only decrease the prospects of it taking on a more responsible role.

This is critical because if there is one set of sensitivities that clearly could lead China off the straight and narrow when it comes to embracing the international community, it would be any provocation of aggrieved nationalism in China. Such perceived incitement could only trigger an internal political dynamic leading to an aggressive Chinese posture both in China's immediate neighborhood and perhaps globally.

Finally, another key factor for the emergence of a more responsible China is its ability to maintain domestic stability and steadily build its capacity to meet the economic and social needs of its citizens in an accountable and responsive way. Conversely, a China that is plagued by domestic instabilities—or that is incapable of meeting the rising expectations of its people—will likely be a far more suspicious and far less cooperative partner on the international scene.

## How Will We Know When China Is a Responsible Stakeholder?

In the following pages, we identify eight important challenges to the international system and examine how China might approach them. By looking at these key issues, we can gain a sense of how to "measure" China's ongoing evolution as a responsible stakeholder. These key issues are:

- political evolution at home;
- peaceful resolution of territorial and sovereignty disputes;
- international economics, trade, and investment;
- international institutions and public goods;
- regional hotspots;

- military affairs;
- climate change and ecological degradation; and
- energy consumption and conservation.

## Political Evolution at Home

Contrary to conventional wisdom, China has undergone a remarkable political evolution. It is clearly the case that China today is more open, not just economically, but also politically, than it has been in the past. But for China to assume even greater international responsibility—and make a greater contribution to the global order from which it has gained so much—continued political liberalization will have to be a part of the picture.

This is not to say that China should precipitously adopt Western-style political arrangements. Rather, a China that in its own self-interest continues on a path of increasing pluralism, equity, and justice will also recognize the value of these norms in other countries. In addition, a China that is more responsive to the needs of its own citizens will be a more stable, constructive, and less fearful international partner, better able to help with the challenges facing the international community.

There are some signs that Beijing understands these possibilities, at both the domestic level and with respect to its international relationships. Officially, Beijing continues to eschew "interference" in the internal affairs of other states. At the same time, Beijing recognizes that poorly governed states (i.e., those that do not deliver steady economic and social development) are prone to instability and thus may require some international assistance and possibly intervention. For example, the joint statement from the EU-China summit in November 2007 "confirmed their full support" for the good offices of UN Secretary-General Special Advisor Ibrahim Gambari "with a view to advancing democracy in Myanmar."[2]

China's continuing opening at home—to include inner-party democracy; anti-corruption measures; improvements in administrative law; empowerment of citizenry; rule of law; more transparent and accountable governance; improved treatment of minorities, religious groups, and civil society organizations; and poverty alleviation—will be important markers along its path toward more responsible stakeholdership.

## Peaceful Resolution of Territorial and Sovereignty Issues

China has been embroiled in territorial and sovereignty disputes with many of its neighbors and on numerous occasions has used military force to push its claims, such as with Taiwan, Vietnam, Philippines, India, and Russia.

Tensions continue to this day over competing claims with Japan, Taiwan, and with claimants to islets, reefs, and seabed resources in the South China Sea.

In the last fifteen years, China has taken steps to resolve several disputes peacefully, and to shelve others indefinitely. The long-standing border disputes with its Central Asian neighbors, including Russia, have been almost entirely settled, and in some instances China actually ceded over 90 percent of disputed territory. At the 2002 China-ASEAN summit the two sides agreed to a "Declaration on the Conduct of Parties in the South China Sea," which stated, in part, that the parties would

> resolve their territorial and jurisdictional disputes by peaceful means, without resorting to the threat or use of force . . . in accordance with universally recognized principles of international law, including the 1982 UN Convention on the Law of the Sea [and] to exercise self-restraint in the conduct of activities that would complicate or escalate disputes and affect peace and stability.[3]

The agreement created a political framework for managing these unresolved offshore territorial disputes. Similarly, China and India have in recent years conducted a regularized dialogue to settle their disputed borders, as the bilateral relationship has blossomed into a "strategic partnership." Chinese President Hu Jintao's state visit to Japan in May 2008 appeared to spur a process for the two sides to find a settlement to their disputed territorial claims in the East China Sea. Early indications suggest China is prepared to engage in peaceful discussions and implement a range of confidence- and security-building measures with Taiwan following the election and inauguration of Taiwan President Ma Ying-jeou.

Further diplomacy to resolve China's territorial and sovereignty disputes will be an important indicator of its willingness to be a responsible stakeholder.

### International Economics, Trade, and Investment

China's economy is one of the fastest developing in history and poised to be the world's largest by mid-century. Following three decades of explosive economic growth, China is now a top trade partner of virtually every significant economy in Asia and around the globe—becoming the European Union's second-largest external trading partner in 2005, the United States' second-largest trading partner in 2007, Japan's largest trading partner in 2004, and South Korea's in 2002.

And although there is no denying that China has made great strides in joining the international economic order since the late 1970s, full commitment to free-market principles would require a proactive, rather than a defensive, leadership posture within the World Trade Organization that leverages the WTO for further liberalization of both international and domestic markets.

Another key indicator will be Chinese efforts toward multilateral trade liberalization, as opposed to weak bilateral free-trade agreements. It is apparent that the aim of many of the bilateral trade agreements pursued by Beijing is largely to improve strategic and political relationships with partners, rather than to advance a more liberal regional or global trading regime. Rather than devote energies to these kinds of agreements—which have the effect of balkanizing the international trade regime without significantly promoting liberalization—Beijing would affirm its stake in free trade by taking a leadership role in ensuring the success of global trade talks rather than contributing to their failure. Greater support for the more inclusive, trans-Pacific regional free trade aims of the Asia-Pacific Economic Cooperation (APEC) group—rather than a narrower and exclusive Asia-based free trade area—would be another indicator of a more comprehensive, forward-looking, and responsible approach to free trade.

A softening of Chinese protectionism for merchandise and service markets also will be a good marker of Chinese commitment to a liberal international economic order; such a shift would help both the global trade system and China's own growth. Likewise, a reorientation on intellectual property rights to show a willingness to enforce the rights of others, even at some cost to itself, would be a clear sign to the international community that China is adopting a new role in international economic affairs.

China's approach to its currency also raises many concerns and does not signal a responsible approach to international financial and monetary affairs. By continuing its substantial intervention in the foreign exchange market to maintain the undervaluation of its currency, China contravenes its commitments to the International Monetary Fund (IMF), while amassing huge current account surpluses. After agreeing in 2005 to a managed floating exchange rate, there has been some recent appreciation of the renminbi against the dollar, but no meaningful change in the currency's undervaluation on a trade-weighted basis. These policies seem to contradict China's growing role as global financial player and risk triggering a greater protectionist backlash from major trading partners such as the United States and European Union—thereby complicating an increasingly troubled global financial situation. China could act more in accordance with its global economic role by meeting its IMF commitments while working closely with the United States and other major economic partners to avert the worst of a looming global financial crisis.

In this connection, making greater contributions to the work of major global economic institutions such as the World Bank and the International Monetary Fund also would be commensurate with the country's wish to be seen as a "responsible great power." Furthermore, Beijing could propose how it might play a bigger part in the G-8 process, either as a possible member of the G-8 (if such arrangements can be created) or as a founding member of a new global economic leadership forum that more accurately reflects China's burgeoning role in the world economy.[4]

## International Institutions and Public Goods

China's approach to institutions and the provision of international public goods will be another indicator of its evolution as a responsible member of the international community. One way to measure this is to track Chinese engagement in institutions like ASEAN, ASEAN+3, ASEAN Regional Forum (ARF), APEC, Shanghai Cooperation Organization (SCO), East Asia Summit (EAS), and the six-party talks (as well as the potential development of a Northeast Asia Peace and Security Mechanism). Indeed, Chinese leadership in the development of a NEAPSM is a very good example of China's willingness to contribute to maintenance of regional and international order. But the focus in evaluating China's position as a responsible stakeholder should now be on Chinese efforts to equip global and regional institutions to meet the challenges of the twenty-first century.

China's position as a permanent member of the UN Security Council (UNSC) gives China not only international prestige, but also a position at the heart of high-stakes diplomacy, where its every move is scrutinized. Beijing's response to the challenge of North Korea's nuclear program showed the highly constructive role of which it is capable. The question is whether it will adopt a similar approach on the council toward challenges like Sudan, Iran, and Burma. Such a move would indicate China's willingness to uphold international order and contribute to the greater good, rather than being interested exclusively in its own position, power, and influence.

Likewise, China's orientation toward UN Security Council reform and enlargement debates will provide an indication of Chinese self-assuredness with their own international position. A China that recognizes the need to draw in and work alongside other key stakeholders such as India and Japan—even at potential cost to its own direct short-term interests—will be a China that has taken to heart the lessons of what it takes to be a responsible great power.

The China of the twentieth century and initial years of the twenty-first has been, despite its great power aspirations, a net taker of public goods, be it navigation and maritime rights, international humanitarian response, or development assistance. It has often been a free rider. A China that adopts a problem-solving orientation toward the maintenance of the global order will be a China that starts to contribute international public goods, both in its region and on a global scale, commensurate with its growing power, riches, and capabilities.

### Global Health

Health issues might be a good way to gauge China's willingness to serve as a provider of public goods. To cite two examples, China's willingness to let Taiwan join the WHO (in an appropriate way) and becoming a net contributor to the global fight against infectious diseases would signal that China now is committed to the spread of genuine human security.

Likewise, a more responsible and open approach at home to the threat of infectious disease would be another important indicator. China's initial cover-up of the emergence of Severe Acute Respiratory Syndrome (SARS) led unnecessarily to the disease's deadly spread. China today accounts for some 10 percent of the world's cases of extremely drug-resistant tuberculosis (XDR-TB) and is a perennial source for widespread outbreaks of avian influenza. Given China's integration into a globalizing world, outbreaks of infectious disease within China can quickly spread well beyond its borders. Consequently, China's internal response to these problems will signal its willingness to protect the international system from which it has so greatly benefited.

### Humanitarian Assistance and Developmental Aid

China traditionally has been an important benefactor of countries in the developing world, especially providing assistance in the form of education and training, the extended deployment of doctors and other public health officials in Asian and African countries, and the provision of public buildings and other basic infrastructure. Today, China's development aid is expanding to the provision of low-cost or interest-free loans and other grants. During the 2006 Forum on China-Africa Cooperation in Beijing, for example, China, among other pledges, offered to send one hundred senior Chinese experts on agriculture to Africa and set up ten agricultural demonstration sites on the continent; establish a China-Africa Development Fund gradually amounting to US$5 billion to support investment in Africa by "well-established and reputable companies," US$3 billion of preferential loans, and US$2 billion of preferential export buyers' credit to African countries; train fifteen thousand professionals from African countries in three years; establish one hundred rural schools and double the number of scholarships for African students to four thousand; open ten hospitals and thirty antimalaria clinics, while providing RMB 300 billion (approximately US$37.5 million) for the purchase of antimalarial drugs; and double development assistance to Africa by 2009.[5]

These are all encouraging steps and mark an effort to make a more significant contribution to global development. Looking ahead, China's fellow international donors expect Beijing to be more transparent in the amounts and methodologies of its development aid, to adopt emergent best practices of good donorship, and to coordinate more closely with other donors to leverage resources more effectively, and to avoid redundancy and waste. A China that seems to have learned the lessons of its less-than-outstanding reaction to the 2004 tsunami—where its initial offer was for US$60 million in assistance and one medical team—and raises the level of its humanitarian assistance surely will be seen more widely as a responsible great power.

*Peacekeeping*

Over the past ten years, China has dramatically expanded its contributions to United Nations peacekeeping operations. Up to the late 1990s, China contributed approximately fifty observers to UN missions such as in the Golan Heights and on the Iraq-Kuwait border. As of early 2008, China has a total of more than one thousand soldiers, observers, and police in thirteen out of seventeen current UN peacekeeping missions. China is most active as a troop contributor to missions in Africa, including its most recent contribution to the deployment in the Darfur region of Sudan. By expanding its involvement in UN peacekeeping, Beijing demonstrates a willingness to take some risk and accept some cost that benefits more than only its own narrow self-interest.

China could take a number of steps that might deepen its involvement in peacekeeping. One is a continued expansion in the number of troops it contributes to UN missions. Another step would be to increase China's commitments to the UN Standby Arrangements System. Currently, China has made a "level 1," or lowest level, commitment, providing a basic list of potentially available capabilities. According to the Chinese defense white paper of 2002, this "level 1" commitment means China is "ready to provide the UN peacekeeping operations with engineering, medical, transportation and other logistical support teams at appropriate times" and "is able to provide these operations with 1 UN standard engineering battalion, 1 UN standard medical team and 2 UN standard transportation companies."[6]

Yet another indicator would be for Beijing to show greater flexibility on peacekeeping when the Taiwan issue is involved. China has a history of bringing its Security Council veto to bear on resolutions for peacekeeping operations in order to protest states' establishment of diplomatic ties with Taiwan. For example, after Haiti invited Taiwan's vice president to its presidential inauguration in 1996, China held up a subsequent peacekeeping operation to Haiti for several weeks. After Guatemala recognized Taiwan in 1997, China vetoed a proposed UN peacekeeping mission to the area, although it subsequently reversed its vote. During the 1999 Kosovo crisis, Macedonia established diplomatic relations with Taiwan, and China vetoed a proposed resolution to extend the UN Preventative Deployment Force (UNPREDEP) that was safeguarding Macedonia's borders at the time.[7] China seemed to change course significantly, though, in 2004 when it sent civilian police officers to take part in the UN Stabilization Mission in Haiti (MINUSTAH), despite Haiti's diplomatic relations with Taiwan.[8]

In the future, observers also should watch to see how willing China is to send UN forces, including its own soldiers, into more dangerous and destabilized situations.

*Nonproliferation and Arms Control*

Since the early- to mid-1990s, China has taken an increasingly constructive approach to nonproliferation. China has steadily reduced its exports of conventional and unconventional weapons, instituted a more effective domestic export control system, and joined and complied with nearly all the major global nonproliferation treaties and many of the supply-side export control regimes. China also entered into a number of bilateral agreements with the United States—such as agreeing to halt new nuclear cooperation with Iran—going beyond its multilateral commitments.[9]

Potential future mileposts might include a continued reduction of its sensitive exports to such countries as Iran, Pakistan, and North Korea. China could exert greater pressure on Iran to fully comply with demands of the international community regarding its nuclear capabilities and intentions. China also could demonstrate greater concern over its long-standing ally, Pakistan, and the safety and security of that country's nuclear programs and materials.

International arms control efforts may well see a resurgence in the coming years, and it will be important that China demonstrates its willingness to actively contribute rather than stand on the sidelines. Potential, if not likely, elements of the agenda are efforts to assure a successful Nuclear Nonproliferation Treaty review conference in 2010, establishment of a fully safeguarded multilateral enrichment facility, and demonstrable steps to further reduce the salience of its nuclear forces.

## Regional Hotspots

As China's global influence and national capacity grows, so too should its obligation to steer regional hotspots toward stability, development, and human security. The Asia-Pacific region is a natural test bed for China's shift from a traditionally inward-directed to an engaged power. But China's approach to developments further afield—as in Sudan and in Iran—also will tell us how prepared Beijing is to engage responsibly within the international system.

### China's Approach to Regional Security Mechanisms

China's deepened strategic engagement in multilateral organizations such as the ASEAN+3 and the East Asian Summit, as well as the emergence of the Shanghai Cooperation Organization as a more open and inclusive institution, would demonstrate Chinese willingness to join and sustain a web of thick political and institutional arrangements in the region. Such a commitment would entail China boosting its influence while also accommodating the views, interests, and norms of others.

Another key indicator of China's rise as a responsible stakeholder would be further indications of its acceptance of an ongoing role in the western Pacific for the United States and its alliances and other security partnerships—not just tactically while China bides its time, but as a strategic affirmation of the stabilizing role those forces play in the region.

### Korean Peninsula

China's role in serving as host and facilitator for the six-party talks, in helping hammer out the September 2005 joint agreement among the parties, and to bring North Korea back to the negotiating table following the DPRK's nuclear test in October 2006 stand out as precisely the kinds of actions one could expect from an engaged and responsible player. China's leadership on the shared agenda of a nuclear-free Korean peninsula is a positive leading indicator of a China accepting, internalizing, and upholding the vital norm against the spread of weapons of mass destruction that is consistent with China's own national security interests.

### Japan

The China-Japan relationship was characterized by a great deal of tension in the early years of this decade, as both countries grappled with shifting regional- and global-power realities. The direction China takes in its relations with Tokyo will be a prominent indication of its approach to the region as China gains greater and greater influence. But China will have ample opportunity to move beyond stale debates over history, focus on a practical agenda, and show respect for Japan's stature in Asia as well as globally—with potential cooperation on economic and energy and possible support for Japan as a permanent member of a reformed UNSC.

The possibility of placing relations with Japan on a new footing does pose a test of whether China can break a historical pattern and overcome the understandable anxieties it harbors following its experiences from the late Qing through World War II. These anxieties have shaped the worldview of four generations of postrevolution Chinese leaders, compelling them to "stand up" and play the nationalist card against Japan to garner sympathy and support both within the Chinese people and from other Asian populations. As China becomes more confident and secure, perhaps it will not need to base its politics and policy on historical, nationalistic grievances.

## India

As with Sino-Japan relations, a Chinese posture of stakeholdership must accommodate a major role for India in both regional affairs and in global affairs. Indeed, the quandary of how two countries with populations over one billion and Organization for Economic Cooperation and Development (OECD) levels of income will coexist is one of the key challenges to the future global order. China can show its goodwill across a number of issues, including: Tibet (where China and India rub up against each other both physically and metaphorically), the resolution of territorial and border issues, joint management of water issues (given the crucial role that the Tibetan plateau plays as the watershed of several of India's major rivers), and India's possible candidacy for the UN Security Council and other major international bodies.

## Burma

The decisions that confront China regarding Burma also will indicate to the outside world how and whether China is ready to help bring a more peaceful, prosperous, and secure future for the Burmese people. China's record to date has been decidedly mixed—at times trying to prod the junta to act in a more responsible fashion, and at other times using its veto power as a permanent UNSC member to shield Burma from stronger pressure from the international community. China supports the Burmese junta in part because of natural gas interests and the help China needs from Rangoon to crack down on cross-border narcotics traffic.

But other near-term interests, such as the threat of pandemics and other cross-border health issues also may push China to seek to develop a more multilateral approach to Burma. Indicators of such an approach would include stepped-up efforts to bring the parties within Burma together for constructive dialogue and increased, but still quiet, Chinese pressures and inducements to spur the Burmese leadership to make concessions to the will of its neighbors and the international community and to see the lives and livelihoods of the Burmese people improved.

### Taiwan

Although China views the Taiwan question as an entirely "internal" affair, other major powers in the region—especially the United States—have their own commitments, stakes, and interests vis-à-vis Taiwan. Consequently, developments across the Taiwan Strait have serious implications for regional security and prosperity, and all interested parties have a stake in seeing that differences across the Taiwan Strait are resolved peacefully and with the consent of the peoples of China and Taiwan.

With the election and inauguration of Ma Ying-jeou as Taiwan's president in 2008, a new window of opportunity may be opening for a more constructive approach by Beijing, as well as by Taipei. Key features of such an approach might include a Chinese willingness to reengage in dialogue and cross-strait confidence-building measures, a build-down of the armaments arrayed opposite Taiwan, a reconsideration and even recision of the Anti-Secession Law passed in March 2005, and continued clear statements of Beijing's long-term intention to engage Taiwan peaceably. In a word or two, a responsible approach to the situation would see China taking actions to induce Taiwan to see it as a constructive partner.

### Sudan

As a global power, China has increasing obligations as a stakeholder in Asian hotspots. But China has yet to engage in a similarly proactive way on some of the other major challenges beyond its own region, including the situations in Sudan and Iran. How China orients itself on these issues in the years ahead will be crucial. China has invested heavily in Sudan, for example, in part to ensure its energy security and diversity of supply. And despite Sudan's record as a state sponsor of terrorism and the genocide in Darfur, China continues to serve as a major supplier of armaments to the country. China has taken some positive steps in recent years—for example, encouraging Khartoum to accept a hybrid UN–African National Union peacekeeping force in Darfur. But Beijing can and should do much more to enable more effective UN and African National Union action and demonstrate a genuine concern for the security, prosperity, and dignity of the people of Darfur.

### Iran

China's relationship with Iran is likewise a challenge to China's status as a responsible stakeholder. China's interests and relations with Iran are complex and involve more than simple access to energy. Nevertheless, as a permanent member of the UN Security Council—and with an increasingly constructive approach to nonproliferation—China will need to balance its near-term interests against Iran's threat to the very viability of the nuclear nonproliferation regime. The support China provides the United Nations and the International Atomic Energy Agency (IAEA) in addressing Iran will provide important clues to China's own understanding of its role in maintaining a rules-based order.

### Military Affairs

The rapid military buildup that has accompanied China's economic rise has sparked considerable worry by some who view it as part of an aggressive Chinese design to remake East Asia and the globe. Although certain Chinese weapons systems are worrisome because of their destabilizing natures, the critical issue for China is less specific systems per se and more the question of whether China will give greater transparency to its strategic intentions and actions. Indeed, in looking at the historical precedent of "successful" instances of peaceful rising power—such as the "handoff" from the United Kingdom to the United States to take a leading role in maintaining maritime order—a key element has been the transparency of intentions and actions that allowed one (waning) power to accept the greater role played by the other (rising) power. Critical to this equation, of course, is the established power's acceptance of the legitimacy of the armed forces' modernization by the rising power and a folding in of those military capacities into the regional and global order.

Several potential indicators of greater Chinese strategic transparency will need careful observation. Perhaps the most important indicator will be an increased Chinese willingness to fully engage in a robust regime of confidence- and security-building measures with its neighbors. This would include more transparency for its military doctrine, force structure and operations, and defense budgets—taking the published form of more detailed, comprehensive, and regularized open source "white papers" and other formal publications, as well as reciprocal official exchanges of defense-related information and briefings between China and its principal security partners. Other steps should include increased military-to-military exchanges, defense college exchanges, port visits, joint exercises, and senior-level dialogues between both uniformed and civilian counterparts on military and security matters. With time, these measures can build mutual trust and further establish the Chinese military as a more responsible regional player.

Another place to look might be in the domestic Chinese policy discourse about the very issue of military transparency and confidence-building measures. Chinese analysts tend to dismiss such efforts as being disadvantageous to weaker states since the discourse might reveal too much about vulnerabilities, while being advantageous for more powerful countries for which such information can have a deterrent effect. If Chinese military analysts introduce less rigid attitudes toward transparency, showing appreciation for the advantages it can offer in easing security dilemmas and strategic mistrust, it could be an early indication of a positive evolution.

### Climate Change and Ecological Degradation

In the years ahead, China faces a huge challenge stemming from the environmental impact of its growth, which has created significant problems for the country's people, health, and landscape. China remains the world's largest consumer of coal (an energy source that is among the worst in its production of greenhouse gases), and its energy needs will only increase as China continues to develop. Some studies estimate that unremediated environmental degradation and pollution could cost the Chinese economy between 8 and 12 percent of GDP annually.[10]

The implications of China's environmental degradation are far-reaching and serious, both for China and for the world. Climate change spawns refugees, floods, energy crises, poverty, and conflict over scarce resources—issues that either already affect the United States and China or will affect them in the coming years.

China thus has a shared interest in addressing these critical issues. Having failed to ratify the Kyoto Protocol, China has the dubious distinction of joining the United States as one of the top two emitters of carbon gases. Along with India, China also is now the fastest growing market for oil. The associated implications and stakes are thus critical for the world as a whole. Given that China almost certainly will be the world's largest carbon emitter by mid-century, it must be fully engaged with the issue nationally and internationally, or it will be impossible for the world to deal effectively with climate change.

In fact, capping greenhouse gas emissions, with its development and growth trade-off, could be *the* premier test of China's new global role. To a great degree, international debate hinges on how China addresses the demands and needs of its own people. It confronts structural challenges of divisions between rich and poor, new demands for governance (i.e., capacity-building), and the need to either license or develop clean energy and efficiency technologies. How China chooses to respond to these difficult trade-offs will be an indicator of the country's broader approach to global affairs.

To be effective, any climate change regime must commit developing countries, including China, to a reasonable set of targets and timetables for reducing their greenhouse gas emissions. China's approach at the recent Bali conference indicates that it may be edging toward an affirmative decision to play a much more constructive role in combating climate change. Chinese delegates at Bali brought several proposals, including suggestions to increase fuel-efficiency standards—a pronounced shift from past talks where China took hard-line, defensive approaches. China's openness to aspirational greenhouse gas emissions targets in a post-Kyoto climate framework and to measures that are "reportable and verifiable" are positive steps, but its willingness to commit to binding obligations remains the ultimate marker of China's readiness to meet the challenge of climate change with serious action.

Meaningful Chinese leadership on combating climate change would show other developing countries that, rather than harming developing economies, sustainability and environmental stewardship are the only real paths to growth in the twenty-first century.

### Energy Consumption and Conservation

China today has the largest annual increases in oil consumption in the world—around five hundred thousand barrels per day—and the percentage of its consumption that it imports is growing rapidly. It is clear that China must search actively and cooperatively for solutions to its energy consumption and conservation challenges. As competition for energy threatens to become more intense in the years ahead, a China that reinforces free markets and global trade in energy would be a great boon for the liberal economic order.

Given the implications for China's domestic economy and growth rates, major new investment in less energy-intensive industries would signal Chinese willingness to be a global leader in energy conservation. Beijing has announced a number of positive and ambitious steps toward such goals under the rubric of a "scientific development concept," and any further implementation will be strong indicators of a more globally responsible approach. In cooperating internationally to spur innovation in energy technology and to develop efficient alternative energy resources, China can address directly a source of tension between PRC energy needs and the needs of others in the international community.

China's leadership increasingly recognizes that its country's foreign relations are deeply affected and even damaged by the country's energy consumption and is looking for ways to address the energy and foreign policy problem. In fact, Chinese President Hu Jintao's new energy policy announcement in 2007 stressed openness to international cooperation in part in recognition of these issues.

## Challenges for the Leaders of China and Its Partners

The global reaction to the rise of China has been varied. For example, a number of countries in the developing world have welcomed Chinese investments and Beijing's "no-strings-attached" approach to aid as well as its support for noninterference in internal affairs. Some still have their doubts about whether China will be a constructive or destructive force in the global community in the decades ahead; others have a more optimistic outlook on the long-term prospects for a more responsible China.

Like other rising powers before it, China is certainly flexing new muscles and seeking new influence around the world. But China also has shown that it is susceptible to international pressure and that it does not wish to be an outlier in the international system—especially at the cost of estrangement from key partners with which it desires stronger ties. The question still remains, whether China's aim is merely to do the minimum necessary to evade international criticism and reap near-term benefits, which would indicate that it neither rejects the current international order nor fully buys in. Put another way, such a stance leaves China a beneficiary of the current world order but also leaves China with the option to diverge from the current order should China choose.

For the United States and others in the international community, the notion of China as a responsible stakeholder can serve as the basis of a progressive policy toward China and also point toward the objective of an international order in which China understands the true measure of its stake. There is a possibility that an ascendant China will follow in the path of other rising powers before it and seek to rewrite the rules of international politics and economics. The gains to be realized from China assuming a more constructive role in international affairs are hardly insignificant, and offer the hope that, managed wisely, further Chinese integration will benefit all.

Broadly speaking, China has made encouraging progress along a path toward becoming a more responsible stakeholder in international affairs. But far more still can and should be done to help urge China along this path. At a minimum, interested observers and policymakers should heed the "six assumptions" at the outset of this chapter as the surest foundation from which to work with China. This process will be neither quick nor easy. It will demand steady and prudent statesmanship on the part of the Chinese leaders and their key partners abroad, along with regular stock-taking and clear communication with Beijing along the lines we have suggested.

In the end, we are not in the least sanguine, and are at best cautiously optimistic, that such an approach can solidify China's role as a pillar of a stable, secure, and prosperous community of nations. We appreciate the obstacles and drawbacks that may lay ahead, not least those within China itself. But by clearly defining what is meant by "responsible stakeholdership," carefully identifying the steps that indicate movement in that direction, and pragmatically working within a framework of common interests as a basis for those steps, we can improve the prospects for a more peaceful and prosperous world.

⌒

## Wu Xinbo's Reaction

### Facilitating China's Rise as a Responsible Stakeholder through Constructive Interactions

One of the perennial challenges confronting international politics has been the management of the rising powers. As China and other countries rise to a more preeminent position in the world arena of the twenty-first century, a hot topic of the moment is how to turn them into pillars of a rules-based international order. Although behaviors of the rising powers are mainly shaped by their respective internal dynamics, in a world of globalization and interdependence, the outside world can exert significant influence—for better or for worse. Therefore, whether China can become a responsible player depends, in part, on how the outside world will interact with it. In this regard, three questions are relevant: First, in what context does the outside world engage Beijing? Second, are the demands from the outside world reasonable? And finally, can the existing major powers such as the United States set a good example?

### A More Constructive Framework

Any effective approach to China must address its core concerns: economic growth, political stability, and territorial integrity. One of the six strategic understandings laid out by Gill and Schiffer, "acknowledge and work with the one-party political system," addresses Beijing's concern with political stability, while another, "clear acceptance by the international community of the territorial unity and integrity of China," helps alleviate Beijing's concern over its territorial integrity. However, Gill and Schiffer did not explore adequately how to address China's concern about its economic growth, which affects both China's political stability and international status.

The truth is that Beijing made strenuous efforts to join the World Trade Organization, hoping to secure a stable and favorable international economic environment, but soon became disillusioned by frequent trade frictions with the United States and Europe. Indeed, the growing protectionist mood in those regions has led Chinese leaders to reexamine the external economic environment and rethink its international economic policies. Frankly speaking, China's integration into the international system and its responsible international behavior are largely contingent on the rewards it reaps from an open and free international economic system. Therefore, to encourage China to behave as a responsible player in world affairs, the United States and Europe should resist their economic protectionist impulses and help create a stable and amicable economic order.

The authors' argument for recognizing China's uniqueness is also important. From the Chinese perspective, this uniqueness has two implications. On the one hand, it means that China's domestic development may not follow the "Washington Consensus"—i.e., market economy plus a multiparty political system. While some in the West have labeled China's development model the "Beijing Consensus," Chinese leaders prefer the notion of "socialism with Chinese characteristics." On the other hand, it means that China's rise may not follow the past pattern in which the rise of major powers often led to major wars and conflicts. This squares with the Chinese notion of "China's peaceful rise." Indeed, international affirmation of China's uniqueness would send Beijing a reassuring message that the West respects China's search for its own development model and will abstain from imposing the Western version on China.

## Gauging China's Behavior Reasonably

Overall, Gill and Schiffer offered quite sensible yardsticks to measure China's ongoing evolution as a responsible stakeholder. Still, I would like to offer the following thoughts to endorse or supplement their points.

### Political Evolution at Home

To be sure, the West has its own set of expectations for China's political evolution. Even the Chinese acknowledge that their political system should be improved. However, when the West tries to sell the value of "democracy" to China, the Chinese are always skeptical. From the Chinese standpoint, democracy is a strongly ideological and narrowly defined notion. It is too much of a holdover legacy of the East-West confrontation during the Cold War and reflects the U.S. aspiration of spreading its values and political model throughout the world in the post–Cold War era. Moreover, democracies do not necessarily lead to good governance. In Asia, as in other parts of the world, there are both successful and unsuccessful—or functional and dysfunctional—democracies. From a functionalist perspective, what really matters to people is whether they have good governance—that is, conditions of political stability rather than chaos, social harmony rather than conflict, and economic prosperity rather than poverty. Instead of using democracy as the sole and rigid indicator of China's political evolution, Gill and Schiffer adopted a more sophisticated and pragmatic approach, such as inner-party democracy; anticorruption measures; improvements in administrative law; empowerment of citizenry; rule of law; more transparent and accountable governance; improved treatment of minorities, religious groups, and civil society organizations; and poverty alleviation. These indicators make more sense to the Chinese and are more pertinent to the orientation of China's political development.

### International Economics, Trade, and Investment

As the Chinese economy continues to grow rapidly and energy consumption rises, a stable supply of affordable energy is all the more important. In recent years, China has conducted active diplomacy to broaden its access to overseas energy resources. However, Beijing was criticized by many in the United States for adopting an "increasingly mercantilist approach to locking up energy resources," and they suggested that China should use transparent market-based solutions to address energy issues. From a Chinese perspective, however, the international oil market is neither open nor reliable. The U.S. and British oil companies have control over a sizable chunk of the oil trade on the international market. Meanwhile, the United States has been pursuing an aggressive policy of dominating the flow of oil in the Middle East and beyond. As we saw from the spurned bid of the China National Offshore Oil Corporation (CNOOC) for Unocal Corp., oil is not an ordinary commodity, and access to it is inevitably complicated by political and strategic considerations. For China, investment in overseas oil production can help alleviate its concern over dependable access to the international oil market. Unless China's energy concern is adequately addressed, Beijing very likely will continue to pursue long-term oil purchase agreements, invest in established foreign oil companies, and obtain concessions to develop oil fields as well as rights to explore for new fields.

*Regional Hotspots*

Gill and Schiffer suggested that China's attitude toward the United States, its alliances, and other security partnerships in the western Pacific also should be a key indicator in assessing China's willingness to be a responsible stakeholder. The problem is that Beijing has its reasons for viewing the U.S.-centered security alliances with suspicion—seeing them as the product of the Cold War, and therefore obsolete, and intended to check a rising China. In fact, China looms large not only in the redefined and strengthened U.S.-Japan alliance, but also in other U.S. security partnerships in the region—for instance, the fast-growing U.S.-Indian security ties. It is therefore unrealistic to expect Beijing to embrace such security arrangements when China is their major target.

Relations between a rising China and a more assertive Japan remain a sour spot in the diplomacies of both countries, despite their recent improvement. To place bilateral ties on a solid basis would require some tough grand bargaining between Beijing and Tokyo. To reach such a deal, Japan would need to take a more serious and responsible attitude toward the history issue. Tokyo also needs to overcome its psychological peevishness over having to live with a strong neighbor for the first time in its modern history and adopt a more accommodating posture toward the emergence of a more powerful China. From Beijing's side, it should discard its long-held contempt of Japan and show more respect and recognition of this neighbor. For instance, Beijing could acknowledge openly the Japanese contribution to China's economic growth and broader global prosperity. China also should be more sympathetic to the Japanese desire to play a large role in both regional and global affairs as long as such a role is constructive and stabilizing.

*Military Affairs*

Gill and Schiffer emphasized the importance of strategic transparency in China's responsible security behavior. Although transparency is not part of

China's military traditions, it is likely that improvements to Beijing's military capability will give the People's Liberation Army (PLA) the confidence to increase its transparency. In addition, Beijing has become more active in pursuing confidence- and security-building measures with its neighbors in recent years. So far as the United States is concerned, however, the real questions on China's military modernization are twofold: whether the United States recognizes the legitimacy of China's defense modernization, and whether the United States can accept China's growing military capability.

To be sure, as China's economy continues to boom, Beijing will be able to devote more resources to its defense establishment and to building a modern and more capable military machine. Also, as China's national interests rise along with its power, it will need to protect those interests. Yet some in the United States may point at China's rising defense budget and question Beijing's pledge of "peaceful development." More importantly, as the PLA's capability grows and its geographic parameter of activity expands, the United States may feel not only slippage in its overall military superiority, but a challenge particularly to its dominance of the western Pacific. As a result, the Pentagon may square off against the PLA as its major rival and launch a Cold War–style arms race with China. This will of course conversely factor into Beijing's defense planning and provide more stimulus to the PLA's modernization drive. It will also undermine China's willingness to increase its military transparency.

*Exemplary Behavior*

As Gill and Schiffer correctly noted, China has shown itself to be "susceptible to international pressure." It is also true that other major powers' behavior, good or bad, will have an important impact on China's thinking and behavior. Given its preeminent position in the current international system, the United States is the most important point of reference for China in framing its policies. It is therefore crucial that the United States and other major powers set good examples for China and other rising powers through their own international behavior.

In a world of globalization and interdependence, multilateralism is not only necessary to deal with many transnational issues and common challenges, but a value that should guide the behavior of the members of international community. Multilateralism entails respect for the views and interests of others and compromise of one's own. Major powers, and particularly a superpower like the United States, may choose unilateralism when deemed necessary to pursue its narrow national interests, as the George W. Bush administration did. Such destructive behavior not only undermines international order and the spirit of international cooperation, but also sends a message to other countries that multilateralism is merely a matter of convenience.

Undoubtedly, a neoliberal world order has to be based on an open and free international economic system. Despite globalization's successes in promoting economic development, its harmful side effects—trade imbalance, relocation of the production base by the transnational companies, and uneven competitiveness among countries—have generated social and economic pressures and sparked protectionism in both developing and developed worlds. Some politicians, for the sake of their own political interests, may pursue economic nationalism. Such actions not only would undermine the liberal economic order, but would also hinder cooperation among the major powers on political and security issues, thereby undercutting any basis for a neoliberal political order.

Finally, a neoliberal world order should be one of strategic stability and free of major power competition. The United States risks an arms race and strategic instability if it tries to exploit its superior economic and technological prowess and aggravates the security dilemma by developing both advanced offensive and defensive capabilities. Also, a U.S. effort to strengthen and expand its security alliances and partnerships in pursuit of a favorable power balance will only create geopolitical tensions and undercut mutual confidence among the major players. The twenty-first century calls for genuinely new security thinking and practice. Indeed, the world will look to the United States to set a good example by pursuing relative security instead of absolute security, strategic confidence instead of military preponderance, and security cooperation instead of balance of power. The United States should define its greatness in a progressive, rather than regressive, way.

## Notes

1. Bonnie S. Glaser and Evan S. Medeiros, "The Changing Ecology of Foreign Policy-Making in China: The Ascension and Demise of the Theory of 'Peaceful Rise,'" *China Quarterly* 190 (2007): 291–310.

2. See "Joint Statement of the 10th China-EU Summit," November 28, 2007, accessed at www.eu2007.pt/UE/vEN/Noticias_Documentos/20071202CHINA.htm.

3. Declaration on the Conduct of Parties in the South China Sea," November 4, 2002, accessed at www.aseansec.org/13163.htm.

4. C. Fred Bergsten outlines a number of steps China and the United States should take as more responsible leaders in world trade and financial markets in "A Partnership of Equals: How Washington Should Respond to China's Economic

Challenge," *Foreign Affairs* (July/August 2008), accessed at www.foreignaffairs.org/20080701faessay87404/c-fred-bergsten/a-partnership-of-equals.html.

5. On China's recent activities in Africa, see Bates Gill, J. Stephen Morrison, and Chin-hao Huang, *China's Expanding Role in Africa: Implications for the United States* (Washington, DC: Center for Strategic and International Studies, January 2007), accessed at www.csis.org/component/option,com_csis_pubs/task,view/id,3714/type,1/.

6. *China's National Defense in 2002* (Beijing: State Council Information Office, December 2002), 35.

7. See, for example, Barbara Crossette, "UN Mission to Haiti Is Reprieved," *New York Times*, March 1, 1996. See also UN Document S/PV.3982 (25 February 1999), and Deborah Kuo, "MOFA's Wu Stresses Taiwan-Macedonia Ties Firm, Solid," *Taiwan Central News Agency*, February 22, 1999, in FBIS *Daily Report: China*, February 22, 1999.

8. "China to send anti-riot peacekeepers for Haiti," *Xinhuanet*, June 4, 2004; "Chinese Riot Police Head for Haiti Mission," *China Daily*, November 22, 2004.

9. Evan S. Medeiros, *Reluctant Restraint: The Evolution of China's Nonproliferation Policies and Practices, 1980–2004* (Stanford, CA: Stanford University Press, 2007); Alastair Iain Johnston, *Social States: China in International Institutions, 1980–2000* (Princeton, NJ: Princeton University Press, 2008).

10. Elizabeth C. Economy, *The River Runs Black* (Ithaca, NY: Cornell University Press, 2004).

# India: The Ultimate Test of Free-Market Democracy

*Barbara Crossette and George Perkovich*
*With a Reaction by C. Raja Mohan*

Among the countries that emerged from the anticolonial movements of the last century, India was unusual in possessing the outlines of a grand national strategy based on a democratic polity and economic self-reliance at home and an active international political role. National self-confidence and a fierce pride in Indian culture and history ran high after a relatively smooth transition to independence, marred, of course, by the Hindu-Muslim violence that followed the partition of British India. But then came disappointments, as the economy stalled and then declined, and India's hopes of becoming a global political player dimmed. Only now, as one of the fastest-rising nations in the developing world, India finally seems poised to achieve the prize that many Indians believe has been too long denied to them: a place at the table of power. The way in which India uses its newfound influence will be one of the most interesting stories of the twenty-first century. New generations, both in age and outlook, have the freedom, the cosmopolitan experience, and the training to transform India internally and make it a positive international force on many fronts.

For decades a nation with relatively little power—hard or soft—in international affairs, India is now nuclear armed, economically dynamic, technologically advancing, and increasingly influential in organizations such as the World Bank, the World Trade Organization (WTO), and the United Nations, where it persistently seeks a permanent seat on the Security Council. There has rarely been a better moment for the international community to engage India on issues ranging from nuclear nonproliferation to economic integration, the strengthening of democracy globally, the race against climate change, the reduction of world poverty, and the protection of universal human rights. India, with more than 1.1 billion people, will in a few decades become the world's most populous nation. India therefore cannot be ignored. The twenty-first century's major challenges cannot be met without the active and positive involvement of India (and, of course, China). Ever more self-assured in its outlook, India matters.

In a world that has often seen India as the dissident, there are now signs of a new Indian approach to international cooperation, both in its own South Asian region and among global stakeholders. In what may have been a bellwether moment in December 2007, India stepped in to break a deadlock at a critical climate change conference in Bali, Indonesia, allowing nations to enter a new phase in planning how to limit greenhouse gases following the expiration of the Kyoto Protocol in 2012. Delegates in Bali had watched the United States defy to the bitter end the wishes of all others by demanding that all major polluters, not only industrial nations, be held accountable for reduced emissions under a new regime, removing the blanket exemption for developing countries. With the conference already in overtime and tempers frayed, India intervened on behalf of the Group of 77—which, despite its name, consists of 130 developing nations and China—to propose a sliding scale of responsibilities and capacities among poorer countries, with India and China, among the top ten polluters, prepared to make concrete pledges to reduce emissions. The United States, saying it had been heartened by the compromise, reversed course and agreed to join the consensus, and the conference was saved. Seven months later, however, Prime Minister Manmohan Singh, laying out India's climate change policy, did not include the reduction of carbon emissions.[1]

The degree to which India continues in a constructive spirit in international environmental, nuclear, and economic regimes will depend on the balance between global commitments and domestic political demands that can be struck by the central and state governments in a diverse and democratic society.

## The Road India Has Traveled

In the heady days following its independence from Britain in 1947, India enjoyed a certain international stature rooted in spiritual and moral leadership as the land of Mohandas Gandhi and the nonviolent Quit India movement. Jawaharlal Nehru, India's aristocratic first prime minister, was undeniably a global figure. By the mid-1950s, he had become a founder of the Non-Aligned Movement (NAM), which was formed to serve as a third force in a polarized world of East versus West. Nehru deftly maneuvered within the new United Nations, sending high-profile representatives there. He looked for opportunities to extend a hand across borders and continents to aid like-minded friends. In 1956, for example, the acerbic diplomat V. K. Krishna Menon was dispatched to Egypt to advise its government during the confrontation with Britain and France over the Suez Canal. Nehru clearly had a global vision.

But while India managed to exert some influence in its early decades through the mobilization of NAM, the country lacked the capacity to motivate or compel others to shape the international system to its own liking. Rather, Indian leaders had only enough power to say "no" to keep others from imposing their will on India. Moreover, during the tenure of Indira Gandhi, Nehru's daughter and political heir, the Indian National Congress slipped from its lofty status as a liberation movement to a political party steeped in petty corruption and misuse of power, pandering to "vote banks" and preoccupied by domestic political turbulence. India saw some of its international luster fade.

During the Cold War, Indira Gandhi, never the towering figure her father had been, appeared to cast her lot with the Soviet Union. This undermined her professed nonaligned stance and reflected her wariness of the West, particularly the United States, which she saw moving closer to Pakistan, to India's disadvantage.

Other causes of India's eclipse stemmed from a domestic economic policy of democratic socialism, reflecting the need of a political democracy to respond to the fears of a majority that had always been poor and agrarian. As the population more than tripled between 1947 and 2000, not enough jobs were created in industry or services to absorb the workers who would be displaced by any consolidation of profitable larger-scale agriculture. Consequently, except for pockets of prosperity such as Punjab during the "green revolution," farming remained low-tech, low-income, and heavily subsidized; in fact, the value of subsidies today is four times that of public investment in the development of agriculture.[2] Agricultural growth, at about 2.7 percent annually, is still only a fraction of the national economic growth rate of between 8 percent and 9 percent, a source of concern to Indian and international development economists.

Protectionism not only of agriculture but also industry under the politically resonant banner of self-reliance—swadeshi—kept India from becoming much of a global economic player until the early 1990s. At that point, following the Soviet collapse and the loss of its preferential trade status with

Moscow, India faced a foreign reserve crisis that compelled the government to undertake major policy changes. Led by then–Finance Minister Manmohan Singh and under successor governments, India opened its economy and looked toward the West and Japan for trade and investment. Only in the past decade or so has India begun to muster the power to press its desires in the international community and not just in economic spheres.

The end of the Cold War system created a space for major regional powers to gain stature in the global order. China's rapid advances pose competitive challenges for India, but it also makes the United States, Japan, and European nations want to assist India in gaining the economic, military, and soft power to balance China. Major transnational challenges in the twenty-first century—foremost among them climate change and infectious diseases—cannot be managed without India's full cooperation, and India will not cooperate unless it plays a role in the policy-formulation process. As a result, India necessarily will gain influence.

Many, for instance, see nuclear energy—realistically or not—as an important technology to limit the growth in greenhouse gas emissions. India, with the strong encouragement of the United States, France, and Russia, hopes to expand its nuclear electricity production. Yet, if the global expansion of nuclear industry is not guided by new rules, the risks of weapons proliferation will grow dangerously. India thus can either facilitate or wreck international efforts to strengthen nonproliferation rules. Likewise, if the global economy is to continue modernizing and expanding, rules will need to be negotiated to manage trade in services. WTO negotiations have not ventured into this territory yet, but when they do, India will be an exceptionally important player.

## Nuclear India and Global Regimes

The international nuclear order is in the greatest state of flux since its inception forty years ago. India is one cause of this turbulence. At the same time, it can be a major contributor to the renovation needed to make the nuclear order viable over the next four decades.

In the 1960s the United States and the Soviet Union joined in building the framework of the international nonproliferation regime. The two superpowers competed in many domains, but by the mid-1960s neither wanted other states to acquire nuclear weapons. On the basis of this shared interest, the United States and the Soviet Union took the lead in negotiating the Treaty on the Nonproliferation of Nuclear Weapons (NPT). This treaty rested on three bargains. States that had not tested nuclear weapons agreed not to acquire such weapons. In return, the five states that had already tested and acquired nuclear weapons promised to not help others obtain them, pledged to assist others in enjoying the peaceful benefits of atomic energy, and committed to the eventual elimination of all nuclear weapons. In essence, the treaty recognized a de facto (if not permanent and legally mandated) dichotomous nuclear order in which there were five "haves" and a huge number of "have-nots" and sought to stabilize this order against further proliferation by promising that it was a transition to a much more equitable order in which no state would possess nuclear weapons and everyone would benefit from the peaceful use of nuclear energy.

India was one of the leading states in the negotiation of the NPT and led the call for equity under the treaty. In the end, India refused to sign it because New Delhi viewed the disarmament commitment by the five recognized nuclear weapon states as too weak and disingenuous, so India would therefore keep its own nuclear options open.

The NPT took effect in 1970, without India, Pakistan, and Israel among its signatories. Other developing countries also stayed out of the treaty and instead launched nuclear weapons programs that were either halted before they came to fruition (Argentina and Brazil) or were dropped after having produced nuclear weapons (South Africa). France did not join the treaty until 1992, in part because it believed that the disarmament commitment under the treaty went too far. China also joined only in 1992, while contributing before and after that to Pakistan's nuclear weapons program, which was directed against India. In 1974 India announced the detonation of what it called a "peaceful nuclear explosion." This prompted the United States to launch an international campaign to strengthen the nonproliferation regime by creating cartels of nuclear technology and material suppliers that would establish rules to limit exports to states prohibited by the NPT from having nuclear weapons.

### The Dilemmas of Nuclear Testing

Contrary to the expectations of many foreign officials and experts, the Indian government did not authorize more nuclear tests by its military for another twenty-four years. There were many reasons for this restraint.[3] Indian nuclear scientists and some military leaders urged prime ministers to approve proposed tests, but the politicians refused, largely in the belief that India had higher economic and political priorities and that international backlash against further nuclear tests would divert leadership energy from these priorities—and possibly incur heavy penalties.

By 1998, however, multiple interests converged in favor of nuclear weapons tests. A nationalist political party—the Bharatiya Janata Party (BJP)—led the government and wanted to flex its muscles at home and abroad. Only the strong get respect, the party believed, and nuclear weapons could show India's strength. India's closest strategic rival, China, was now heralded as the next great world power. China had earned this respect not by moralism of the old Indian sort but by acting defiantly and assertively in its national interest. The world's hegemonic power, the United States, gave communist China more respect than it did democratic India, in part because China challenged the United States and flexed its muscles, while India feebly protested in moralistic speeches. It stood to reason, therefore, that India should be more like China and speak the language of power that U.S. leaders respected. If India did not demonstrate to itself and its neighbors that it was capable of producing sophisticated nuclear weapons, according to this line of thought, it would not be strong enough to keep a growing China from trying to push it around.

India also had to test to stay ahead of a U.S.-led international effort to establish nonproliferation norms and treaties that would substantially increase the associated political and economic costs. In 1995, to the surprise of Indian leaders, the state parties to the NPT had agreed to extend the treaty indefinitely, without a requirement for steps toward disarmament from the nuclear weapon states. The following year, the Comprehensive Test Ban Treaty (CTBT) was signed and pressure mounted for India to join it. (Ultimately, Chinese and U.S. failure to ratify kept the treaty from entering into force.) In sum, any further delay by India in testing a weapon and proclaiming its capabilities would only make it politically much harder to do so later. As another factor, India's nuclear establishment—the influential and relatively unaccountable strategic enclave of scientists and engineers—was by then apoplectic over its political leadership's refusal to authorize tests more than two decades after the 1974 explosion. They argued that the generation that had designed and built India's early nuclear devices was retiring and that if tests were not authorized, India could be left without the technical expertise needed for a nuclear deterrent. Tests also would lure gifted young scientists and engineers into the nuclear enterprise.

These multiple Indian interests in nuclear testing are catalogued here because they offer a case study of how values and international events interacted with Indian politics and interest groups to produce behavior. For example, international norms crafted by big powers that then campaign to impose them on others can indeed be influential, but rather than dissuade India (and possibly other big developing countries) from consequential threshold steps, the pressure can actually spur them to accelerated action before a new norm or rule takes effect. Indeed, a good rule of thumb is that if a norm creates a hierarchy or multiple tiers in the international system, India generally will resist locking itself into a lower tier but will either hold out or force its way into the top tier.

## India's Separate Nuclear Deal

Soon after the Indian and Pakistani nuclear tests, the George W. Bush administration came into office, bringing in key leaders—including John Bolton, Dick Cheney, Douglas Feith, and Steve Cambone—who were convinced that the rules-based nonproliferation regime would never prevent the most dangerous actors from seeking and perhaps acquiring nuclear weapons. Even worse, in their view, in order to win international acceptance of rules (which they considered inadequate in the first place), the United States had to accept constraints on the quality and quantity of its own nuclear arsenal. Instead of wasting time and political capital negotiating incremental improvements in ineffectual global nonproliferation rules, the Bush administration developed a strategy predicated on regime change. Revising earlier bipartisan first principles, they did not view nuclear weapons as the problem; the problem was bad guys with nuclear weapons. Rather than try to eliminate the weapons, it made more sense to eliminate the bad guys. That way the good guys could keep their weapons; a world in which the good guys have nuclear weapons and the bad guys are gone is more than tolerable.

The strategy, reminiscent of nineteenth-century realpolitik, established a good frame for what became the U.S.-India nuclear deal. In July 2005 President Bush hosted Indian Prime Minister Manmohan Singh and announced the intention to set aside all U.S. and international restrictions on nuclear cooperation with India and, instead, to encourage full cooperation to help India develop its nuclear industry. The desire to remove what had, in effect, been sanctions on India for acquiring nuclear weapons reflected a larger U.S. purpose. The Bush administration now sought to help India become a major power for intrinsic reasons but also for the instrumental purpose of balancing China's power in Asia. Some in the administration even welcomed the prospect of India increasing the size and quality of its nuclear arsenal and the quality of its ballistic missile delivery systems and platforms. Thus, the president's instructions for the interagency process on the deal insisted that nothing in the resulting agreement should constrain India's strategic capabilities in any way. This ruled out limitations on or an end to Indian production of fissile materials for nuclear weapons—a key objective of those concerned with upholding the global nonproliferation regime.

France and Russia emphatically support the U.S.-led effort to exempt India from nonproliferation constraints. Their nuclear industries are naturally eager to export reactors, fuel, and related goods and services to India. These commercial interests are an additional source of the international nuclear order's state of flux; the very terms and expectations of exemplary steward-ship seem to be under constant revision.

India has thus had a conflicted and sometimes conflictual relationship with the rules-based nuclear order, which itself is evolving. India began by genuinely loathing nuclear weapons and advocating nuclear disarmament but now proudly proclaims itself as a nuclear weapon power and demands the accompanying international status and rank (a crude form of hard power that Indian leaders once denounced as inhumane). India began with great determination to be self-sufficient in production of nuclear energy but sixty years later pleads for rule changes to allow it to receive extensive imports of nuclear fuel and reactors. These shifts, in one sense, reflect the failure or at least the waning of idealism. India and other sources of moral or political suasion could not persuade the early nuclear weapon states to pursue nuclear disarmament; Indian technological skills and economic infrastructure could not self-sufficiently overcome some of the challenges of extracting large amounts of electricity from the nuclei of uranium and plutonium atoms. In another sense, India has moved from being a naive or self-righteous outside critic of other states' nuclear practices to being a conformist.

### Terms of a New Nuclear Order

If a new nuclear order is currently under construction, its main contours are emerging, but there is also much doubt as to whether cooperation among key states will put the elements of the order into place or if noncooperation will allow more dangerous trends to prevail.

- It is assumed and/or advocated that large numbers of new nuclear power plants will be built, both in nations that do not currently have any and in those that do.
- This expansion of nuclear energy production, however, must/will feature proliferation-resistant technologies and more robust rules and procedures to prevent proliferation.
- The key nonproliferation imperative is to prevent uranium enrichment and plutonium separation capabilities from spreading to states that do not now have them, out of concern that these capabilities put their possessors too close to having nuclear weapons.
- Ideally, binding rules would be set to stop the spread of fuel-cycle tech-nology, and in return there would be strong guarantees of international supply to make it more economically attractive to forego indigenous fuel-cycle operations.

- However, some nonnuclear weapon states adamantly resist any new rules that discriminate between nuclear "haves" and "have-nots." They complain that the United States, Russia, Israel, and other possessors of nuclear weapons have failed to pursue nuclear disarmament seriously. The nonnuclear weapon states thus will block establishment of important new nonproliferation rules absent a genuine push toward nuclear disarmament and more equitable sharing of peaceful nuclear technology.
- Recognizing this resistance, the United States, the International Atomic Energy Agency (IAEA), and others are suggesting that instead of new rules, voluntary incentives should be developed to make reliance on international fuel supply the obvious choice for new possessors of nuclear power plants.

Clearly there is a circular problem impeding the construction of a more durable new nuclear order. To correct dangerous flaws in the old order, updated nonproliferation rules are needed, especially as the nuclear industry expands to new countries. No new rules, however, will be accepted unless the possessors of nuclear weapons take more serious steps to disarm. Yet the United States, Israel, and other states with nuclear weapons will not move toward nuclear disarmament without clear indications that nonproliferation rules will be fully enforced and proliferation will be prevented. The U.S.-India nuclear deal further confuses this fluid situation, as many states see the United States as loosening existing rules for India as its new favorite, while simultaneously tightening the rules for everyone else.

Despite the contested and uncertain state of the rules-based system into which India would be integrated, there are nonetheless clear standards of basic responsible nuclear stewardship—fundamental requirements irrespective of what nonproliferation rules are eventually agreed on. First and most simply, a responsible state would devote all the resources and high-level attention needed to implement state-of-the-art laws controlling exports of sensitive nuclear equipment, material, and know-how. UN Security Council Resolution 1540 in April 2004 made such national controls mandatory on all states to block proliferation to nonstate entities; India and others should also extend their controls to prevent states, not merely nonstate actors, from acquiring nuclear weapons. This goes beyond enacting comprehensive laws; it requires training and motivating customs officials, border and port monitors, and private producers of relevant equipment and materiel. It also means cooperating with other countries' intelligence services and with the IAEA to pursue any leads that flag one's own state as a potential locus of proliferation activity.

Indian officials and champions of the U.S.-India nuclear deal abroad have insisted that India has a sterling record in keeping its technology from leaking out. These advocates implicitly, and sometimes explicitly, suggest that nuclear cooperation should be the reward for this good behavior. This seeks to have it two ways: because India is virtuous, the United States should drop any barriers to doing nuclear business with it; if it doesn't, India might grow so frustrated it could do something less than virtuous. The truth probably lies somewhere in the middle. Indian leaders, including those of the nuclear establishment, have indeed been careful stewards and genuinely abhor the spread of nuclear weapons. Meanwhile, new inducements would probably help persuade these leaders to invest more energy, resources, and credibility in implementing export controls.

Beyond ensuring that a nation's own entities do not actively contribute to proliferation, a responsible steward must operate its nuclear facilities—civilian and military—according to the highest standards of safety and security. This is easier said than done. The operative norms of safety that are in place for human health and the environment and capabilities to ensure compliance tend to be part and parcel of the overall technological and administrative picture for the given state. India is still a poor country with insufficient infrastructure and inadequate regulation of workplace safety and environmental protection. India's nuclear industry is admirable in many ways but does not operate with capabilities and standards comparable to those of, for example, France. The leadership of the Indian nuclear establishment has tended to avoid international cooperation (and scrutiny) partly out of sensitivity to being judged as backward by peers from France, the United States, Japan, and other countries. Indeed, one tacit reason why Prime Minister Manmohan Singh wants to open India to international cooperation and contracting is to foster interactions and competition that will expose the shortcomings of the indigenous nuclear establishment and require it to improve or be displaced by international partners that can produce electricity more efficiently, safely, and securely. The broader point here is that all nuclear establishments should seek—or be pressed to seek—to operate at state-of-the-art standards.

A third measure of responsible stewardship is to lower the salience of nuclear weapons in international politics and national security policies. Parties to the NPT recently have established this as a political obligation, even though governments including the United States, Russia, and France arguably fail to uphold it. At the very least, then, the standard should be to keep from *boosting* the value of nuclear weapons for security—as happens through nuclear saber-rattling, using nuclear weapons as a currency for domestic political gain or to flex muscles for international stature, and announcing national security doctrines that highlight the role of nuclear weapons. On this count, Indian leaders have been conscientious. While public debate over nuclear posture and policy is appropriate and necessary in a democracy, Indian leaders since the 1998 tests have been careful to refrain from demagoguery. Nor have Indian leaders rattled their nuclear sabers. Instead, they tend in a rather exemplary way to portray these devices not as useable weapons but as political-psychological warnings to possible enemies not to commit suicide because, as a last resort, Indian leaders would be willing to destroy those who would destroy India. India insists that it would not use nuclear weapons first, which is another measure of self-restraint. By maintaining its nuclear weapons under civilian control physically separate from their delivery vehicles, which are under military control, the Indian system further emphasizes the exceptional political character of these weapons. By contrast, the United States and Russia even today maintain thousands of nuclear weapons on high alert, deployed with their delivery systems and poised for launch within minutes.

**India as a Pillar of Nonproliferation**
Going beyond followership, what would Indian leadership in the global nuclear realm entail? Perhaps most important would be actions and words to downgrade the perceived value of nuclear weapons. India already contributes by not maintaining nuclear weapons in a launch-ready mode. It could do even more by declaring that, because the world already has too many nuclear weapons and too much nuclear weapons material, India is prepared to join the United States, Russia, China, France, the United Kingdom, Pakistan, and Israel in a mutual cessation of their production of highly enriched uranium and separated plutonium outside of IAEA safeguards. India's pledge to join a global moratorium on nuclear weapon fuel production would be more meaningful than India's support of negotiations over a fissile material production cut-off treaty. Treaty discussions have been snarled for more than a decade over issues that pose no obstacle to the relevant states halting their own production of more fissile material well in advance of a formal treaty.

More likely, India could lower the perceived value of nuclear weapons by reinvigorating its traditional diplomatic advocacy of nuclear disarmament. Indeed, Prime Minister Manmohan Singh pointed in this direction in a June 2008 speech calling for other nuclear-armed states to join India in a time bound series of steps leading to the elimination of all nuclear arsenals.[4] Yes, it is somewhat hypocritical for a state to muscle its way into the nuclear weapons club and then turn around and urge nuclear disarmament. But India can honestly say that it always preferred nuclear disarmament to proliferation, yet its calls went unheeded by its neighbors and the superpowers. Nuclear disarmament could make strategic sense for India. In a world without nuclear weapons, India's capacity to deter Pakistani intervention in its internal affairs would be more secure than it is when Pakistan possesses nuclear weapons. Also, India has the conventional military capacity to defend its border with a nuclear-disarmed China.

Indian leadership in advocating the devaluation and phased abolition of nuclear weapons could incur the wrath of the U.S. and French governments—privately expressed, of course—but this only proves that the impetus to strengthen a rules-based international system will not always come from the United States or Europe.

Looking far down the road, India's role in shaping the future nuclear order could affect its prospects of obtaining permanent membership in the UN Security Council. India deeply wants such a seat and has many valid arguments to back up its claim. Given the Security Council's role as the ultimate enforcement authority of the NPT, though, how would it work to have a nonparty to the NPT as a co–chief enforcer?

To be sure, the current permanent five nations also possess nuclear weapons so the current system already reflects a double standard. If India abides by its pledge in the deal with the United States to fulfill all the obligations that the traditional nuclear weapon states do, then the double standard should be no more problematic for India than for the United States, Russia, China, France, and the United Kingdom. This would require India to sign the CTBT, as the others have, and accept the general commitment to disarmament undertaken by the treaty's nuclear weapon states parties.

Unfortunately for India, these have not been the prevailing terms of the debate over Security Council reform. A large segment of international opinion in fact wants to break the one-to-one correspondence between veto-wielding Security Council members and the club of nuclear powers and indeed keep any nuclear weapon states from becoming permanent members. This issue would only grow in prominence once real progress toward Security Council reform began to materialize. Optimally, global nuclear disarmament would free India from this problem: if all possessors of nuclear weapons eliminate these arsenals, India could join the NPT as a nonnuclear weapon state. In the nearer term, Indian leaders could consider how leadership in defining and advocating a process of nuclear disarmament to be joined by all the other possessors might improve its prospects.

Meanwhile, the severe challenge posed by Iran to the old nuclear order highlights the central requirements of a new order. The magnitude of changes necessary in rules governing nuclear technology depends on whether Iran continues to get away with defying enforcement of the old rules it has flouted. If Iran can be persuaded to suspend its fuel-cycle activities long enough to resolve the outstanding questions and build international confidence in the peaceful purposes of future nuclear activities, then rules restricting access to uranium enrichment and plutonium separation capabilities need not be as exclusive as those that will be needed if Iran continues expanding uranium enrichment without convincing the world community of its benign intentions. Given the stakes involved, India's posture in the effort to bring Iran into compliance with nonproliferation and UNSC rules may speak volumes about its international stewardship in general.

India has steadfastly defended Iran's "right" to benefit from atomic energy, while at the same time insisting that Iran comply with all its NPT obligations to use atomic energy exclusively for peaceful purposes. As evidence of Iran's noncompliance with its IAEA safeguards obligations mounted and Iran failed to provide the full transparency demanded by the IAEA, India defended the IAEA's position.

India historically had played a leading role in negotiating the IAEA statute and setting up the agency, and Indian officials express a strong interest in protecting the agency's role. But when U.S. leaders conditioned support for the then-proposed U.S.-India nuclear cooperation agreement on Indian support in an IAEA board decision to refer Iran to the UN Security Council, elements in the Indian polity bristled at this attempt at coercion. For its part, Iran capitalized on this discord to press for India to defend Tehran's position. In the end, India joined with many other IAEA members in reporting Iran to the Security Council, but the public U.S. pressure actually made the decision more difficult than it otherwise would have been.

India clearly does not want Iran to acquire nuclear weapons. Such a development would contribute to insecurity in the region and complicate India's relations with the Gulf Arab states. Any prospects of conflict could threaten the safety of Indian nationals in these states and require contingency plans for Indian action to protect and evacuate them. Like other nuclear weapon states, India would see Iran's acquisition of nuclear weapons as a devaluation of the nuclear currency India has obtained. Iran's proximity would force Indian strategic planners—more than those in other nuclear weapon states—to look at the impact of an Iranian arsenal on its military operations within range of Iranian missiles. Moreover, to the extent that the United States and other states, particularly the Gulf Arabs, sought to contain and deter Iran via closer countervailing security arrangements, India could be asked to contribute in ways that it would rather avoid.

Absent brazen Iranian aggression, India will neither support nor participate in military action to stop Iran's nuclear activities. Nor should India be expected to support sanctions on Iranian energy exports. While India would not affirmatively "accept" Iran's illegal acquisition of nuclear weapons, it would see war with Iran or an energy embargo as more threatening. Nor would India support efforts to force a change in the Iranian regime—a reflection of its long-standing position that holds the principle of noninterference in internal affairs sacrosanct. India's own struggle for independence and its deep anticolonial sensibility cause it to favor self-determination over coercive democracy promotion.

These perspectives and interests have led India to support only diplomatic efforts to change Iran's behavior, most prominently to persuade Iran to comply with all IAEA demands for transparency and cooperation to resolve outstanding doubts that all its nuclear activities are exclusively for peaceful purposes. Indian officials carry no brief for Iran, but they can relate to its perspective as an independent civilizational and regional power. They argue that patient, quiet diplomacy and provision of face-saving options are the only way to persuade Iran to comply with international demands.

India's own nuclear energy aspirations also affect its perspective toward Iran. The proposed U.S.-India nuclear deal represents an unprecedented opening of India's nuclear sector to the outside world. Even though the terms of the deal are highly favorable to India, the Indian nuclear establishment and polity have resisted the loss of autonomy they think it entails. To the extent that Russia, the European Union, and others press Iran to accept the multinationalization of its fuel-cycle operations, India will not lend its support. The Indian nuclear establishment and others—not only the Left parties that oppose the U.S.-India deal—would be chary of creating a new norm against national fuel-cycle operations.

## A Role for India in Global Security

India is bound to play an increasingly important role in the international security system. Whereas the nuclear nonproliferation regime is a well-established, detailed, rules-based milieu, international security more broadly is largely anarchic. While India is a not insignificant player in this domain, its role here is much less significant than in the nuclear arena. To the extent there are rules or norms in international security, the first is "don't start wars or commit aggression." Here India has been exemplary, especially given its size. Pakistan has initiated each of its four wars with India: 1948, 1965, 1971, and 1999. The Sino-Indian clash of 1962 could be ascribed to both countries, though India's culpability had more to do with incompetence and hubris than with aggression. The list could go on, but the point is that while India can be a difficult neighbor, it is not an aggressive power.

As China and India gain in global power and influence, the world will have a greater stake in them avoiding a clash with each other. This may seem a strange formulation because India and China should, of course, focus on their own interests and manage competition peacefully for their own reasons. Yet, for a cooperative, rules-based international order to develop, the two most populous countries in the world must not be preoccupied with or engaged in armed conflict of any significant scale. Managing Sino-Indian relations and military competition is only complicated by Pakistan's involvement in an emerging triangular security dilemma. Pakistan has threatened India's security more directly, frequently, and intensively than China has, so India must simultaneously develop capabilities to meet long-term Chinese strategic threats and also develop and deploy military capabilities to deter Pakistan. As the Pakistani military traditionally assesses the Indian threat, it assumes that India is building up in order to dominate Pakistan, discounting the extent to which India's preparations are related to China. Making matters more difficult, China has been a Pakistani ally and provided vital help to Pakistan's nuclear and missile programs.

The three parties have recently managed their multidirectional relations well. India has been courted by both the United States and China. The United States wants India as a strategic partner in part to balance China's growing power. China would prefer that India "date" but not "marry" the United States. Indian leaders have recognized the benefits of maintaining good relations with both the United States and China—giving neither a sense of exclusive commitment, while welcoming the overtures of each. This reflects the core imperative of India's national and strategic identity: autonomy. In this way, India and China continue to improve their diplomatic and economic relations, even as they compete decorously in building military capabilities. Pakistani and Indian leaders at the highest levels profess to understand, now that they have nuclear weapons, that war is no longer a rational alternative, and they must find a way to make peace. Behind-the-scenes diplomacy to formalize a resolution of the Kashmir issue has been stalled by political turbulence in Pakistan and India, but each side recently has shown a determination to avoid crisis.

To the extent that a desired international order will be less militarized than recent decades have been, India can be an exemplar among major powers. Historically, India has spent a lower percentage of its GDP on the military than have most major powers, with its leaders striving to keep the level below 3 percent of GDP. India's rise to global power—explicitly sought from the mid-1990s onward—has included a conscious buildup of military strength, yet defense spending as a percentage of GDP has actually dropped in the past few years (see table 5.1).

Nonetheless, the BJP and an emergent national security elite, buoyed by the perceived gain in status and self-confidence following the 1998 nuclear tests, have concluded that the militarily strong nations in this world gain not only security but also political respect and international prestige. As India's economy has enjoyed unprecedented rates of growth, India has become a major purchaser of advanced military technology. India is the leading purchaser of arms from Russia, it has a major defense partnership with Israel, and it is considering major defense purchases from the United States, with the encouragement of the U.S. government and defense contractors. This trend does not mean India is more likely to threaten its neighbors or commit aggression. It simply means that India will behave more like the United States, China, and Russia in valuing and acquiring military power.

India has no compunction about joining the United States in speaking of a "war on terror," unlike others who think "war" is the wrong conceptual framework and way of speaking of the challenge of terrorism. India had experienced terrorism long before September 11 and suffered the deadly attack on its national parliament shortly thereafter. India is willing to cooperate with the United States and other states in sharing intelligence and otherwise resisting and targeting terrorism. India's main complaint—which complicates U.S., UK, and other NATO states' foreign and antiterrorism policies—concerns Pakistan's role as the principal source of terrorist threats and a failure by the United States, the United Kingdom, and others to press Pakistani authorities hard enough to eradicate terrorist networks and to stop nurturing them as an instrument of Pakistani competition with India.

Insofar as a key source of the overall terrorist threat is Muslim disaffection exploited by antimodern political movements, India can contribute to global order and progress by proving that Muslims can prosper in societies where they are a minority, like India. The formation of Pakistan during the bloody partition of British India, and the intercommunal tensions that preceded it, are reminders of the charged nature of this issue. This history has continued with contemporary communal massacres and pogroms, generally led by Hindus against Muslims—as in Ayodhya in 1992 and Gujarat in 2002—which have helped perpetuate the cycle of brutal vengeance. Even more alarming over the long term are the growing disparities in educational and economic achievements of India's Muslims and Hindus. The Sachar Report, named after the chairman of the government-sponsored panel that wrote it, painted

**Table 5.1.   India's Military Expenditure as Percentage of GDP, 1990–2007**

| Year | Military Exp. (% of GDP) | Military Exp. (billion USD) |
|------|--------------------------|------------------------------|
| 2007 | 2.4 | 28.5 |
| 2006 | 2.5 | 23.9 |
| 2005 | 2.8 | 22.2 |
| 2004 | 2.6 | 19.2 |
| 2003 | 2.8 | 18.7 |
| 2002 | 2.9 | 18.2 |
| 2001 | 3.0 | 18.3 |
| 2000 | 3.1 | 17.7 |
| 1999 | 3.1 | 17.1 |
| 1998 | 2.8 | 14.8 |
| 1997 | 2.7 | 14.1 |
| 1996 | 2.6 | 12.8 |
| 1995 | 2.7 | 12.6 |
| 1994 | 2.8 | 12.1 |
| 1993 | 2.9 | 12.1 |
| 1992 | 2.8 | 10.7 |
| 1991 | 3.0 | 11.2 |
| 1990 | 3.2 | 12.0 |

a bleak picture of Muslim life in India. While the panel found that India had done well as a secular nation in providing religious freedom and had made great strides against poverty, "not all religious communities and social groups . . . have shared equally the benefits of the growth process. Among these, the Muslims, the largest minority community in the country, constituting 13.4 percent of the population, are seriously lagging behind in terms of most of the human development indicators."

Among other findings that point to low development in many Muslim communities, the report said that Muslims suffer from the highest rates of stunted growth and the second-highest rate of underweight children. Their literacy rate in 2001 was 59.1 percent compared with the national average of 65.1 percent. The report also found that as many as 25 percent of Muslim children in the six- to fourteen-year-old age group have either never been to school or have dropped out, a figure higher than that of any other disadvantaged group. Although Muslims have gained prominence as craftspeople, athletes, and entertainers, as a whole their poverty rates are close to those of the lowest Hindu castes and outcaste communities; they make up only 4 percent of students at top universities and hold only 5 percent of government jobs.[5] All of these factors, along with serious political errors by the government in Delhi, contributed significantly to the Kashmiri uprising.

Moreover, many of India's 150 million Muslims see an ambivalence, or cynicism, in the way that they are treated—they are courted and appeased by politicians seeking votes (India was the first country to ban Salman Rushdie's novel *The Satanic Verses*), then marginalized, distrusted, and harassed by law enforcement officers. "In general," the Sachar Report concluded, "Muslims complained that they are constantly looked upon with a great degree of suspicion not only by certain sections of society but also by public institutions and governance structures. This has a depressing effect on their psyche." Against this background, a respected United Nations rights monitor and leading Pakistani human rights lawyer, Asma Jahangir, said at the conclusion of a visit to India in early 2008 that the country could face more deadly violence between sectarian communities if much more is not done to deter religious hatred and prevent politicians from exploiting tensions.[6]

Many nations and societies struggle to reverse growing inequalities between minority and majority populations; in Europe, especially, the condition of Muslim minorities has become an acute, if poorly redressed, concern. This challenge is one in which India and other leading states with diverse populations could benefit from candid exchanges among scholars, journalists, communal leaders, parliamentarians, and other officials. This is an extremely sensitive issue—especially when representatives of the majority population are doing most of the talking—but ways must be found to reach a deeper understanding of the problem.

A rules-based international order must have ways to stop conflict and make peace. Indeed, this was the founding principle of the United Nations. India, of course, is not a permanent member of the Security Council, so its role in UN peace*making* has been slight and ad hoc. Relatively few conflicts in recent decades have been clear cases of state-on-state aggression (as when Iraq invaded Iran in 1980 and Kuwait in 1990). Most have murkier origins in intrastate struggles, and India's passionate insistence on noninterference in the internal affairs of nations thus makes it a reluctant peacemaker. The principle of noninterference cherished by India (and China and most other postcolonial countries) collides with newer precepts such as the "responsibility to protect," which members of the United Nations endorsed at a 2005 summit. This nascent norm grows from the recognition that the internationally accepted injunction against genocide and other abuses of civilian populations is not self-enforcing, and that when governments do not act to protect their own people, the world at large has the right, and perhaps the obligation, to act. India's emphasis on noninterference in internal affairs will make it resistant to international action in such cases.

Peace*keeping*, in contrast, is a different matter entirely. India has long been a major contributor of military leadership and troops to UN peacekeeping operations. Indian leaders and the public are proud of this role. Indeed, they sometimes rankle at the lack of commensurate recognition from the international system's leading powers. More concretely, Indian officials will insist on being involved in the broader policy decisions for the situations in which their peacekeepers are deployed. Indian officials privately resent, for example, that U.S. and French leaders decided policies related to Lebanon, where Indian peacekeepers are deployed, without consulting Indian leaders. New Delhi will not long settle for being a mere passenger on the aircraft of global peacekeeping; it will want to be in the cockpit where strategic decisions are made.

## India as an Engine of Global Growth

Economists and development experts frequently recall that on the eve of the Industrial Revolution in Europe, India was the world's second-largest economy, with 20 percent of global output. Two centuries later, by the late 1970s, its share of the global economic pie was down to a miserable 3 percent. Now, not even a half-century later, India has rebounded. Some forecasts of its future global role are truly stunning. A recent report from the Goldman Sachs Global Economics Group has predicted that India has the ability to sustain annual economic growth rates of around 8 percent until 2020 and will surpass the United States in gross domestic product by 2050.[7] That would restore India to its former place as the world's second-largest economy, though Goldman Sachs and others warn this growth will have to translate into better lives for most Indians.[8]

Several important factors have combined to make India a potentially powerful player in the international economy. The first to gain the attention of many outsiders was India's enormous and still-growing middle class, usually counted in the hundreds of millions, though exact figures are a matter of dispute. The new spending power of so many Indians, coupled with the gradual reduction of trade and investment barriers since the early 1990s, has been an irresistible lure to exporters wanting to sell to India and to companies eager to establish operations in the country.

As Indians abroad—in Silicon Valley, on Wall Street, and in commercial centers across America—began to demonstrate their impressive skills, Western technology companies became aware that there was a reservoir of talent back in their homeland, having been cultivated in the Indian Institutes of Technology and the Indian Institutes of Management as well as in American and European universities. Soon enough, the outsourcing rush was on. Tens of billions of dollars in business have poured into India, not only in offshore call centers but also in software writing, other high-tech work, and lately in research and development. Moreover, successful Indians in the United States send a greater volume of remittances back home than members of any other immigrant group. The World Bank says that Indians sent home $27 billion from the United States in 2007, compared to $25.7 billion by Chinese and $25 billion by Mexicans.[9]

Within India, domestic industry has expanded and worker productivity is rising, and an important bridge has been crossed. India is now part of a globalized economy; it has every self-interested reason to lend its weight to making globalization work to the benefit of all, most importantly to the poor.

Indian companies are becoming multinational. Among the significant recent takeovers of foreign companies by Indians are Mittal Steel's acquisition of Luxembourg-based Arcelor to create ArcelorMittal, Tata Steel's purchase of the Anglo-Dutch Corus Group, and Tata Motors' winning bid for the Jaguar and Land Rover divisions of the Ford Motor Company. These are just the beginning. Large international banks, investment houses, and accounting firms are expanding within India. The Indian government is putting its officials and world-class diplomats to work worldwide to build goodwill for India in the competition with China and other industrial nations for raw materials and new markets for exports. Africa and Latin America in particular are playing host to a newly energized Indian presence. India's long track record of diplomatic support for developing nations in NAM and the Group of 77 will give it an advantage here.

India is also one of a set of emerging or reemerging nations with the potential to forge a new global economic order acceptable to rich and poor nations—that makes globalization work for all—though the associated consensus-building will require Indian representatives in international forums to make compromises. Both India and China are seen as inevitable candidates for membership in the Group of Eight leading world economic powers. The participation of these two Asian giants would inevitably alter the dynamics of what would then be the G-10. India is already part of the Group of 20, a forum of finance ministers and central bank governors formed in 1999 to broaden consultation on and stewardship of the global economy. Most of these rising nations have already moved away from being traditional closed economies and are becoming steadily more like the open economies of the industrial world—with which they are increasingly integrated.

This integration, however, poses challenges for developing nations, perhaps for India most of all because of its enormous uneducated, unskilled, impoverished population. Among the rising economies, India falls behind South Africa, all of Latin America, and most of Asia (including Bangladesh) in the percentage of skilled labor as a share of the total labor force.

In January 2008, as the final make-or-break phase of the Doha Round of global trade talks neared, Sandra Polaski of the Carnegie Endowment calculated what India had to gain or lose in the next stage of negotiations with richer nations in Europe and North America.[10] She concluded that India would have more to gain from a global trade pact under the Doha Round than through free-trade agreements with China, the United States, or the European Union. Even given this comparison, the gain from Doha, involving the lowering of Indian agricultural tariffs, would still be very small, adding only about 0.25 percent to the Indian economy and creating perhaps no more than four million new jobs in a country with more than forty million people out of work. Against these modest gains, India will have to weigh other significant factors. For a country whose enormous rural population earns its livelihood from commodity crops, "[a] decrease of even 25 percent in the world price of rice, which has happened repeatedly, would negatively impact all but the top 10 percent of Indian households, with the poorest households losing the most," Polaski wrote. A lowering of income from agricultural tariffs would, Polaski points out, diminish the overall tariff income that accounts for 11 percent of the government's total revenues. Even in a global market, it is not clear whether the Indian agricultural sector is aligned with the international economy as a whole. It is not certain that Indian agriculture can realize a sustained benefit from high global prices. Simulating domestic demand while keeping open the options of using tariffs to shield farmers from deeper poverty might, Polaski argues, make more sense than getting locked into a rigid, rules-based global trade order. India adopted this course by banning many food exports as global prices rose sharply in 2008.

In the longer run, prominent factors in India's growth reflect its evolution as a globalizing economy and its steady integration into a free global market, where it finds benefits. An International Monetary Fund report in February 2008 attributed India's recent robust economic performance to a strong investment climate—with capital inflows reaching $45 billion in 2006–2007—as well as to rising corporate profits and a boost in business confidence.[11] Indians are part of the global mix and can no longer retreat from the world at will. When the effects of the American mortgage crisis began to reverberate in Europe and East Asia in early 2008, some financial experts in Mumbai were saying flatly that India was immune to these distant problems. Yet uncertainty about world trends contributed to a 23 percent loss in the benchmark Bombay Stock Exchange Index in the first quarter of 2008.

## Growth and Human Development

Behind India's growth still lurk human development factors demanding urgent attention: low literacy, high malnutrition, and serious social and economic discrimination against women. The Indian private sector and nongovernmental organizations (NGOs) offer potential capacity to help decentralize human services and thereby insulate them from corrupt or indifferent local politicians. Global partners of all kinds, along with international development organizations, are also already at work on human development issues. Private philanthropies such as the Bill and Melinda Gates Foundation and numerous Indian charities and research organizations such as the Sir Ratan Tata Trust, the Infosys Foundation, the Azim Premji Foundation (created by the chairman of Wipro), and the LNM Group Foundation (endowed by the steel magnate Lakshmi Mittal) are investing in health and education programs; it is in their interest to build a better labor force.

In its tenth five-year development plan, for 2003 to 2007, India set ambitious targets that would meet or exceed the United Nation's Millennium Development Goals. The government hoped to raise overall literacy from 65 percent to 75 percent and establish universal primary education. There were also targets for reversing environmental degradation and widespread pollution of natural water systems, along with programs to teach awareness and prevention of HIV/AIDS. After most of these targets went unmet, the 2008–2012 plan shifts responsibility to the states, recognizing that state and local governments usually bear the blame for unfulfilled policy directives or misused budgetary resources.

Indian governments at the state and national levels will both have to reprioritize budget spending, including on family planning, which is far too weak for a country that is supporting four times the population of the United States on one-third of the land area. India is already experiencing severe stresses on its natural environment, including falling water tables in the agricultural areas and the rapid loss of forest cover and habitat for wild plants and animals. Implementation of programs is often very poor or riddled with corruption, and government subsidies often exacerbate waste. In early 2008 the World Bank acknowledged that it had uncovered the diversion of up to $600 million in funds allocated for the Indian health sector due to corruption.[12] This in a country with significant levels of HIV/AIDS; endemic diseases such as polio, malaria, tuberculosis, and leprosy; tropical fevers such as kala-azar and dengue; and a range of respiratory and diarrheal infections that are killing small children. Infant and maternal mortality rates also remain high.

### India and Peer-to-Peer Development

Countless Indian NGOs are at work on projects to improve the lives of the poor, albeit often on a modest scale that is dwarfed by the magnitude of the challenges. Given more resources, these groups have the know-how to tackle problems, not only to do more in India but also throughout the developing world. India already assists other, poorer countries with economic development. A new Indian organization similar to, but larger than, the U.S. Peace Corps or UN Volunteers would be a major force in reducing poverty and spreading education and the use of new technologies worldwide. India clearly has the expertise. An Indian scientist, Rajendra Pachauri, director-general of the Indian Energy and Resources Institute, led the United Nations Intergovernmental Panel on Climate Change, which shared the 2007 Nobel Peace Prize with the former U.S. vice president, Al Gore, for groundbreaking work on threats to the global environment. In his Nobel acceptance speech, Pachauri cited an ancient Indian admonition that "the whole universe is one family" in his blueprint for the future.[13] A few months later, another Indian, Jagadish Shukla, who now teaches at George Mason University in the United States, won the International Meteorological Organization Prize for his work in environmental science and hydrology. India also has a strong technical base to be able to lead in fields such as solar power and other alternative sources of energy.

## Maneuvering in a Diverse Democracy

India's democratic governance will shape its approaches to global rule-making in ways that are frequently not appreciated in wealthier or more homogeneous states. Indian decision-makers have to be sensitive to Indian voters in unimaginably diverse circumstances. Wealthy new economic elites in the major cities of a few states—Mumbai, Bangalore, Chennai—have a more international vision and set of interests than do landless laborers in Bihar or Uttar Pradesh and their notoriously corrupt (and often criminal) political leaders. Lower, generally poorer castes now play a huge role in Indian politics, particularly in state governments, with priorities that are not frequently heard at the World Economic Forum in Davos. The definition and articulation of India's interest in shaping the international system will be complex and at times seem irrational from the outside. Internal negotiation and competition often make mixed signals and fitful movements unavoidable. The multiple pressures on politicians in India thus make it more difficult to predict and deal with than most other nations.

India's recent economic growth and the emblematic appearance of its tycoons on global lists of the superwealthy give an aura of inevitability to its rise to world power. But the symbols at the elite level that are earning India a seat at the "high table"—wealthy and brilliant corporate leaders, booming information technology and medical sectors, and lauded writers and film-makers—are more than balanced by another India. This India cheers for the gains and acclaim of its "high table" compatriots, but it measures success less by the prosperity of those at the top of the economic pyramid than by the well-being of the hundreds of millions at the bottom. Economic growth and global influence are great, but how equitably are the benefits and costs of growth distributed, and how are global gains shared with Indians living in the village?

Neither is rural India's persistent deprivation inevitable or incurable; failures of leadership have allowed the problem to fester. Political decisions to subsidize water, for example, have put a strain on aquifers, and subsidized power supplies have similarly led to waste and inefficiency. Indian agricul-tural exports have risen as the domestic market has grown, but at a time of soaring global food prices, the dominance of small-scale farming in India has kept it at a disadvantage against food-exporting nations such as Argentina, Australia, Brazil, Canada, and the United States. There is no shortage of suggestions from Indian experts and international development organiza-tions for easing the double rural burden of uncompetitive agriculture and poor infrastructure. The World Bank, which has $2.6 billion invested in rural India, recommends (as do many Indian experts) stepped-up investment in agricultural technology and nonfarm entrepreneurship.[14] More broadly, the bank calls for "systemic reform" of public sector service providers, more accountability, the decentralization of services, and an expanded role for nongovernmental actors.

For the foreseeable future, however, the tension between the top and the bottom of the Indian pyramid will constrain Indian decision-makers. Moreover, there are and will always be Indian politicians, on the left and right, who question how cooperative India really should be in building global consensus on a range of issues, fearing an associated cost in sovereignty or cultural and economic losses. In a democratic system where political coali-tions have become the norm, such skepticism must be taken into account, along with the voices of the rural poor, who vote in enormous numbers. Among some political leaders there is also a tendency to carry on old de-mands for a new economic order, putting economic rights ahead of civil and human rights in the development efforts of international organizations. At a meeting of NAM ministers in Malaysia in 2006, Anand Sharma, a minister of state for external affairs, reiterated this approach when he called on his colleagues to resist a new "East-West collusion" in the international economic realm and to press ahead instead with reforming the Bretton Woods institutions and the WTO in line with the views of the global south. Stating a clear distaste for the instruments of the Washington Consensus, he said "this should be [the] first step of the United Nations recovering its central place in the economic agenda which it had in the 1970s."[15]

For their part, international financial and development organizations suggest that India, still with the largest number of people living in extreme poverty and home to 40 percent of the world's poor, faces an urgent need to reinvigorate its own human development policies—health and education in particular—raising them to a level befitting a more developed country. Among other things, India needs to ensure that the "youth bulge" of the next few decades becomes the "demographic dividend" that Prime Minister Manmohan Singh and others have anticipated—i.e., the productive work force needed for further growth as an industrialized nation.

### Democracy and the Question of Universal Values

While the number of nations calling themselves democracies has risen exponentially since the end of the Cold War, many wear the label in name only. India, in contrast, has a long history of commitment to true democratic governance, marred only by Indira Gandhi's suspension of civil rights in the 1975–1977 emergency. Yet the Indian government does not believe that democracy can or should be imposed by or fostered in a country by outside powers, but can only be generated internally. This is of a piece with its prioritization of state sovereignty and national self-determination above all, and its resistance to interference in internal affairs. Therefore India does not use its power and influence to try to promote democracy where it does not now exist. The U.S. experience in Iraq only reaffirms the Indian view.

There are those who argue that individual human rights can be distinguished from democratic governance. Here India's record clearly could use improvement—though it could be worse, as China's and Russia's are, among fellow major powers. Protection of human rights certainly cannot be squared with the Indian state's failure to prevent or contain the massacre of Muslims in Gujarat in 2002. Indeed, the state government was deeply complicit in the organized killing, and the central government, including multiple political parties, did little credit to human rights in its post facto handling of the atrocities. The Indian constitution, rule of law, and political rights that allow NGOs and a free press to operate provide a framework for protecting human rights, even though violations are disturbingly frequent.

Because India is a democracy with freedom of expression and participation in the making of policies—unlike China and Russia—more is often expected of it. India is party to numerous international conventions but does not always act on them, at home or abroad, a pattern for which it should be held more accountable. The Indian state is more intent on pursuing realpolitik interests in its neighborhood, including competing with Chinese influence in Burma, for example. If all of the major powers, including China, were actively pressing for human rights in Burma, would India do likewise? Of course. But given that nondemocratic China expresses little interest in human rights in Burma and seeks to extend its influence on India's eastern flank, Indian leaders place greater priority on India's economic and geostrategic position than on the human rights of the Burmese people.

More important than India's role advocating human rights in other countries is its record in the protection of religious minorities—especially in Kashmir but also in the Indian northeast—and in the lingering discrimination based on caste. Since the mid-1980s, the Indian-administered part of Kashmir, still an internationally disputed territory, has been a cauldron of bitter resentment toward New Delhi among Kashmiri Muslims, leading to an armed uprising that Pakistan was eager to fuel. India has not always given human rights groups unfettered access to the Kashmir Valley, the center of Kashmiri Muslim culture. Since the late 1990s, the International Committee of the Red Cross (ICRC) has been permitted to meet Kashmiri detainees and observe their conditions, which it has asked India to improve. Kashmiri families continue to press the Delhi government and the ICRC to investigate thousands of disappearances and cases in which Indian security forces have been accused of killing people in what Indian human rights groups call "faked encounters." A 2006 report from Human Rights Watch documented a "culture of impunity" in Kashmir under which torture was found to be common.[16]

Because India is a democracy, much of the information on shortcomings of government, human rights abuses, or development failures reaches the world via the reporting and writing of Indians. When the Indian media, particularly television, was freed from government monopoly in the 1990s, it quickly became a significant force for change. With the combination of Asia's most freewheeling NGOs and think tanks, world-class high-technology centers, and the recently unleashed economic power of the private sector, there should be no lack of momentum to propel India through the decades ahead. A challenge to world powers is to urge India to close the gap between the expertise and vision of its citizenry and the performance of its politicians.

There is a paradox that India will struggle to balance as it ascends into the rarefied climes of the global powers. However global in its economic clout and active in its engagement in international institutions, India has not been a truly cosmopolitan society. Although it has a degree of ethnic diversity, it is not multicultural in the sense that Europe, the United States, Canada, and Brazil combine European, African, Middle Eastern, and East Asian populations. Many Indian families have their first taste of multiculturalism and diversity only when they move abroad, and the experience is often jarring, as testified in the books that emerge from the Indian diaspora. There are no large foreign-born communities in India beyond those of expatriates in international business and diplomacy, and virtually no immigrants beyond other South Asians. The number of foreign tourists traveling in India pales in comparison to the numbers attracted by China or even much smaller countries in Asia, such as Thailand and, lately, Vietnam.

Scholarly exchanges with India have occasionally been made difficult by the Indian side. The U.S. Department of State, in its human rights report for 2007, noted that the Indian government "continued to apply restrictions to the travel and activities of visiting experts and scholars." Yet Indians—intellectuals, professionals, and private sector leaders—thrive on freewheeling give and take. Engaging them as widely as possible in international debate in years to come may help them open official thinking at home. The attempt to control intellectual exchanges risks playing into the hands of Hindu extremists who are eager to keep Western ideas and practices out of India.

Official India has not been receptive to international criticism. It sometimes bars international human rights monitors and goes into diplomatic overdrive to keep Indian practices such as caste discrimination off the agenda of UN human rights meetings. As India's star rises in global affairs, it is likely to find—as the United States and, more recently, China have—increasing attention focused on its record. Scrutiny is part of the territory of being a major power.

A different future is already in sight. New generations of Indians are travelers, at home around the real world and in every corner of the cyberworld. Students, business leaders, designers, writers, musicians, and movie stars are more cosmopolitan than any of their predecessors since independence. They have brought India into the world's imagination in amazing new ways. Among the newly cosmopolitan are many who are also acutely aware of the need to help India live up to its potential and to invigorate politics, not by looking back, but by looking forward and outward.

In the twenty-first century, there will be more new democracies, continuing a trend that began in the last century with the end of colonialism

and accelerated after the Cold War and the collapse of European communism. There will also be many more people—98 percent of them born into
the poorest nations—and the strains on democratic governments will be
great, stemming from the competition for resources and decent livelihoods
and sometimes leading to conflict. Many nations will be tempted to ditch democracy. In this not-so-distant future, the world will need an India that can
show how a powerful, still poor, yet democratic country can be made to work
to the benefit of all. No rich industrial nation or one-party state, however
efficient, can provide a more relevant model for the century in the making.

⌒

## C. Raja Mohan's Reaction

### A Future Unlike the Past

In their insightful assessment of India, George Perkovich and Barbara Crossette rightly underline the enormity of the unfolding transformation that
pervades India's national life—from economy to foreign policy and from
social mores to attitudes about the outside world. One consequence of this
extraordinary change is that India's future behavior on the world stage cannot be predicted on the basis of the traditional precepts of its external relations. Yet, as the home to one of the world's oldest continuous civilizations,
India is bound to retain some enduring elements of its worldview.

To complicate matters, some of the more recent trends in India's national
decision-making indicate both the potential for radical change and the
weight of inherited ideological baggage. Many new recent diplomatic initiatives—especially toward Pakistan, China, and the United States—suggest
that India's foreign policy is no longer simply reactive. That these initiatives remain to be converted into breakthroughs points to the dead weight
from the past. Any sound judgment on India's future role as a major power
will have to differentiate parts of its national genetic code from intellectual
baggage that might seem fundamental but is in fact dispensable in light of
changed circumstances.

One theme of modern Indian nationalism is the belief that holds "India's
importance to be singular and self-evident, an entitlement that does not
need to be earned, proved or demonstrated."[17] The Indian elites of the early
twentieth century who rediscovered their country's rich cultural heritage
were convinced of their nation's "exceptionalism." The point was stressed
by India's first prime minister, Jawaharlal Nehru, who was instrumental in

shaping the country's international perspective in the two decades preceding independence: fate had marked India out for big things, and it was entirely natural for New Delhi to take a leadership role in world affairs. Writing well before independence, Nehru was convinced that India would eventually emerge as one of the world's six powers along with the United States, a potentially united Europe, Russia, Japan, and China.

This burning ambition to be a great power playing a shaping role must be differentiated from the variety of other ideas widely viewed as essential to India's mental makeup—such as nonalignment, an anti-Western orientation, and Third World solidarity.[18] In fact, India's adoption of these ideas and postures was the product of specific historical circumstances. A major error that is often made in the analysis of India's foreign policy behavior is to treat these themes as unchangeable parts of a belief system.

### Indian Liberalism and Realism

A second theme in the Indian worldview is an unending but powerful tension between the allure of idealism and the imperatives of pragmatism. As products of a nationalist movement that won its independence from the British by arguing from the first principles of Enlightenment, the Indian political classes took to liberal internationalism like a duck to water. The spirit of universalism that so pervaded the Indian nationalist movement was manifest in its solidarity campaigns with other anticolonial movements, the rejection of power politics, and a strong commitment to the notion of global collective security.

After independence, the Indian constitution, as part of its directive principles, underlined this important dimension. Article 51 of the constitution asks the state to (a) promote international peace and security, (b) maintain just and honorable relations between nations, (c) foster respect for international law and treaty obligations in the dealings of organized people with one another, and (d) encourage settlement of international disputes by arbitration.

This Indian commitment to liberal internationalism, seen by many as the defining feature of modern Indian foreign policy, however, is balanced by a less noticed but equally vigorous realist streak. Contrast Nehru's proclaimed idealism with his government's willful unification of nearly 545 princely states; reinvention of the British protectorate system for Nepal, Bhutan, and Sikkim; forcible liberation of Goa from Portuguese colonialism (in defiance of his own prescription of peaceful settlement of disputes); expansive territorial claims on the frontiers of China; and determination to keep Jammu and Kashmir in India.

Nehru's daughter and India's third prime minister, Indira Gandhi, was more clearly identified as a realist. Her use of force to liberate Bangladesh, integration of Sikkim into India, and a generally muscular policy toward the neighbors are seen as examples. Yet it was during her tenure that nonalignment acquired its ideological character, and the anti-Western orientation congealed as part of a leftward drift that saw the incorporation of the word *socialism* into the preamble of the constitution and an alliance with the Soviet Union abroad.

Over the last six decades, India's strategic posture has shown a continuous admixture of realism and idealism. That this is rooted in India's worldview can be seen from the contrast between the amoral realism of Kautilya's *Arthashastra* and the extraordinary emphasis on normative universalism under Emperor Ashoka just a couple of generations later.[19]

A third enduring element of India's polity is the capacity to innovate and develop unique national solutions. India has shown a remarkable tendency to defy conventional wisdom, as demonstrated by its choice of nonviolence and noncooperation as strategies to win independence, adoption of universal suffrage, creation of linguistic states, development of nonalignment as a foreign policy strategy, and its unique path to nuclear weapons development. Although the creative dimensions of India's policy seemed to fade after Nehru, the new vibrancy within Indian civil society and an increasingly globalist orientation of its elite now point toward the possibility that India might once again surprise the world. Perkovich and Crossette's skepticism about India's ability to contribute to the management of world affairs seems prudent in the context of India's past policies, but it is not necessarily an accurate reading of New Delhi's future direction.

The authors are correct in affirming that most of the world's problems cannot be solved without an effective contribution from India. They also recognize that important recent changes have been the narrowing gap between India's global ambitions and its lack of strategic resources. The high growth rates of recent years, which signal a structural change in the Indian economy, offer it the hard power capabilities to emerge as a great power.

But equally important has been the emergence of a fundamentally altered international environment much more favorable to India. Unlike during the Cold War when the international system severely constrained India's freedom of action, now, as Prime Minister Manmohan Singh often says, the world wants India to do well.

Indeed, India's most significant challenges lie at home.[20] The newly favorable international environment is evidenced most dramatically by the willingness of all the major powers of the world to change the nuclear rules to accept India's nuclear weapons program and renew civilian nuclear cooperation with New Delhi. Yet the domestic difficulties India has had in implementing a deal that was loaded in its favor reinforces one of the basic propositions of Perkovich and Crossette: that the pace and direction of India's engagement with a variety of international regimes "will depend on the balance between global commitments and domestic political demands that can be struck by the central and state governments in a diverse democratic society."

The rest of this chapter will examine how India might navigate the three consequential areas for India's future behavior identified by the authors—nuclear nonproliferation, global security, and international economic order. I conclude with a discussion of the authors' assessment of the interplay between India's diversity and democracy.

### Nuclear Weapons: From Conformism to Leadership

In their brief but accurate overview of India's nuclear history, Perkovich and Crossette capture its essential features—restraint and responsibility—in terms of its own nuclear program and its attitudes toward global proliferation. The authors also rightly emphasize the transformation of India from a notable dissident on nuclear affairs for many decades to an adherent of the traditional tenets of nuclear orthodoxy.

This important shift must be explored a little further to determine whether or not India will be able to assume a leadership role on nonproliferation issues. So long as India had remained ambivalent about the relevance of nuclear weapons for its national security, it was stuck in the blind alley of championing "all or nothing" solutions to the problem. Its normative emphasis on complete nuclear disarmament and nondiscriminatory nonproliferation regimes were of little or no relevance in the real world. Other nuclear weapon powers were not ready for it, and India itself was neither prepared to accept a nonnuclear status nor to abide by regimes that restricted its nuclear options.

Only when it ended its nuclear ambiguity in 1998 by declaring itself a nuclear weapon power did India find the domestic political space to negotiate partial and less than comprehensive "arms control" measures. India's nuclear diplomacy since 1998 has seen a series of incremental shifts, with India willing to accept some restraints (in the form of a test moratorium) and negotiate a fissile material cut-off treaty, move from a declaratory commitment to prevent outward proliferation to an operational framework for export controls, abandon its rejection of any regional arms control with Pakistan and undertake a series of nuclear and conventional confidence-building measures, support the principle of keeping new countries from obtaining enrichment and reprocessing technologies, and vote with the international community against Iran twice at the International Atomic Energy Agency during the years 2005–2006.[21]

New Delhi's engagement on nuclear matters with Washington since 1998, culminating in the civil nuclear initiative of July 2005, demonstrates that as India becomes reassured that its own nuclear weapons program will not be a target of the global nuclear order, it will eventually accept significant restraints. It is possible to argue, as the authors do, that India could have accepted more obligations than it did. Nor is there any doubt that the entrenched fears of the Indian atomic energy establishment about external manipulation and the Indian political class's accumulated distrust of the United States impelled New Delhi to overnegotiate and minimize any constraints on it. At the same time, it is important to recognize that the U.S. bureaucracy, too, found it hard to sustain the original framework of the July 18, 2005, understanding between Bush and Singh, and Congress complicated it by injecting a whole range of conditionalities. This prompted charges in India that the United States was moving the "goalposts" of the nuclear agreement, thus reinforcing traditional suspicions of the United States.

What is most noteworthy, though, was the determination of the foreign office to battle this old-think in New Delhi and Mumbai. Even more important was the willingness of the Manmohan Singh government to put its political future on the line by persisting with the nuclear deal and the transformation of relations with Washington amid constant accusations of having abandoned the traditional pillars of Indian foreign policy.[22]

These massive internal bureaucratic and political battles over the nuclear deal confirm that India is in the midst of significant change. They also suggest that once the nuclear initiative is implemented, and India is fully integrated into the world order, the domestic opposition to India's participation in the global nonproliferation regime will steadily diminish. Whether the issue is better safety standards on the civilian nuclear program, reducing the global salience of nuclear weapons, expanding controls over the quality and quantity of the existing nuclear arsenals, or opposing proliferation, an India at greater ease with the United States and the international system can be expected to be a strong partner in the management of the global nuclear order. This orientation is reflected in India's enthusiastic response to the Shultz-Kissinger initiative on nuclear disarmament in 2008.[23]

There has been considerable anxiety in the United States about India's presumed relationship with Iran and whether New Delhi can take the lead in persuading Tehran to give up its nuclear ambitions. From its own vantage point, India's hesitation is completely understandable. First, given the

United States' own deep internal split over policy toward Iran, it would have been unwise for India to have offered strong support for a policy that could well undergo significant changes in the near future. The difficult domestic politics of India's large Muslim constituency also make Indian leaders want to avoid being seen as camp followers of the United States in the Middle East. So looking at the future, India cannot assume an international leadership role by merely tailing the U.S. policy at its every twist and turn.

It is equally important to recognize that, for all the domestic posturing in New Delhi and U.S. fears of an Indo-Iranian strategic partnership, Tehran is by no means the central element of India's Gulf policy.[24] India's rising profile in the Persian Gulf is centered on cooperation with Saudi Arabia and the smaller Arab kingdoms. India's future role in the Persian Gulf, now facing the challenge of a resurgent Iran, will be rooted in New Delhi's contributions to the construction of a new regional security order that will lend both deterrence and reassurance to the weaker Arab Gulf States. Such a role will also be in tune with the Muslim sentiments within India.

**Global Security: From Autonomy to Responsibility**
Strategic autonomy is widely considered the central tenet of independent India's foreign policy. Yet despite the long tradition and passionate emotion attached to the notion of autonomy, one could legitimately ask whether the emphasis on autonomy is a self-evident truth of Indian foreign policy or merely a by-product of India's relative weakness in the global arena. The emphasis on strategic autonomy was natural for India when it emerged from colonial rule in the middle of the last century. Yet the nation's founding fathers had a vision for India's decisive future role in world affairs. As a weak postcolonial state, India had a strong desire to prevent other powers from limiting its room for maneuver. Six decades later, as India inches toward becoming the world's third-largest economy and presides over a large and powerful armed force, the notion of autonomy is likely to fade as a central tenet of India's foreign policy.

The concerns of Perkovich and Crossette can be boiled down to one question: How soon and effective might India's transition from autonomy to responsibility be?[25] Many in India have begun to recognize that becoming a great power entails sharing the costs of managing the international order rather than merely avoiding the discipline of its current rules.

One area where this change is manifest is in India's neighborhood policy, as the authors have pointed out. After decades of emphasis on "bilateralism" with its smaller neighbors of South Asia and a deep suspicion of regionalism and attempts to keep other powers out of its region in the name of a Monroe

Doctrine, India has taken a different tack, promoting economic regionalism (through unilateral concessions, if necessary), resolving bilateral political disputes, and working with other powers to resolve regional conflicts.[26] On China, too, New Delhi has overcome many of its post-1962 traumas and embarked on a wide-ranging cooperation with Beijing. In the coming years, India—fully conscious of the dangers of a hostile relationship with China—will construct its own unique policy of simultaneously engaging and balancing Beijing.

On the new and larger questions of global security, Perkovich and Crossette articulate the recent Western liberal disenchantment with India's obsession with the principles of absolute sovereignty and nonintervention. Given India's own record of military interventions in other countries, including Bangladesh (1971) and Sri Lanka (1987–1990), and its significant military contribution to UN Peacekeeping Operations (PKO), it would be inaccurate to suggest that nonintervention is a high principle in India's worldview. To be sure, the emphasis on "nonintervention" has been an integral part of India's rhetorical toolkit at the Non-Aligned Movement and at the United Nations. It has also been central to India's rejection of third-party intervention and mediation in its conflicts with its neighbors. This tradition must be understood, however, as part of India's determination to consolidate its own sovereignty as a newly independent nation and a recognition that national freedom was, in essence, about an autonomous foreign policy. For India the real issue was not about the principle of "intervention" but its implications for its own territorial consolidation and national integration. It was this determination to protect itself from being the target of international intervention that drove India's positions in the post–Cold War international security debates. India, however, had no hesitation in using force in its own presumed sphere of influence—the subcontinent—against genocide in East Pakistan and in favor of minority rights and federalism in Sri Lanka.

The political will to use force in pursuit of regional foreign policy ends, and the eagerness to contribute to international security by contributing to PKO far from its shores, reflect an important tradition in Indian foreign policy. India's military role in regional and international security, however, has rarely received the attention in India's internal public policy discourse that it deserves. The Indian use of force beyond its borders has been an important legacy of the British Raj. Although the initial focus of the armed forces under colonial rule was on domestic constabulary functions and the defense of the frontiers, the British also used it in an expeditionary mode within and beyond the region for colonial missions. Until seven decades ago, the Indian army was at the very heart of the British imperial defense system in Asia and the Indian Ocean regions.

That India as well as Pakistan and Bangladesh became the biggest contributors of international peacekeeping forces during the Cold War and beyond underscored the subcontinent's "military surplus." India in particular contributed quite substantially to the international PKO under the aegis of the United Nations from its very inception in the early years of the Cold War. As peacekeeping and peace enforcement operations proliferated after the Cold War, India has refused to participate in any military operations that lacked the United Nations seal of approval.[27] This again was not a high principle, but a prudent posture to avoid provoking unwanted international controversies.

Once the United States recognized and sought India's potential contributions to peace and stability around the world, New Delhi began to ease the near-theological emphasis on a UN mandate. In a demonstration of its political support for the U.S. intervention in Afghanistan, India agreed to escort U.S. naval ships through the Malacca Straits. In 2003 the Indian government vigorously debated the U.S. request to send troops to Iraq. While fear of a domestic political backlash prompted New Delhi to demur, it was significant for the idea even to have received serious consideration. As the tsunami disaster hit the eastern Indian Ocean at the end of 2004, India quickly decided to join with the navies of the United States, Japan, and Australia in providing relief and rehabilitation. In June 2005 India signed a ten-year defense framework agreement with the United States that involved a broad range of bilateral cooperation in addition to participation in multinational military operations. New Delhi came under sharp criticism from the communist partners of the government and foreign policy traditionalists for agreeing to join U.S.-led military coalitions outside the United Nations.

In sum, the Indian debate on using force beyond borders remains an unfinished one, but it has broken out of the restrictive confines of the past. An India that reemerges as a great power, with significantly expanded capabilities, is bound to reconsider even further the terms and conditions under which it will use force beyond its primary area of concern.

As the Indian security establishment debates which international security tasks it might undertake, the policy shift is likely to be gradual, given the deep risk aversion of the political establishment and ideological opposition on the left. A number of factors will affect this transition. First is the readiness of great powers to accommodate India to the management of international security. The problem here goes well beyond the mere expansion of the UN Security Council or the G-8. It is about constructing a new concert of great powers that is in tune with the changing international distribution of power. Second, despite the current popularity of the "liberal wars," the debate on when, where, and how to use force has hardly been clinched. For all the enthusiasm for such notions as responsibility to protect, the military capacity and political will available to the international system is finite and limited. Post-Iraq, there is considerable popular skepticism even within the United States about using force abroad. One way or another, the world will eventually have to develop a less ambitious and more effective set of guidelines for using force abroad that does not attempt to right every wrong in the world. Third, as India's own power position in the world improves, there will be ever greater demands on its growing military surplus. India's own interests—economic and security—clearly demand more vigorous Indian foreign and military policies in regions far beyond its shores.

Within India, the navy has already begun to take a more global view of the nation's security interests and the air force is following in its footsteps. As the Indian army's burdens of internal security and territorial defense ease in the coming decades, it is bound to rediscover the expeditionary legacy of the British Raj. As in the United States, those demanding greater caution, if not isolation, will rightly counterbalance the internal advocates for a larger external security role. More fundamentally, as it becomes stronger, India will have fewer incentives to remain "rent-a-force" for the United Nations or other great powers. An India with a greater say in setting the terms of use of force and in executing it could, however, be a major contributor to international peace and security.

### Global Economy: From Free Rider to Stakeholder

Perkovich and Crossette highlight the gap between India's expanding economic power in the current wave of globalization and its ability to take a leadership role in making the global economy work for everyone. The Indian negotiating strategy and tactics at the World Trade Organization have come under some valid criticism.[28] Here again it is important to assess the nature of the transition that is unfolding in India. As it becomes integrated with the world economy for the first time since independence, the internal balance between protectionists and free traders is clearly shifting. Indian industry, battened under the protectionist era, has been loath to cede its market space to outsiders absent what it would consider to be a level playing field. The Department of Commerce, which has the lead role in international trade negotiations, has often been accused of being under the thumb of the corporate sector. In the last few years, however, a split has emerged within the

Indian capitalist class. Some segments now have a large stake in opening up markets elsewhere rather than keeping the domestic one closed to outsiders. As the weight of this sector grows, India's negotiating positions on market access are bound to evolve.

If the ideology of liberal trade has had a limited following in the Indian industry, it had none at all in rural India, where the majority of the population continues to reside. With the dominance of the rural voters in the electoral process, few political factions have been willing to support free trade. This too is beginning to change. For one thing, small but dynamic sections of the Indian farming community are starting to produce for the global market rather than only for the domestic market.

Meanwhile, an important tension—that of balancing the interests of the rural food producers in receiving good prices and those of the urban populace in keeping food affordable—may be resolving itself. India's traditional approach of subsidizing both at great cost is clearly unsustainable. Other factors are also spurring change. Rapid urbanization is bound to compel the political class to find a new balance. In any case, an imperative of economic development has historically been to shift labor from agriculture to industry and services. The mounting shortage of skills in the urban sectors should also accelerate this shift.

One key to this will be cooperation with the United States in improving agricultural productivity. Four decades ago the "green revolution," undertaken with American assistance, helped stabilize India. A similar revolution, but much larger in scope, is needed to facilitate not just the transformation of India but also the creation of conditions favorable for accelerated globalization.

From a broader perspective, India's large poor population is not the only challenge to the further liberalization of global trade. Amid the rise of China and India, opponents of globalization have acquired a new strength within the West. As many key constituencies in the developed world begin to see themselves as losers under globalization, the pressure on political classes to step back from free trade is bound to intensify. This trend line is visible even in the United States, which has long been the main economic and political impetus for globalization. The integration of China and India into the global economy, then, requires some conceptual leaps in reorganizing the world trading regime.

The same is even truer of the new challenges of global warming and energy security. The answers might lie less in diplomatic negotiations about who cuts what and when, than in technological breakthroughs that alter the very structure of energy production and distribution.

Meanwhile the shift in interests within India toward the global economy has been fundamental. After decades as a marginal player in international trade, and campaigning for such impossible goals as a "new international economic order," India has become an important player in the world trade negotiations as well as a key promoter of regional free trade in the subcontinent and across Asia.

## Toward a Global India

The best way to understand India's future role is to look at the comparative experience in another large, diverse, and democratic nation—the United States. The American experience of the last century is a good guide to divining India's direction. For one, there will inevitably be a lag between acquiring great power capabilities and the international policies to go with them. The first decades of the twentieth century saw massive internal struggles and failed domestic negotiations in defining an American foreign policy that was commensurate with its real weight in world affairs. A similar complex negotiation is underway in India today, and its recent results show slow and painful progress toward assuming greater international responsibilities.

Second, the problem of "two nations" within one is not unique to India. Uneven development has always and everywhere been part of the history of modern capitalism. As late as the sixth decade of the twentieth century, the United States had to embark on the Great Society program to reduce internal inequalities. The resources for that program could not have been generated without the creation of an affluent society in the 1950s. In China, too, Deng Xiaoping was right in coming up with the bold idea of "letting some people get rich first." As India becomes more affluent, it will have resources to address the massive internal disparities. It is not mere charity from the top, but rather the dynamics of mass democracy that will in fact force things in that direction.

Third, the tension in Indian foreign policy between idealism and realpolitik, too, is not very different from that in the United States. Both nations have been obsessed with the notion of sovereignty and the democratic refusal to open domestic matters to outside interference. Both nations have had to use significant force at home to unify their nations. Having constructed an exceptional nation, defined by extraordinary diversity, India—like the United States—will take its own time and demand its own space to balance the imperatives of realism and the higher calling of universalism. It is unlikely to accept tests of "stakeholdership" from outsiders, but will be constantly under pressure to prove its international standing to its own citizens. Given the complexity of the internal negotiation within India, it makes sense to focus on what India finally does rather than what its leaders say it might do.

Perkovich and Crossette are correct in underlining the consequential nature of the India project. The political trend lines since India began to reconnect with the world have been essentially positive. After decades of pessimism, a new optimism now guides a changing nation's thinking about itself and the world. Although the many problems that confront it at home are massive, a globalizing India is better equipped than ever before to address them. Externally, India must be expected to contribute more significantly to the construction of global regimes. But do expect India to negotiate hard, very hard, on terms of its engagement with preexisting global structures, and look for it eventually to take the initiative in building new ones.

## Notes

1. "India Unveils Climate Change Plan," BBC News, June 30, 2008.

2. World Development Report, "World Bank Calls for Agricultural Renewal to Reduce Rural Poverty in Transforming Economies Like India" (The World Bank, 2008). Available online at www.worldbank.org/wdr2008.

3. For a detailed account, see George Perkovich, *India's Nuclear Bomb: The Impact on Global Proliferation* (Berkeley: University of California Press, 2001).

4. "India Seeks Convention to Destroy Nuclear Weapons Within Timeframe," Indo-Asian News Service, June 9, 2008.

5. Carin Zissis, "India's Muslim Population," Council on Foreign Relations, June 22, 2007. Available online at www.cfr.org.

6. "India at Risk of Renewed Communal Violence, UN Human Rights Expert Warns," www.un.org/apps/news, accessed on March 20, 2008.

7. *BRICs and Beyond*, Goldman Sachs Global Economics Group, November 2007. Available online at www2.goldmansachs.com/ideas/brics/BRICs-and-Beyond.html.

8. "India's Report Card Fails to Make the Grade," *Financial Times* (June 18, 2008).

9. Dilip Ratha and Zhimei Xu, *Migration and Remittances Factbook 2008* (The World Bank, 2008).

10. Sandra Polaski et al., "India's Trade Policy Choices," Carnegie Endowment, Washington, DC, January 2008.

11. "IMF Executive Board Concludes 2007 Article IV Consultation with India," International Monetary Fund, Public Information Notice No. 08/09, February 4, 2008.

12. "World Bank Disgrace," *The Wall Street Journal*, January 14, 2008.

13. R. K. Pachauri, "The Nobel Lecture," Oslo, Norway, December 10, 2007. Available online at nobelprize.org.

14. "India Country Overview 2007," The World Bank, www.worldbank.org.in.

15. Anand Sharma, Minister of State for External Affairs of India, General Debate of the Ministerial Meeting of the Coordinating Bureau of the Non-Aligned Movement, Putrajaya, Malaysia, May 29, 2006. Available online at www.in.int/india/india_nam.pdf.

16. "'Everyone Lives in Fear': Patterns of Impunity in Jammu and Kashmir," Human Rights Watch, September 2006. Available online at www.hrw.org.

17. Rodney W. Jones, "India's Strategic Culture," prepared for Defense Threat Reduction Agency, SAIC, Washington, DC (October 31, 2006), 7, available at www.dtra.mil/documents/asco/publications/comparative_strategic_cultures_curriculum/case%20studies/India%20(Jones)%20final%2031%20Oct.pdf.

18. Baldev Raj Nayar and T. V. Paul, *India in the World Order: Searching for Major-Power Status* (Cambridge: Cambridge University Press, 2003).

19. Benoy Kumar Sarkar, "Hindu Theory of International Relations," *American Political Science Review* 13, no. 3 (August 1919): 400–14.

20. C. Raja Mohan, "Poised for Power: The Domestic Roots of India's Slow Rise," *Strategic Asia 2007–08: Domestic Political Change and Grand Strategy*, ed. Ashley Tellis and Michael Wills (Seattle: The National Bureau of Asian Research, 2007), 177–207.

21. C. Raja Mohan, "India's Nuclear Exceptionalism," *Nuclear Proliferation and International Security*, ed. Morten Bremer Maerli and Sverre Lodgaard (London: Routledge, 2007), 113–51.

22. Somini Sengupta, "A Test of Friendship for the Indian Leader," *The New York Times*, July 24, 2006; "Closer Ties with the United States Could Cost India's Prime Minister His Government," *The New York Times*, July 20, 2008.

23. Prime Minister Manmohan Singh, "Towards a World Free of Nuclear Weapons," speech given to mark the twentieth anniversary of Prime Minister Rajiv Gandhi's initiative on global nuclear disarmament, New Delhi, June 9, 2008; available at www.pmindia.nic.in/speech/content4print.asp?id=688.

24. C. Christine Fair, "Indo-Iranian Ties: Thicker Than Oil," *Middle East Review of International Affairs* 11, no. 1 (March 2007): 41–58; C. Raja Mohan, "The Charade on Iran," *Indian Express*, May 11, 2007; and Harsh V. Pant, "India-Iran Ties: The Myth of a 'Strategic' Partnership," *India in Transition*, February 11, 2008, available at casi.ssc.upenn.edu/print_pages/pdf/print_Pant.pdf.

25. Xenia Dormandy, "Is India, or Will It Be, a Responsible International Stakeholder," *The Washington Quarterly* 30, no. 3 (Summer 2007): 99–115; C. Raja Mohan, "India's Great Power Burdens," *Seminar*, no. 581 (January 2008).

26. Charu Lata Hogg, *India and Its Neighbours: Do Economic Interests Have the Potential to Build Peace?* (London: Chatham House, 2007); Christian Wagner, "From Hard Power to Soft Power? Ideas, Interaction, Institutions, and Images in India's South Asia Policy," *Heidelberg Papers in South Asia and Comparative Politics*, no. 26 (March 2005).

27. Kabilan Krishnasamy, "The Paradox of India's Peacekeeping," *Contemporary South Asia* 12, no. 2 (2003): 263–80; Christine C. Fair, "U.S.-Indian Army-to-Army Relations: Prospects for Future Coalition Operations," *Asian Security* 1, no. 2 (April 2005): 157–73.

28. Amrita Narlikar, "Peculiar Chauvinism or Strategic Calculation: Explaining the Negotiating Strategy of India," *International Affairs* 82, no. 1 (January 2006): 59–76.

~

# Russia's Place in an Unsettled Order: Calculations in the Kremlin

*Andrew Kuchins and Richard Weitz*
*With a Reaction by Dmitri Trenin*

## Russia's Turnaround

Russia has traveled a tumultuous path since the collapse of the Soviet Union nearly seventeen years ago. Hopes that Russia would recast itself as a democracy and align with the West were soon dashed as the Russian economy collapsed in the 1990s, and federal and local state power deteriorated. Russia lacked the capacity to act as a "responsible stakeholder" during a period when the survival of the Russian state itself was hardly guaranteed. Then, almost as suddenly as the Soviet Union disintegrated, Russia experienced an extraordinary economic recovery. In the decade since the 1998 Russian financial collapse, the country's gross domestic product (GDP) rose from slightly less than $200 billion in 1999 to more than $1.3 trillion in 2007. This figure probably will reach $2 trillion by 2010—a stunning 1,000 percent growth in just over a decade. Earlier this year, the Ministry of Economic Trade and Development published very ambitious plans for continued economic growth pointing toward a GDP of approximately $5 trillion by 2020, which would make it the largest economy in Europe and the fifth-largest in the world.[1]

Russia's recovery is only part (albeit an important part from Moscow's perspective) of an ongoing dramatic tilt in the global economic balance of power toward large emerging market economies and hydrocarbon producers—two categories in which Russia figures prominently. Thirty years ago when the G-7 was formed to manage the global economy, its member countries constituted more than 60 percent of the world economy; today those countries make up just a bit more than 40 percent of global GDP.

Given the breathtaking change in Russia's "stakes," it is no surprise that Moscow has been rapidly reevaluating its interests in the international system and what it means to be a "responsible stakeholder." President Vladimir Putin's famous February 2007 speech at the Werkunde Security Conference in Munich made two points: that the United States was behaving in an "egoistic" rather than responsible manner in managing global affairs, and that an international system of global American hegemony was evaporating and being replaced by genuine multipolarity. Most commentary focused on the first point and missed the import of the second, which Putin summarized:

- The combined GDP measured in purchasing power parity of countries such as India and China is already greater than that of the United States.
- A similar calculation with the GDP of the BRIC countries (Brazil, Russia, India, and China) surpasses the cumulative GDP of the European Union (EU). According to experts, this gap will only increase in the future.
- There is no reason to doubt that the economic potential of the new centers of global economic growth will inevitably be converted into political influence and will strengthen multipolarity.

Putin and his colleagues elaborated on this theme in a number of important speeches in 2007. The call for a "new international architecture" of global governance also became one of the campaign themes of the Russian parliamentary/presidential electoral cycle.[2]

While Russians are right to point out the anachronistic and often ineffective institutions of global governance, their own capacity to contribute toward a solution is constrained by an emotionally charged view of what has happened in the international system during the past twenty years. Moscow views many of the changes that have occurred since the late 1980s as illegitimate, since Russia was too weak to assert its positions. In this narrative, the West, and mainly the United States, took unfair advantage of Russian weakness through NATO expansion, Kosovo, promoting regime change (color revolutions) on Russia's borders, abandoning the Anti-Ballistic Missile (ABM) Treaty, and other policies.[3]

The Russian elite clearly views these Western moves in the 1990s as detrimental to Russia's national interests, but it is hardly realistic—nor would it be in anybody's interests, including Moscow's—to reverse the changes in the international system simply because Russia was temporarily weak. It is somewhat understandable that Russians are reveling in their resurgence, but too often this is manifest as "the Russia that can say 'no,'" rather than cooperating to build a better world. The sometimes obstinate and cocky Russia was reflected in Putin's personality as well as Russia's meteoric recovery during his presidency. Russian *schadenfreude* was also notable as Moscow watched the trials and travails of the United States in Iraq and in the global financial system, sparked by the subprime crisis.

### Resurgent Russia Asserts Itself

The tensions between Russia and the West, and especially between Moscow and Washington, became tragically evident with the August 2008 war in Georgia. The prevailing narratives in the United States and Russia regarding the provocation for the war were almost diametrically opposed. Putin, on the basis of the flimsiest evidence, even accused the Washington administration of orchestrating the conflict, while President Bush castigated Russia for violation of Georgia's territorial integrity, behavior that is impermissible in the twenty-first century. Russian Foreign Minister Sergey Lavrov gave the Russian view in a speech in Moscow on September 1:

> Should the United States and its allies choose to back the regime of Saakashvili, who has learned nothing at all, it will be a mistake of historic magnitude. . . . America's military aid to Saakashvili's regime never became a leverage with his government. On the contrary, it encouraged this irresponsible and unpredictable regime to proceed along the road of escapades.

For the analytical task at hand, it is not the proximate causes or immediate consequences of this war, but rather the implications for Russia's future role in the evolving international system that is of interest. As Russian elites themselves discuss this issue, it should be noted how little they talk in terms of "public goods" and "norms." Russians describe their foreign policy as ultimately pragmatic and interest-driven. U.S. and European references to values and norms are received at best cynically, but often with defensive hostility about our "double standards." The default interpretation in Russia of American efforts to promote its "values" is to view them as hypocritical justifications for the promotion of U.S. interests—and, ultimately, for influence and hegemony.

But the norm that the Russian government has held dearest—that of national sovereignty—is itself very selectively applied by Moscow. And Russian policy is also rife with double standards when it comes to the sovereignty of countries like Georgia and Ukraine. President Medvedev made this eminently clear in September 2008 remarks on Russian TV, when he presented the five principles that would guide Russian foreign policy:

- First, Russia will comply in full with all of the provisions of international law regarding relations between civilized countries.
- Second, Russia believes in the need for a multipolar world and considers that domination by one country is unacceptable, no matter which country this may be.
- Third, Russia is naturally interested in developing full and friendly relations with all countries, including Europe, Asia, the United States, and Africa. These relations will be as close as our partners are ready for.
- Fourth, Medvedev sees protecting the lives and dignity of Russian citizens, wherever they may be, as an indisputable priority for our country, and this is one of our foreign policy priorities.
- Fifth, Medvedev thinks that like any other country, Russia pays special attention to particular regions, regions in which it has privileged interests. We will build special relations with the countries in these regions, friendly relations for the long-term period.

This formulation, which many analysts quickly dubbed "The Medvedev Doctrine," is a striking contrast with the idealistic universalism that marked Mikhail Gorbachev's "new political thinking" of the late Soviet period. At the same time, it bears a strong resemblance to a traditional "realist" balance of power that allots special spheres of influence to great powers.

Rather than "norms" and "public goods," Russian leaders and political analysts frame Russia's terms of international cooperation as realpolitik bargains and "trade-offs" of interests.[4] For example, if Washington wants Moscow to take a stronger position to isolate Iran, then the United States is expected to compensate Moscow by halting NATO enlargement or deployment of missile defense systems in Poland and the Czech Republic. One of the most oft-repeated grievances is the U.S. betrayal of the "gentleman's agreement" supposedly struck between George H. W. Bush and Mikhail Gorbachev in 1990 to allow the unification of Germany as long as NATO would not expand and deploy new bases on the territory of former Warsaw Pact countries.[5]

That said, there have been indications, however slight, of a Russian willingness to be more cooperative and constructive. In the early months of the Medvedev administration, prior to the conflict with Georgia, the new Russian president employed distinctly different language regarding the challenges of global governance, offering positive proposals rather than litanies of complaints. For example, in a speech in Berlin in June 2008, President Medvedev—rather than griping about Kosovo, missile defense, NATO expansion, and other issues that usually arouse Moscow's ire—proposed that the United States, Europe, and Russia should draft a binding treaty on European security.[6] After the clash with Georgia, though, the tone and content of Medvedev's rhetoric has echoed the tough sharpness and occasional vulgarity of his prime minister, former President Putin.

This chapter will first discuss how Russia's domestic goals shape its interests in stability in the international system. We will then consider those interests in light of global challenges in key areas, such as international nuclear and security policy, regional security, energy, managing the global economy, and democracy/human rights.

### Russian Economic Goals and Their Implications

We must remember that while Russia's recovery over the last decade has been unexpectedly impressive in its speed and magnitude, from the perspective of the Putin/Medvedev team, this is still a relatively early phase. In 2008, per capita income should reach $12,000. The goal for 2020 is $30,000, and for 2030, $50,000. These are daunting, but achievable, goals that will depend as much on external conditions as on the Kremlin's policies. But even in the best-case 2020 scenario, Russia's share of global GDP will only rise from 2.3 percent to 3.5 percent. So even if Russia follows this ambitious trajectory, it is hardly poised to serve as the counterweight to the United States in a bipolar Cold War–like world.

Moreover, the only reason that the Soviet Union was able to compete militarily with the West during the Cold War was because it devoted at least one-fifth of its economy to military spending—ultimately paying the price of the disintegration of its economy and the Soviet state itself. By comparison, Russian military spending, while it has grown in tandem with Russian economic growth, has remained fairly constant as 3–5 percent of GDP.[7] Such growth is certainly not insignificant, but Russia still will face tremendous constraints and challenges in military modernization.

Growing international arms sales will also remain a high priority for the Russian government. Unless Russia can reach its desired sales figures via improved access to Western markets, the United States should expect to find Russian arms in the arsenals of dubious clients like Iran, China, Venezuela, and other problematic regimes. The Russians will defend their sales by, among other arguments, pointing to Western arms deals with such authoritarian governments as Saudi Arabia and Pakistan.

## Strategic Arms Control and Nonproliferation

Nuclear security and nonproliferation are areas in which we expect Russia to continue to be a responsible stakeholder. Indeed, the Russians would argue that they have been more responsible in this regard over the past eight years than the Bush administration. Even though Russia became more reliant on its nuclear deterrent due to the deterioration of its conventional forces in the 1990s, the continued aging of its nuclear arsenal leads Moscow to be more interested in deeper cuts in strategic weapons than Washington. While the Russian economy is recovering, we need to keep in mind that, from a strategic military standpoint, Russia remains in decline. Although the United States is mired in Iraq and Afghanistan, to Russia the United States still looks as though it's on the march—developing missile defenses, outspending Moscow by a ratio of 10:1, enlarging NATO, and calling for new bases in former Warsaw Pact countries. Russian policymakers still perceive stabilizing the strategic competition with Washington and its allies as being in Moscow's interests.

In the April 2008 meeting at the Russian Black Sea resort of Sochi, President Vladimir Putin and U.S. President George Bush issued a "Strategic Framework Declaration" aimed at "moving the U.S.-Russia relationship from one of strategic competition to strategic partnership." While such a development would clearly go far toward making Russia (and the United States) more responsible international stakeholders, the Russian and American governments have fundamentally different perspectives on how to control strategic offensive nuclear weapons.

Since March 2007, Russian and American negotiators have been discussing the contours of a new bilateral arms control accord to replace the 1991 Strategic Arms Reduction Treaty (START), set to expire in December 2009. In their more recent 2002 Russian-American Strategic Offensive Reductions Treaty (SORT), Washington and Moscow committed to reducing their nuclear arsenals to between 1,700 and 2,200 "operationally deployed strategic warheads" by December 31, 2012. This figure is lower than some of the limits imposed by START, but SORT's verification depends heavily on the extensive on-site inspections, data exchanges, and other compliance measures found in START. Thus, if START expires without a new agreement, both governments will, as of December 2009, be severely hampered in their ability to verify any strategic arms control.

Russian negotiators have pushed for a new legally binding treaty that would replace START and supersede SORT. The Kremlin wants the new accord to be more detailed than SORT, whose limits Moscow sees as insufficient to ensure predictability and parity in the Russian-American strategic balance. Russian representatives also seek to require the United States to eliminate the warheads that are removed from its active stockpile, rather than simply place them in storage. Russian leaders are concerned that the earlier agreements leave the United States with the ability simply to "upload" these warheads back onto U.S. strategic systems, thereby quickly reconstituting its pre–START II force.

Although the outgoing U.S. administration would prefer an agreement with fewer constraints on U.S. nuclear forces than desired by Moscow, Barack Obama has advocated a position regarding START that is in better accord with Russian preferences. Even if the Obama administration adopts a more flexible negotiating position once in office, that would not address another problem with the two governments' approach to nuclear arms control. Moscow and Washington affirm in the Strategic Framework Declaration that any reductions in the size of their nuclear arsenals will represent "a further step in implementing our commitments" under the Nuclear Nonproliferation Treaty (NPT). Yet, under NPT Article VI, "Each of the Parties to the Treaty undertakes to pursue negotiations in good faith on effective measures relating to cessation of the nuclear arms race at an early date and to nuclear disarmament, and on a Treaty on general and complete disarmament under strict and effective international control." Given the NPT's call for nuclear weapon states to relinquish their arsenals, many other governments and international security analysts believe that the Russian Federation, the United States, and the other nuclear powers must make more drastic reductions— with many calling for total elimination—to meet their NPT obligations.

Another lingering nuclear arms control problem is intermediate-range nuclear weapons, those with ranges of 500–5,500 kilometers. The 1987 Intermediate-Range Nuclear Forces (INF) Treaty bans the two countries from developing, manufacturing, or deploying ground-launched ballistic and cruise missiles with these ranges. Russian dissatisfaction with the INF Treaty stems in part from how this bilateral agreement uniquely discriminates against Russia and the United States. In October 2007, Putin warned that Moscow would find it difficult to continue complying with the INF Treaty unless other countries ratified the agreement as well. Washington and Moscow subsequently agreed jointly to encourage other countries to join the INF Treaty, but this has not amounted to anything more than issuing an appeal at the UN General Assembly. From the perspective of becoming a more responsible international stakeholder, it would be much better for Moscow to work with Washington to pull other countries into the INF Treaty than to abandon yet another arms control agreement without offering anything in its place. Indeed this might represent a broader arms control opportunity to find additional means to curb the proliferation of ballistic missiles.

## Missile Defense

Russian political, military, and other leaders have stridently denounced American plans to erect a comprehensive ballistic missile defense network extending beyond the U.S. territory. In particular, Moscow objects to early U.S. steps to deploy ballistic missile defense (BMD) systems in Poland and the Czech Republic. Russians are dubious of the stated U.S. justification for the BMD deployments—that the systems are needed to defend the United States and European countries against an emerging Iranian missile threat. Moscow argues that Iran and other potential proliferators have yet to develop long-range missiles or the nuclear warheads that would make them truly threatening. Russian representatives further maintain that the best way to discourage countries from pursuing weapons of mass destruction (WMD) is to deal peacefully with their underlying security concerns rather than take military steps likely to trigger aggressive counteractions. Instead, Russian leaders insist that the true object of these deployments along Russia's periphery is to intercept Russian intercontinental ballistic missiles, which may require the cooperation of other (and possible future) NATO governments—including Ukraine and Georgia—to build a more extensive and effective BMD system.

Russia's response to U.S. missile defense moves in Central Europe has been creative. As president, Putin broached a number of potential cooperative approaches to the technology and the emerging threat from Iran. For its part, the Bush administration, while expressing general interest in expanding BMD cooperation with Moscow, discounted Putin's specific offers because they would require abandoning its near-term plans. In any case, the two governments need to address both the specific issue of the East European systems and the more important longer-term issue of how to integrate strategic defensive and strategic offensive systems in a manner that promotes, rather than worsens, international security in general. Nevertheless, converting these concepts into operational arms control limits has proven extremely difficult, with each side doubting the sincerity and intentions of the other. And, although both the Polish and American governments deny it, the Russian military intervention in Georgia clearly spurred both parties to hurry their protracted negotiations to a conclusion. The United States met Warsaw's long-standing demand for a pledge to come to Poland's immediate defense should it be attacked by another country.

In a classic, distinctly ironic, instance of strategic crossed wires, Russia's decision to intervene militarily in Georgia was at least partially intended as a protest against U.S. disregard of Russian security interests in expanding eastward with the deployment of missile interceptors and other military facilities. Regardless of merit, Moscow's decision to respond militarily in Georgia has accelerated this trend.

## Cooperating on Nuclear Technology and Nonproliferation

The Russian-American Strategic Framework proclaims that "our two countries will provide global leadership on a wide range of cooperative efforts that will advance our common nonproliferation goals. These will include new approaches focused on environmentally friendly technologies that will support economic growth, promote the expansion of nuclear energy, and create a viable alternative to the spread of sensitive nuclear fuel cycle technologies." The document then affirms Moscow's and Washington's commitment to address key elements of this nuclear nonproliferation agenda—expanding the use of nuclear energy while limiting the spread of sensitive fuel cycle technologies, an accelerated timetable for nuclear security upgrades in Russia, and the Proliferation Security Initiative, together with other measures aimed to limit the spread of weapons or technologies to countries of proliferation concern and nonstate actors.

Moscow has also been working with other countries on parallel, but separate, initiatives to control sensitive nuclear enrichment technologies via an internationalized supply of nuclear fuel. These initiatives use market incentives, rather than coercive methods, to induce countries to lease nuclear fuel from designated provider states and then send the resulting waste back to the supplier for reprocessing and disposal. These incentive systems represent the positive complement to these countries' negative nonproliferation measures in the mode of denial and coercion. Such a balanced approach reflects the full imperatives of responsible stakeholdership in discouraging nuclear proliferation.

The tensions between Russia and the United States over Georgia have claimed—temporarily, one hopes—a significant nonproliferation casualty: the U.S.-Russia Agreement for Peaceful Nuclear Cooperation, which had been completed earlier in 2008 after nearly two years of negotiations. The proposed accord (known as a "123 Agreement"), would have lasted thirty years, and facilitated the flow of technologies, materials, equipment, and other components used to conduct nuclear research and produce nuclear energy. Section 123 of the U.S. Atomic Energy Act of 1954 requires the United

States to negotiate a separate bilateral accord with each country before it can cooperate on commercial nuclear projects. These accords obligate the recipient country to obtain Washington's approval to use any U.S. nuclear material or equipment for uranium enrichment or reprocessing, or to transfer any items to a third party.

Representatives of the Russian government and nuclear industry have eagerly sought the cooperation agreement to enhance their ability to expand Russia's role as a provider of international nuclear fuel services. Russia has considerable excess capacity to manufacture or reprocess uranium fuel for foreign customers. Yet a majority of the world's nuclear fuel originated in the United States. Until a 123 Agreement is in place, countries are prohibited from sending their U.S.-origin nuclear fuel to Russia. Despite the possibility of increased competition, many representatives of the American nuclear industry endorsed the proposed Russia-U.S. agreement. They also want the options of both importing Russian nuclear technology and selling American services and equipment directly to Russian buyers—providing that the Russian government commits to opening its nuclear market to foreign competition and establishes a comprehensive liability regime for commercial nuclear activities.[8]

Several arms control experts who backed the accord emphasized the importance of giving Moscow some financial benefits and other incentives to increase its cooperation with Western countries to contain Iran's feared nuclear weapons program. They had hoped that offering Russian nuclear energy companies new markets in the United States and elsewhere, the Russian government would have found it easier to reduce nuclear cooperation with Iran.[9]

Perhaps the Obama administration can renew momentum in this area despite the fallout over Georgia. Russia's support may not be a sufficient condition for preventing nuclear terrorism, but it is a necessary one. Along with the United States, Russia possesses more nuclear material suitable for manufacturing weapons—along with more expertise in disciplines useful for preventing illicit nuclear diversions or use—than any other country. Since terrorist groups, unlike nation-states, cannot manufacture highly enriched uranium or plutonium, they need to steal, buy, or otherwise acquire these materials from other sources. For years, experts have considered the hundreds of tons of fissile material located in the former Soviet Union to be the most vulnerable to falling into the wrong hands.

Even after years of Russian government effort and outside support, concerns remain about the present condition of the materials, as well as their possible diversion during the chaotic years following the Soviet Union's collapse.[10] Although some Russians, including those involved in the country's nuclear and security community, deny that Russian "loose nukes" present a major security problem, the Russian government has generally been quite helpful and active in countering these threats. For example, Russian officials still claim pride of authorship in submitting the original text in 1997 that served as the basis of the International Convention for the Suppression of Acts of Nuclear Terrorism, which the UN General Assembly adopted by consensus in April 2005.

The Strategic Framework Declaration also commits both countries to "expand and strengthen" their joint Global Initiative to Combat Nuclear Terrorism (GI). The initiative aims to improve the coordination of nonproliferation programs that contribute to averting nuclear terrorism. Current priorities include:

- Decreasing the availability of nuclear material to terrorists.
- Improving the capabilities of participating nations to counter trafficking of such materials.
- Promoting information sharing and other cooperation between law enforcement agencies engaged in combating nuclear terrorism.
- Improving legal and regulatory frameworks in this area.
- Minimizing the use of highly enriched uranium and plutonium in civilian activities.
- Strengthening national capabilities to manage the consequences of a nuclear terrorist attack.

Although the global initiative began as a bilateral Russian-American initiative, it has since gained widespread international support. More than fifty countries joined the GI in its first year; as of July 9, 2008, seventy-five countries were full partners.

After the initial U.S.-Russian Cooperative Threat Reduction (CTR) effort helped Russia and other former Soviet republics dismantle unwanted Soviet-era strategic weapons systems, focus shifted to enhancing the safety and security of residual weapons against illicit trafficking by terrorists and other nonstate actors. The newest CTR priority in recent years has been joint efforts to lessen third-party proliferation threats. This new focus holds the most promise for future Russian-American threat reduction cooperation because it moves from the donor-recipient dynamic of earlier CTR programs to one of joint partnership against common threats. Russian and American experts have already engaged in periodic discussions about applying CTR-like programs to other countries, especially in North Korea and Pakistan.[11]

## Iran and North Korea

Since Moscow has better relations than the United States with Iran and other nuclear aspirants, Russian leverage offers significant potential to help resolve nonproliferation issues with these countries. In addition, Moscow and Washington could develop joint programs designed to share lessons with representatives of less experienced nuclear weapon states, such as India and Pakistan. Such initiatives could focus on securing nuclear weapons and related materials against being diverted into illicit transnational criminal or terrorist networks—a recurring worry in chaos-prone Pakistan. And if Iran and North Korea ever follow Libya's example and renounce nuclear weapons, they might prefer to work on sensitive verification measures with a joint Russian-American program rather than with the United States alone.

In an effort to avert near-term challenges posed by Iran's nuclear program, Russia and Western governments continue to urge Tehran to comply with UN Security Council resolutions to suspend its enrichment and reprocessing activities. While Russia joined with other UN Security Council members in supporting sanctions in 2006 and 2007, Moscow remains an unenthusiastic backer of punitive measures. Russian diplomats often work to weaken proposed sanctions. In addition, they have always defended Iran's right to pursue nuclear activities for peaceful purposes, such as civilian energy production. Russian officials have also been especially stubborn in denying that Tehran is currently seeking a nuclear weapon or is developing long-range missile technology. Although Russian nonproliferation experts are genuinely concerned about preventing Iran from developing the capacity to manufacture a nuclear bomb, other influential Russians place a higher priority on possible arms sales and nuclear energy deals with Iran. As a responsible stakeholder, Russia would continue to oppose Iran's acquisition of nuclear weapons and prove willing to impose whatever multinational sanctions are necessary to achieve this end, even if that required Russian firms to end their lucrative sales to Iran. For leaders already ambivalent about helping the United States with the Iranian nuclear issue, the Georgia war has only lessened their appetite for cooperation with Washington.

In the case of North Korea's denuclearization, the Strategic Framework proclaims the commitment of Russia and the United States to the six-party talks, the implementation of UN Security Council Resolution 1718, and "the ultimate goals of the denuclearization of the Korean Peninsula." Although U.S. and Chinese officials have assumed the lead role in negotiating with the North Koreans, Russian representatives have also encouraged Pyongyang to roll back its nuclear program. In addition, Russia chairs the six-party working group responsible for addressing regional security issues. Its chairman,

Deputy Foreign Minister Alexander Losyukov, has declared his government's long-term objective of establishing a more permanent institution than the six-party talks to address northeast Asian security issues.

Russian leaders clearly oppose North Korea's acquisition of nuclear weapons. The Russian delegation to the six-party talks has demanded that the Democratic People's Republic of Korea (DPRK) dismantle its nuclear facilities at Yongbyon rather than simply suspend operations at the facility in order to ensure the country's nuclear disarmament. Nevertheless, Russian policymakers remain more concerned about the potential immediate collapse of the North Korean state than about its leader's intransigence on the nuclear question. Given these concerns, Moscow could best serve as an international stakeholder regarding Korea by contributing Russian diplomatic support and, ideally, nuclear expertise to assist with implementing the denuclearization agreement, as well as use its role in the six-party framework to help establish a more durable security environment in northeast Asia.

## Regional Security Issues

Throughout 2007 and early 2008, Russian government officials brandished their Security Council veto against any proposal on Kosovo that the Serbian government in Belgrade opposed. Russia's position probably contributed toward stiffened Serbian recalcitrance. Some analysts suspected that the Russian government hoped that such tactics of delay and slow rolling would provoke frustrated Kosovars to once again resort to mass violence, thereby turning the international community against their independence.[12] As events unfolded, the EU decision (backed by NATO) to circumvent the UN Security Council and support Kosovo's independence on its own authority to the Russians seemed like an exact replay of the 1999 Kosovo war.

More problematically, some Russian officials threatened that if Kosovo succeeded in asserting its independence other separatist regions in Europe would intensify their efforts to follow suit. In January 2008, Russian Deputy Foreign Minister Grigory Karasin warned of the potentially far-reaching and "unpredictable consequences" of sanctioning Kosovo's independence "given that presently about 200 regions are seeking self-determination in one form or another." Subsequent Russian moves to enhance ties with the pro-Moscow enclaves in Georgia's regions of Abkhazia and South Ossetia might be traced in part to Moscow's frustrations over being unable to block Kosovo's independence. During his last news conference as president, Putin said European governments that recognized Kosovo's independence should feel "ashamed" for "having these double standards." Putin also warned that Moscow would not necessarily consider Kosovo a special case: "We have Abkhazia, South Ossetia, Trans-Dniester, and they say Kosovo is a special case?"

At first, Russia responded merely by strengthening its ties with Serbia, denouncing Western actions, and withholding formal recognition of the new Kosovan government and preventing it from joining international organizations, such as the United Nations. Responsible stakeholdership would restrain Moscow from adding further provocation, such as encouraging Belgrade to reopen the issue of Republika Serpska in Bosnia. Russia should also have ceased threats to retaliate by supporting separatist aspirations in other breakaway regions, such as Abkhazia and South Ossetia in Georgia.

## Fallout over Georgia

Although the precise catalyst for the war between Russia and Georgia in August 2008 is unclear, the risk of escalation was always present given the years of tension and the diplomatic stalemate over the status of the pro-Russian separatist regions of Abkhazia and South Ossetia, as well as Georgian aspirations to join NATO. The question was whether Moscow would exploit its local military superiority to compel Georgia's formal dismemberment or would instead hold the threat of armed interventions in reserve in an attempt to influence Georgian foreign policy without jeopardizing Russian-Western relations. Ultimately, in August 2008 Russian policymakers decided to accept the risks of armed confrontation in the expectation that, given the already poor state of Russian-Western relations, they would suffer minimal added costs while achieving some enduring security benefits.

Although Russian Foreign Minister Lavrov has denied that Moscow seeks "regime change" in Tbilisi, the Russian Ambassador to the United Nations, Vitaly Churkin, observed that "Sometimes there are democratic leaders who do things which create great problems for their country. Sometimes those leaders need to contemplate how useful they have become to their people." Other Russian officials have referred to the Georgian government as a "criminal regime," while Putin told the media that Tbilisi had effectively lost its moral right to govern the two regions. President Medvedev referred to Georgian President Saakashvili as a "political corpse." The military punishment inflicted on Georgia is also presumably a signal to the Georgians and other countries, including Tbilisi's allies, of Russia's military revival. Although Russian defense spending has increased in recent years, analysts remained uncertain whether the Russian military had achieved genuine improvements in operational capability, given its poor performance in Chechnya, morale problems, and lack of actual combat experience. Russian leaders have now demonstrated dramatically that they have both the capacity and the will to use the country's armed forces to advance Russia's security goals.

Earlier in 2008, many NATO governments resisted formally strengthening their ties with Georgia and with the alliance for fear of further antagonizing Moscow at a time when Russian-NATO relations were already strained over U.S. plans to deploy ballistic missile defenses in Eastern Europe and Russia's moratorium on implementing the Conventional Armed Forces in Europe Treaty. Some European leaders also expressed concern about Saakashvili's alleged authoritarian tendencies. The declaration adopted at the April 2008 NATO summit in Bucharest nevertheless stated that the allies eventually expected Georgia to join the alliance, but the recent fighting has underscored the risks of actually bringing Georgia into the alliance since no NATO government is prepared to engage in a war with Russia on Tbilisi's behalf. On the one hand, Putin pointedly warned that "Georgia's aspiration to join NATO . . . is driven by its attempt to drag other nations and peoples into its bloody adventures." On the other hand, some NATO leaders have worried that a weak alliance response, such as an offer of dialogue unaccompanied by threats of punishment, would encourage further Russian aggression. The resulting compromise consisted of a formal statement by the foreign ministers that NATO could no longer "continue with business as usual" toward Russia following its invasion of Georgia. They therefore suspended meetings of the NATO-Russia Council—a move reciprocated by Moscow—until Russian troops withdrew from recently occupied Georgian territory back to their prewar deployments. The ministers also agreed to create a special NATO-Georgian Commission to help coordinate allied support for Georgia's postconflict reconstruction, including rebuilding Georgia's military infrastructure.

Yet Russian leaders have had little success in rallying other governments to their side. Despite intense Russian lobbying, the political declaration adopted at the Shanghai Cooperation Organization (SCO) summit shortly after the conflict with Georgia does not blame Tbilisi for causing the war or refer to its alleged acts of "genocide" in South Ossetia, the alleged pretext for Russia's intervention. The other SCO members also distinctly opted against following or even supporting Russia's decision to recognize the independence declarations of the pro-Moscow leaders of South Ossetia and Abkhazia.

The Central Asian countries in the SCO—with borders drawn by Soviet leaders for their own administrative convenience and as part of Moscow's divide-and-rule strategy—all have ethnic minorities and potentially contested boundaries. Their leaders have no interest in sowing doubts over these frontiers, encouraging secessionist sentiments among their ethnic minorities, or giving Moscow an excuse to intervene on behalf of Russian citizens. They also fear that openly siding with Moscow on Georgia would antagonize their Western partners, some of whom already see the SCO as a potential anti-NATO bloc of Eurasian authoritarian states. Even the Chinese leadership was evidently reluctant to endorse the principle that governments can militarily support secessionist movements in other states.

Until recently, it appeared as though mutual concerns about Afghanistan's security would sustain a modicum of Russia-NATO cooperation. After the NATO summit, however, Lavrov suggested that Russia might suspend Moscow's transit agreement with NATO for the transport of nonlethal equipment through Russia—and through consenting Central Asian countries—for use in Afghanistan. The Russian foreign minister pointedly told reporters in Sochi that "[t]he fate of NATO is being decided in Afghanistan" and "Russia needs cooperation with NATO no more than NATO needs Russia."

When Russia and the West begin looking for areas to restore their relationship, the situation in Afghanistan and Central Asia may offer greater opportunities than many others. Russian policymakers express less unease about the Western military presence in Central Asia than they do about NATO military activities in Eastern Europe, Ukraine, or the Southern Caucasus. Of course, it helps that no influential voices in Brussels or Washington call for extending full alliance membership to the current Central Asian governments. In addition, Russia and NATO share an interest in preventing a Taliban resurgence in Afghanistan. For several years, Putin and other Russian officials have urged NATO to cooperate with the Russian-led Collective Security Treaty Organization (CSTO) on joint operations to counter Afghan narcotics trafficking.[13] Since NATO is still struggling to ensure security in that country, heightened cooperation with Russia to curb terrorism and narcotics trafficking and promote reconstruction only makes sense. As a responsible stakeholder, the Russian government would continue to support international efforts to curb Afghan narcotics trafficking and stabilize the Afghan government. Russian officials would also refrain from exploiting the crisis to establish hegemony over its Central Asian allies or displace Western influence from the region.

## Energy Security

Russia's role as a major player in global energy security—especially as a gas supplier in Europe—has attracted a great deal of attention and heated debate in recent years. This debate has only intensified since the war in Georgia prompted accusations that the Russians were merely using the conflict as a pretext to strengthen Moscow's dominance of the Caspian Basin's energy transit infrastructure. The Russian government vehemently denies this charge, but certainly other governments in the region—notably, energy-rich states like Azerbaijan, Kazakhstan, Turkmenistan, and Uzbekistan—are watching with great trepidation.

The extraordinary rise in oil prices has transformed Russia in less than ten years from virtual bankruptcy to one of the world's largest creditor nations. When oil prices were high, the value of oil and gas production was about $500 billion annually, or nearly half Russia's current GDP. This hydrocarbon-generated revenue stream is the most important driver of the Russian political economy and its foreign policy projection. The two most significant events of the Putin years for Russia's domestic and foreign policies both find their roots in oil and gas: the Yukos affair and the 2005/2006 gas dispute with Ukraine. The Yukos affair marked a dramatic power shift and the recentralization of political and economic authority away from the business oligarchs back to the Kremlin. In Vladimir Putin's campaign to regain state control over the massive financial flows in the energy sector, the destruction of a company that five years ago was Russia's most highly valued and the jailing of its CEO Mikhail Khodorkovsky was a considerable show of strength.

The early 2006 gas dispute with Ukraine—culminating with Gazprom's decision to shut off gas supplies for a day to that country (and consequently to many of Russia's European customers)—raised the question of Moscow's reliability as a supplier. The coincidence that Russia took this step on the very day that it assumed chairmanship of the G-8, with energy security as its main theme, only added to the fallout. U.S. Secretary of State Condoleezza Rice was one of the first international figures to accuse the Russian Federation of using energy as a "political weapon." Regardless of the merits of Gazprom's negotiating positions, cutting off gas supplies was a public relations fiasco for Moscow. Concern in Europe about excessive dependence on Russia and the need to diversify supplies has been intensifying ever since, and the echoes are loud in Washington as well.

That said, much of the controversy surrounding the gas cut-off to Ukraine obscured the underlying roots of the problem: the growing tightness between supply of and demand for Russian gas. Price hikes to Ukraine were part of an overall picture of price increases, albeit not evenly applied, to all of Moscow's former Soviet customers as well as its consumers at home. The dispute was particularly sharp with Ukraine because it appeared Moscow was punishing Ukraine for the Orange Revolution and for the rejection of Moscow's favored candidate for the presidency. In fact, the Ukrainian gas dispute is an excellent case where Russia's political and economic/commercial interests, as viewed from the Kremlin, coincided. In purely economic terms, though, production growth has been nearly stagnant at Gazprom for years, while the demand for Russian gas both abroad and at home is steadily increasing. (Production growth for Russian independent gas companies, though, has been far more impressive.)

This brings us back to the Yukos case and the push for increased state intervention in the energy sector. The essential question is whether the Russian state is "killing the goose that lays the golden egg." Or, put differently, is the current Russian ruling elite more concerned about growing the energy sector pie—or merely getting larger pieces for themselves? The most pressing issue for defining Russia's contributions to regional and global energy security is twofold: whether the dependence of consumers of Russian oil and gas (mostly European) makes these entities vulnerable to Moscow's political whims, and, perhaps more importantly, whether the Russian companies and state are taking adequate measures to sustain and even grow supply capacity to meet domestic and foreign demand commitments. There is no question that Russia does not develop supply relationships on a purely commercial basis.[14] Russia naturally takes advantage of Europe's inability to act collectively on energy by providing attractive terms to politically favored clients like Germany, France, Italy, and others. Whether Europe will be able to develop energy policy toward Russia in a more unified manner in the wake of the recent war in Georgia remains to be seen. Certainly there is now increased desire among EU members to act with greater consensus.

Russian efforts to dominate transport infrastructure of gas and oil from Russia and the former Soviet Union to European and Asian markets have also sparked outcries in Europe and the United States. Russia views efforts to develop alternative pipeline routes that bypass Russia as overtly hostile. Disputes between Russia and the West over the Baku-Tblisi-Ceyhan, and more recently plans for the Nabucco and Trans-Caspian pipelines, have been sharp. Russia has responded to the U.S.-led "happiness is multiple pipelines" policy with a concerted strategy to augment Russian domination of pipeline infrastructure. Related disputes have prevented Russia and Europe from agreeing on the Energy Charter Treaty, which Moscow has refused to ratify, principally because of Gazprom's refusal to renounce its monopoly of domestic gas pipelines.

Whether Russia will behave as a responsible stakeholder on energy security may well depend on where you sit. Germans are more likely to answer this question in the affirmative, for example, than Ukrainians, Poles, residents of the Baltic States, or Georgians. However, Russian behavior is not so different from that of other large hydrocarbon suppliers when a high-price environment enhances their leverage. At times when prices are skyrocketing, Russian companies are hardly alone in revisiting contracts, production sharing agreements, and equity stakes that had been negotiated when prices were much lower. The recent demonstration, however, of Moscow's willingness to use force outside its constitutional borders marks a new development bound to affect calculations of all neighboring states on a wide variety of issues, including energy.

## Global Economic Stewardship

When President Bush met with President Putin and then with President-elect Medvedev in Sochi in April 2008, the foremost question on Russian leaders' minds was not on the official agenda: the future strength of the U.S. dollar. Looking back to the 1990s, if there was a currency issue between the two countries, it was the plummeting value of the ruble. This new concern of Russian leaders reflects the extent to which Russia is now integrated into the global economy, with commensurate stakes in global financial stability.[15]

It stands to reason, then, that global financial stability is the area where one can expect to see the most constructive Russian approach. Unlike the security and political realms, this set of issues is not heavily burdened by the legacy of the Cold War. In fact, the Soviets remained outside the Bretton Woods process during and after World War II as a matter of their own choice. Six decades later, as the existing financial system struggles with current challenges, the Russian leadership is determined not to repeat the mistake of their Soviet predecessors. The first significant Russian foray, in 2007, was to push former Czech Finance Minister Josef Tosovsky as a candidate for managing director of the International Monetary Fund as an alternative to the EU candidate, Dominique Strauss-Kahn. While most of the media coverage portrayed the move as yet another Russian obstruction or geopolitical game, *The Financial Times* recognized the validity of Russia's position on its merits:

It is depressing when the Russian executive director speaks more sense about the future of the International Monetary Fund than does the European Union. Yet Alexei Mozhin did so when he criticized the European Union's decision to foist Dominique Strauss-Kahn, a former French finance minister, on the IMF. Only those who want the Fund to be irrelevant can applaud the decision. This is the wrong candidate, chosen in the wrong way. Mr. Mozhin was right when he said "the IMF is facing a severe crisis of legitimacy." He was correct to insist that "we must select the best candidate" if the institution is to remain relevant for developing countries.[16]

The "crisis of legitimacy" is especially acute at the IMF where the voting power quotas are so convoluted and archaic that China's quota is less than that of either Great Britain or France, and where India's share is less than Belgium's. Global wealth is moving east and south while the IMF distribution of voting power harkens back to the colonial era. This deficit of legitimacy also implicates the World Bank, given the cozy arrangement that for sixty years put an American at the head of the World Bank, while a European leads the IMF. Many in the U.S. government recognized that Tosovsky was a stronger candidate than Strauss-Kahn, but the decision to go along with the European Union's French candidate showed how reluctant Washington was to upset the old arrangement, which, after all, had put the Bush administration's own Robert Zoellick in the bank's top job. While the Russian candidate did not prevail in the IMF contest, the fact that Tosovsky was defeated despite the support of China, India, and many other developing and emerging market countries laid bare the inequities of an anachronistic system and boosted the chances that the structural challenges to the IMF to maintain legitimacy will be addressed sooner rather than later.

President Medvedev has continued to elaborate on the need for reform of global financial institutions in light of the weaknesses exposed by problems in the U.S. financial system. In his speech to the XII St. Petersburg International Economic Forum, Medvedev pointed to three challenges for a regulatory system in a globalized market: better coordination between regulatory institutions, improved evaluation of various financial instruments, and new systems for more reliable information disclosure, including strengthening the role of rating agencies. He also contrasted the responsible approach of Russian companies and investors with the "economic selfishness" of other international actors that has contributed to the dramatic increase in food prices in 2008.

## Democracy and Human Rights

The long tradition of democracy promotion as a hallmark of U.S. foreign policy can impede Americans from being aware just how distinctive that tradition is—and how strange it is to other political cultures. Indeed, with support from China and a host of other authoritarian governments, Russian leaders have sought to break the momentum of color revolutions that appeared to be sweeping Eurasia when George Bush spoke so eloquently about democracy and peace in his second inaugural address in 2005.[17] As Thomas Carothers argued in 2006, "The growing backlash has yet to coalesce into a formal or organized movement. But its proponents are clearly learning from and feeding off of one another."[18] From Eurasia to Africa to the Middle East, the promising wave of democratization of only a few years ago appears to have lost momentum, while the authoritarian capitalists have mobilized.

There are striking similarities in the maturing ideological foundations of contemporary Russian and Chinese outlooks. Russians often referred to the emerging ideology promoted by the Putin administration as *sovereign democracy*.[19] To understand the Kremlin's idea, it is important to appreciate that they view the decade of the 1990s as a modern "time of troubles" when domestically Russia was in chaos, very weak internationally, with foreign powers and organizations exerting too much influence over Russian domestic and foreign policies. In this narrative, Vladimir Putin has restored stability to Russia and set it on the road to recovery, not by abandoning market democratic values and institutions, but adapting them to Russian values and traditions, which appear to have little in common with Western notions of democracy.

These Russian perspectives match quite well with Chinese ideological formulations. The so-called Beijing Consensus poses counterarguments to American and Western ideological hegemony that align very closely with the Kremlin's *sovereign democracy*. First, there is not just one correct path to development. A country must innovate and experiment to find the path best suited for its cultures and traditions, and no country or organization should seek to impose external models. The majority of Russians today view the advice of Western advisors and multilateral organizations as bad medicine that only exacerbated Russia's socioeconomic problems. The typical Chinese interpretation of Russian development of the past fifteen years suggests that Moscow took the wrong path in the 1990s, but that the Putin administration has learned many things from the Chinese reform experience and instituted much-needed corrections to reconcentrate power in the hands of the state.[20]

Russia's liberal approach to economic integration starkly contrasts to the Kremlin's posture in the debate between national sovereignty and international intervention to promote democracy and to address human rights abuses. While the Russian government has scaled back foreign involvement in designated "strategic sectors" of the Russian economy, essentially Moscow's approach has been very open. But on human rights and democracy promotion, as Sarah Mendelson has argued, Russia under Vladimir Putin has developed a sense of "hyper-sovereignty."[21] This strain was certainly evident in the 1990s with Russia's sensitivity to criticism over its war in Chechnya and vehement opposition to NATO's Kosovo war. Somewhat incongruously, however, just as Russia was, in actuality, becoming more financially sovereign,

Putin spoke ominously about Russia being besieged by foreign enemies who sought to weaken it. In response to criticism of Russia's authoritarian drift and accusations of human rights violations, corruption, and other abuses, Russian officials countered with a loud and steady refrain of "double standards." Unfortunately, the combination of the bizarre spectacle of the 2000 U.S. presidential elections, rash of corporate scandals symbolized by Enron, and disgraceful U.S. treatment of detainees, the Russians had a lot of ammunition. But the Russian concerns about violations of national sovereignty are also very selectively applied. Moscow shows few qualms about violating the sovereignty of its neighbors, especially Ukraine and Georgia. It was reported that, in a dinner discussion at NATO's April 2008 summit in Bucharest, Putin told Bush that Ukraine was not a real country.[22] Although some observers claim that destruction of Georgia's nascent democracy was one of the Kremlin's goals in prosecuting the recent war, we believe that Russian policymakers mainly sought to prevent what they viewed as encroachment on their geostrategic sphere of influence rather than oppose the spread of democracy through military action.

Russia has also made systematic efforts—often in alliance with China and others—to highjack the agenda in international organizations responsible for establishing and defending norms on human rights. Russia's relationship with the Organization for Security and Cooperation in Europe (OSCE), for instance, has been tense for years, as Moscow has aggressively sought to reduce the organization's role in election monitoring and human rights protection. Increasingly, practitioners and academics working on democracy promotion and human rights view Russia more as a determined spoiler than a responsible stakeholder.[23]

## Factors in Russia's Trajectory

The extent to which Russia plays the role of a responsible stakeholder in the evolving institutions of global governance will depend primarily on how the country develops domestically. We would welcome Russia's transformation into a liberal democratic regime like that of Western Europe, but such a transition looks improbable for the next few years. Ultimately, we do accept the proposition that a more solidly democratic Russia will display more responsible behavior. But for the period covered by this chapter and its companions—the next decade—Russia will still be in a transitional phase. It is very hard to imagine Russia in 2018 having completed its democratic transformation.[24] However, a Russia that remains on a relatively stable development path for the next decade will likely be a more accommodating and responsible Russia—especially as the trauma of the Soviet collapse and the perceived humiliation of the 1990s recede from the forefront of the Russians' national identity.

In addition to domestic considerations, Russia's participation in the international system will be most affected by the behavior of other countries, especially the United States and, to a lesser degree, Europe. Perhaps even more so than the behavior of other countries covered in this series, Russians will respond to U.S. policies given the recent and decades-long history of bipolar Cold War confrontation with Washington. The Russian political elite still has a tendency to benchmark itself against the United States, though this practice is diminishing as the Cold War recedes into history and newer elites emerge who do not carry their elders' historical and psychological baggage. The shadow of the Cold War looms most heavily over security issues, especially those involving nuclear weapons, where American policies indeed have a decisive impact on Russian strategies.

The overall challenges of reforming institutions of global governance also fall most heavily on the United States, since Americans played the lead role in creating the existing system. But the "unipolar moment" is fading, as is the broader historical dominance of the West that has lasted for nearly three hundred years. Russia is not very different from other large emerging powers in that its behavior will likely be more responsible to the extent that its leaders believe they participate in the shaping (and reshaping) of international political, security, and economic institutions. Russians appear eager to play a more leading and vocal role, including championing the interests of other powers that were not involved in crafting the existing institutions. They are also not shy about contesting U.S. leadership—even if, at times, their rhetoric and actions aim more at posturing than policy.[25]

For the next decade, we believe that the likelihood of Russia playing the role of responsible stakeholder will vary considerably, depending on the area. At present, the most promise lies in the areas of strengthening global economic institutions and promoting nuclear nonproliferation. On energy security, Moscow's status as a supplier country will strongly color its approach. Current tense relations with some of its European customers will likely persist. Finally, Russia's relations with its neighbors will likely prove the most problematic, particularly on issues relating to regional security ties and democracy promotion.

We leave the reader with a question. What if Russia is very successful in achieving its economic growth goals, yet still feels unsatisfied with its global role? This is a distinct possibility given that, even in the best-case economic scenario for 2020, Russia's proportional weight in the global economy would only increase from today's 2.3 percent to about 3.5 percent in that year. More-over, the continued rapid economic growth of China and India will probably result in these countries pulling further ahead of Russia. The relatively large economies of Japan and Brazil might also outperform that of Russia. Even in the realm of providing a counterweight and contesting U.S. and Western leadership, China and India may soon seize the initiative from Moscow. Given the current ambitious aspirations of the Russian leadership, some dis-appointment and disillusionment seem inevitable.

∽

## Dmitri Trenin's Reaction

The Kuchins-Weitz chapter is well researched, lucid, and insightful, leading them to quite useful policy conclusions. There is virtually nothing in the chapter with which I would take strong issue. Rather than use this commen-tary to nitpick, I will amplify some of its key arguments, and perhaps offer added perspective.

As Russians see it, the very concept of responsible shareholders is a U.S. project aimed at locking the world's key players into a new compact largely drafted by the United States. The concept tries to lure other countries, including Russia, into taking an ownership "stake" in the system, yet the system itself would essentially remain under the United States' supervision.

The Russian reaction to such an arrangement over the years has been ambivalent. From the 1990s to the early 2000s, Moscow actively, though unsuccessfully, sought Washington's recognition of its legitimate interests and its role as a valuable, even strategic, partner to the United States. It did not challenge U.S. post–Cold War global hegemony and only claimed to be part of the decision-making loop.

This changed in the mid-2000s, as the Russian leadership, after a series of strategic shocks—the Iraq war, Yukos affair, Beslan school tragedy, Georgian and Ukrainian color revolutions, and dual "big bang" expansion of both NATO and the European Union—concluded that integration into the U.S.-led system as America's junior partner is neither feasible nor especially desirable.

### What Does Russia Want?

In recent years, Moscow has been trying to bring the United States into a new deal with Russia. The terms would include Washington's acceptance of

Russia "as is," its willingness to treat it "as an equal," and mutual respect of each country's interests. This was the essence of Putin's infamous Munich speech. In other words, rather than trying to fit into the Western system, Russia announced its independence from the West.

This evolution of the Russian attitudes stems from very palpable changes in Russia's financial status, economic well-being, and self-esteem. It took Russia a full twenty years to recover from the latest of its periodic historical crises, but the recovery is real, even if today's Russia is hardly the superpower that the Soviet Union was. Kuchins and Weitz richly document this trajectory.

Russian policymakers interpret the Bush presidency as the beginning of the decline of U.S. hegemony. America's problems in the Middle East and with its own financial system mean that the unipolar moment has truly passed. For the time being, the United States will remain the world's premier power, but it will have to contend with ever-stronger competition from other players, mostly from the non-Western world.

Moscow is eager for the post–Cold War order, forged when Russia was flat on its back, to fade. The Georgia war marked a watershed: Russia is prepared to fight, literally, to defend its interests. Moscow's "armed response" was not aimed solely at Tbilisi; it was also intended as a warning to Washington not to cross certain red lines—most important, no U.S. permanent military presence or NATO expansion anywhere in the post-Soviet space.

Russia's foreign policy, as the authors correctly point out, prides itself on being pragmatic. Gorbachev's apparent altruism in conceding Soviet interests to the West is now widely derided, even reviled. The West no longer carries, in the Russian eyes, the moral authority it enjoyed at the end of the Cold War. Rather, it is seen as a collection of assorted players, some rather arrogant, some quite impotent, with a number of sensible ones thrown in—but all of them guided by their own perceived interests, despite trying to dress them up in ideological or rhetorical wrapping. Consequently, Russia's approach to Western counterparts is to appealing to their self-interests.

As the existing order is visibly crumbling, Moscow wants to be present at the creation of its replacement. Essentially a strategic loner, Russia is trying to renegotiate the terms of engagement with the powers in decline (i.e., the United States and the European Union), build strong ties with Asia's emerging powers (China and India), reach out to the forces of moderation in the Muslim world, and exploit other geopolitical shifts, from Venezuela to Vietnam, Mexico to South Africa.

While insisting on its great-power status, Russia has dropped the Soviet Union's superpower ambitions as an aberration. It sees itself as one of an approximately half-dozen major powers shaping the future of the global system.

In a way, Moscow views the system as an oligarchy. Thus, when Russian leaders talk about the primacy of the United Nations in the global order, what they really mean is the primacy of the UN Security Council, where Russia has a veto.

Russians are fully aware of the failings and failures of the UN system, and the notorious difficulties of reforming it. Equally content to work both formally and informally, Russians value their G-8 membership not only as a status symbol, but also as a means of reaching understandings that can then be translated into UN Security Council decisions. Call it the global Politburo or the Board of World, Inc., Russians want to be in the G-8. To them, it is in line with a long tradition dating back to the Concert of Europe.

Rather than seeing themselves as a responsible shareholder in the U.S.-led system, Russians want the United States to be a responsible normal great power in concert with the other elite few. Moscow is irritated by the United States imposing its law, its notions of right and wrong, and its military forces anywhere it chooses. Russia does not want confrontation with a still immensely more powerful America, but it hopes that a combination of the U.S. decline and other powers' rise will eventually lead to a more equitable international arrangement.

In the meantime, Russia will need to focus on its own problems. The Georgia war was followed, in quick succession, by the global financial crisis, which wiped five years' worth of growth out of the Russian stock market. It should be fully apparent to the Russian leadership that unless the country modernizes, it will not be able to compete in the rapidly changing world. Russia's mammoth problems, from infrastructure to demographics, will have to be tackled for the country to stay above water. The triumphalism of the Putin years has no place in today's circumstances.

Asking whether Russia can be a responsible shareholder in some still-undefined global system is not the right question. The real issue is whether Russia can be a partner to the United States in solving important global and regional issues and, if so, under what conditions. This is what Kuchins and Weitz are actually asking—since they presume, of course, that the system of global shareholders is U.S.-led.

The authors' answer to that question is a general "yes," and this commentator agrees. This answer needs to be qualified, though, by one major consideration. Russia would likely act responsibly and in good faith toward the Unites States and its interests, but only if the United States reciprocates by treating Russia respectfully, and as a serious player. And from Moscow's vantage, they have yet to see it.

## How the United States Can Help

The problem with the prevailing U.S. view of Russia is that since the latter is not a democracy—and Russia's present regime is indeed a mild form of autocracy, or "authoritarianism with the consent of the governed"—then, in this day and age, its government is not fully legitimate. And if Russia's leadership lacks legitimacy, it follows that Moscow's pursuit of its national interests is likewise not fully legitimate. The early heightened hopes after the abandonment of communism and dismantling of the Soviet Union could be partially to blame for this, as well as the fairly light commercial traffic between the two countries. Nevertheless, it is a problem that needs to be solved.

The United States could move toward solving that problem in several ways. One concerns the question of Ukraine and NATO. There is no need to kowtow to Russia on that issue, but there is a clear need to let the Ukrainian people sort out where they want to belong. According to recent opinion polls, only one in five Ukrainians want to be in NATO, and more than half would prefer to abstain. This does not mean that they favor an alliance with Russia, which is definitely not in the cards. But as regards U.S. policy, refraining from pushing for MAP (Action Plan for NATO Membership) and encouraging the European Union to be more open and generous to Eastern Europe's largest nation is not only the right Ukraine policy, but also the right approach to Russia.

Another key issue is missile defenses. As Kuchins and Weitz highlight, Moscow has long supported European theater missile defenses. Yet the Bush administration decided against working with Russia on a system clearly oriented toward Iran, and instead proceeded with ballistic missile defense (BMD) deployments in Central Europe—which Moscow views as part of a global BMD system that ultimately would only undercut Russia's strategic deterrent. When the Russians, as a fallback position, sought permanent monitoring arrangements at the U.S. installations, they were essentially rebuffed.

To restore a modicum of mutual confidence in strategic matters, which is also a U.S. national security interest, the United States needs to review its stance. In fact, accepting Russia's offer of theater missile defense collaboration would send perhaps the most powerful possible signal to Tehran, while laying the foundation with Moscow of a strategic partnership worthy of the name. If that is still too much to dare, a more sensitive approach to missile defense that responds to Russian concerns would at least halt any further deterioration of U.S.-Russian relations in the area of strategic arms.

Kuchins and Weitz are correct that Russia is ready to work toward a new agreement regulating long-range offensive weapons. Moscow has a clear interest in seeing the START treaty, which expires in December 2009, be succeeded by a new legally binding document. Constructive work on a new set of rules in this highly sensitive area would also help spur joint U.S.-Russian efforts in the field of nuclear nonproliferation, which brings us back to the subject of Russia having no interest in seeing Tehran armed with nuclear weapons. Moscow, however, cannot be expected to jump on Washington's bandwagon on policies decided without its active input. U.S.-Russian collaboration on Iran-related issues would require genuine and close work in tandem (as part of broader international cooperation) and as equals.

### Russia's True Stakes

Russia has just awakened from the strategic equivalent of a coma. The trauma of the last quarter-century is still exceptionally painful. In response, its leaders have adopted an inordinately jaded approach, characterized by realpolitik, jungle law, and black-and-white. There is too much emotion vis-à-vis the United States and too much *schadenfreude* when it fails. The fact remains, though, that Russia is much more part of the wider world than it has been at any point in its history. It wants to succeed, and to advance in that world. It wants to take part in making the rules, not just observing them. It wants all others, meaning the mightiest nations, to follow the same rules. All of this makes Russia a difficult country to deal with—too big for the West to integrate and too small to compete with the West as an equal.

As a member of this wide world, Russia is becoming increasingly aware of its limitations. Its population is smaller than Pakistan's and will fall below Turkey's. Its modernization is contingent on its access to Western technologies. Its conventional military is no match for the alliance on its western borders, or the great power rising in the east. With a massive piece of terrestrial real estate populated by too few people, Russia is bound to have a growing interest in some kind of order in the world—a set of rules and norms and a system of governance. Its capacity for being responsible grows in proportion to its stake, which cannot be described as anything other than existential.

### Notes

1. *Concept in the Long-term Socio-economic Development of the Russian Federation,* 6. For analysis of the international implications for the Russian economy of the 2020 program, see Andrew Kuchins, Amy Beavin, and Anna Bryndza, "Russia's 2020 Strategic Economic Goals and the Role of International Integration," July 2008.

2. For more on this point see the article by Clifford Gaddy and Andrew Kuchins, "Putin's Plan," *The Washington Quarterly* (Spring 2008): 117–29.

3. This argument is set forth in "Putin's Plan." See reference above.

4. Interestingly, President Medvedev spoke out against consideration of such "trade-offs" as detrimental to Russia's interest in a major speech he gave in Berlin in June 2008. See "Speech to Political, Parliamentary, and Social Representatives," June 5, 2008, www.kremlin.ru/appears/2008/06/05/1923_type63374type63376type63377_202133.shtml. In reality, such "trade-offs" on really major issues seems fairly rare in international relations. In the case of perhaps the most significant such example during the Cold War, the U.S. withdrawal of nuclear forces in Turkey to resolve the Cuban Missile Crisis, we did not learn of this until decades later.

5. The incident shows the problem with such unwritten exchanges, since U.S. officials contest the Russian interpretation of this period.

6. Medvedev, "Speech to Political, Parliamentary, and Social Representatives."

7. Personal communication from Keith Crane, RAND Corporation.

8. Jack Spencer, "Russia 123 Agreement: Not Ready for Primetime," Heritage Foundation, May 15, 2008, www.heritage.org/Research/EnergyandEnvironment/wm1926.cfm.

9. Richard Lugar and Sam Nunn, "Help Russia Help Us," *The New York Times*, May 30, 2008. See also Miles A. Pomper, "Bush Sends Russia Nuclear Energy Pact to Hill," *Arms Control Today* (June 2008), www.armscontrol.org/act/2008_06/Russia Energy.asp.

10. Matthew Bunn and Anthony Wier, *Securing the Bomb 2007* (Washington, DC: Project on Managing the Atom, Harvard University, and Nuclear Threat Initiative, 2007). belfercenter.ksg.harvard.edu/publication/17525/securing_the_bomb_2007.html.

11. David E. Hoffman, "Lugar, Nunn Push Arms Security Program," *Washington Post*, August 28, 2007, www.washingtonpost.com/wp-dyn/content/article/2007/08/27/AR2007082701395_pf.html.

12. Morton Abramowitz, "Kremlin Making Mischief in the Balkans," February 7, 2008, search.japantimes.co.jp/cgi-bin/eo20080207a2.html.

13. See, for example, the exchange in "Remarks by Secretary of State Condoleezza Rice, Secretary Robert Gates, Russian Foreign Minister Sergey Lavrov, and Russian Defense Minister Anatoly Serdyukov," March 18, 2008, www.state.gov/secretary/rm/2008/03/102362.htm.

14. Vladimir Milov, "Russia and the West: The Energy Factor," IFRI, CSIS (July 2008).

15. This argument is developed at length in "Putin's Plan," by Clifford Gaddy and Andrew Kuchins.

16. "Not Strauss-Kahn," *Financial Times*, August 27, 2008, www.ft.com/cms/s/0/90b5c5d6-54fe-11dc-890c-0000779fd2ac.html?nclick_check=1.

17. Much of the discussion on democracy promotion is derived from Andrew Kuchins, "État Terrible," *The National Interest* (September/October 2007): 92–96.

18. Thomas Carothers, "The Backlash against Democracy Promotion," *Foreign Affairs* 85, no. 2 (March/April 2006): 55–68.

19. As is typical of emerging ideologies, there has been considerable controversy over the term *sovereign democracy* and its meaning. In fact, Dmitri Medvedev was a critic of the term when it emerged during Putin's presidency in 2005/2006. Deputy head of the presidential administration, Vladislav Surkov, was the most vocal proponent of the notion, and his behind-the-scenes role has been compared to that of Mikhail Suslov during the Brezhnev years. Surkov laid out his understanding of Russian sovereign democracy in a fascinating, nearly stream-of-consciousness speech he gave at a party meeting for United Russia in February 2006; "Vladislav Surkov's Secret Speech to United Russia," *Moscow News*, July 7, 2005, www.mosnews.com/interview/2005/07/12/surkov.shtml.

20. Kuchins heard this view expressed many times in visits to China in May, October, and December 2006.

21. See Sarah Mendelson's testimony before the U.S. Commission on Security and Cooperation in Europe "Russia Today: In Transition or Intransigent?" May 24, 2007, www.csis.org/index.php?option=com_csis_congress&task=view&id=231.

22. "Putin Hints at Splitting Up Ukraine," *Moscow Times*, April 8, 2008.

23. Mendelson, op. cit.

24. For a fuller treatment of the likely development trajectories of Russia, see Andrew C. Kuchins, *Alternative Futures for Russia to 2017* (Washington, DC: Center for Strategic and International Studies, 2007).

25. For example, an interesting new grouping is the BRIC countries (Brazil, Russia, India, and China), the foreign ministers of which met together for the first time separately at a summit meeting in Yekaterinburg in May 2008.

# PART 3

# BELLWETHERS

~

# Turkey's Identity and Strategy:
# A Game of Three-Dimensional Chess
## Zeyno Baran and Ian O. Lesser
### With a Reaction by Hüseyin Bağcı

Modern Turkey sees itself as a responsible stakeholder, keen to adhere to international norms. Indeed, republican Turkey's national experience has been closely entwined with the issue of the country's identity, and with the explicit aim of becoming fully part of the West, including its norms and institutions. This drive for convergence with Western attitudes and practices in fact began well before Atatürk's secular revolution and the establishment of the modern republic. Turkey has been part of the European system for centuries, and this geopolitical "membership" has had significant internal and external policy implications. The Turkish case is compelling in the context of the "stakeholdership" debate because these issues of identity, affinity, and behavior remain unsettled, and because the country has entered a period of pronounced social and political flux.

A few factors and dynamics are discernible as constants in the Turkish experience with regard to norms, stakes, and behavior on the global scene. First, the interplay of domestic and external factors is critical. The more problematic aspects of the Turkish case arise mainly in the internal arena, where questions of incomplete democratization, human rights, and identity politics are central to Turkey's own debate about norms. And these are even more central to the Western debate about Turkey in light of the country's troubled EU candidacy. With a few notable exceptions—such as the Cyprus intervention of 1974 and periodic cross-border operations in northern Iraq— Ankara's foreign policy behavior has been considerably less controversial.

197

Second, there is a continuous tension between Turkey's desire for full integration with leading institutions on the one hand, and an extraordinary sensitivity to any infringement on national sovereignty on the other. Turks across the political spectrum tend to be highly patriotic, and their notion of Turkish nationalism is often of an unreconstructed variety. Most Turks, including those in official circles, remain uneasy with the weaker, postmodern concept of national sovereignty popular within the European Union. Where Turks see risks to national interest, especially in the area of national security, the ideal of multilateral action can be cast aside. In this and other aspects of Turkish strategic culture, there are some notable similarities with the United States. This sovereignty-consciousness sometimes manifests as a wary, highly legalistic approach to international affairs in Ankara. Even sophisticated Turks can be hypersuspicious about Western intentions toward their country, and an abiding fear of threats to that Turkish sovereignty and territorial integrity lies just below the surface.

Third, the question of responsible stakeholdership for Turkey is only partly about the Turks themselves. Many Turks believe that for all of the country's interest in adherence to international norms and institutions, it is unclear that the West is prepared to accept Turkey as a full member of the club. Europe is deeply ambivalent about Turkey, and many Europeans see Turkey as emblematic of the historic "other." Muslim opinion, especially in the Arab world, is just as mixed. Russia may see practical value in closer relations with Turkey, but, in geostrategic terms, the two countries are traditional competitors. The U.S. also takes a strategic interest in Turkey, but is hardly a trustworthy sponsor from the Turkish perspective. So where does Turkey really fit? Should we even expect it to fit? After all, the sense of distinctiveness (evident in another famous Kemalist slogan, "we resemble ourselves") is an important theme in Turkish discourse.

Measured against the full spectrum of international behavior, Turkey is a conservative, status quo actor: slow to move unilaterally and firmly attached to international norms. Turkey belongs to leading Western organizations, including NATO, the OECD, and the Council of Europe, and is a candidate for EU membership. Yet in recent years there has been a perceptible shift in Turkey's foreign policy, toward what some call a "neo-Ottoman" approach, in which Islamic identity and Middle Eastern interests play a greater role. According to this vision, which is popular across the ideological spectrum, Turkey should draw on its special cultural, historic, and religious links to its former possessions and rise to major power status through deeper involvement across this vast geography. This view calls for Turkey to act independently in accordance with Islamic or Turkic culture and norms—not necessarily

Western ones. The widespread support for this approach has, for instance, pushed Turkey toward a more active role in non-Western institutions such as the Organization of the Islamic Conference (OIC), which brings together fifty-seven mostly Muslim-majority countries.

As part of this self-confident vision, Ankara aims to take part in the full panoply of intergovernmental institutions. For example, Turkey has put itself forward as a candidate for a two-year elected seat on the UN Security Council in 2009 (it succeeded). In its associated diplomatic campaign, Turkey has established unprecedented government, business, and civil society relations with countries in Africa, South Asia, and Latin America, including Caribbean and Pacific states with few if any previous ties to Ankara.

Looking ahead, we believe the key areas to watch are Turkey's internal evolution, the related consequences for Ankara's foreign and security policies, and the completeness of Turkey's integration in the West, and possible alternative postures.

## Kemalist Turkey and the Pressures for Change

Ever since its founding, the Turkish state defined Kurdish separatism and Islamic fundamentalism as existential threats to the Republic. The Kemalist establishment has swung into action—at times with military force—when any perceived "red lines" were crossed on either of these issues. These two issues are also at the heart of the Turkish debate on political and human rights, including freedom of speech and minority rights, as well as general reform initiatives.

The reforms that began with Turgut Özal in the 1980s were interrupted when an Islamist party came to office in 1996 in a coalition and then was ousted by a "postmodern" coup a year later. The 2002 elections brought to power its more moderate successor, the Justice and Development Party (AKP), which garnered enough seats to rule without coalition partners. The AKP owes its success partly to other parties' loss of legitimacy as well as to its own pro-EU, pro-reform, and pro-economic liberalism platform. The AKP received strong support from reform-minded democrats and from the business community, which had suffered greatly during the economic crisis of 2001. Turkey had endured a string of no fewer than seven tumultuous coalition governments stretching back to 1983. This degree of political instability is deadly to investment; as a result, the Turkish economy tottered along a roller coaster track—though on average, in the decade between 1991 and 2001 annual real GDP growth averaged 3.7 percent. The AKP heavily promoted and then successfully implemented the economic recovery program introduced in

March 2001 by former World Bank vice president and later economy minister Kemal Dervis. In 2004, inflation fell to single digits for the first time since 1976. Average growth during the AKP's first five years in office was 7.4 percent. Following a fairly strong five-year record of economic performance, the AKP was returned to office in July 2007 with an unprecedented 47 percent of the vote.

Most importantly, the AKP campaigned on themes of hope and optimism for the future. Clearly, the opening of EU accession talks made Turkey attractive to foreign investment, and overall global market trends certainly helped. But what is most significant is that the AKP government showed unprecedented openness to privatization. Business interests were pleased with the AKP's pro-EU policies and the boost that they gave to international investment. Liberal democrats also looked to EU norms and saw Turkey's future rightful place as being within the European Union. Even though the European Union's favorability rating among Turks has wavered—going from some 58 percent in 2004 to 27 percent in 2007, and roughly 41 percent in late 2008—businesspeople, liberals, and Islamists still consider the European Union one of their best levers against what they see as the rigid Kemalist establishment.[1]

The AKP has also been most eager to integrate the traditionally marginalized Kurds and Islamists into the mainstream—as part of what the government has declared to be a much-needed process of "normalization." Following the arrest of PKK leader Abdullah Ocalan in 1999, there were attempts at extending wider political and cultural rights to ethnic Kurds. Then–Prime Minister Mesut Yılmaz went so far as to declare "the road to the European Union goes through Diyarbakır." During a landmark August 2005 visit to Diyarbakır, Prime Minister Erdogan broke further ground in forthrightly stating that Turkey has a "Kurdish problem" that could only be solved by "more democracy, more civil rights, and more prosperity." Kurds were pleased by the premier's apparent recognition that the issue transcended the terrorism and national security concerns with which it was usually framed. Many of them voted for the AKP in 2007 elections. In addition, for the first time since 1991, a pro-Kurdish party (Kurdish Democratic Society Party—DTP) was able to gain a position in the Grand National Assembly—at a time when Turkish patience with PKK terrorism had reached its limits.

The third and most important support base for the AKP has come from a nexus of devout Muslims and Islamists. Disappointed in the AKP's first term, they wanted "one of their own" to be elected president, and expected the party during its second term to deliver on unfulfilled promises—above all, constitutional changes to permit women to wear the Islamic headscarf.

As concerns arose about AKP having a "hidden Islamist agenda," mass demonstrations took place against the election of an AKP president that would extend the party's power to full control over the executive and the legislature along with the ability to influence the judiciary, effectively putting an end to the separation of powers. Following the military's so-called e-coup, which backfired, the soldiers took a low profile. The most memorable slogan of these rallies—"No *shari'a*, no coup!"—perfectly summed up the two poles pulling the country apart and the desire of the majority for a democratic consensus. In 2007, the main split was between those whose greatest fear was the threat to democracy (from a military coup) and those whose greatest fear was the threat to secularism (from the Islamists).[2]

The Islamist base was emboldened after the July election results and chose confrontation instead of compromise on a number of issues. A president with an Islamist past, Abdullah Gul, was chosen right after the parliamentary elections—thus opening a new chapter in Turkey's democratic evolution. For the first time, the Turkish Republic has both a president and a prime minister from Islamist backgrounds whose wives wear the Islamic headscarf. With no time to digest such a major change, the AKP commissioned the drafting of a new constitution. While many people wanted to see a new "civilian" constitution eventually replace the one drafted by the military after its 1980 coup, the timing and the process aroused concerns about a religious agenda. In the event, AKP focused heavily on the headscarf issue, neglecting other significant reform proposals, including on issues of concern to liberal Muslims. For example, the Alevi community, some 20 percent of Turkey's population, has been mostly ignored; Alevi children still have no choice but to follow the Sunni religious curriculum. Civil liberties such as freedom to dissent came under increasing attack from nationalist circles, civil service promotions appeared to be based increasingly on piety rather than merit, and more and more establishments stopped serving alcohol to prove their Islamic credentials—an anathema for secular Turks.

In March 2008, Turkey's chief prosecutor filed a case with the Constitutional Court, charging that AKP had become "a center of anti-secular activities" and asking that AKP be shut down and seventy-one of its members banned from elected office for five years. In June the court overturned the controversial headscarf law. But contrary to domestic and international expectations, on July 30, 2008, the court opted to sanction rather than close AKP. A further closure case is pending against the Kurdish DTP, accused of praising and aiding the PKK and also of serving as "a center of activities aimed at damaging the independence of the state and the indivisible integrity of its territory and nation." The threat of an AKP closure provoked a complex debate inside and outside Turkey about norms and practices, especially in the context of Turkey's EU candidacy. The consensus among observers across the spectrum is that the deeper social and political divisions behind the political crises of 2007–2008 are unlikely to be resolved by the July 2008 verdict. The potential for further political and legal clashes over secularism remains very real.

In recent years, the nationalists and the AKP have found themselves on opposite sides of almost all of Turkey's most sensitive issues. As the AKP's position has often been aligned with that of the West, anti-AKP groups evolved into anti-Western ones. Some key points of contention have included the AKP's willingness to reopen the Greek Orthodox seminary in Halki (secular nationalists fear this will set a precedent for opening new Islamic institutions outside the control of the state), and the AKP's acceptance of the Annan Plan for Cyprus—a deal that nationalists view as a "sellout" of Turkish interests.

As ethnic and religious identities become bigger drivers of politics (and conflict) the world over, Turkey is in the midst of a clash of its multiple identities; the outcome of this battle will shape the nature of its international "stakeholdership." One clash is between Western and Islamic identities, with the Islamic periphery coming to the center, and Islamists gaining influence in many Muslim societies. In addition, Turkey's strong state is also challenged by forces of globalization, which benefit transnational Islamist groups among others. In the short term, there is likely to be a continued backlash from the secular and nationalist establishment, and this will certainly not lead to a more liberal political culture.[3]

The prevailing mood of Turkish nationalism and xenophobia is reflected in the latest Pew poll results.[4] Those with a positive view toward the United States stand at 12 percent—up from 9 percent in 2007, but still the lowest in the world. Those with a negative with toward the United States stand at 77 percent. The percentage of Turks who consider the United States an "enemy" stands at 70 percent, and only 8 percent consider it to be "partner." By way of comparison, 60 percent of Pakistanis, 39 percent Egyptians, and 34 percent Russians consider the United States to be an "enemy." These figures, worrisome in their own right, take on added significance in light of the steadily growing role of public opinion in Turkish foreign policy—a point of convergence with Western societies.

## Geostrategy with a Diversified Portfolio

With relatively few exceptions, Turkish foreign policy has been essentially moderate, predictable, and multilateral. A highly professional and well-respected diplomatic service has also enabled Turkey to "punch above its weight" in many settings. Outside of some rarefied liberal circles, the notion of international relations as a source of public goods is not central to the Turkish debate. Turkish foreign policy is much closer to the realist approach, with a healthy dose of suspicion and ambivalence toward the other players thrown in. But even these concerns about identity and orientation have prompted Turks to keep an eye on the country's international reputation and on opportunities to play a constructive regional role. This component of Turkish foreign policy has expanded in recent years—a process that started with the Özal government's forward-leaning stance in the 1990–1991 Gulf War coalition.

The AKP government took this approach several steps further by broadening the scope of Turkish foreign policy to build closer relations with the Arab and Muslim worlds, and Eurasia. Leading advisors in the AKP government, notably Ahmet Davutoglu, have argued for a policy of "strategic depth," balancing relations with the West and immediate neighbors with new relationships, mainly economic and political, further afield.[5] This policy has had its controversial aspects, most notably in Ankara's close contacts with Hamas and Iran. In August 2008, Iranian President Ahmadinejad made a controversial, high-profile visit to Istanbul. The visit had little tangible significance, but AKP supporters and detractors alike trumpeted the symbolism of the event. Other steps have been more positively received, including Turkey's ongoing role as a facilitator in negotiations between Jerusalem and Damascus, and between Israel and Lebanon's Hezbollah. Sometimes, though, this desire to act as interlocutor can seem ill-considered or haphazard, as in the widely criticized visit of the Sudanese president to Ankara in January 2008.

Turkey values its self-described role as a "bridge" between continents and cultures, and within limits, seeks a leadership role in international initiatives around this theme. Turkey co-chairs, with Spain, the UN-sponsored Alliance of Civilizations, and the AKP government has been more eager than its predecessors to embrace the country's Islamic, Middle Eastern, and Eurasian identities, alongside engagement with the West. Without question, the Turkish public has become more interested in international questions affecting Muslim interests—most notably the Palestinian issue, but also in Chechnya and the Balkans.

While officials in Washington and Europe have generally been keen to see Turkey play the role of civilizational interlocutor, it is a role that makes many members of Turkey's secular foreign policy establishment profoundly uncomfortable. For these traditional elites, a new emphasis on relations to the south and east can only come at the expense of Turkey's Western orientation.

## Turkey's Immediate and Extended Neighborhoods

Since 2002, Turkey has also embarked on a policy of "zero problems with neighbors." More a slogan than a fully operational policy, it nonetheless captures a trend toward relaxation of traditionally tense relations with neighbors such as Bulgaria and Syria. Even more significant has been the rapprochement between Ankara and Athens, breaking with a long history of confrontation stretching back to the birth of modern Greece and Turkey. The détente followed a period of dramatic brinksmanship over the Aegean and Cyprus in the 1990s. The initial political opening was engineered by Turkish Foreign Minister Ismail Cem and his Greek counterpart Andreas Papandreou following the "earthquake diplomacy" of 1999, and has been reinforced by successive governments in both countries. The internationally minded Greek and Turkish business communities have also played an important role, alongside military leaderships keen on risk reduction and, in the case of Turkey, eager to focus on threats from other quarters. The backdrop for this Aegean détente has been Turkey's European candidacy, and observers now worry that rising nationalism and friction in relations between Ankara and Brussels could erode the progress of recent years.

Turkish external policy beyond the Aegean shows a combination of tendencies—generally cautious and favoring the preservation of the territorial and political status quo, but with some persistent frictions and occasional forays into intervention and unilateralism. To Western eyes, Cyprus has, for instance, been the setting for some of the most problematic Turkish behavior. Turkey's 1974 military intervention may have protected the Turkish population of the island from absorption and abuse, as Ankara has asserted, but it also left in its wake a permanent Turkish military presence and a political entity, the "Turkish Republic of Northern Cyprus," recognized (and subsidized) only by Turkey. Other repercussions of this show of force included the imposition of UN sanctions, a U.S. arms embargo, and decades of congressionally mandated scrutiny.

Cyprus has been a nationalist cause par excellence for Turks, and the Cyprus problem continues to bedevil Turkish relations with Europe. Indeed, notwithstanding an improved situation on the island itself, the costs of the Cyprus issue have arguably grown, rising to a strategic scale, particularly as Turkey has become a candidate for EU membership. Cyprus is now a political rather than a security question for Turkey and others. It is also a focal point for the tension between Turkish nationalism and the requirements of integration with Europe. Ankara may regard the accession talks with Europe as a negotiation, a search for a mutually agreeable solution, but, in fact, Turkish accession is contingent on the assent of other EU members, including the

Republic of Cyprus—in other words, a nonnegotiable item and a *sine qua non* for membership. As it seeks the proper balance between national interest and international responsibility, Turkey is still burdened with the costly legacy of 1974. Ankara's willingness to make further compromises in the interest of a Cyprus settlement will thus be a key specific "milepost" for Turkey over the next decade.

Other neuralgic aspects of Turkish policy concern relations with Armenia, Syria, and Iraq. Together with the Cyprus dispute, the debate over the history of the Armenian "genocide" has been among the most problematic points of friction between Turkish policy and international opinion. The Turkish narrative regarding the events of 1915 and the years following still contrasts strongly with perceptions in Europe and Canada, where several parliaments have adopted Armenian genocide resolutions, some with legal force. In the United States, the annual congressional debate over the issue has strategic as well as normative dimensions. While successive U.S. presidential administrations have been sensitive to the threat such resolutions pose toward bilateral relations, there is growing awareness within Congress of what is at stake, given Turkey's vital logistical contribution to operations in Iraq and Afghanistan, and in assistance to Georgia.

On the ground, the border with Armenia remains closed, if rather porous. Bilateral political dialogue between Ankara and Yerevan has been vociferously opposed by the Armenian diaspora—even as Turkey's own debate over the Armenian question actually has become more active and open. Turkish President Gul even visited Yerevan in September 2008 at the invitation of his counterpart, officially to watch the soccer match of their national teams. This first ever visit to Armenia by a Turkish president has created optimism among the liberals who hope for the establishment of bilateral relations. Yet the Armenian issue, in both its historical and contemporary dimensions, remains a leading obstacle to the liberalization of Turkey's international posture, and will be another test of Turkey's evolution in the coming years.

Until very recently, Turkey has tended to see the Middle East more as an area of risk than opportunity.[6] The Kurdish issue remains the principal lens for Turkish perceptions of the region, particularly for policy toward Iraq, Syria, and, to an extent, Iran. The PKK insurgency and counterinsurgency led to some forty thousand deaths on all sides in the 1990s and the displacement of large numbers of people. This searing experience contributes to the continued focus on PKK violence and the existence of safe havens for insurgent activity across the border in northern Iraq.

In the 1990s, Syria was the leading supporter of the PKK, the leadership of which was based in Damascus. In 1998, at the height of Turkey's confrontation with Syria over the PKK, Ankara openly threatened large-scale military operations if the Assad regime did not close down the PKK presence (it did). This episode illustrated Turkey's willingness to act unilaterally where its security, and especially internal security, was at stake. Since 2003, northern Iraq has been the focal point for Turkish concerns about the PKK and Kurdish separatism. Despite the large-scale Turkish economic presence in northern Iraq, the idea of an independent Kurdistan remains a "red line" issue for Turkey, at least as a matter of declared policy. The international community's stance toward the future fate of Kirkuk is therefore seen as critically important. In the 1990s, Turkish forces launched a series of ground and air operations across the border to create a security zone to fend off PKK infiltrations (Israeli strategy in southern Lebanon was a model). In 2007–2008, Turkey has conducted further cross-border strikes—although on a smaller scale, and with the tacit approval of the United States.

Ankara is well aware of the negative reaction these operations have sparked in Europe and the United States, but the high stakes for Turkey's internal security and the neuralgic Kurdish issue has placed the government and the military establishment under strong pressure to act, regardless of international sentiment. Looking ahead, it is hard to imagine that Turkey's sensitivity to security risks emanating from northern Iraq will diminish, barring a comprehensive approach to the Kurdish problem in Turkey and the region—the sort of grand bargain advocated by some Western and a few Turkish analysts. Arrangements of this kind could well involve international guarantees, and possibly a role for NATO or other institutions in monitoring the border: all representing significant sovereignty compromises for Ankara.

It is worth stressing the singular nature of Turkish policy where the Kurdish issue is concerned. These are issues on which Turkish nationalism and national interest are at their most intense. The Kurdish dimension is perceived as "existential" for the Turkish state and society. (Cyprus, while still an emotive issue, is no longer in this category for most Turks. This may be because the issue has been frozen for some time. Cyprus could once again become a major issue, if, for example, NATO accession talks begin.)

The Iraq war illustrates other aspects of Turkey's perspective on international stakeholdership as well. Turkey's failure to agree with Washington on the opening of a northern front in Iraq in 2003 stemmed from a combination of political mismanagement in Ankara, a clash of negotiating styles, and American failure to convince strategic elites in Turkey. It is also clear that Turkish public opinion, as in Europe, played a part; both were deeply opposed to the war. The absence of a UN or NATO mandate further complicated Turkish decision-making. Turkish thinking and behavior might have been quite different against the backdrop of a solid international mandate (as in 1990). For Turkey as a regional stakeholder, American efforts to "shake things up" in the Middle East, through regime change or vigorous democratization efforts, run contrary to Ankara's interest in stability and the territorial status quo in the neighborhood.

The Turkish perspective on Iran reflects similar concerns. Turkish security elites are concerned about Iran's nuclear ambitions, and some observers worry about the export of Iran's revolutionary Islamic ideology. But regime change is far from the Turkish mind, and Ankara has a long tradition of peaceful relations with Iran, including significant economic ties. While Ankara is concerned about the rising Iranian influence in the region, Turks often mention that their long border with Iran has remained unchanged since 1639. Ankara is also increasingly inclined to cooperate directly with Tehran in Kurdish matters, including coordinated strikes against the PKK (and PJAK). Therefore Turkish policy toward Iran is likely to remain firmly in the European mainstream—with a strong preference for engagement over confrontation.

In the Balkans, the Turkish approach will probably continue to be shaped by affinity politics and cautious multilateralism. During the 1990s, and through successive Balkan crises, Turkey emerged as a far more prudent and constructive actor than many in the United States and Europe imagined. In the Bosnian crisis, where Turkish affinities with Bosnian Muslims were involved, American policymakers were especially concerned that conflict along religious lines could pull Greece and Turkey into the fray. In the event, no such spillover occurred. Both Athens and Ankara demonstrated a marked preference for working within an international framework, and both contributed to multinational peacekeeping and humanitarian operations. This remains the Turkish approach to the region, with Ankara playing a leading role in NATO and regional security initiatives. Notably, Ankara extended diplomatic recognition to Kosovo, despite the associated precedent with regard to borders and self-determination—a sensitivity Turkey shares with Russia and others. Affinity with the Muslim Kosovars is part of the explanation; the existence of a general European and Western consensus on the issue is another. Here again, international opinion plays an important role in Turkish thinking.

## Energy Security and a Modern "Silk Road"

A similar calculus operates with regard to the Black Sea, the Caucasus, and Central Asia, tempered by even sharper sovereignty concerns. Turkey has been a leader in supporting the development of strong regional organizations in this area, most notably Black Sea Economic Cooperation (BSEC, headquartered in Istanbul), and in Black Sea Harmony, a maritime collaboration with Russia and others. Ankara has been firmly resistant, though, to any expanded role for extra-regional powers, for instance opposing the extension of NATO's Operation Active Endeavor (in the Mediterranean) to the Black Sea. Looking ahead, Turkey could be quite open to a Turkish-Russian condominium for the region, with strict attention to the existing legal regime governing passage through the Turkish Straits. That said, Turkey has welcomed, even sought, international opinion and organizations as part of is campaign to limit the environmental consequences of increased tanker traffic through the Bosporus.

In the Caucasus, Turkey has a long-standing special relationship with Azerbaijan. The two countries share so many historic, cultural, religious, and ethnic links that they often refer to each other as "one nation, two states." Turkey closed its Armenian border during the war between Azerbaijan and Armenia over Nagorno-Karabakh in 1993, and is unlikely to open it until the conflict progresses toward resolution.

Bilateral relations with Azerbaijan were really solidified with cooperation on two new major oil and gas pipelines to carry Azeri hydrocarbons to Turkey via Georgia. Turkey looks toward expansion and extension of regional energy pipelines, especially penetrating further into European markets, in order to become a major energy hub. The Russian invasion of Georgia, and the prospect of heightened Russian-Western friction, certainly clouds the prospects for new projects of this kind.

These pipelines are but one element of a wider vision for an east-west "new Silk Road" corridor including highway, railway, and pipeline connections from Central Asia to Europe via Turkey. The transportation of Azeri and Central Asian (mainly Kazakh and Turkmen) energy to Europe is nonetheless at the core of this vision. There is already a line connecting Turkey with Greece, and it will be further extended to Italy in the coming years. There is also a massive gas pipeline project called Nabucco that would stretch from Turkey to Austria, passing through Bulgaria, Romania, and Hungary. This pipeline could contribute significantly toward the European Union's energy diversification strategy and would reinforce Turkey's interdependence with Europe. Georgian stability and sovereignty—now in question—have been seen as critical for the east-west corridor, and Turkey has supported the notion of Georgian and Ukrainian membership in NATO.[7]

Nor Turkey does want to limit its efforts to east-west pipelines; it is also actively cooperating with Russia, Iran, Iraq, and Egypt to transport their gas to European markets. While Turkey's increased energy cooperation with Iraq (especially the Kurdish region) is widely praised, its burgeoning partnership with Iran and Russia raises eyebrows in both Europe and the United States.

The Turkish approach to relations with Moscow is complex and informed by a long history of geopolitical competition and mutual wariness. The economic relationship with Russia, both energy and nonenergy, has burgeoned over the last fifteen years—Russia is now Turkey's largest trading partner—and this has been accompanied by an expanded political relationship. Some Turkish strategists even argue for a strategic relationship with Moscow as preferable to what they view as hollow and unpredictable ties to the West. It should be quickly added that this is still a minority, even eccentric, view. Turkey has a long-term stake in reassurance and deterrence vis-à-vis Moscow, especially given current uncertainties regarding relations between Russia and the West. In the wake of the Russian operations in Georgia, a more confrontational Russian posture would only reinforce the Turkish need for a predictable NATO guarantee, as any new east-west competition would likely unfold in Turkey's immediate vicinity this time around.

The Turkey-Russia relationship actually offers prospects for convergence in their posture toward "stakeholdership," on the grounds of their common nationalist/realist approach and the search for an alternative to Western liberalism on the one hand, and unfettered globalization on the other. As a matter of shared historical roots and evolution, the Leninist and Kemalist systems emerged at roughly the same time with some similar characteristics, including a statist policy bent and a tough-minded approach to sovereignty questions. The potential combination of a hollow EU candidacy, estrangement from the United States, and a continued rise of nationalist sentiment in Turkey (and elsewhere) could propel a drift away from Western values and institutions, and even a growing affinity for Moscow. A more confrontational relationship between Russia and the West could pose difficult dilemmas for Turkey, with growing tension between the country's economic and security interests, and sharply competing visions of Turkish identity and orientation.

The two already share concern about U.S.-backed "color revolutions" across Eurasia and the broader Middle East. Both are traditionally status quo powers and dislike change—especially if change runs counter to their interests or promotes instability of a more general kind. At the same time, leaders in both countries (Putin and Erdogan) have shown new activism in their neighborhood. Russia would like Turkey, for instance, to join the Shanghai Cooperation Organization (SCO) as an observer. While Ankara has stayed away from the SCO thus far, a growing number of Turks seem to view the SCO countries as more aligned with Turkey's interests than either the United States or the European Union is. They call for a close partnership with Russia coupled with a strong but pragmatic policy in Eurasia, giving priority to economic ties over pan-Turkic sentiment. This new Russo-Turkish rapprochement and partnership in Eurasia holds an appeal for some conservative Islamist groups, secular nationalists, and as well as members of the millitary leadership. In this vein, retired General Tuncay Kilinc, a former secretary-general of the National Security Council, even said that "Turkey should quit NATO" and he singled out Russia as Turkey's most logical strategic partner. The Turkish discussion on these questions is set to become more pointed and difficult after the August 2008 Georgia crisis—and in light of looming debates about NATO's strategic concept, relations with Russia, and the costs and benefits of further enlargement.

## The West, Turkey, and Its Alternatives

The overwhelming thrust of Turkish strategy since the end of World War II has been to align with the West, via membership in NATO, a close strategic relationship with Washington, and aspiration to full membership in the European Union. The durability of these ties over the next decade will be a key factor determining Turkey's commitment to responsible international stakeholdership, informed by Western norms. Turkey's EU prospects may well be the most critical factor. The long-term and open-ended nature of the accession path offered to Turkey and growing ambivalence on all sides cast real doubts over Turkey's prospects for full membership. The pace and extent of reform in Turkey is one factor in the equation. The evolution of the European Union is another. A tighter, more integrated Europe—tired of costly new enlargements and with close attention to norms and behavior—will be a tough Europe for Turkey to join. A looser, multispeed European Union tolerant of a range of political practices will be an easier fit for Ankara. Overall, the future of Turkish convergence with Europe in key sectors (norms, practices, policies) may be more important than the question of membership per se. Few observers in Turkey or the West would disagree that "Europe" has been a key incentive for change in Turkey's internal and external behavior.

Europe's critique of Turkish behavior will likely continue to focus on internal developments and deviations from accepted European norms. The AKP closure case episode illustrated this concern, as does the controversy over the infamous article 301 on insults to "Turkishness." With the notable exception of Cyprus, Europe is much less inclined to criticize Turkey's foreign policy behavior. On the contrary, periodic European Commission reviews underscore the close alignment between Turkish and European policies. On Iran, the Middle East peace process, Iraq, the Balkans, and other issues, Turkey is very much in the European mainstream, and often far closer to Brussels than to Washington.

The relationship with the United States, seen as strategic on both sides, has experienced marked but not unprecedented strain since 2003. These strains have been extensively analyzed and debated in Turkey and the United States.[8] They are the product of proximate policy disagreements, most notably on Iraq, as well as structural problems in a relationship predicated on security and strategic real estate rather than true partnership based on affinity and shared values. Public opinion has been another key element. Public sentiment matters in contemporary Turkish policymaking, and as noted above, this sentiment has turned starkly anti-American in recent years. As striking, and perhaps more consequential, has been the deterioration in elite attitudes toward U.S. leadership, and the deepening suspicion among Turks of diverse background.

What has filled this vacuum of alliance and affinity? Polling and much anecdotal evidence suggests that this "space" has been filled in part by rising Turkish nationalism and a more inward-looking disposition. Turks have become more suspicious of the international community as a whole: Americans, Israelis, and Europeans, above all, but also Russians, Iranians, and even Palestinians.[9] Turks are intently focused on their own questions of identity, religion, class, and power, and these long-simmering tensions are unlikely to be resolved any time soon. The result may be a distracted and less engaged Turkey—a less active and responsible stakeholder by default rather than inclination.

Since September 11, and especially after the Iraq war, the Islamic coloration of Turkish perceptions and policy has increased. There is a widespread awareness now among Turks of their Islamic identity, culture, and norms. With the United States increasingly seen by Turks as a negative and less influential force, and with the European Union focused on its own identity and enlargement issues, Turkey has stepped up its diplomacy across the former lands of the Ottoman Empire. Almost all the ethnic groups of the Middle East, Balkans, the Caucasus, and Central Asia are also significantly represented within Turkey's own population. Davutoglu and other AKP advisors argue that any instability in these regions is consequential for Turkey, requiring Ankara's active commitment to regional security and development. The underlying objective is to boost Turkey's influence as an "independent" actor and recognized interlocutor for the Muslim east and south. Turkey's recent activism in the OIC and other Islamic groups is a clear element of this strategy (in 2005, the OIC elected its first Turkish secretary-general).

One prominent Turkish foreign policy analyst has characterized Turkey's entrepreneurial diplomacy with Lebanon, Hezbollah, Syria, and Israel as "the return of the Ottomans."[10] For Davutoglu and other members of the neo-Ottoman school, the main argument against joining directly in the Iraq war was that Turkey should not be aligned with powers that would inevitably be perceived as occupiers. He considers this strategy to have paid off. Similarly, Turkey's initiative to bring Israel and Syria together has shown that at a time when the United States is not able to exert effective influence in the region, countries like Turkey can go their own way to good effect.[11] Influential Turks close to AKP as well as nationalist circles are becoming convinced that the norms and institutions defined by the West during the Cold War are no longer working and outmoded for an emerging international order in which Asia, the Muslim world, and the global south are gaining much greater influence. In other words, Turks who aspire to a leading role in this new—less Western than before—geopolitical order will be working with a different concept of stakeholdership.

## How Ankara Looks at Threat Assessment

Turkey is a security-conscious state, and the security dimension weighs heavily in Turkey's international calculus. As noted above, Turkey does not shrink from using its substantial military strength unilaterally in the Middle East, but has adopted a much more cautious and multilateral posture elsewhere. The Turkish approach to the use of force carries broad international significance, though, not least because Turkey's ability to project power and the breadth of its diplomatic reach extend its influence across several critical regions.

Turkey will continue to value its NATO membership, including the nuclear guarantee and article V commitments. Nonetheless, Turks worry about the credibility of the NATO commitment in relation to the extra-European and nontraditional risks they confront. The slow NATO response to Turkish requests for air defense reinforcements in both Iraq wars has, however, left a bitter residue of doubt and mistrust. Because Turkish contingencies are so prominent in contemporary NATO planning, and most of these contingencies have focused on the country's Middle Eastern borders, Ankara has favored revisions to the NATO strategic concept to enhance the Alliance's ability to act rapidly outside Europe. After initial ambivalence, Turkey has also emerged as a supporter of NATO enlargement, in the belief that a wider NATO will stabilize areas on the periphery of Europe—i.e., Turkey's neighborhood. The experience of Russian military intervention in Georgia could serve as a spur to renewed emphasis on core NATO article V commitments and the capacity for territorial defense.

Turkey is also the NATO member most affected by proliferation trends in the Middle East, with Iranian and Syrian missile programs a particular concern. Most Turkish population centers are within reach of Syrian and Iranian missiles. Turkey's well-developed strategic relationship with Israel, expanded in earnest in the 1990s, was aimed largely at the containment of Syria, then a major backer of the PKK. Turkish-Israeli cooperation has included intelligence sharing and air defense coordination in relation to Iranian WMD risks as well as extensive defense industrial cooperation. Absent a direct threat to Turkish territory, Ankara is highly unlikely to help with any Israeli or American strikes against Iranian WMD facilities, but Turkish strategists might quietly favor such an action.

For decades, Turkey has lived with nuclear weapons on its borders, and the Turkish reaction to the prospect of a nuclear or near-nuclear Iran tends to be restrained. But Turkish concern is mounting, not least because of the potential for one or more new nuclear powers in the region to profoundly alter the strategic equation, with cascading effects on military perceptions and balances in multiple directions. Turkey is unlikely to respond to a nuclear Iran by pursuing a nuclear capability of its own—as long as the NATO guarantee remains credible—even though the country possesses the technical wherewithal to pursue a weapons program.

Détente with Athens has eased a major challenge for Alliance cohesion in the eastern Mediterranean, and Ankara retains a strong stake in NATO membership as a hedge against high-end threats emanating from Russia and the Middle East. Turkey has also been a good NATO "citizen" with regard to peacekeeping operations in the Balkans and Afghanistan. In other respects, Turkey's position is more complex and less helpful to Alliance objectives. Most notably, Ankara continues to obstruct closer defense coordination between NATO and the European Union in protest over Turkey's exclusion from European Security and Defense Policy (ESDP) decision-making. It is also strongly opposed to Cyprus becoming a NATO member without prior resolution of the island's status. These situations are added signs of Turkey's incomplete integration, and its effect on Turkey's own strategic perceptions and behavior. The vexed matter of Turkey's EU candidacy, and the potential for further estrangement from Europe, suggest that the standoff over NATO-ESDP cooperation will persist for some time to come.

Over the next decade, Turkey's security priorities are likely to be driven by more tangible concerns such as counterterrorism and irregular warfare. Turkey has not been immune to the threat of Islamic extremism, as bombings and assassinations in Istanbul and elsewhere attest (most notably the 2003 bombings of the British consulate, a synagogue, and the headquarters of HSBC in Istanbul). Homegrown groups such as Turkish Hizbollah, as well as networks with al-Qaeda links are active within Turkey, although heavily monitored and contained by the Turkish security services. The return of jihadists from Iraq and Afghanistan in the coming years could also affect the security situation in Turkey and elsewhere. Turkey continues to face a low-level terrorist threat from extreme leftist and nationalist networks as well. More serious, especially in terms of Turkey's European ties, has been the growth of diverse criminal networks involved in drug smuggling and human trafficking.

Foremost, the absence of a comprehensive approach to the Kurdish problem suggests that Turkey will continue to face a threat from the PKK or related groups. This threat is unlikely to be eradicated without the close cooperation of Kurdish leaders in northern Iraq, where the local Kurdish leadership has shown little inclination to incur the costs of closing down PKK operations on their side of the border. As a result, Turkey will likely be in the counterinsurgency business for some time to come, and the containment of the PKK and its offshoots will be difficult or impossible without substantial help from Turkey's allies. The European Union will be critical to curtailing PKK fundraising and organization, much of which takes place in Europe. The U.S. will be key on the intelligence and operations side of the equation in Iraq. Iran, too, will be an important partner for Ankara. In short, the leading security challenges facing Turkey over the next decade will require a considerable degree of engagement with international partners. National approaches by themselves are unlikely to suffice.

## Turkey and Globalization

Despite strong opposition from nationalist rivals, the AKP government has advanced Özal's program of large-scale privatization, and has generally emphasized economic engagement in regional and global settings. In addition to a steady flow of European investment, in recent years Turkey has attracted unprecedented levels of investment from Arab states, especially from Qatar, the UAE, and Saudi Arabia.

The groups that have benefited most visibly from AKPs liberal economic policies are those from Anatolia, and small- and medium-size enterprises from Turkey's heartland have forged partnerships with companies all over the world—Africa, Latin America, Japan, and China. This can also be seen as a risk diversification strategy: if talks with the European Union come to a halt, then Turkey may reconsider the Customs Union agreement, which has served as a constraint on Turkish business outreach and strategic partnerships. In addition to forming regional free trade zones and joining existing organizations, there is also talk of Turkish participation in a proposed trans-Atlantic free trade agreement (TAFTA).

Turkish small- and medium-scale businesses, and new NGOs, have all taken full advantage of globalization to help build Turkey's soft power. Through economic and cultural links, Turkey's influence and standing is growing throughout many parts of the world. Turkish television draws audiences across Eurasia and the Middle East and in the Turkish diaspora in Europe. The schools that Islamic cultural groups such as the Gulen movement have established throughout the world focus on the spread of a Turko-Islamic worldview. In 2008, the sixth Turkic Olympics were held in Istanbul with participation from 110 countries. Students, mostly from Gulen schools, demonstrated their Turkish language skills and their knowledge of Turkish folk culture.

This new soft power is reverberating, above all, through South and Central Asia. Turkey is taking a lead role in reconstruction efforts in Afghanistan and helping improve Pakistan-Afghanistan relations via economic cooperation along the border. Turkish troops are not deployed in combat zones like Helmand province, instead focusing on building infrastructure and supporting health and administrative services. Turkey and Pakistan are close political partners, often taking common positions in international platforms such as the United Nations and OIC. With India, too, Turkey recently established a strategic partnership—and there is growing Indian investment in the Turkish energy sector. The possibility of sending oil from Kazakhstan and Azerbaijan via the existing Baku-Tbilisi-Ceyhan or the planned Samsun-Ceyhan oil pipeline and onward via Ashkalon to India is being discussed.

Under AKP, Turkey is opening entirely new frontiers of economic partnership. Foreign Minister Ali Babacan explained to an American audience that in 2007 it became an official "Strategic Partner" to the African Union, and Turkey is planning to open fifteen new embassies in sub-Saharan Africa.[12]

Turkish businesses see Brazil as a gateway for increased ties with the rest of Latin America. Ankara hopes that its support of Brazil's bid for permanent UN Security Council membership will be repaid with Brazil's support for its own campaign for a rotating seat. A similar gambit is being tried in East Asia with Japan. In all these regions obtaining support for its UN Security Council membership bid also played a significant role in expanding business and cultural links.

In the years since the AKP assumed power in 2002, economic growth has averaged 7.5 percent. Inflation has fallen from 70 percent to just below 10 percent. The net public debt ratio has been cut in half, and banking system indicators have improved. Turkey's GNP is now around $400bn. Sustained growth boosted the country's per capita income to an impressive $5,000. A successful privatization program not only reduced government spending, but also brought additional revenues, significantly shrinking the budget deficit and public debt. Foreign investment also rose from $6 billion to over $100 billion during the AKP government's tenure. These results are mostly the product of aggressive reforms anchored to Turkey's application for EU membership and its loan program with the IMF. Like other emerging markets, Turkey has benefited from a strong world economy and favorable external financing conditions—both questionable in the years ahead.

All that said, any future economic stability and growth will be closely linked to continuing political stability, progress in EU accession talks, and keeping a lid on domestic and foreign debt during a downward global cycle. Rising oil and food prices, a return of inflation, and slower growth could pose the most serious threats to the Turkish economy. The global economic slowdown that began in the summer of 2007 has already affected the Turkish economy negatively: GDP growth dropped to 4.5 percent in 2007 and is forecast to dip further, to 3 percent, in 2008. The rapidly growing current account deficit, which ballooned due to the expansionary fiscal policy of the past few years, as well as the mounting trade deficit, has heightened Turkey's vulnerability to global shocks. Turkey continues to attract large inflows of "hot" money, but, given the nature of this capital, any elevation of political risk and deteriorating external conditions could trigger a quick liquidation of assets held in Turkish lira. Such conditions could bring the boom in Turkish prosperity and globalization to a screeching halt.

### The Diverging Roads Ahead

Looking ahead, Turkey will likely remain a responsible international stakeholder, however flawed and ambivalent on occasion. Turkey's foreign and security policy outlook strikes a careful balance between an essentially national and realist approach and a long-standing concern for the country's Western identity and reputation, along with a basic commitment to international norms. At the same time, Turkey seeks to update these norms to reflect the interests of the Muslim world and the "south" more broadly. Regardless of its orientation, Turkey will almost certainly continue as an essentially conservative, status quo nation rather than a revolutionary actor in international affairs.

The most problematic aspect of the Turkish case concerns the country's internal evolution and governance, rather than its foreign and security policy. With the exception of Cyprus and northern Iraq, it is Turkey's internal social and political struggle, and the haphazard progress toward European standards of democratization and governance, that inhibit Turkey's full participation in an international liberal order. More narrowly, these same factors will determine the European and American response to Turkey, and potentially limit Turkish integration within Western institutions such as the European Union. Many of the key "mileposts" over the next decade will, thus, be internal—including civil-military relations, the Kurdish issue, and resolution of the country's deepening religious-secular divide. Externally, Turkish policy on Cyprus, Armenia, and northern Iraq will be the key tests. On Russia, Turkey is apt to be wary and ambivalent toward any harsher NATO policies. On energy, Turkey will pursue its interest in becoming a hub and transit country for Caspian and Middle Eastern energy.

In a grand strategic sense, possible further convergence with the European Union, and ultimately, the outcome of the membership process, will have the most profound effect on Turkey's posture with regard to international norms. Depending on the evolution of Turkish politics and identity over the next decade, Ankara could be drawn to alternative norms and international alignments, possibly centered on Eurasia or the Muslim world. If the country's essentially secular orientation holds, Turkey will almost certainly remain part of the transatlantic community, with external policies informed by Western norms—notwithstanding a balanced Turkish foreign policy with deeper Eurasian engagement. Yet growing Islamic identity in Turkish society and politics could point the country in a different direction, in which case the neo-Ottoman impetus, and its associated values, could become more entrenched and significant in determining external behavior. A more serious risk stems from potentially virulent Turkish nationalism, estrangement from the West, and the emergence of a more sovereignty-conscious, inward-looking Turkey—in short, a fundamental difficulty in undertaking international cooperation and less responsible stakeholdership by default.

## Hüseyin Bağci's Reaction

Indeed, Turkey sees itself as a responsible stakeholder, as Baran and Lesser rightly emphasize. Turkish foreign minister Ali Babacan said as much in a July 2008 major policy speech in which he offered the carefully crafted formulation that Turkey aims to become a global player using her soft power capabilities as a regional hard power.

Turkey's geographic location has always offered strategic advantages, but in the last twenty years it has been particularly effective at making the most of its position as a bridge country in every direction; in the process, it has enhanced its reputation as an internationally responsible actor to a higher level than ever in its modern history. It's true that Turkey is a country faced with complex questions of identity, alignment, and governance, but within these issues also lie significant opportunities.

The pursuit of Turkey's maximal integration internationally remains a cornerstone of Turkish foreign policy, and it is unlikely that any Turkish government in the coming decades will renounce this traditional goal. Turkey's supposedly "urgent" candidacy for the European Union is no longer really expected to succeed, and in a sense is irrelevant since the associated democratic and economic reforms have succeeded enough to acquire their own momentum. The process may have left Turkey in the position of "the other" with regard to Europe, as Baran and Lesser put it, but it is also clear that for the foreseeable future, the European Union needs Turkey as much, if not more, than Turkey needs the European Union. The EU debate over Turkey's candidacy certainly arouses concerns among Turks—and prompted a dramatic decline in Turkish public support for EU membership—but that does not change the fact that Turkey is firmly on a course of convergence with Europe. In the words of an old Turkish proverb, the EU caravan still goes on with Turkey behind it despite the belling dogs.

The authors portray Turkey as a conservative, status quo actor, but that isn't quite accurate. In fact, Turkey is a fast changing, liberal and active player, especially in recent years. The idea of "neo-Ottomanism" in Turkish foreign policy remains more of a fantasy than a real policy option. Turkey's foreign policy ambitions have indeed found a conducive environment, or larger playground, due to regional and global changes, but Turkey's Western drive continues unchanged contrary to expectations that Turkey would adopt more "Islamist" policies. Turkey is not Iran, and, with her involvement in Western institutions from Council of Europe to NATO and many others, will not become like Iran. And while Turkey's new orientation after the end of the Cold War prompted concern among Western countries, Turkey's democratic process made it a model to be emulated rather than feared. Today's Turkey is much more reliable, manageable, and responsible than thirty or twenty or even ten years ago.

It is not an exaggeration to say that there is a new Turkey and new Turks with more management capabilities in domestic as well as in foreign policy matters. Turkey's domestic and economic reforms since the early 1980s under Turgut Özal had a deep impact on the country, engendering strong self-esteem and self-confidence. In the 1990s, Turkey had a series of coalition governments, but the political stability since 2002 under the AKP government has borne fruit, in the economic field particularly. Turkey's exports exceed $136 billion, with a total GDP of more than $600 billion. In a few years Turkey will reach a $1 trillion economy. Globally Turkey is already the world's fifteenth-largest economy, and in sixth place in the European Union.

The second term of the AKP government will be much harder than the first term. Baran and Lesser highlight the problems which AKP will face and, in the process, overestimate the dangers. Turkey's domestic reform and likewise its economic reforms will continue. And whatever role emerges for Islam, Turkey is nowhere near anything resembling *sharia*, which, given the country's social composition, would be impossible. Even the debate on a new constitution has run aground and thus doomed prospects for a new constitution in the foreseeable future. The AKP government is highly pragmatic and is bound to recognize that pressing a religious agenda will only threaten its domestic political survival. The religious views of the AKP government will more likely be "secularized" by the pressure from a strengthening opposition. The 2007 election giving the AKP government a 47 percent plurality was deemed by some observers as a social revolution, but instead of revolution, there are more tensions—brought on by terrorism, corruption cases, and the Constitutional Court's verdict on the AKP's Islamist policies (a ruling that, as the Turkish public suspects, was political rather than juridical).

As to other threats and factors, PKK terrorism remains as the most important problem, with no solution in sight. The current spike in anti-Americanism is superficial and not as deeply rooted as in other countries. There is no enduring tradition of hatred toward the United States, but rather a fluctuation from one U.S. administration to the next (President Clinton was, after all, quite popular). Turkish nationalism is still limited and poses no danger for neighboring countries. Indeed, contrary to expectations or perceptions, Turkish nationalism is not on the rise. That said, however, Turkish nationalism is a given and could at any moment be aroused by PKK terrorism or other provocation.

### Turkey's Foreign Policy

Turkey's foreign policy confronts a wide range of challenges at multiple international levels and from various geographic directions. On the other hand, Turkey's role as a "civilizational bridge" has contributed to Turkey's positive image worldwide; indeed, Washington and Europe consider this role essential for Western-Islamic relations. Baran and Lesser rightly emphasize Turkey's new policy, "zero problem with neighbors," which has significantly changed Turkey's image in the region. Its efforts to serve as an honest broker in several regional conflicts have also enhanced Turkey's image as a peacemaker. Another indication of Turkey's enhanced international stature was its election into the UN Security Council as a nonpermanent member after a forty-seven-year wait.

Even so, a number of concerns linger. Turkey's relations with its neighbors are not yet resolved permanently and are likely to remain so for some time. Time will tell whether the Cyprus issue, Armenian issue, and Syrian-Turkish relations will remain relatively calm or flare up. If nothing else, the uncertain situation in Iraq and the future of the Middle East is increasing Turkey's international stakeholdership. Turkish-Iranian relations are quite good at the moment despite the nuclear issue. Iran is second only to Russia as a source of oil and gas imports. This does not mean the most Turks agree with Iranian policies, but in broad terms, Iran enjoys the highest level of political sympathy since the heyday of former president Hatami's reform push. Also, Turkey and Iran face PKK terrorism as a common threat and they will continue to do so.

In the wider region, the Balkans, Black Sea, Caucasus, and Central Asia will enjoy increased focus in Turkish foreign policy. President Gül is de facto foreign minister and he will develop presidential foreign policy to those regions as the former presidents (with the exception Ahmet Necdet Sezer) such as Turgut Özal and Süleyman Demirel have followed. Indeed there is a strong back-to-the-future element to Turkish policy in those regions—part of a more broadly ambitious geostrategic posture since the end of the Cold War of increased cultural, economic, and political influence and an attempt to be the leading power in that regional arc. This ambition only makes Turkish-Russian relations more attractive as an area of opportunity. For the first time in contemporary Turkish perceptions, Russia has a very positive image, and is in fact Turkey's top trading partner. (Conversely, Turkey is Russia's fourth-largest trade partner.)

That said, the relationship with Russia is not an alternative to Turkey's EU membership aspirations. The chapter authors portray Russia and the West as an either/or dilemma for Turkey. Yet despite the minority view of some intellectuals that the Shanghai Cooperation Organization is an alternative alignment, Turkey will not be forced to choose between good relations with Russia and its rock-solid overall alliance with the West. As a NATO member and integrated in nearly all the Western institutions, the Turkish government considers the European Union and United States as absolutely fundamental, and the AKP government itself has repeatedly reaffirmed that EU membership remains Turkey's ultimate goal. And from a security point of view, the

United States and Turkey remain, despite ups and downs in their relationship, bound to each other. From a responsible stakeholder standpoint, Turkey has long been an important peacekeeping troop contributor country both for NATO and the United Nations—deploying troops in several missions since the 1990s, from Somalia to Afghanistan. This is very much a neglected area where Turkey's contribution is overlooked or underestimated.

It is true that since September 11 Turkey discovered the "Islamic card" and has played it very successfully. All the talk about a new Ottomanism, however, proved to be more amusing speculation than operational Turkish diplomacy. No doubt, the AKP has strong connections with all Islamic states and organizations, and Prime Minister Erdogan enjoys the most political sympathy any Turkish foreign minister ever enjoyed. Therefore, it does not qualify Turkey as a "neo-Ottoman state"; on the contrary, Turkey is a democratic state with realistic aims.

Despite the continuing extended delay in Turkey's accession to the European Union, Turkey's relevance for EU security is on the rise. Therefore, both the United States and Europe remain Turkey's security pillars, particularly the U.S. security umbrella, including Turkey's security and the fight against terrorism.

**Turkey as a Global Player**
Turkey's international economic and social activities are key drivers of its growing prominence. Its success in attracting foreign investments is thus an important quantifier of its regional and global impact. Baran and Lesser are correct that Turkey's economic and political reforms will enhance it as a global player and soft power. Turkish nongovernmental organizations, small- and medium-size business, and even recently the television and film industry are all contributing to Turkey's international image. In the scientific and technological fields, Turkey has made huge strides in recent years and is one the few Islamic countries with satellites in the orbit, which will be added to significantly in coming years.

Turkey also became a donor country in recent years, providing technological and economic help to Third World countries. As an emerging market and soft power, Turkey is considered in the "second circle," just below the G-7 countries, of economies with strong prospects. Given Turkey's strong economic performance, one can say that Turkey is one of globalization's principal winners. The recent global financial crisis has only confirmed the wisdom of the economic and banking reforms of the last eight years. In the context of the EU process, Turkey will certainly continue these reforms. Since 2005, Turkey has been a relatively expensive country for foreign investment, but at the same time it has been a real center of attraction for foreign capital. And as the privatization process in Turkey continues to progress, this will only encourage further investment, which has already broken all the records in her economic history.

Turkey's challenges are daunting, but with her strong liberal economic and political system and record, Turkey remains a responsible international stakeholder. Turkey will remain squarely on a path to the West, but it will also retain significant influence in the south and in the Islamic world, as well as in Africa in particular. Turkey's role as a Mediterranean power will also help make the Mediterranean Union a strategic success.

In sum, Ankara's policies are not splintering but rather the continuation of "traditional realistic policies" of the Turkish Republic. Far from undergoing an Islamization of its foreign policy, Turkey is preserving a realistic and pragmatic one. In the final analysis, Turkey aspires to become a global player, but she continues to juggle all her advantages as well as limitations.

Turkey seeks more democracy, more prosperity, and more security in a world that each day seems to get more and more insecure. Turkey absorbs her fair share of these negative developments, but still remains indispensable for the European Union and the United States—not to mention the neighboring countries, which seem very happy with the soft power of Turkey and her new policy of "zero problems with the neighboring countries."

## Notes

1. See German Marshall Fund of the United States, *Transatlantic Trends*, 2008.

2. Zeyno Baran, "Turkey Divided," *Journal of Democracy* 19, no. 1 (January 2008).

3. One example is the fate of article 301, criminalizing the denigration of Turkishness, the republic, and the foundation and institutions of the State. It is a major concern for freedom of expression, and one the European Union and the United States have urged AKP to amend. In the face of nationalist opposition and priorities elsewhere, the reforms to article 301 introduced by AKP have been haphazard, and more cosmetic than real.

4. pewglobal.org/reports/display.php?ReportID=260.

5. Ahmet Davutoglu, "Stratejik Derinlik. Ankara: Küre Yayınları," 2001; "An eminence grise," *The Economist*, November 15, 2007, www.economist.com/world/eu rope/displaystory.cfm?story_id=10146653.

6. This point has been emphasized by Alan Makovsky in various analyses and is captured in Soli Ozel's writings about the perils of a unilateral Turkish policy in the Middle East ("on not being a lone wolf").

7. In late August 2008, Turkey approved the passage of American vessels through the Turkish Straits to deliver humanitarian assistance to Georgia. The possible delivery of military assistance will pose more difficult dilemmas for Ankara.

8. See Ian O. Lesser, *Beyond Suspicion: Rethinking US-Turkish Relations* (Washington, DC: Woodrow Wilson International Center for Scholars, 2007).

9. See GMF, *Transatlantic Trends*, 2007 and 2008.

10. Cengiz Çandar, "Yeni Ortado u denklemi, Lübnan'daki Türkiye, Türkiye'deki Türkiye," *Referans*, May 27, 2008, www.referansgazetesi.com/haber.aspx?HBR_KOD=97873&YZR_KOD=15.

11. David Ignatius, "Going Their Own Way in The Mideast," June 1, 2008, www.washingtonpost.com/wp-dyn/content/article/2008/05/30/AR2008053002517.html.

12. "Turkey: 'Silent but Effective' Partner," speech by Foreign Minister Ali Babacan at the Atlantic Council of the United States, www.acus.org/about-news-Turkish-PM.asp.

~

# Brazil's Candidacy for
# Major Power Status

*Paulo Roberto de Almeida and Miguel Diaz*
*With a Reaction by Georges D. Landau*

## Aspiring to Global Greatness

Brazil has long believed that it was destined for greatness. This exalted sense of importance has been based on pride in the country's geographical size, its natural beauty and resources, and its heritage as part of Portugal's great seafaring empire. At various points in its history, greatness seemed within Brazil's reach, only to flitter away—mostly as a result of Brazil's own missteps. Now, once again, Brazil is presenting itself to the world as ready to assume its rightful place among the leading global stakeholders, and its case has never been stronger. The success of this bid depends in part on the international community's response, yet the responsibility still rests with Brazil's governing elite.

Much to Brazil's consternation, the great powers have repeatedly rebuffed Brazil's many recent requests to join their ranks, in particular denying Brazil the holy grail of a permanent seat on the UN Security Council. The prevailing perception by world powers was that Brazil had little to offer to help resolve important issues on the world agenda. Even within Latin America, Brazil has not received the deference commensurate with its size and economic clout. Spanish-speaking Latin America has largely been indifferent to its giant neighbor, perhaps kept at a distance by the language and geographical divide that effectively makes them two separate worlds. Undoubtedly, the large shadow that the United States casts over Latin America has also altered the dynamics of the region's natural relationships.

In rejecting Brasilia's overtures, the global powers simply judged that the country was unprepared to assume global leadership, given the chronic political and economic crises that plagued the country for much of the twentieth century. Brazil is not a "serious" country, French President Charles de Gaulle is alleged to have once said, and he was probably not alone in that opinion. Its predicament was perhaps best captured in the oft-used quip: "Brazil is the country of the future and it will always be."

But by the dawn of the twenty-first century, Brazil was no longer being derided, despite some lingering skepticism about Brazil's capacity to lead. In a 2004 National Intelligence Council report looking at the world in 2020, the authors stopped short of grouping Brazil with India and China as a future great power, instead hedging with the caveat that "perhaps" Brazil can rise to the ranks of the global elite. The American intelligence community even doubted that Brazil could assume regional leadership. "Brazil will likely have failed to deliver on its promised leadership in South America, due as much to the skepticism of its neighbors as to its frequently overwhelming emphasis on its own interests," the report read.

### Making a Grand Entrance

Brazil seems to be proving the skeptics wrong. In the last year or two, Brazil has stepped onto the international stage and has dazzled—prompting a euphoria about the country's prospects that has been unseen since the 1970s and sparking new debate about Brazil's readiness for global leadership. Investors and the media have feted Brazil, the latter having recently christened the country "the awakened giant." The established global stakeholders have apparently taken notice as well and have begun extending Brasilia the diplomatic accolades and courtesies for which it has long yearned. In a 2007 speech, U.S. Secretary of State Condoleezza Rice referred to Brazil as a regional power and a global partner, a compliment not readily offered in the past. Since 2003, the global elite have even made arrangements to include Brazil in their G-8 deliberations, along with other important emerging economies, such as China, India, Mexico, and South Africa.

As a result, the discussion has shifted from the issue of whether Brazil will be a global stakeholder to the question of how it will play such a role. Indeed, in some areas—such as the fight against hunger and the spread of pandemic diseases—Brazil is already exercising global leadership. The question of how to facilitate and maximize Brazil's contribution to a rules-based international order is squarely on the foreign policy agendas of the major global powers. The challenge is particularly great for Washington, which historically has had an awkward and testy relationship with Brasilia. The task is further complicated by Brazil's own peculiarities and challenges and the state of flux in which the world governance system finds itself.

For its part, Brasilia is struggling to come to grips with the political, financial, and diplomatic burdens that accompany being a global stakeholder. As it is, Brazil's foreign policy bureaucracy, Itamaraty, appears overstretched in its international commitments and at times conflicted, if not bewildered, regarding which international objectives it is supposed to pursue. Itamaraty's complex task has been magnified by the split of the decision-making process among the minister, the international advisor of the presidency (a pro-Cuba Party apparatchik), and the secretary-general of the foreign service, an old-style nationalist, and the activist diplomacy conducted directly by the president, who is inclined to assert his leadership credentials in the region and beyond. As to be expected, the pressure to toe the official line has had a detrimental effect on morale, the openness and vitality of internal debate and, ultimately, the soundness of policy. Itamaraty's greater emphasis on Third World "solidarity" and periodic outbursts of anti-Americanism can be explained, in part, by these pressures. Beyond question, though, is the damage to Itamaraty's long-cherished reputation for professionalism and objectivity, raising doubts about Brasilia's ability to navigate the uncharted diplomatic waters that lie ahead.

Meanwhile, the Brazilian public has not even begun debating the ramifications of Brazil's new prominence, not to mention examining the potential costs and commitments involved. For their part, Brazil's myopic political elite and media certainly have not encouraged such a debate. Neither have academic institutions and the few foreign policy think tanks in the country stepped forward to host and orchestrate the kind of national debate that their U.S. counterparts generally take for granted.

Notwithstanding this lack of preparedness, the convergence between Brazil's and the world's interests is inevitable and offers, in addition to the costs and risks, great benefits. Consequently, it is incumbent upon Brazil and the international community to work in concert to ensure that Brazil reaches its potential as a stakeholder—with the onus clearly on Brasilia in the near term to demonstrate initiative and commitment, which it is just starting to do. As with other world powers' leaders, the most difficult shift facing Brazilian leaders is to rethink their country's international role and begin expecting and encouraging Brazil to think and act as a global stakeholder, with all the requisite humility, gravity, and selflessness. It may not be exactly the sort of greatness that Brazil had in mind when it first dared to dream decades ago, but it is indeed the very opportunity to lead that lies, at last, within Brazil's reach.

## Brazil's Strategic Fundamentals

It is hard not to think of Brazil as a full-fledged world power, given its sheer size. It is the world's fifth-largest country in territory, the fifth-largest in population (nearly 190 million inhabitants), and has the tenth-largest economy. Brazil is an urban, cosmopolitan society, home to world-class cities, like Sao Paulo, and many other mega-cities of which most Americans have never heard. It has almost as many mobile phones as people, and Internet connection rates are rising at a double digit pace. While a large percentage of the population lives in poverty, Brazil is a truly modern society, Western in its orientation and without the religious or ethnic cleavages that are tearing other nations apart.

Like the United States, the country is a melting pot of cultures and ethnic and racial groups. Brazil boasts the world's largest number of Afro-descendants outside of Africa and the largest population of Japanese origin outside of Japan. Between the late nineteenth century and early twentieth century, it also welcomed hundreds of thousands of Italians, Germans, and other European immigrants who started as small peasants and laborers on coffee farms and later led the country into the industrial age. Millions of Middle Easterners—mostly from Lebanon—and hundreds of thousands of South Americans from across the continent have made Brazil their home as well. While Brazil has always celebrated its diversity, it has fallen short of its professed ideal of racial harmony, especially with regard to integrating the Afro-Brazilian population into the economic and social mainstream. Nonetheless—and again, much like the United States—Brazil has not stopped striving for the melting pot ideal and has made more progress toward that end in recent years than in its previous five hundred years as a nation.

Brazil's bounty of natural riches is second to none. Within its borders lie the planet's last major tropical rainforest, its largest renewable freshwater reserves, and its greatest biodiversity. The country has large deposits of precious metals, such as iron ore, gold, and aluminium. To top it off, Brazil has shown exquisite timing with the discovery of vast offshore reservoirs of oil deposits that could catapult Brazil to the top ranks of the world energy producers within a decade. (Brazil is also giving a tremendous boost to its sugarcane ethanol, which already fuels most of its hybrid cars.) Not to be minimized as an element of national identity, Brazil sees itself as aesthetically gifted, claiming one of the world's most beautiful cities in Rio de Janeiro and scores of beautiful people who have no qualms about spending more on cosmetic surgery per capita than any other country in the planet. Of course, Brazil is also an internationally acclaimed powerhouse in soccer, the only true world sport. Among Brazil's many "exports" these days are plenty of soccer players and fashion models. Its unique music has also found significant popularity outside its borders.

Beyond these generally recognized attributes, the Brazilian government has been developing in key areas necessary for global leadership. Brazil is taking the right steps to ensure economic and political stability, as well as carrying out diplomatic outreach to raise its profile internationally and cement its reputation and commitment to multilateralism. All of these changes are taking place within a new global environment in which the pending issues—climate change, global health and pandemic diseases, nuclear nonproliferation, the potential for failed states, and so on—only enhance Brazil's international relevance. Absent these issues, a major power like the United States could understandably continue to overlook Brazil's global position. Yet, given the emergence and urgency of this new agenda, and Brazil's centrality to them, Washington would be ill-advised to overlook its giant hemispheric neighbor any longer.

## Coming of Age as a Global Stakeholder

The prevailing opinion is that no single transformative episode propelled Brazil to international prominence, but rather a combination of internal and external developments converged to make an already uniquely gifted nation into an even more viable candidate for global leadership. Still, any explanation of Brazil's ascendance must begin with the 1985 return of democracy and the political and economic stabilization that has been achieved since. In just two decades, Brazil has gone from being a political and economic basket case—even by Latin American standards—to one of the strongest democracies and most dynamic economies in the region, if not the world.

### Economic Stabilization
This progress is probably easier to measure in economic terms. In less than twenty years, Brazil went from hyperinflation (with an astronomical 2,300 percent annual inflation rate in the early 1990s) and regular cycles of debt default to the economic wonder that it is today—with single-digit inflation, stable (if not robust) growth, and the accumulation of more than $200 billion in foreign exchange reserves (a sum now in excess of the country's stock of foreign debt).

The current recovery differs from previous economic booms in several important ways. For starters, this time, the vast majority of Brazilians—not just a privileged few—are benefiting. Brazil can now proudly claim to be the first country to have met its Millennium Challenge targets of reducing poverty by half. Thanks to the Fome Zero anti-hunger initiatives, which provide a minimum income for an estimated forty-five million people, many poor Brazilians no longer go to bed hungry and are able to send their children to school. They now also receive a modicum of medical care when sick and, in treating some diseases, Brazil has stood out. For instance, the government's response to AIDS has been trendsetting, and contrasts sharply with the way other developing countries have handled the outbreak. Thanks mostly to the improved lot of those at the bottom of the economic ladder—according to the Rio-based Getulio Vargas Foundation, the income of the bottom 10 percent of the population rose by 58 percent between 2001 and 2006—steady progress is also being made in narrowing the country's embarrassingly wide income gap and in absorbing the historically marginalized black population into the economic mainstream.[1]

The rich and powerful are also faring well, as revealed in data showing that those in the top 10 percent income bracket saw their incomes rise by 7 percent between 2001 and 2006.[2] Brazilians have now joined the ranks of Forbes's wealthiest individuals, and Brazilian multinationals are thriving as never before, with many executives crisscrossing the world looking for acquisitions. In the fields of mining and commercial aviation equipment, Brazilian companies, like Vale, Usiminas, and Embraer, are dominant players in their fields. And the highly regarded government-owned oil company, Petrobras, has become a major player in the energy field. Other large Brazilian companies, in steel, metal processing, footwear, meat and poultry, and textiles and apparel, are also acquiring global reach and are beginning to raise funds in the international capital markets.

Also setting Brazil's economic recovery apart is the way it was achieved. The key was disciplined implementation of orthodox economic policies sustained across two consecutive presidencies, a rare feat in Brazilian history. Particularly remarkable was the decision of President Lula—a former labor union leader and longtime militant of the Left—to stick to the liberal economic program put in place by his predecessor. Although discontinuing the privatization process initiated a decade earlier, Lula maintained the three pillars of his predecessor's orthodox model: fiscal responsibility (with a primary budget surplus of about 4 percent of gross domestic product [GDP]), a free-floating exchange rate regime, and inflation targeting—the latter in the minds of many Brazilians being the bedrock of macroeconomic stability. So diligent has been the government's commitment to its inflation-targeting policy that it can only be explained by a collective determination to do everything necessary to avoid a return to hyperinflationary chaos. To this day, the government's inflation reports make the front pages. For the millions of

Brazilians who lacked hope that life could be better for themselves and their children, Brazil's own version of the American dream is emerging, in which hard work, ingenuity, and playing by the established rules of the game can be counted upon to lead to prosperity.

Brazil has walked a fine line with its embrace of liberalization. Current policy is marked by its embrace of globalization, although not wholeheartedly. By international standards, Brazil's economy is still relatively closed, with the percentage of trade relative to GDP only about 25 percent. Making up for this has been an increase in fiscal spending and an explosion in domestic consumption, fueled by job growth, a rise in real income, and expansion of credit. However, with a deteriorating international environment for exports, limited options for fiscal stimuli (Brazil's overall tax burden is already near Organization for Economic Cooperation and Development [OECD] levels of 38 percent of GDP), and growing signs of consumer debt overextension, the government is coming under pressure to undertake a second wave of reforms geared toward further privatization and deregulation to maintain the economic momentum.

The reform agenda before the government is indeed daunting and inevitably controversial. Brazil watchers are looking to see if Brasilia follows up on its commitment to cut some of the infamous red tape that entrepreneurs encounter in starting a business and paying taxes. Economists would also like to see some progress in reducing the public debt burden and the size of government. Just in the last six years, the country's bureaucracy has grown from 900,000 to more than 1.1 million people, and more than thirty-seven new state companies or public agencies have been created since 2003. Furthermore, a significant share of the economy is still conducted on an informal basis. By one estimate, some 40 percent of GDP and almost half of the workforce operate in the informal economy. The public pension system is also long overdue for an overhaul. So with nearly 20 percent of Brazil's population still living in dire poverty, Brasilia certainly does not have the luxury of resting on its laurels.

With a clear reform agenda and generally favorable economic and political conditions, economic policy poses a test to the Lula administration. Clearly, the moment of truth has arrived for Lula to show whether he is truly a free market convert, or merely one when politically convenient. With the government still enjoying a high level of popularity—mostly on account of the economic good times it has delivered—the expectation is that Brasilia will pursue economic progress by buckling down and plowing through the next phase of reforms.

Surely investors, both local and foreign, share this sanguine view of the country and are voting with their capital. In 2007, nearly $37 billion in foreign direct investment flowed into the country—almost twice as much as in 2006 and second only to that of China—and the data through the first six months of 2008 show a doubling of the amount relative to the same period in 2007. Meanwhile, the Bovespa stock market index continues its erratic ascent since Lula came to office in 2002. If these positive economic trends continue, Brazil could vault even higher up the list of the world's largest economies. Goldman Sachs estimates that if Brazil were to grow an average of 3.6 percent in the next twenty years—an ambitious but plausible scenario—Brazil's GDP will go from being the world's tenth to the sixth largest by 2050. If that holds true, Brazil would overtake Italy by 2025 and pass the economies of France, Germany, and the United Kingdom by 2031.

In sum, the about-face in Brazil's economic fortunes and its transformation into an economic powerhouse is truly remarkable. Although Brazil has stopped short of the deeper economic reforms undertaken by Chile, it has nevertheless laid much of the foundation needed for sustainable growth. As recently as 2002, many observers thought that Brazil would default on its debt, as its next-door neighbor, Argentina, eventually ended up doing. Instead, six years later, Brazil has been awarded an investment grade rating on its foreign currency debt by Standard and Poor's and other rating agencies.

The irony was not lost on the Brazilians when their finance minister recently chastised the developed countries at the annual spring International Monetary Fund (IMF) meeting for the lack of transparency and regulatory oversight that allowed the U.S. subprime crisis to explode into a global economic crisis. Less than ten years earlier, the IMF chided Brazil for similar imbalances and regulatory lapses and forced the country to take bitter medicine as a remedy. As far as Brazilians are concerned, Brazil has come full circle, has learned its lessons well, and is now teaching its former teachers.

## Brazil's Political Renaissance

It was not a given that democracy would blossom in Brazil over the last twenty years. Indeed, the 1985 return to democracy got off to a rough start with the death of the first elected president a few days before his inauguration and the second elected president forced from office on grounds of corruption. It was not until 1994 that Brazil's democracy finally found its footing with the election of Fernando Henrique Cardoso. A former sociology professor and political activist who had spent the years of military rule in exile, Cardoso came to national and international prominence as the foreign minister in the Itamar Franco government. However, it was as finance minister in the same administration where he made his mark by authoring and executing an economic plan that halted hyperinflation in its tracks.

Riding a wave of popular acclaim for slaying the dragon of inflation, Cardoso was elected president the first time in an easy race against Luis Inacio Lula da Silva and reelected four years later by an even wider margin of victory. And although his countrymen will remember him for his economic management, his political legacy will be even more enduring. Easy-going, understated, and consensus-seeking by nature, Cardoso brought much-needed civility to Brasilia. Moreover, his personal reputation for probity helped restore the public's faith in government. The esteem he brought to public service, in turn, drew talented people to his administration. Probably the most positive thing that can be said about the Cardoso years is that governing became a relatively mundane affair, in contrast to the high drama to which the world had grown accustomed. In short, Brazil at last became a normal country.

And if that was not enough, Cardoso passed the ultimate test of a true democrat—knowing when to walk away from power. This was an exceptional move in Brazilian history. Having raised eyebrows by amending the constitution to allow for a second consecutive term—which, as noted, he easily won—he resisted pleas from his supporters to support another constitutional amendment to clear the way for a third term. Instead, he improved the election prospects of Lula by, among other things, distancing himself from the contest and reaching out to Lula and his supporters to present the merits of his economic policies. The message must have gotten through, as Lula gave the necessary signals to avoid the feared stampede to the exits by investors.

President Lula's election has been beneficial for Brazil's democracy on a number of levels. First of all, it vindicated the Left's decision to play by the rules of the democratic game. Indeed, a number of high-ranking officials in Lula's administration, though not Lula himself, were former guerrillas. It also affirmed the political evolution of Brazil's Left, which has come to accommodate market-friendly policies. Lula's uplifting personal story also inspired millions of men and women who share his modest origins to have faith in the democratic process and become involved. The result is an active civil society movement that is beginning to make its mark on the country.

## Diplomatic Overdrive

The rise in Brazil's international stature can also be attributed to the diplomatic offensive waged by the country's highly regarded foreign diplomatic service, Itamaraty. Alternately prodded and assisted by two presidents who enjoyed and excelled at hobnobbing with the world elite, Itamaraty has worked assiduously in the last five years, entangling Brazil in a thicket of coalitions, organizations, and initiatives. And when circumstances high-lighted the need for new networks to be created, Brazil has taken the lead in creating them. Brazil's predisposition to work through multilateral coalitions was prominent once again when Brasilia reportedly gave a positive response to Russia's Vladimir Putin's suggestion of a G-13. At Russia's previous in-vitation (and with China and India), Brazil helped to transform the BRICs from being merely an analytical exercise by Goldman Sachs into an actual multilateral concert of rising powers, one poised to challenge G-8 dominance of the global political agenda—as well as G-7 dominance of the global eco-nomic agenda.

Making sense of this blitzkrieg of diplomatic activity has strained the ana-lytical powers of Brazil watchers, who have yet to render their full verdict. Even so, a hazy logic at least can be discerned among the diplomatic en-tanglements. For one, the agreements show a clear proclivity to coalesce with similarly promising emerging powers, such as India, South Africa, and China, ostensibly to present a common front against traditional powers, notwith-standing the divergence of positions and interests among them. One particu-larly high-profile example was Brasilia's leadership in the constitution of the G-20 at the 2003 World Trade Organization (WTO) ministerial meeting in Cancun, despite clear trade policy differences within its ranks that in the end were readily apparent in the August 2008 collapse of the WTO Geneva talks. Nonetheless, the agreements have served to deepen relations among the large emerging economic powers, and the setback at the WTO will probably not derail this trend. Trade among the four countries has expanded dramati-cally in recent years and represents an increasingly important source of global economic growth. In other words, Brazil may not be too happy with Beijing and India scuttling the WTO talks in Geneva, but it fully understands the benefit and the promise that both markets represent for Brazil.

It is not as if Brasilia has neglected relations with the traditional powers, only that is has cultivated them selectively and on a strategic basis. Dur-ing Lula's first term, for example, Brazil joined France in a global campaign against the spread of AIDS, tuberculosis, and malaria, and collaborated with Japan to arrest climate change. Of course, there is the much-publicized mul-tiyear commitment to cooperate with the United States on expanding the use of biofuels. All in all, Brazil is in the enviable position of having friends in all corners of the world and no enemies to speak of, although it may be friendlier to some than to others.

As we end the first decade of the twenty-first century, Brazil has made impressive advances in harnessing its natural resources and developing its human capital. Moreover, Brazil's government has made a quantum leap in achieving social, economic, and political stability compared to its turbulent past. As a result, Brazil has reached a higher economic plane that minimizes the danger of a return to its past chaos. Brazil has also made great strides to develop global diplomatic outreach, which, while still perhaps needing some refinement, indicates that Brazil has started to put its domestic challenges in a global context.

### The Times Are Changing

A change in the international constellation of power has also factored into Brazil's ascendance. Most importantly, the loss of America's hegemonic influence in Latin America (and elsewhere) has enabled a once-tentative Brazil to assert itself, regardless of Washington's views. In effect, Brasilia finally feels liberated to play the rightful role that its size, resources, and diplomatic persona portended, but felt it lacked the latitude to exercise. In particular, Brasilia more and more plays the role of convener and peacemaker—for instance, in mediating a standoff between Venezuela and Colombia over the latter's March 2008 military action in Ecuador.

The change in the world's agenda has also made Brazil's participation indispensable. The emergence of global warming as a top-tier issue, for example, has changed the world's calculus on the importance of getting Brazil's buy-in to deal with this major global challenge. The same applies to a similar degree to the world's efforts to grapple with the food crisis, for Brazil is one of the few countries with arable land to spare and the technology to utilize it. At the same time, Brazil's own priorities are beginning to coincide more with those of the rest of the world. For example, Brazil is now giving the issue of narcotics trafficking higher priority, having developed a domestic drug consumption problem that is second in the hemisphere only to that of the United States, and suffered the associated consequences of rising crime, loss of productivity, and higher health costs.

## Brazil's Track Record of Leadership

Now that Brazil has emerged as a new global leader, it has started to exercise its newfound power and global influence on a range of regional and global issues such as climate change, trade, and the fight against poverty. The results have been mixed. Brazil is showing itself highly capable in some areas and struggling in others. Undoubtedly, it will take a while for Brazil and the world to discover the competitive advantages that Brazil has to offer to the construction of a rules-based global order. This section outlines how Brazil is managing its newfound role on a regional level, and then investigates those areas where Brazil has distinguished itself beyond regional boundaries, including climate change, world hunger, peacekeeping, and nation-building.

## Latin America

Brazil has emerged as South America's clear leader and is now waging an offensive to extend its influence throughout Latin America—an effort that is beginning to achieve results. This is not a surprise, given Brazil's size and economic clout. It has only helped matters that Venezuela—the latest rival claimant to regional leadership—has seen its star wane, mostly because of self-inflicted wounds. What is surprising are the means Brazil used in pursuit of this objective, and the obstacles it has confronted and is overcoming to cement its position of leadership.

Brasilia's gains in regional leadership were attained in a piecemeal fashion. The outreach began with President Jose Sarney (1985–1990), who, in an attempt to improve ties to Argentina after years of friction, forged a customs union between the two countries that soon expanded to include Uruguay and Paraguay. The Common Market of the South agreement (referred to as Mercosur in Spanish-speaking Latin America and Mercosul in Brazil) was formally inaugurated in March 1991. Despite its economic pretensions—which the agreements have yet to live up to—the real and immediate benefit was in strengthening the political ties between the state parties: the operative assumption being that the member countries are compelled to work through their disagreements peacefully.

Cardoso's administration also distinguished itself as an international peacemaker when it mediated—along with Argentina, Chile, and the United States—a peace agreement between Peru and Ecuador in 1995 and also helped prevent a military coup in Paraguay. Confident that Brazil was ready to exercise South American regional leadership in the waning years of his administration, Cardoso convened the first-ever summit of the region's heads of state in Brasilia in 2000. The summit was an unambiguous success; the final product of the gathering was the South American Regional Integration Initiative (IIRSA), aimed at building better overland lines of communication and transportation to connect the countries.

Brazil's incremental progress to gain regional influence has continued to the present day. President Luis Ignacio Lula da Silva's well-known political history has given him a unique advantage as a regional leader. As the icon of the Left for decades, Lula commanded the respect and admiration of the new class of leftist politicians who were having electoral success in their countries—including Michele Bachelet of Chile and Tabare Vazquez in Uruguay. Even borderline democrats like Hugo Chavez and Evo Morales had little choice but to give Lula his due deference as a man of the Left. At the same time, Lula's orthodox economic policies won him new admirers among center-right governments in the region, like Colombia's, who were taking heat from their own political Left for sticking to the path of economic orthodoxy.

Lula's string of regional diplomatic accomplishments grew in May 2008 when the much-heralded Union of South American Nations (Unasur) came into being. The agreement sets targets for the integration of energy and transportation infrastructure and establishes a South American parliament and a Unasur secretariat. (Plans were also made to create a South American defense council, under the Unasur umbrella.) Itamaraty may be expecting that Unasur, like Mercosur, will not achieve its ambitious goals—such as a free trade area for nonsensitive goods by 2014 and of sensitive goods by 2019—but could nevertheless provide another framework for South American nations to work out their disagreements peacefully, under the tutelage of Brasilia, of course. More recently, Brazil played a leading role in convening South American heads of states in Santiago, Chile, to address the growing political polarization in Bolivia.

Confident that it has gone as far as it can in South America, at least for the time being, Brazil has recently sought to extend its influence elsewhere in Latin America, where the political soil seems fertile for change. This push is already showing promising results. Brazil has taken a leadership position in Haiti as the head of the UN Stabilization Mission in Haiti (MINUSTAH), a role that has won Brasilia new esteem in the Caribbean. In a second move, Brazil has won kudos in Central America with its decision to include El Salvador in the global ethanol initiative on which it has been collaborating with Washington. Region-to-region summits have been another outlet for Brazil's international leadership, including two that it organized since 2005 between South American and the Arab and African world leaders. There is no doubt that Brazil has become an able spokesman for South America.

Even so, regional leadership, as Brazil has learned, is neither cheap nor trouble free and cannot be taken for granted. There is no shortage of competition for the mantle of leadership, the latest and most prominent being Venezuela's Hugo Chavez, who is hoping to take advantage of his country's oil windfall to enhance the regional appeal of his Bolivarian project. Truly, he has taken every opportunity to try to cut Brazil down to size. Painting Brasilia as a lackey of Washington appears to be his latest tactic. For example, in 2007, Chavez and his Cuban, Nicaraguan, and Bolivian allies lambasted Brasilia for its collaboration with the "empire" on biofuels, contending that it is the principal cause of the current food crisis. Brazil's neighbors, such as

Paraguay and Suriname, regularly take it to task for failing to deliver on its many promises of aid—complaints that are only bound to increase as Brazil's coffers fill with newfound oil wealth.

Nevertheless, it is hard to bet against Brazil's long-term prospects for regional leadership. The political stars are clearly aligned in its favor, with its economy pointed in the right direction and steady inroads being made in addressing the country's huge social deficit. A healthy economy seems Brasilia's strongest calling card, as is indicated by the increasing number of fellow Latin Americans who are flocking to Brazil—legally and illegally—to work and the number of Brazilian companies expanding their presence all throughout Latin America. According to recent government figures, remittances from fellow South Americans working in Brazil have now surpassed $1 billion and are growing at a healthy clip.

Brazil seems to harbor no false illusions about the need for ongoing care and maintenance to retain its leadership position. Lula is already urging his countrymen to show greater generosity toward their neighbors, going as far as suggesting to Brazilian businesses to buy from within the region, even if not economically optimal. The government has set the example by making concessions to Bolivia's government, even after the latter nationalized significant Petrobras oil and gas resources, and is similarly expected to accommodate the new Leftist government in Paraguay by paying higher royalties for the electricity it receives from the Itaipu hydroelectric dam. (Some quibbles have appeared with Ecuador over activities of Brazilian enterprises, including Petrobras, in that country.) At the same time, Brasilia is expected to be more aggressive in challenging Chavez's antics and not simply absorbing his criticism. Brasilia recently, for instance, decided to opt out of Chavez's grandiose regional gas line project.

In sum, a new political and economic geography has clearly emerged in Latin America, with Brazil playing a starring role. In Latin America at least, Brazil's place as a stakeholder has been assured. No other country can replace it. It is an indispensable piece of the puzzle to any Latin America–wide initiative and, for a number of regional challenges, the only country that can provide effective leadership. At some point in the future, even Brazil's two historical competitors for regional leadership, Argentina and Mexico, will resign to this new reality and accept, albeit grudgingly, that Brazil is the natural choice to represent Latin America before the world.

## Climate Change

Brazil is a major contributor to global warming, but also a potentially significant contributor to its resolution. Brazil ranks as the world's seventh-largest emitter of greenhouse gases—behind China, the United States, the European Union (EU), India, Russia, and Indonesia—mostly due to deforestation (70 percent) and changes in land use. Indeed, according to the World Wildlife Federation, the burning of the Amazon (about 70 percent of which lies in Brazilian territory) makes up about half of the world's annual greenhouse emissions from deforestation, which, in turn, contributes about 20 percent of world greenhouse emissions.

At the same time, Brazil is a leader in the use of alternative fuels and is likely to remain so for decades to come. With oil prices reaching new highs in 2008, Brazil's energy matrix is the envy of the world—drawing 47 percent from renewable resources, such as sugarcane and hydroelectric plants, and ethanol now making up 40 percent of the fuel used by light vehicles.

And then there is pride of place that goes with having hosted the first world environment summit in Rio de Janeiro in 1992. Brazil has been a signatory to all the important environmental treaties, including the Kyoto Protocol, and is a mainstay at all the important environment deliberations, including the ongoing UN-sponsored negotiations to construct a post-Kyoto protocol. President Lula campaigned on the promise to be an environmental president and has spearheaded the forming of alliances with the key global leaders, such as Japan, on the issue. According to John Ashton, the United Kingdom's special representative for climate change, the importance of Brazil on the issue of climate change can no longer be denied. He stated: "[It] is unthinkable to have an (environment) agreement without Brazil playing a significant role in it."

Notwithstanding these signal advances, Brazil's domestic environmental policies continue to disappoint. Under the Lula government, deforestation, after having declined for two years in a row, has surged upward in the last year. In total, 15 percent of the surface of the rainforest has been cleared since 1970. The culprit appears to be the government's inability to clamp down on illegal loggers in some Amazonian states, who often collude with local authorities. The government is also being assailed by radical environmentalists for permitting genetically modified soybeans to be sown in the south of the country and for violating the Cartagena Protocol for Biosafety by approving the cultivation of transgenic maize.

For many environmentalists the last straw was the resignation in May 2008 of the minister of the environment, Marina Silva, an icon in Brazil's environmental movement. Frustrated after losing one environmental battle after another, she claims to have had no other alternative but to resign in protest. Despite the Lula administration's effort to contain the political fallout, the damage has been done and, in the view of a growing number of environmentalists, Brazil is clearly not yet ready for leadership on environmental issues. One area in which Brasilia has been faulted is its failure to influence the world's two fastest-growing polluters, China and India. These are two countries that Brasilia has tended not displease in the past and to which it has tied its diplomatic future. Yet Brazil's honored place at the table is assured, and the hope is that Brasilia will soon live up to its rhetoric of being a leader in the global effort to combat climate change.

**Fight Against Hunger**

In contrast to its stumbling approach to leadership on environmental issues, Brazil has become a true leader in the fight against world hunger, both by its example and by its diplomatic deeds. Although not without its critics, the government's Fome Zero anti-hunger initiative, in which poor families receive a direct cash transfer to buy food, is seen as a model worth replicating. Most recently, India has turned to Brazil for advice in establishing a similar program. President Lula's professed objective is to eliminate hunger in Brazil by the end of his term in 2010.

Brazil has also done a remarkable job in bringing the issue of hunger to the international agenda, and could not have had a more effective champion than President Lula. Born poor and having suffered the pangs of hunger himself, he has brought an urgency and legitimacy that few world leaders can match. A diplomatic high point in his global anti-hunger campaign was a speech he gave at the fifty-eighth session of the General Assembly of the United Nations in September 2003 in which he referred to the "eradication of hunger in the world as a moral and political imperative."[3] The following year, Brazil took the lead in organizing a world summit on World Hunger in the United Nations during which more than one hundred countries committed to contributing to a fund to eradicate hunger. The United States was one of the few countries that opted out of the commitment, on the pretext that economic growth is the long-term solution to hunger and poverty. Brazil is doing its diplomatic share and is also contributing directly to assist countries hit by emergency food crises, such as Haiti in the spring of 2008. In sum, unlike many other countries, where the rhetoric outstrips actions, Brazil has matched its rhetoric with substantial financial commitments—and the world has recognized its leadership in this area, particularly the many grateful recipients of Brazil's largesse.

**Peacekeeping and Nation-Building**

Brazil has limited military capabilities, with a standing army of just two hundred thousand and a budget of 1.5 percent of GDP or $15.3 billion in 2007[4] (about 2.65 percent of that of the United States). But Brazil has put the military capability it does have to good effect in the important work of peacekeeping and nation-building. In recent years, under the United Nations' umbrella, Brazil has sent troops or observers to fellow Portuguese-speaking African countries, such as Angola and Mozambique, and, as already noted, taken a leadership position in the United Nations' pacification and stabilization mission in Haiti. More recently, the United Nations has asked Brazil to lead a peace-building mission to bring about political reconciliation and economic consolidation in another war-ravaged Portuguese-speaking African country—Guinea-Bissau.

This new role for Brazil has not been without its costs. Brazilian troops have given their lives in the service of their peacekeeping/nation-building mission, and large sums of money have been spent. But Brasilia is driven by the conviction that it is incumbent for Brazil, as a good global citizen, to provide this kind of contribution. Suffice it to say, Brazil has played the role of peacekeeper and nation-builder with distinction, an accomplishment made easier thanks to Brazil's nonpartisan reputation.

Moreover, Brazil is leading the effort to get other developing countries to collaborate to fill similarly needed security gaps worldwide. In May 2008 Brazil's armed forces joined those of its IBSA partners (South Africa and India) to conduct a military exercise off the coast of Capetown aimed at combating the growing problem of piracy and terrorism in the high seas. Brazil is planning similar military exercises with other emerging powers.

Paradoxically, Brasilia has had greater difficulty in expanding military cooperation with its Andean neighbors, as evidenced by the fate of the proposal for a South American Defense Council submitted by Brasilia at the Unasur summit. After contentious debate, the proposal that would have established a consultation forum for security affairs was remanded to a committee for further study. Further complicating the prospects for Brazil leading the region in cooperating militarily has been the incipient arms race in Latin America that seems to exceed the periodic need to replace outdated hardware. Much of the blame for this situation is being directed at Hugo Chavez, who under the guise of preparing for an imminent U.S. attack, ostensibly in concert with Colombia, has gone on a military spending spree. Whether he is doing so to prepare for war or merely to solidify his control of the military is a subject of debate. The fear of many, especially among Brazil's military brass, is that Chavez will take the next step and join the nuclear club. Certainly, he has the financial means and friends who know the technology.

In short, Brazil may not be a military superpower, but it is not militarily irrelevant, either—using what it has to good effect in response to twenty-first-century global security challenges. After having cut its teeth in Haiti, Brazil's military will be undaunted by whatever its mission. Brazil is willing and able to engage militarily on a global basis, if it believes in the mission. World War II was one such campaign. Iraq is not. The litmus test that Brasilia will likely continue to use in deciding to deploy troops is whether such action is sanctioned by the United Nations.

## World Trade

Trade is a high priority for Itamaraty, which historically has managed the issue—and, increasingly, for other interested constituencies such as agro-industrial leaders, state agencies, and labor unions who are demanding more input in policymaking. It is easy to see why. Trade has fueled much of Brazil's recent economic growth, rising from $58 billion in 2001 to almost $200 billion in 2008, about half of which was raw material goods. Brazil currently ranks first in the world in the export of coffee, sugar, soybeans, and oranges. Brazil's principal trading partners are the European Union, China, the United States, and its South American neighbors, with important growth in trade in recent years with Africa and India, as well as other Asian countries.

On world trade issues, Brazil is generally perceived as punching above its weight, given that its share of world trade is a miniscule 1 percent of total trade, which puts it in the twenty-fifth position in the world. Moreover, the country has a relatively skimpy track record of trade agreements, all of which it has undertaken as part of Mercosur. Most noteworthy are the preferential trade agreements that Mercosur has signed with Mexico and the Andean countries, and outside the region with India, South Africa, and, as of December 2007, with Israel.

Nonetheless, Brazil was a key player in the Doha trade round, operating on the same plane with the major trading powers. Its high standing came about on account of having joined India in organizing the G-20 (a group of twenty countries collectively representing 60 percent of the world's population and 22 percent of agricultural output) in the run-up to the 2003 Trade Ministerial in Cancun. Although the G-20 is more consensual in its offensive agenda (the lowering of trade barriers in industrialized countries) than in its defensive agenda (the retention of tariffs on industrial and farm goods), it has become a real protagonist in multilateral trade negotiations.

That was the case, at least, until the collapse of the WTO talks in Geneva in the summer of 2008. As of this writing, there is a fair amount of soul-searching going on in Brasilia as to who is to blame for the debacle in Geneva and whether it could have played its card differently. Ultimately, the G-20's success will hinge on its ability to reconcile the interests of agricultural systems whose consolidation enable them to compete internationally (e.g., Brazil and

Argentina) with systems based on small landholders that need protection from the global market (China and India).

## Brazil's Past and Future Commitment to the Rules-Based Order

As we can see from the previous review of Brazil's response to the full range of twenty-first-century challenges, few countries can match its commitment to a rules-based international order. Moreover, Brazil has come to rely on global principles to support its own agenda. For starters, Brazil has eschewed the acquisition of a nuclear capability and, beyond that, has no designs on its neighbors as a military hegemon. Instead, Brazil is looking toward a rules-based order as the best means available to gain stature. Since its participation in the Second International Peace Conference at The Hague (1907), Brazil has endeavored to base its foreign policy on a set of values and assumptions rooted in the principles of international law (especially noninterference in internal affairs) and the practice of true multilateralism and collective action dating to the very inception of the United Nations.

Brazil's commitment to a rules-based international order also draws from a long-standing outlook that views progress as closely associated with order. For Brazilians, the last decade of political stability and growth is merely the latest affirmation of this widely perceived link. Indeed, Brazil wears the mantra of order and progress literally on its flag and believes that a multilateral system can provide the orderly framework for the most broadly shared progress possible.

Multilateralism also plays to Brazil's cultural strengths and prejudices. Unlike many of its neighbors in Latin America, Brazil inclines toward a gradual approach to change. Its culture emphasizes compromise and give-and-take, which is indeed woven into the fabric of daily life. This has been its secret in avoiding the bloodshed and bedlam that have marked the political history of most of its neighbors.

Last but not least, Brazil has relied on multilateral solidarity to check the other, more militarily potent, giant in the hemisphere—the United States. As to be expected, Brasilia is quite wary of the U.S. penchant for imposing its will on others, particularly in Latin America. These concerns have been heightened by the Bush administration's adoption of a doctrine of preemption and its decision to go to war in Iraq. Given this precedent, many find it highly ironic that Brazil must prove its bona fides to join the UN Security Council or other august international bodies. As far as most of the world is concerned, Brazil has long ago passed the multilateralist test.

## Stability, Stability, Stability

Brazil must remain politically and economically stable if it is to remain engaged in the construction and management of a rules-based international system. Fortunately for Brazil, there does not appear to be any imminent political threat to its essential stability. For the most part, the economy's fundamentals also look to be in fine shape, or at least investors—both domestic and abroad—appear to think so.

Also heartening is the fact that the usual causes of institutional crises are under control, principally hyperinflation and the military. In the case of the former, the dozen years of low inflation, coupled with the economic reforms that have been instituted—such as a fiscal responsibility system and a free-floating exchange rate regime—have insulated the country against a return to its history of chronic high inflation. Meanwhile, Brazil's military is safely ensconced in the barracks, making due with limited resources and trying to recover from its legacy of misrule. Nowadays, the military has been kept busy with policing and peacekeeping duties, although it is safe to assume that the threat posed by a militarized Venezuela is increasingly drawing the attention of the military top brass.

This does not mean that Brazil is home free and invulnerable to democratic backsliding—no country in Latin America can claim that. Ironically, the more politically and economically stable Brazil becomes, the higher the public's expectations for its leaders. To say the least, though, Brazil has faced far more difficult challenges—and unlike in other periods, Brazilians can now use democratic mechanisms such as a free press, the right to strike and, ultimately, elections to express their dissatisfaction.

Its current political and economic stability notwithstanding, Brazil faces other domestic challenges that, if not addressed, could spark an institutional crisis. Of these, rampant crime (mostly in metropolitan areas) and corruption are by far the most serious. Also of continuing concern are the narrowing, yet still too-wide, gap between rich and poor, the health crisis associated with a rising rate of drug abuse, and the degradation of the environment.

## 2010 Elections

Given the relatively short history of Brazil's political stability, the international spotlight will no doubt be on its 2010 presidential elections. It will just be the sixth election since the return to democracy and is the next major milestone of the country's democratic maturity. How smoothly the elections are run, the quality of the campaign debates, and, ultimately, who gets elected will be the main benchmarks to watch.

At first glance, there is nothing on the horizon that gives cause for worry. The two leading political groupings are preparing themselves for the contest, and none of the candidates that are being paraded prompts a major concern. They are known figures whose democratic credentials are beyond dispute and who have submitted themselves at one time or another to the judgment of the electorate.

Yet a number of questions loom ominously in the background, many of them relating to Lula personally. Here at the end of his second term, President Lula should not, by law, be engaged in a third run for the job. It is not clear, however, if he will imitate other populist leaders in the region and seek a change in the constitution to allow for another term. While Lula himself has repeatedly discounted this rumor, it continues to have currency, and many in his party are actively working on it. Probably a more serious concern is what would happen to the PT party once Lula departs from the political stage. Will Lula's departure divide the party into a centrist and militant wing? If that happens, how committed to the democratic process will the latter be?

## Who Matters

One cannot underestimate the damage to a country's international reputation that can result from a poor choice for president, nor the potential benefits associated with the election of a leader of high quality. In President Lula and President Cardoso, Brazil was fortunate that they were both already seasoned and wise in international matters when they assumed the presidential sash. In reviewing Brazilian history, though, statesmen such as Cardoso and Lula are rarities, and a cursory look at the discernable contenders reflect the dearth of international exposure that is typical of Brazil's political elite. Undoubtedly, whoever will be the next president of Brazil will find him- or herself in stewardship of a highly evolved foreign policy and with relatively little time to get up to speed.

This situation points toward the need for a support network of institutions to help Brazilian presidents think through and, ultimately, implement, a comprehensive foreign policy strategy. Save for Itamaraty, the next Brazilian leader has little to work with, and Itamaraty itself has been hemmed in by political guidelines that often espouse some old (Workers' Party) PT beliefs.

Moreover, the media, the political parties, and the intellectual class do a relatively poor job in developing their own views on Brazil's international posture or even in vetting candidates for their views on foreign policy. There is no equivalent in Brazil, for example, of a *Foreign Affairs* magazine or a Council on Foreign Relations—with the possible exception of a still-emergent Rio de Janeiro–based Cebri, Brazilian Center for International Relations, which works closely with many practitioners. The founding in 2006 of the academic Brazilian Association of International Relations (ABRI) is certainly a welcome development, but the progress has been gradual and uneven. So there has been some progress in the development of institutions that can serve as national foreign policy sounding boards.

## Economic Milestones

On the economic front, the expectation now is that the government has to deliver more than just macroeconomic stability—i.e., low inflation. Foremost, the imperative is to improve the condition of the 20 percent of the population who still live on less than $2 per day and who are anxious to reap some of the benefits that their fellow citizens have been enjoying. Strongly interlinked with that objective is the maintenance of government social service programs, particularly those that provide direct cash support to those at the bottom of the economic ladder.

Meanwhile, the growing and newly empowered middle class is also now pressing its own set of demands. Many middle-class citizens, having enjoyed for the first time the benefits of credit, would like to see further progress in the democratization of access to capital. By world standards, interest rates on mortgages, credit cards, and other loans are still extraordinarily high, some would say usurious. The middle class has also grown accustomed to their own set of subsidies—some in the form of free public universities, for instance, or high pensions—and are keen to defend them in the streets if any are threatened.

Then there is always the suspicion that Brazil will again be contaminated by a foreign crisis. The sense of economic vulnerability to outside forces runs very deep in Brazil and will undoubtedly take a long time to heal. The upside, however, is that it has impelled the government toward extraordinary measures to protect itself—the accumulation of over $200 billion in foreign exchange reserves is a good example—from contagion. Given how well Brazil fared relative to other countries during the latest subprime scare, the preventive efforts seem to be paying off. However, the real test for Brazil will be the inevitable correction in the prices of commodities, still a major component of Brazilian exports and the impending (as of this writing) shockwaves from the severe financial crises in major markets.

## Crime

Like elsewhere in Latin America, the issue of crime will be uppermost in the electorate's mind in the upcoming elections, and for good reason. The latest statistics are shocking, with per capita murder rates spiking from already high levels essentially on a par with countries at war. The government and the media claim that much of the violence is drug related, but even setting aside drug-related murders, the problem is still critical.

The deeper challenges posed by runaway crime come in various forms. It can open the doors to fringe candidates—for example, former military leaders calling for a return to the "order" that prevailed under their reign, even if that entails a cost to human rights and political freedoms. No such political faction has yet emerged in Brazil, but they have certainly been prominent in neighboring countries with similar crime problems. There is also the risk that crime syndicates—already rampant in the poor neighborhoods of the large cities—can grow to pose a challenge to the authority of the state, as in Mexico. In many shantytowns throughout the country, for example, the drug gangs are already so dominant and violent that they effectively imprison residents in their own homes.

Thus far, the federal government is clearly losing the battle against crime and has yet to show that it is even beginning to get its hands around the problem. Previous hopes that economic growth and the reduction in income inequality would take care of the problem have fizzled out. The Lula government is now pinning its hopes on a $3.9 billion, five-year program focused on the training and the elimination of corruption within the police to do the trick. The early results of this latest approach are inconclusive.

## Corruption

Corruption is another scourge that, if not addressed systematically, could threaten Brazil's stability if it provoked virulent populism (à la Venezuela) at a cost to the basic legitimacy of the state. The corruption charges against members of Lula's inner circle showed very clearly that no party is immune to temptation and should put an end to the sanctimonious posturing that the PT has used in past electoral campaigns. Corruption is a problem that permeates life in Brazil today and unfortunately still colors international perceptions of the country. According to the Transparency International 2006 rankings, Brazil rates 70 out of 133 globally.

What is also clear, though, is that the Brazilian people have become less tolerant of corruption. The days have now passed when a former governor of a prominent state could get away with boasting "he stole, but still delivered." Moreover, it is important to note the enduring impact of having a sitting president—for that matter the first popularly elected president after the return to democracy at that—hounded out of office on corruption charges. Even so, little has been done to systematically root out corruption. For example, members of Congress facing corruption charges are prosecuted not in the regular judicial system, but in special courts not known for their transparency and efficiency. Meanwhile, the legal system remains overburdened and still highly susceptible to external influences. Brasilia may have signed its share of anticorruption treatises, but on the ground, the problem remains as grave as ever.

## Delivering on Leadership

Before it can assume new prominence on the world stage, Brazil will have to make good on the responsibilities it has already assumed. To begin with, the international community is counting on Brazil to play a particularly constructive role—if not a decisive one—in bringing the global trade and environment negotiations to a successful conclusion. It may be a heavy burden, but it is a role that Brazil has played successfully in the past—particularly in 1997 in helping break the political logjam that led to the Kyoto Agreement—and one it embraces as part of the effort to become a major global stakeholder. Unfortunately, Brazil has taken on two of the thorniest items on the international agenda, and it is not clear that even the most masterful rising power could drive them toward a successful conclusion.

If nothing else, the metrics of success in this area is clear and simple: there will either be agreement or no agreement; there is no middle option. In that light, the failure of the WTO talks in the summer of 2008 obviously was a major setback for Brasilia, leaving the question of when, if ever, negotiations will resume. The good news—if there is any—is that the global environmental discussions are still very much alive and indeed are entering the critical stage. On the one hand, the stated aim of the participants is to present a fully vetted proposal at the December 2009 Copenhagen summit, so as to have enough time to make a transition to the post-Kyoto era. On the other hand, the ideological position that Brasilia has staked out for itself leaves little room for compromise—with Brazil being among the most persistent and vociferous in placing the responsibility for environmental rectification squarely, and solely, on the developed world. In addition, Brasilia has shown little interest in really pressing China and India (not only the two fastest-growing polluters, but also important markets for Brazil's exports) to make economic sacrifices for the sake of the global environment. Suffice it to say that Brazil's professed prowess in intermediation and compromise is facing its most daunting test ever, on the biggest stage possible.

Even if Brazil somehow manages to succeed, though, the legacy from past work as an international consensus-builder bears a cautionary note. Brazil's past accomplishments can easily be quickly forgotten. The diplomatic accolades, for example, that Brazil won for its efforts to improve the transparency and inclusiveness of the WTO's decision-making process have given way instead to recriminations and even to Brazil being made a scapegoat. Most disconcerting to Itamaraty, Brazil has acquired a reputation, among many of the developing countries that it claims to represent in the G-20, of being uncooperative, unreliable, and, worse, self-serving. For a country that prides itself in being on good terms with everyone, it must be particularly discomfiting to be blamed by many small and poor developing countries for not trying hard enough to persuade the trade giants (i.e., the United States, European Union, and Japan, as well as China and India) to find common ground to deliver a trade deal. Brazil may be able to afford the perpetuation of the status quo, many of these developing country leaders complain, but they cannot.

Brazil also faces a challenge in giving its foreign policy greater strategic coherence. If there is any strategic logic to the many foreign policy initiatives undertaken by the Lula administration—in particular the thicket of agreements, coalitions, and initiatives that Brasilia has signed on to in the last few years—it is hard to decipher and even harder to do a cost-benefit analysis of them. Currently, the government gives the impression that it is trying to straddle the many political and ideological fences that divide the world, at times literally, as when Lula has shuttled between Davos and the World Social Forum. The diplomatic acrobatics may help preserve the country's good graces all around, but it does generate confusion about the country's core values. This is especially notable in the way Brasilia has flip-flopped on a number of international issues, for instance on the merits (or failings) of some global institutions, where the government's position seems contingent upon the selection of Brazilians for leadership posts. In looking at the recent diplomatic record, the best that can be construed from the cacophony of declarations coming out of Planalto (Brazil's presidential palace) is that we know more about what Brazil stands against, than what it stands for.

### Building Domestic Consensus

Moving forward, Brasilia not only must project a better sense of direction of where it wants to go internationally, but it also needs to rally public support for its policies. This will be new, as Brazil has never had much need to muster a consensus for any foreign ventures, except perhaps its involvement in World War II. The assumption was that foreign policy was better left to the professionals, a view that no doubt Itamaraty was only too happy to let stand. Not even Congress stuck its nose in international matters, since foreign policy rarely, if ever, required budgetary action—Congress's only real leverage. Otherwise, its function was limited to ratifying the few agreements and treaties that came its way.

If there is one villain for the lack of consensus on foreign policy, however, it is the Brazilian electorate itself. Uninterested in the subject, voters never have demanded that politicians show competence in the matter. Rarely has a foreign policy question ever featured prominently in a presidential election and never in congressional or state elections. Politicians have only been too happy to oblige, until now. Moving forward, Brazil's political class must make a better effort to build consensus for its foreign policy. The increasing financial and personnel commitments that will be associated with the responsibilities of stakeholder will require it. Certainly, the Brazilian Congress—which has the ultimate word on fiscal spending and sending troops abroad—will naturally be drawn to the subject.

To its credit, the Lula government is already doing a good job of engaging the increasingly important civil society sector, particularly on the environment, many elements of which have links with international affiliates. One would hope that Brasilia would be able to take advantage of the public's current favorable disposition toward globalization to put other foreign policy questions on the domestic political agenda. Indeed there are important questions for the public regarding what it means to be a global stakeholder. The associated issues of sovereignty and responsibility have been difficult for a number of current and potential stakeholders, but probably more so for Brazil. A key question that Brazil will have to answer sooner or later is what would be the right trade off between the new global priorities (e.g., the imperative to confront climate change) and the country's single-minded focus on development.

Two related issues appear to be causing Brazil particular trouble. One is how to reconcile its historical commitment to noninterference in other countries' affairs with the demands of being a global stakeholder, which by definition connotes a willingness on the part of the global powers to intervene in the affairs of others, stakeholders or not. Brasilia's reticence to speak out on recent events in Zimbabwe, Myanmar, or Sudan has underscored the point. A second related issue deals with Brazil's historical phobia with respect to the Amazon, most recently displayed by the government's legislative proposal to limit who is allowed to enter and leave the rainforest. In the past, Brazil's baffling insecurity about foreign intervention in the Amazon has risen to the level of defining its national defense policy. It is a phobia that defies any simple explanation, but one that has raised doubts about Brazil's ability to see its place in the world through a new paradigm in which traditional national demarcations have less relevance.

### Brazil's Bright Prospects

By now, Brazil may finally be ready to overcome the old adage of forever being the land of the future and able to say that Brazil's moment is at hand, though this depends in great part on Brazil fulfilling its promise as a global stakeholder. The world, and the United States in particular as the perceived gatekeeper to the world's most exclusive governing bodies, have an important role to play in facilitating Brazil's emergence. Fortunately, the starting point for the new Obama administration is a good relationship with Brasilia.

Nonetheless, the onus is clearly on Brazil's political elite, and the new administration that will be assuming power in January 2011 to take Brazil on the last leg of the diplomatic marathon to join the elite ranks of major powers. Whoever leads Brazil next will also have a solid footing to build upon thanks to the transformative policies carried out, first by Cardoso and more recently by Lula—assuming, that is, that Lula takes advantage of his remaining time and the current favorable political environment to deepen free market economic reforms and orchestrate a smooth transfer of power.

Ultimately, the burden rests with the Brazilian public to shift from thinking of their country in strictly nationalistic terms to that of a global citizen. Only such a shift of mind-set will enable Brazil to make the tradeoffs and sacrifices that are expected of a stakeholder, with Brasilia's management of the Amazon being perhaps the most important litmus test. Brazilians are not alone in struggling with this adjustment; other current and aspiring stakeholders are grappling with similar issues. What sets Brazil apart—and gives hope for its success—is its long-standing self-image as a world leader. Brazil has long believed that it was destined for greatness and belonged at the table of great powers. It is a vision that has sustained the country through difficult times, driven the dramatic turnaround of the last twenty years, and fortifies Brazilians with the confidence to take on the challenges that lie ahead.

## Georges D. Landau's Reaction

### Assessing President Lula—Substance v. Style

The Almeida-Diaz chapter takes a quite laudatory view of Brazil under Lula's stewardship, ascribing to his presidency many of the successes that more properly belong to his predecessor, Fernando Henrique Cardoso: economic stability, the fight against inflation, liberalizing policies including the extinc-tion of state monopolies, and privatization of state enterprises. It is undeni-able that Brazil is today in much better shape than it was when Lula took office in 2003—given the widespread domestic and international fear that the leader of the Workers' Party (PT) would reverse the achievements of his predecessor and institute a socialist regime with the full PT platform devel-oped during twenty-three years in militant opposition. Some of the successes of Lula's administration, it should be noted, are also due to the exceptionally high growth rates in the global economy during most of the 2000s. Brazil was fortunate to be on the "right" side of the commodity supply chain.

Instead, Lula, ever the pragmatist, had the singular good sense to follow the essential features of Cardoso's economic program, and Brazil blossomed. However, that program has run its course. Inflation has been brought under control, thanks to the Central Bank's austere monetary policy, and new poli-cies are now needed. But the government does not seem to have any in store. No structural reforms have been implemented, and they are vitally needed. What is worse, in Lula's second term (2007–2010), there has been a distinct statist and nationalist slant, as evidenced by Lula's handling of the energy sector. Lula has not only stopped the privatization program initiated in the early 1990s, he has reverted to the creation of new state enterprises. He has also shackled operational independence of the regulatory agencies. The only area in which, from day one, Lula's policies differed from those of the preced-ing administration is that of foreign policy—where the president has been consistently pursuing a south-south approach that is ideological instead of pragmatic, and this policy has yet to yield dividends.

The chapter does mention these issues, but as a matter of emphasis does not highlight them. Lula is a highly charismatic politician adept at captivat-ing the masses and charming the elite, but he has little appetite or concern for the dreary task of governing this complex country. And it shows.

The chapter refers to a number of highly appealing programs that Lula has launched with great fanfare. Yet it fails to mention that he never fol-lowed through on them. Fome Zero is an example, environmental protection another, education, public security—there are plenty of illustrations. Dilma Rousseff, his chief of staff, is charged with managing the administration, but her views are stuck in the 1960s. The real issue is that the Brazilian economy and its entrepreneurs seem ready for a new engagement with the world economy, but the country's political leadership, especially the PT po-litical program, is clinging to the same old nationalistic assumptions about north and south, the pseudo-dichotomy between developed and developing economies, us versus them, and so on. Lula, the former trade union boss, is forever a candidate and forgets that, as an elected leader, he must get down to brass tacks, but they simply don't interest him. He attends the conclaves of world leaders, but doesn't do his homework. Appearances are everything. It is enough just that he is there and speechifies. Domestically, too, he seems to think that to solve a problem he merely has to make a speech about it. But Brazil is more than Lula. It has a role to fulfill as a responsible global stakeholder. The question is whether the current government is up to the task. The chapter answers mostly in the affirmative, but serious misgivings are warranted.

### Brazilian Political Culture's Deeper Roots

The chapter does a fine job of analyzing the historical context of modern Brazil and how it got where it is. Similarly, it is insightful regarding the critical differences between Brazil and the other Latin American nations. What Almeida and Diaz miss is a critical sociocultural difference between Brazil and the United States that explains essential aspects of Brazilian political culture. Whereas the United States began as a nation and became a state—with residual powers granted by its components—Brazil is heir to the Iberian centralist-monarchic tradition, in which the sovereign state is the great provider, an end unto itself, around which everything else gravitates; hence its ponderous, stifling, bloated public bureaucracy. The distinction is fundamental, and the authors, for instance, do not give sufficient credit to the private sector for overcoming the obstacles put in its path by the government and securing for Brazil the status of a major player in the global economy.

Almeida and Diaz frequently use the word *consensus*. However, in the Brazilian system of government, no consensus is needed, the president has imperial powers; consequently the crucial concept of *accountability* simply does not exist. In fact, the Portuguese language does not have an equivalent for the word. To be sure, there is an elaborate collection of agencies and mechanisms to control public accounts, but the government can still do what it wishes, and the Congress, more often than not, meekly follows. In practice, in the political realm, consensus means the acquiescence of the legislative to the executive branch. And therein lies another Brazilian idiosyncrasy: form matters more than content. Everything is permissible, provided the outward formalities are preserved.

### Brazilian International Leadership—Achievement or Prospect?

The authors ascribe a leadership role to Brazil. Potentially, the country may indeed be doomed to lead. That leadership, though, should be an expression of internal strengths. And these strengths do exist: an extraordinary, if not unique, endowment of natural resources (enough to make Brazil a granary for the world); strong democratic institutions; a high degree of social tolerance; economic stability; a dynamic industrial and services sector and a sophisticated financial sector; an orderly, ethnically integrated population that will stabilize at 220 million within three decades; and an enormous consumer market. But there are intrinsic weaknesses as well: staggering income inequality, backward rural areas, a deplorable educational standard that is a mortgage on the country's future, a dilapidated infrastructure, a still fairly closed economy with a high degree of state interventionism, exorbitant taxation to finance snowballing public expenditures (without corresponding services to the population), and a "diplomacy of generosity" that the country can ill afford. So, the record is mixed. Brazil will eventually emerge as a strong leader, but it will require a colossal effort and synergy, neither of which is yet in sight.

Meanwhile, Brazil's earnest endeavors—such as its participation in peacekeeping efforts in Haiti and East Timor—have not secured it a permanent seat either on the UN Security Council, or on a G-8 expanded to a G-13, nor indeed to grant it success in the Doha trade round, where its friends in the G-20 pulled the rug out from under it. Brazil would be welcome as a member of OECD, but it would rather not, for fear of alienating its developing country friends. Moreover, the government is unwilling to undertake the requisite incremental next steps in economic opening and trade liberalization. Within South America, Brazil's leadership is consistently challenged by Venezuela's Hugo Chavez and his petrodollar diplomacy, and, for emotional reasons, by Argentina.

Of all these challenges, the most serious setback—for the time being, because it could be reversed—occurred at Doha, which is much more than a round of trade negotiations. The global trade talks symbolize the principle of rules-based multilateralism in the WTO, to which Brazil is deeply committed. Thus, if the country's proactive participation (what the authors call "diplomatic overdrive"), under Lula as a stakeholder in international affairs, enabled it to score some gains, there are as many instances where attempts at leadership were less successful. Proactivity is not the same as leadership.

Another caveat is that there are certain issues of global concern in which Brazil has indeed participated, but has so far failed to make a significant contribution. For instance, Brazil's status as a big polluter—not due to fossil fuel consumption, but rather to widespread deforestation in the Amazon region, which it can't control—would seem to spur an obligation to act. Yet Brazil has confined itself mainly to: (1) requesting funds for the conservation of the tropical forest it so jealously guards, and (2) proclaiming the benefits of sugarcane-based ethanol, whose production does not impinge on that of edible crops. Brazil suffers from paranoia with respect to Amazonia, but does virtually nothing to protect or preserve it. On the question of human rights, Brazil has often chosen for ideological reasons to ignore gross violations in such countries as Cuba, the Sudan, Zimbabwe, and China, and indeed has been ineffectual in controlling similar violations on its own territory. The chapter refers to Itamaraty's (the foreign ministry) perplexity on these issues, but stops short of insisting that, as a responsible international stakeholder with aspirations to regional and global leadership, Brazil should have a principled, rather than an ideological, code of conduct.

## The Unfulfilled Reform Agenda

Summing up, Almeida and Diaz make a convincing case for the growing solidity of Brazil's economy. This is true even though the country's imports are now twice that of the growth of its exports, and it has a steadily increasing deficit in current accounts, as well as a swiftly rising fiscal deficit. On social issues, the authors highlight the pervasive criminality and public insecurity with which the underprivileged classes must contend, though the government is powerless in the face of these realities. The chapter also refers to the issue of corruption, which is an endemic cancer in Brazilian society that will only be overcome through sweeping reforms in the political culture and system. Moreover, the authors rightly underline the importance of institutional stability, but downplay the critical need to ensure accountability. There has been little more than lip service from the Lula government or Brazil's other political parties to indicate a serious reform agenda.

Nor do the authors analyze the increasingly nationalistic—indeed, xenophobic—stance of the present administration, which is reflected in the nature of the bilateral relationship with the United States—it is not that it is poisonous, but neither is it constructive. And the chapter gives perhaps too rosy a view of Brazil's participation in international governance, when in fact it is more show than substance.

The chapter invokes the well-worn joke about "Brazil, the country of the eternal future," but does not really delve into the underpinnings for such a future. Since the public sector does not have the abundant revenues it would take to simultaneously improve education, restore physical infrastructure, finance job-creation programs, add technological value to exports, and so on, then Public-Private Partnerships (PPP) would seem absolutely critical for any progress. However, perhaps as a corollary to PT's fundamental distrust of private enterprise, the federal PPP program has not a single project to show for itself three years after it was launched, while a number of states across the country have successfully embarked on similar programs.

A related issue is that of Brazil's international competitiveness, especially in the face of the overwhelming capacity of China and India. Brazilian entrepreneurs are aggressive and successful in penetrating foreign markets for goods and services, but these businessmen pray that the bungling federal bureaucracy stays well out of the way of their creative strategies. To be sure, the government has policies (such as the Program for Industrial Policy, PDP) aimed at helping the overseas expansion of Brazil's private sector and a very capable financial agency (BNDES, the national development bank) to assist it. But the agency's purview is confined to Latin America, when entrepreneurs' real challenge is the conquest of the North American, European, and Asian markets. The government thinks too small.

This brings us to the possibility that—thanks to Petrobras's recent discovery of enormous oil and gas deposits in the offshore pre-salt layer—Brazil may become one of the world's leading producers (and exporters) of hydrocarbons. This will generate unprecedented wealth, and the government is perplexed as to how it should be handled. While no final decisions have yet been taken, President Lula is on record as favoring the creation of a 100 percent state-owned public enterprise that would be parallel to Petrobras, yet unencumbered by private, let alone foreign, capital. This represents a significant retrogression to the government's erstwhile nationalist-monopolistic stance, which had been superseded by the Petroleum Law of 1997 that enabled Petrobras to partner with foreign enterprise and achieve Brazil's self-sufficiency in petroleum production. The pre-salt could serve as a bridge to Brazil's future, but not if encumbered with a philosophy rooted in the past.

## Notes

1. *New York Times* article quoting Marcelo Cortes Neri, director of the Center for Social Policies at the Getulio Vargas Foundation in Rio de Janeiro: "Strong Economy Propels Brazil to World Stage," Alexei Barrionuevo, July 31, 2008.

2. Ibid.

3. Speech by President Luis Inacio Silvas de Lula at the fifty-eighth session of the UN General Assembly, September 23, 2003, available in Portuguese at www.mre.gov.br/portugues/politica_externa/discursos_detalhe3.asp?ID_DISCURSO=2153 (accessed on July 1, 2008).

4. Military Expenditure Database of the Stockholm International Peace Research Institute, 2008, available at milexdata.sipri.or/result.php4 (accessed on July 1, 2008).

PART 4

# SQUARE PEGS

# South Africa: From Beacon of Hope to Rogue Democracy?

*Pauline H. Baker and Princeton N. Lyman*
*With a Reaction by Khehla Shubane*

South Africa's extraordinary negotiated transition from apartheid to democracy in 1994 was hailed as a supreme example of statesmanship, commitment to democracy, and the triumph of human rights and political reconciliation. Nelson Mandela, whose own struggle for freedom included twenty-seven years in prison, dazzled South Africa and the world by guiding the country back from the brink of a race war with a spirit of reconciliation and a firm commitment to multiracial democracy.

Not surprisingly, therefore, the world looked to South Africa as a beacon of democracy and a champion of human rights—a "rainbow nation," to use Archbishop Desmond Tutu's words—that would embrace all of its black, white, mixed-race, and Asian peoples equally and guarantee their individual rights under the law. Women were given real political power, with quotas in party lists for parliamentary representation. In sum, post-apartheid South Africa was expected to be a principled leader in international affairs, a country whose moral authority would enable it to "punch above its weight," not only in Africa, but also globally. Indeed, Mandela himself encouraged such expectations. On the eve of the 1994 elections, he declared "human rights will be the light that guides our foreign policy."[1]

Human rights was not the only area in which South Africa was expected to play a significant and positive role. Endowed with relatively high levels of industrialization and infrastructure, South Africa was a natural engine of growth for sub-Saharan Africa. The pragmatic, market-oriented economic policies adopted by the country's post-apartheid African National Congress

(ANC) rulers were strikingly farsighted, given the ANC's long-standing espousal of socialist philosophy, enshrined for fifty years in the party's Freedom Charter. South African economic policy was thus presented as a model to other African countries whose statist policies over the previous decades had left them impoverished and debt-ridden. Finally, South Africa, even prior to Mandela's election, had given up its nuclear weapons and submitted to close international inspection of its peaceful nuclear facilities. South Africa thus gained credibility as both a model and a strong advocate of nonproliferation.

South Africa set out almost immediately to play a leading and largely reformist role in multilateral institutions—including the Southern Africa Development Community (SADC), where it soon took over the presidency; the Non-Aligned Movement, which it led from 1998 to 2003; and the Organization of African Unity (OAU), later converted into the African Union (AU). Both Mandela and the South African leadership became deeply engaged in efforts to end several deadly and protracted conflicts in the region, including those in Burundi, Congo, and Sudan. In the 1995 negotiations for permanent renewal of the Nuclear Nonproliferation Treaty (a major objective of U.S. policy), South Africa was credited with overcoming staunch African resistance by brokering compromises that led to a unanimous supportive vote in the United Nations.

Relations with the United States also were expected to be positive. The United States played an influential role in the international ostracism of the apartheid regime when Congress enacted comprehensive economic sanctions against the apartheid government over the veto of a popular president, Ronald Reagan. There also were strong ties between U.S. and South African civil society groups, from the African American community to churches, labor unions, universities, local governments, and corporate shareholders, all of which were actively engaged in the fight against apartheid. Many U.S. companies had unilaterally pulled out of South Africa, as the ANC advocated. In the expectation that these historical ties and political affinity would open doors to American businesses and pave the way generally for cooperation, the Clinton administration set up a bilateral commission with South Africa and designated it one of ten top "emerging markets" for U.S. interests. There was little question that South Africa would become a natural ally of the United States, and assume its role as a responsible global stakeholder on a number of issues. As will be explained below, some of these assumptions were unrealistic, but at the time they seemed entirely reasonable and were regularly reinforced by both sides in high-level visits and official statements.[2]

Fast forward to 2008. A *Washington Post* op-ed in March castigated South Africa for turning its back on all these principles, ticking off a litany of "sins."

> South Africa has actively blocked United Nations discussions about human rights in Zimbabwe—and in Belarus, Cuba, North Korea, and Uzbekistan. South Africa was the only real democracy to vote against a resolution demanding that the Burmese junta stop ethnic cleansing and free dissident Aung San Suu Kyi. When Iranian nuclear proliferation was debated in the Security Council, South Africa dragged out discussions and demanded watered-down language in the resolution. South Africa opposed a resolution condemning rape and attacks on civilians in Darfur and rolled out the red carpet for a visit from Sudan's genocidal leader. In the General Assembly, South Africa fought against a resolution condemning the use of rape as a weapon of war because the resolution was not sufficiently anti-American.

The author proposed a new foreign policy category to describe South Africa: a "rogue democracy."[3] Another *Washington Post* editor writing at the same time dismissed South Africa as the "ever-reliable voting partner" of Russia and China in resisting the UN Security Council's efforts to implement the responsibility to protect, a norm that urges outside intervention when a state cannot, or will not, protect its own people from grievous human rights violations.[4] South African Nobel laureate Desmond Tutu lamented that South Africa seemed to have lost its moral compass.

South Africa had for years also been the subject of wide criticism for its stance on HIV/AIDS—with the government first questioning matters of widely accepted science and then dragging its feet on antiviral treatment and prevention programs, despite having one of the highest infection rates in the world.[5] The government's stance toward Zimbabwe was another target of mounting international criticism. As Zimbabwe's situation worsened steadily after 2003 from political repression and economic collapse, South African President Thabo Mbeki was appointed by SADC as a mediator, but his "quiet diplomacy" failed to avert steady economic and political deterioration under the increasingly despotic rule in its northern neighbor. Many observers did not view Mbeki as a neutral negotiator, as he shielded Robert Mugabe from external pressures. In 2005, President Bush said that the United States would follow South Africa's lead on Zimbabwe. But by July 2008, after President Mugabe was using violence to thwart the opposition during a runoff presidential election, and South Africa led resistance in the United Nations to sanctions, a U.S. ambassador at the United Nations drew a stinging parallel, charging that while Mugabe had used violence to fragment the opposition, Mbeki had used diplomacy to do the same thing.[6]

How could this turnaround happen in less than fifteen years? Has South Africa consciously abandoned the lofty principles it had held dear, becoming narrowly protective of its national interests, its leaders' personal views, and the ruling party's political survival? Should the international community have expected South Africa to become "more normal, less special"? Or has South Africa instead merely arrived at hard conclusions as it moves from liberation to governance? What are its real comparative advantages on the international stage, especially given the burdens of the historical legacy of apartheid and huge domestic challenges? There is actually some truth in all these interpretations as, overall, South Africa faces hard realities, both at home and internationally. In the coming decade, pragmatic factors, not abstract principles, will shape South Africa's performance, whatever global objectives South Africa chooses to pursue.

## The Identity Crisis

While apartheid has been excised from the laws and statutes, the country's post-apartheid transition is far from complete, and the strains of the process have begun to show. South Africa is, in fact, in the grip of a postliberation identity crisis, somewhat akin to Turkey's ambivalence over its Muslim identity and its secularist traditions. In South Africa, though, the conflicting pressures are even more complex.

At the same time, the country is struggling to:

1. Overcome widespread poverty (apartheid's most enduring legacy) while preserving the market-based economy it has nurtured since the advent of majority rule.
2. Mitigate extraordinary income inequality based mostly, but not entirely, on racial lines, while respecting business interests and preserving technical skills.
3. Balance the relatively conservative fiscal and monetary policies that have put it on a sound economic footing since the transition against growing, and well-organized, populist demands for more aggressive state action on the needs of the poor.
4. Compete economically against powerful emerging market rivals globally while dealing with powerful unions and high labor costs domestically.
5. Bear the burden of leading, however tentatively, a continent in distress that is, at the same time, suspicious of potential South African hegemony.

6. Stabilize democracy as the political system transitions from first-generation liberation leaders, most of whom were in jail or exile during the apartheid period and who presided over a one-party dominant political system, to a younger and more diverse generation. Could this transition process, over the next decade, unravel the dominance of the ANC and create rival power centers?[7]

South Africa's identity crisis thus involves a clash of the two worlds that uneasily coexist within the country. There is a developed and a developing South Africa—the former consisting of a minority population of wealthy blacks, whites, and Indians who enjoy the fruits of the developed world, and the latter consisting of the vast majority population, mostly blacks and mixed-race, or "colored," who are still mired in the poverty of the developing world. Awareness of this widening gap between rich and poor is rising at a moment of leadership transition and uncertainty.

At the same time, South Africa still pursues its ambitions to become both a regional and a global leader in international affairs. It wants a seat on the UN Security Council and, in claiming that right, will continue to champion African independence of action against perceived Western or, for that matter, Eastern pressure.[8] It will assert its right to define international leadership and "global responsibility" on its own terms. In this vein, for both practical and principled reasons, it has given greater priority to "sovereign democracy," a term which reflects South Africa's self-image as a champion of the collective voice of the "south" rather than of individual human rights and democratic governance. Thus, here too, there is tension between two identities: one pulls South Africa toward aligning with Western interests and playing a constructive global role in international organizations, while the other pulls it toward solidarity with the causes of the Third World in opposition to perceived Western hegemony.

These seeming paradoxes between mounting domestic pressures, a continuing adherence to democratic governance at home, and a somewhat split personality on international goals will not necessarily cripple South Africa's ability to serve as a responsible stakeholder, but they will likely make South African foreign policy far less predictable. Pretoria will have to factor a number of variables into its policies—domestic demands, party fissures, and the broader emergence of factionalized elites within the political class and closer relations with the G-77 and other African nations, as well as short-term national interests. It might be extreme to describe it as a "rogue democracy," but we anticipate that South Africa will often confound Western expectations and wishes—sometimes seeming headstrong, recalcitrant, or inconsistent as it picks and chooses its way in international politics.

## Internal Strengths

In the first years of the post-apartheid era, South Africa confounded predictions as well, but in the other direction. Even sympathetic observers believed that the combination of nearly unchecked electoral power, accumulated resentment, and pent-up demands among its constituents would propel the ANC into autocracy and reckless economic policies.[9] Neither prediction proved true.

South Africa's post-apartheid leaders produced one of the strongest and most liberal democratic constitutions in the world. It provides for an independent constitutional court and guarantees a free press and other civil and political rights regardless of race, religion, or ethnicity. The constitution established a Human Rights Commission to investigate violations, to check corruption through independent (or relatively so) audit and investigative bodies, to elect a parliament, and to develop a substantial set of economic rights that provide access to such things as housing and health care. Even more remarkable, the negotiations prior to the landmark elections of 1994 affirmed a set of principles that are immutable and beyond the reach of any subsequent legislative changes. These principles include protection of minority rights, a federal system of government, and a constitutional court charged not only with upholding the constitution, but also the preconstitutional immutable principles. This political innovation was instrumental in easing the transition and averting internal conflict, and it has no parallel in any other republic. As a demonstration of its embrace of diversity, South Africa has eleven official languages, with all national laws and the parliamentary debates translated into each one.

Since the adoption of the new constitution, these institutions have remained viable and, in many ways, robust. There have been instances of suppressed investigations of corruption and some attempts to politically influence the judiciary and other purportedly independent bodies. Under previously enforced ANC discipline, the parliament has not acted as a significant check on executive power. Nevertheless, as a credit to the independence and durability of the constitutional court, both the Mandela and Mbeki administrations lost cases before it and bowed to its directives. Mandela even praised the independence of the judiciary when it ruled some of his decisions unconstitutional. The extended court struggles of former South African Deputy President (and subsequently ANC president) Jacob Zuma, and a judicial finding that his corruption charges stemmed at least partly from the politicized interests of the Mbeki presidency, prompted verbal assaults on the judicial system from many quarters. Even so, the judicial system has thus far withstood those pressures and remains a respected pillar of the rule of law. The press remains free and dynamic. Opposition parties are free to operate, raise issues in parliament, and compete for provincial government despite the ANC's dominance.

The Mandela-Mbeki administrations also stuck with conservative economic policies, much to the dismay of the labor and communist constituencies within the ANC. Determined to avoid the mistakes of other debt-ridden African countries, the ANC was fiscally responsible in the extreme. It thus rejected offers of both concessional loans from the World Bank and higher interest credits from Japan and other donors. In the first five years after Mandela's election, the government had reduced its short-term debt by 80 percent, decreased inflation from 15 percent to 6 percent and, in 2001 achieved South Africa's first budget surplus in decades. Annual economic growth has been steady, if not spectacular, since 1994—between 4 percent and 5 percent.

Fiscal prudence since the transition to majority rule did not impede investment and progress in broadly shared development and growing social expenditures. Electricity has been extended to 3.5 million homes, including many in the shantytowns surrounding the country's major cities. Free water is provided to 3.9 million households and water infrastructure now reaches nearly 90 percent of the population. More than 1,300 clinics have been built and 2,300 upgraded. Free medical services are provided to pregnant women and children, with health services receiving 101 million patient visits a year. Perhaps most significant in providing an economic safety net, social security and social assistance grants have been the fastest-growing spending category—reaching $10 billion in 2006, with ten million beneficiaries (fully one-quarter of the population) and constituting 3.4 percent of gross domestic product (GDP).

As a result of these policies, financial institutions have remained strong, and the Johannesburg Stock Exchange has attracted substantial foreign investment. South Africa escaped much of the fallout from the Asian financial crisis of the late 1990s. It has not, however, been immune to the 2008 global financial crisis that originated in the United States and spread worldwide. However, while the global recession is hitting South Africa at a time of political uncertainty, steady stewardship of the economy has made it less vulnerable. Good economic management and banking supervision have so far protected South Africa's banks from the risk of bankruptcy that has gripped banks elsewhere. South Africa was hit with an early 20 percent drop in the stock exchange and a depreciation of the rand, but no banks have failed and, at the time of this writing, financial institutions seem stable. The country could face deeper economic challenges from a possible drop in the price of gold and other commodities, such as platinum and coal, to which the rand's performance is closely tied. There could also be a shortfall in capital flows; by November 2008, "foreigners sold a net 48 billion rand ($6.1 billion) in local stocks, compared with a net buy of 62 billion rand the same time a year before."[10]

Any exodus of investors and professionals skittish about future leadership and policy changes could also be hurtful. Investors will watch the evolving leadership transition to detect sharp swings in economic policies. The public will also feel the sting of higher rates for loans and mortgages as repossession of homes and automobiles rises.

## Economic Challenges

Notwithstanding this impressive record of economic growth and social expenditures and its ability to ride out global economic crises, South Africa still faces structural challenges in overcoming the immense economic and social legacies of apartheid. This is beginning to take a toll on its political stability. Even with steady growth, South Africa by 2006 merely returned to its per capita GDP level of 1980 (the country had poor economic growth during the final fourteen years of apartheid). Annual growth would have had to reach 6–7 percent to make a dent in the country's unemployment. Instead, black unemployment remains between 27–40 percent, income inequality is much greater than in most countries, and the education system remains inadequate to promote real social mobility. For a long time these problems were tolerated by the population out of gratitude to the ANC for political liberation and satisfaction with political freedom. Moreover, before the ANC leadership split, there was no viable alternative to the dominance of the ANC. It is unclear whether a breakaway faction could generate significant support in the short run (i.e., by the 2009 election), but it is a feasible scenario in the long run.

As the wheels of the ANC train have started to wobble, South Africans and others wonder about the direction of future leaders and the nation's ability to manage its heavy burdens. The confluence of several recent events cast doubt over the stability and harmony South Africa achieved for more than a decade after liberation—the rise of a privileged black elite of multimillionaires, indictments of high-ranking ANC officials for corruption, extremely high rates of violent crime, the influx of refugees and economic migrants from other African countries, the scourge of HIV/AIDS, a large bulge in youth unemployment, and an increasingly restive poor population—all of which are breeding popular discontent that is being expressed in violent ways and factionalism in the political class.

The growth of a black middle class is a good example of the dilemma South Africa faces, and the strains that are coming to the surface. The number of blacks in the middle class has risen dramatically, from 300,000 in 2004 to 2.6 million in 2007. In one sense, this is one of the most remarkable successes of the government's economic policies. Indeed, it is singled out as one of the goals of the government's affirmative action program, Black Economic Empowerment.[11] This program also is credited with stimulating the consumer economy and bringing diversity to the upper echelons of corporate boardrooms.

But even Mbeki himself was troubled by the excesses of the so-called black bourgeoisie and its seeming single-minded focus on self-enrichment.[12] Others have joined the chorus, brandishing the list of new (and often ANC-linked) billionaires across the front pages of the newspapers. Public resentment has been inflamed by the extravagant lifestyles of the wealthy, and their fast growth as a class has spurred suspicions about rising levels of corruption. There is an issue, moreover, about whether this development is truly deep-rooted—whether it represents corporate window dressing and special favoritism, co-opting blacks rather than structurally changing the economy. Some black-owned companies are doing quite well, but they still are proportionally much fewer than white-owned business. In all, black-owned firms comprise less than 3 percent of the Johannesburg Stock Exchange.

Another major source of controversy, both within South Africa and abroad, was Mbeki's sustained downplay of the HIV/AIDS crisis in the country, even though South Africa has one of world's largest AIDS-infected populations. The roots of Mbeki's attitude toward HIV/AIDS are explored later in this chapter because it illuminates one of the threads of South Africa's foreign policy. Suffice it to say, the policy severely damaged South Africa's reputation abroad and dismayed South Africans trying to wrestle with this national catastrophe. Only because of strong civil society protests, and the decisions handed down by the constitutional court, did the Mbeki administration finally adopt significant treatment programs. However, even with substantial budgets now allocated to the disease, more than R4.5 billion in 2007, the government had not aggressively tackled the problem. Mbeki remained stubbornly loyal to his discredited minister of health, who insisted on native foods as treatment and who resisted many of the most important advances in treatment until forced to accept them. One of the first acts the post-Mbeki administration of interim president Kgalema Motlanthe instituted was to replace the minister of health, a widely applauded result of the recent political turmoil.

A direct foreign policy consequence of the HIV/AIDS crisis is its impact on the security services. South Africa's contribution to peace processes in its region stems in part from its ability to deploy well-trained and well-equipped peacekeepers; for instance, in Burundi and the Democratic Republic of the Congo. But because South Africa will not deploy service personnel abroad who are HIV-positive, the country's personnel pool has been limited to three thousand peacekeepers. Having maxed out its available pool in ongoing peacekeeping operations, the country will have to limit future foreign policy initiatives.

Another blow to Mbeki's legacy, but even more to South Africa's vaunted economic prowess, has been a severe electricity shortage that erupted in 2008, revealing a lack of forward thinking and needed investment. An administration that had previously been regarded as technocratically competent and administratively sophisticated was revealed to be dismissive of expert admonitions and of warnings regarding the consequences of increased demands for power after a decade of economic growth. The power outages also fed criticism of South Africa's Black Economic Empowerment policies (affirmation action decisions for employment and contracts favoring blacks), with some critics tracing the problem to the replacement of skilled white technicians by less qualified black ones. The power company, Eskom, has tacitly acknowledged this criticism by beginning to hire back recent white retirees. Meanwhile, the power crisis, along with the changing political leadership within the ANC, sent white applications for emigration visas soaring, further undermining confidence in governance. Any continued pattern of crises and mismanagement could risk further brain drain, both black and white.

The power shortage may reflect deeper economic problems and energy insecurity, potentially burdening South Africa financially for several years, lowering growth rates, and requiring massive investment. South Africa has relied on domestic coal supplies for power, but these may no longer be sufficient. One reason for South Africa's ambivalence about Iran's nuclear program is its own contemplation of a major investment in nuclear energy, drawing on the extensive experience and infrastructure associated with its earlier weapons program and its existing modest nuclear power facilities.

If all these developments were not enough, popular frustration over lack of jobs and advancement reached a boiling point in 2008 in the form of surprise attacks on African immigrants accused of taking South African jobs. This was a significant eruption of spontaneous mass violence by a frustrated population looking for scapegoats. Caught off guard by the worst outbreak of internal conflict since apartheid, the government was initially paralyzed. Resentment toward the estimated three million Zimbabwean refugees and other migrants had been building up for some time, and xenophobic riots erupted across the country. To quell the unrest, the government had to call in the military, marking the first the military was used to clamp down on public demonstrations in the post-apartheid era. Though deaths were, thankfully, limited to sixty-five, hundreds were injured; tens of thousands were driven from their homes, many of whom fled back across neighboring borders. This was a sudden eruption of mass rage by the poor and unemployed. Despite Mbeki's denunciation of the violence and apologies to affected African governments, South Africa's pan-African credentials were sorely damaged, along with its reputation for stability. Contributing to the embarrassment, the fleeing migrants came from many countries that during apartheid had offered safe haven to South African exiles.

## ANC Leadership Transition

Finally, there is the instability that emanates from former Deputy President Jacob Zuma's tumultuous rise to power. Mbeki had dismissed Zuma from the number two position in 2005 for alleged corruption, but Zuma fought the charges and built a strong challenge to Mbeki, culminating in Mbeki's defeat in December 2007 for a third term as ANC president. Events moved even more dramatically after a judicial showdown over Zuma's corruption indictment, when his supporters within the party forced Mbeki to resign the presidency of the country. As the new ANC president, Zuma became the presumed frontrunner in South Africa's 2009 presidential elections.

Zuma's labor and radical supporters within the ANC had for some time been sharply critical of Mbeki's market-oriented and fiscally conservative economic policies. In effect, this was a generational revolt, marked more by ideology than by age, with the "populists" displacing the "liberators," especially those who had been in exile during the anti-apartheid struggle and who were perceived as more sympathetic to the black bourgeoisie than responsive to the needs of the underprivileged.

The party split also prompted a great deal of uncertainty about South Africa's future economic policies and its commitment to the rule of law. On economic policy, Zuma has sought to reassure business, as well as the public, on economic policy. The retention of Finance Minister Trevor Manuel, a mainstay of the Mandela and Mbeki administrations, as part of interim President Kgalema Motlanthe's cabinet was helpful in that regard. Of special concern, nevertheless, have been the threats made against the judiciary by the leader of the militant ANC Youth League, which, though refuted by Zuma, raised worries about the independence of the judiciary under a Zuma presidency. And if the indictment against Zuma is eventually quashed due to political pressure from his supporters, who argue for a political rather than a judicial resolution of the corruption allegations, then many would rightly ask what that would mean for accountability for South African leaders. The Zuma wing of the ANC has also successfully pushed for the dissolution of the Scorpions, the anti-corruption police unit that has fiercely pursued its mission, including investigating Zuma's corruption charges. Further concern has been sparked by the call of the ANC secretary-general for changing South Africa's land reform process from "willing buyer and willing seller" to one in which the government could presumably allocate land for distribution and set the terms of compensation.

Zuma himself has worked to allay these worries, pointing out that the longtime presence in the ANC of the South African Communist Party and the ANC Youth League never derailed its pragmatic economic policies in the past. He also expressed faith in the ANC's decision-making process—in which policy proposals are put forward, distributed widely, and debated with the ANC as a whole before making ultimate decisions—claiming that these will, overall, be more pragmatic.[13] But if the moderates in the ANC are sidelined, or leave to form another party, then more radical elements could end up having control over the party.

Indeed, the degree to which the old guard was being purged—most of Mbeki's cabinet resigned with him and provincial premiers were forced to resign in favor of pro-Zuma ones—suggests a new political era is emerging that will see the first serious black party competition to the ANC and wider multiparty politics in South Africa. The process, however, could be messy, lengthy, and potentially destabilizing in the short run.

It would be a mistake, however, to view these events as indicators of a steady downward trend. The country still has exceptional infrastructure and strong political institutions. It plays a major role—as discussed below—in the economy of the rest of the continent. It boasts many skilled people, first-class universities, a vibrant free press, religious tolerance, a strong civil society, diverse cultural heritages, and major achievements in a variety of fields from health to literature. Moreover, the extraordinary political changes of the past year were all carried out under constitutional procedures, a point that Zuma supporters took pains to highlight. The country will indeed be challenged in the coming years, but there is much to admire in South Africa—and grounds for confidence and optimism for the future. It retains a wealth of assets to deal with these domestic challenges and to assume a major role as a responsible global stakeholder. However, the next group of leaders will likely be compelled to balance such aspirations against the imperatives of internal needs, limiting the country's ability to play a prominent role on the international scene.

## The Evolution of Foreign Policy

Despite the lamentations on the part of South Africa's current critics, the country's foreign policy was, in fact, never as purely principled as some of the early rhetoric suggested. While Mandela spoke of his commitment to human rights everywhere, he also maintained strong loyalty to rulers and regimes that had supported the ANC in its anti-apartheid struggle, regardless of their poor human rights records. Under Mandela's presidency, South Africa retained close relationships with Indonesia's Suharto, Libya's Qadhafi, Cuba's Castro, and, after 1996, with China. South Africa opposed resolutions in the UN Human Rights Commission against any of these regimes.

Post-apartheid South Africa also saw its arms industry (the world's tenth-largest) as an attractive source of foreign exchange earnings and political leverage. Despite an oversight committee set up to regulate arms sales according to principles of conflict prevention and human rights, post-apartheid South Africa sold arms to Chad, Indonesia, Rwanda, both sides in Sudan's civil war, Angola, and Algeria. Only strong pressure from the United States led South Africa to cancel a sales agreement with Syria.[14]

Together, these factors made for a foreign policy more complex and more serving of national and political/economic interests than idealists had hoped. For example, in spite of long-standing ANC sympathy for the liberation movement in East Timor, Mandela pledged to sell arms to Indonesia on a state visit there in 1997, and South Africa abstained on Human Rights Commission resolutions regarding Indonesian violence against the Timorese in 1997 and 1998. Soon after assuming power, Mandela also set a pattern that has been a constant in South Africa's posture on the global scene: a strong preference for adherence to a form of multilateralism that tilts in favor of the "south," both as a principle of policy and as a justification for not acting more forthrightly in defense of human rights issues abroad.

Mandela articulated the basis of this approach during his first tour of Southeast Asia in 1997. Questioned about the dubious human rights records of some of the countries he was visiting, Mandela stated that:

South Africa would not be influenced by the differences which exist between internal policies of a particular country and ourselves. . . . There are countries where there are human rights violations, but these countries have been accepted by the United Nations, by the Commonwealth of Nations, and the Non-Aligned Movement. Why should we let ourselves depart from what international organizations are doing?[15]

On this tour, Mandela expressed no qualms over the decision of the Association of Southeast Asian Nations (ASEAN) to admit Burma as a member, nor—astonishingly—did he speak out on behalf of the detained and fellow Nobel Peace Prize laureate, Aung San Suu Kyi, whose years of detention in the struggle for democracy bore obvious parallels with his own experience. Subsequently, the leader of Burma's military regime attended Mbeki's inauguration in 1999.

## Critical Early Setbacks

Three early foreign policy setbacks[16] also played a role in tempering South Africa's view of its global role, narrowing the purposes for which it would use its vaunted global moral position and its regional economic and military strength. The first came in 1995 in Nigeria, which was then under the military dictatorship of Sani Abacha.

When Abacha arrested the prominent political dissident, environmental activist, and writer Ken Saro-Wiwa, Mandela believed he had secured Abacha's commitment not to execute Saro-Wiwa and other activists from the Niger Delta region who protested poverty and opposed the government. But when Abacha did just that, Mandela was outraged and called for an oil embargo against Nigeria. He warned Abacha that he was "sitting on a volcano and I am going to explode it under him." Mandela soon found South Africa quite alone among African countries in its stance on the Nigeria problem. Indeed, the OAU publicly castigated the South African position on sanctions, and no other African country even withdrew diplomatic representation in Lagos or protested the executions. South Africa was accused of breaking African solidarity, being hoodwinked by the United States and the United Kingdom, and acting "pro-Western." South Africa soon backtracked, bowing to a SADC decision to, in effect, take no action against Nigeria. Twelve years later, a South African official would tell a group of interested academics that South Africa had vowed "never again" to allow itself to be positioned outside (and presumably embarrassed by) "the African consensus."

The second setback was the military intervention in Lesotho in 1998. Acting ostensibly under a SADC mandate, South Africa, along with Botswana, sent troops into the small neighboring country to restore order and reverse an attempted coup. Although the intervention succeeded in its objective, it was accompanied by looting, destruction of property, and several deaths that led to a strong anti–South African backlash. Mandela had sought to broaden the remit of SADC beyond economic matters to the collective support of democracy and stability in the region. The Lesotho episode was a painful reminder that South Africa's apartheid-era history of encroaching on its neighbors continued to linger in the minds of other African nations, regardless of South Africa's new democracy.

The third setback came with the collapse in the late 1990s of the Mobutu government in Zaire (later renamed the Democratic Republic of the Congo, or DRC). As a strong rebel force was moving across the country, Mandela sought to bring about a transition government with a "soft landing" for Mobutu. Since Uganda and Rwanda, as well as SADC member Angola, were already heavily engaged in helping the rebel forces of Laurent Kabila to overthrow Mobutu, Mandela's efforts failed. When Joseph Kabila's government a few years later was itself threatened by a rebellion (again supported by Rwanda and Uganda), Zimbabwe President Robert Mugabe came to Kabila's aid with forces he sent on his supposed authority as head of SADC's newly created Peace and Stability Organ. Mandela had opposed any SADC military intervention, but was forced to live with the decision. While South Africa would subsequently emerge as a major negotiator of peace in the DRC, with a sizable contribution of peacekeepers, it had learned the limits of its diplomatic ability to set the policies and actions of its closest neighbors and of its primary regional organization, the SADC, despite its overwhelming economic leverage.

## Redefining South African Foreign Policy

When Thabo Mbeki acceded to the presidency in 1999 he set about reshaping South Africa's foreign policy. One guiding principle was that South Africa would act as much as possible within the African consensus. Beyond Africa, South Africa would link with other influential members of the global south—fellow "advanced" developing countries, such as China and India, which were already players in the global economy but shared the view that the system was still rigged both against them and against the poorer countries. South Africa would walk a fine line, asserting its influence through both its relative economic and military power, and as a natural "bridge" between the industrialized West and the less developed African majority. At the same time, it would remain acutely sensitive to charges from countries in the Non-Aligned Movement that, whether in talking of democracy or negotiating compacts with the G-8, it was essentially acting as a neocolonial power and a stalking horse for the interests of the West. One way to meet this problem was to reformulate South Africa's "mission" to the world from human rights to sovereign democracy, serving as a champion of the larger majority of developing countries in international institutions and in the workings of the global economy. Mbeki has, for example, proposed a "G-8 of the south," a strategic partnership that could bargain effectively with the industrialized powers.

Mbeki laid out this new formulation at a conference of the Department of Foreign Affairs shortly after his inaugural. He set out four priorities: restructuring the OAU/African Union and SADC; reforming international organizations such as the United Nations, the World Trade Organization, the International Monetary Fund (IMF), the World Bank, and the Commonwealth; hosting major international conferences (presumably for South Africa to help shape the priorities of the sponsoring organizations); and advancing peace and security in Africa and the Middle East.

South Africa's controversial vote in the UN Security Council on Burma can be better understood in this context. South Africa officially said that the Security Council was exceeding its mandate and interfering with the ongoing UN negotiations with the Burmese government. But a South African government spokesman explained that the purpose was to send a message that the United States and its Western allies could no longer set a selective agenda for the Security Council, picking which countries to criticize and which issues constitute a threat to international peace and security. The vote also signaled the importance South Africa was giving to its alignment with China on international governance issues. Critics did not miss the irony of this position, since the ANC had called for similar censure of the apartheid government on human rights grounds when it was out of power. Much to the chagrin of anti-apartheid activists worldwide who had fought to promote human rights in South Africa before 1994, Pretoria's international advocacy on behalf of human rights was simply subordinated to other imperatives after the ANC came to power.

But Mbeki's own approach to such issues is even more complex than this strategic formulation suggests. A closer look at the bundle of inner feelings, contradictions, intellectual brilliance, and economic sophistication that were all part of his approach to leadership helps explain some of the seemingly bizarre positions he had taken—for example, with regard to HIV/AIDS, and to the deepening political and economic crisis in Zimbabwe. It also provides insight into his singular foreign policy initiative, the New Partnership for Africa's Development (NEPAD).

This chapter does not permit a detailed analysis of Mbeki's personality, history, and experiences.* Suffice it to say that Mbeki's parents, especially his father, were prominent in the South African Communist Party and militant in the anti-apartheid struggle. Yet they, especially his mother, also spent years working to increase the sophistication and economic capacity of their poverty-stricken rural neighbors—without much success.

Mbeki shared this ambivalence, with a deep desire to see Africa reform and adopt sounder governance, policies of economic modernization, and more effective regional and subregional institutions—reforms he saw as essential for Africa to take advantage of the globalization process and overcome some of the continent's problems of poverty and conflict. Yet Mbeki also carried a deep resentment of what he perceived to be Western, primarily white, condescension toward blacks. So conflicted was he that even his belief in the importance of cooperation with the West for development was tinged with suspicion that whites, whether in their policy recommendations or offers of assistance, simply do not believe Africans can run things.

Mbeki saw malicious intentions behind the association of HIV/AIDS with sexual behavior and its being traced to origins in Africa. These ideas were, as Mbeki saw it, clearly part of a Western attempt to demean Africans as sexually promiscuous and irresponsible. Mbeki portrayed even Africans who advocate more attention to the disease as bolstering such prejudices. Instead, Mbeki represented the disease as just one manifestation of the conditions of poverty and malnutrition, which should be the real priority of both African nations and donors. In the same vein, he saw efforts to spread treatment and newly developed drugs as forcing Africa into dependency on Western-manufactured pharmaceuticals, similarly diverting resources from the fundamental problems of poverty.[17]

The same suspicion of Western motives influenced his approach to Zimbabwe, a policy second only to HIV/AIDS as a source of criticism for South Africa, and particularly of Mbeki. Here, too, it appeared to critics, both within and outside South Africa, that South Africa had turned its back on its commitment to human rights and democracy. Mbeki, however, saw it differently. His perspective was rooted, partly, in his disdain for the Zimbabwean Movement for Democratic Change (MDC) opposition party, which he and

---

*For a fuller analysis of Mbeki's background and approach to policy, see Mark Gevisser, *Thabo Mbeki: The Dream Deferred* (Johannesburg: Jonathan Ball Publishers, 2007); William Mervin Gumede, *Thabo Mbeki and the Battle for the Soul of the ANC* (Cape Town, South Africa: Zebra Press, 2005).

Mugabe both saw as a tool of white interests and as a challenge to the rightful rule of liberation movements, no matter what their mismanagement. Perhaps, as some suggest, he saw parallels between these challenges to Mugabe's ZANU government and the criticisms he was receiving from the labor base of the ANC. Or he might have feared that the same manipulation of the land issue that fueled the conflict in Zimbabwe could erupt in South Africa.

Whatever the reasons, the Mbeki government bristled at Western calls for South Africa to use its significant leverage in Zimbabwe—for example, its control over of Zimbabwe's electrical power lines and transportation links to bring down the Mugabe government. To South Africa, such overt attempts at regime change against a fellow African country would clearly invite charges that South Africa is aggressive and throwing its weight around on the continent, just as the predecessor apartheid government did. In addition, Mbeki noted that the electricity grid supplied not only Zimbabwe, but also other countries in the region, and he could not single out one country without hurting others. Finally, Mbeki was convinced that whatever the hardships associated with Mugabe's misrule, a violent collapse of the country—with millions more migrants and other economic fallout—would land principally upon South Africa, not on those who criticized his policy. Given the harm that he felt would result from stronger sanctions, diplomacy was, as Mbeki saw it, the only recourse.

Add to this, finally, Mbeki's instinctive reaction against Western criticism of Africans. In an apparently emotional letter to President George W. Bush, Mbeki denounced U.S. criticism of the government in Zimbabwe, and its call for stronger action by Zimbabwe's neighbors, as yet another example of white insinuation that black Africans cannot manage their own affairs. To Mbeki, the Zimbabwe drama called for patience and trust and Africans would eventually solve it on their own terms—notwithstanding the toll this position had on his own country, Zimbabwe's population, the region, African solidarity, and Western confidence in South Africa's leadership.[18]

## NEPAD

If Africa is the cornerstone of South African foreign policy, as that country's leaders often proclaim, then the New Partnership for Africa's Development (NEPAD) might be its most important policy initiative. Launched jointly by Mbeki, former Nigerian President Olusegun Obasanjo, Senegalese President Abdoulaye Wade, and Algerian President Abdelaziz Bouteflika, NEPAD was founded in 2001 as a grand bargain of African commitment to good governance, sound economic management, corporate governance, and regional and subregional development paired with the G-8's commitment to increased aid, debt relief, and trade reform. NEPAD was presented to the G-8 at the summit of 2002, where it was warmly praised, and led to the formulation of the G-8 Africa Action Plan, which, in turn, served as the basis of ongoing G-8 Africa dialogue. NEPAD has many facets, but among the most innovative is a program of peer review, whereby African countries submit themselves to review by a panel of Africans from other countries who assess the country's performance under NEPAD principles, with the resulting report debated at the Africa Union summit.

Even with NEPAD, South Africa found itself uncomfortably caught in the continuing tension and mistrust between Africa and the West. Critics in Africa find the NEPAD principles too close to the Washington Consensus prescriptions for economic policy, demanding that Africans hew to a Western agenda of "responsible stakeholdership." As a result, while the African Union did eventually adopt NEPAD, it first changed the peer review system to be voluntary, and its support for the whole program remains tepid.[19] Indeed, African countries have to invite NEPAD review; no country can be subjected to peer evaluation without its consent, a loophole that dilutes the impact of the initiative.

Nor has South Africa's relative initial success with the G-8 built the confidence and partnership that was envisioned. The G-8 in 2005 agreed to double aid to Africa by 2010 and has provided sweeping debt relief to most of Africa's poorest countries, as well as to Nigeria and the Democratic Republic of the Congo. The G-8 also agreed to support the buildup of five African peacekeeping brigades. Western increases in economic and military assistance have been substantial but uneven among its members, and it is not clear whether the 2010 target will be met. Despite increased military assistance, moreover, the world has witnessed the ineffective performance of still undermanned and underequipped AU peacekeeping units sent to Darfur and Somalia.

The area of greatest frustration, however, has been in trade reform, where Africans had hoped for the kind of reductions in EU and U.S. agricultural subsidies and the opening of markets that would make the ongoing Doha round a true "development round." But the collapse of the Doha round in 2008 further undermined fulfillment of the grand bargain. Furthermore, although the aid commitments are significant and there is openness to more donor investment in infrastructure, which is one of NEPAD's priorities, few of NEPAD's infrastructure project proposals have yet received funding.

It would be a grave mistake, however, to attribute South African foreign policy solely to Mbeki or to assume it will change radically under a new government in or after 2009. Presumptive ANC presidential candidate Zuma backed away from his earlier harsh criticism of Mbeki's policy toward Mugabe and defended South Africa's "quiet diplomacy" in the face of the mounting Western condemnations of Mugabe. Zuma instead calls for more action by Africans. At times, Zuma accused Western pressure of undermining South Africa's ability to deal with the situation. In a somewhat surprising move, the Motlanthe government asked Mbeki to continue as the mediator in Zimbabwe, suggesting that either Zuma desires to continue the policy or merely wants to alleviate some of the humiliation that Mbeki endured when he was run out of office.

More fundamentally, an anti-American undercurrent runs throughout the ANC and its allies in the government. Rooted in years of training in the Soviet Union during the anti-apartheid struggle, the sentiment is so pervasive that the United States was slow to support that struggle—indeed, only did so as the Cold War faded and in the face of American popular demands. Many within the ANC view the U.S. government as the embodiment of imperialism and the country as a bastion of exploitative capitalism. This negative view of the United States was somewhat ameliorated after Congress enacted sanctions against the South African government in 1986 and President Clinton vigorously courted South Africa. But anti-American sentiment gained new currency in South Africa during the George W. Bush administration, whose actions reinforced South Africa's view that the principal threat to a rules-based international system did not come from non-Western countries but from the U.S. "exceptionalist" policies that seek to absolve Washington from playing by the same rules that it demands of others.

The result has been a significant decline in relations with the United States despite a number of overtures from Washington. The Bush administration more than doubled aid to Africa, pioneered the widely praised $15 billion, five-year President's Emergency Plan for AIDS Relief (PEPFAR), and lent support to other African programs in health and education. South Africa is also the largest beneficiary under the African Growth and Opportunity Act (AGOA), which allows nearly all African-sourced goods into the U.S. market duty free. To many in the United States, South Africa has pocketed the benefits of its relationship with the United States without giving much back in return.

For example, South Africa has been the most vocal opponent of the U.S. government's new Africa Command (AFRICOM). Pretoria saw it as an audacious attempt to gain a military foothold in Africa to fight terrorism and protect oil supplies. When the South African defense minister publicly commented on the proposal, he said that his government opposed AFRICOM anywhere in Africa, not just in his own country. Moreover, his response was not just "No," but an unequivocal "Hell No."

In another example, South Africa was conspicuously silent on Russia's 2008 attack on Georgia, even though it raised some of the most fundamental issues concerning sovereign rights that South Africa purports to champion in its foreign policy. On the one hand, South Africa is an ardent supporter of the right of countries to defend their territorial boundaries and put down internal political disturbances. On the other hand, South Africa might be sympathetic to Russia's charges that Washington is encircling Moscow.

## The Pillars of South African Policy

Looking ahead, several themes, some of which are contradictory, will shape South Africa's foreign policy in the coming decade:

- Focusing on Africa, especially the general issues of poverty and conflict, which can impinge on South Africa.
- Striking a careful balance between asserting leadership in Africa through its relative economic and military weight, while remaining squarely within "the African consensus" even though this African consensus is showing signs of unraveling.
- Wanting to be at the center of the modern, globalizing process, but, paradoxically, also arguing that it is tilted against the interests of the global south.
- Shifting its moral mission toward reform of the international system in terms of sovereign democracy and inclusive multilateralism, rather than an emphasis on liberal democracy and individual human rights, even though these values are upheld domestically.
- Aligning increasingly with other "middle-level" and rapidly advancing developing countries, such as India, Brazil, and Malaysia, even if (as will be discussed below) this sometimes leads to stances that are not necessarily in the interest of Africa and that favor its own economic competitors.
- Continuing an undercurrent of suspicion of the United States, unbridled capitalism, and "neo-colonialism" reflected in its diplomacy and rhetoric, notwithstanding the fact that this brings it into potential conflict with the U.S. and Western objectives. These currents could be strengthened if the South African Communist Party (SACP) or other radical elements play a more prominent role in a Zuma foreign policy.

Emerging constraints stem from domestic economic and political crises, as well as uncertainties associated with the upcoming leadership change in South Africa.

With these factors in mind, here are the major mileposts that will define South Africa's role as a stakeholder in the international system.

# New Administrations in the United States and South Africa

The 2008 and 2009 elections in both countries may present uncertainties, but the associated reassessment could also be a chance to rediscover common bonds and aspirations. As the focus on the Iraq war fades, and as new leaders in both countries determine their priorities, there may be a window of opportunity to establish greater trust and cooperation. Common interests of the two countries—conflict resolution in Africa, overcoming poverty, climate change, trade and investment, and perhaps new approaches to the peaceful uses of nuclear power—could provide the basis for renewed closeness and a more cooperative partnership in international affairs. A resolution of the Zimbabwe situation, if it comes, could defuse that sharp disagreement. The end of South Africa's term on the UN Security Council, with it the stream of controversies and disagreements, should also allow for a lowering of tensions.

## South Africa's Election

The 2009 South African election will be a watershed. It is the end of the Mandela-Mbeki era—the liberal phase of the historical transition from apartheid to democracy. Staffing within the government and the party and alliances in the parliament started to be reshaped soon after the ANC chose Jacob Zuma over Thabo Mbeki as party leader. But there is great uncertainty about the direction the country will follow whether Zuma takes over or, alternatively, is reindicted and convicted. Some observers fear that the new leadership will embark on state-led economic policies and deficit spending as demanded by the left, damaging South Africa's credit standing. Others predict that the new leaders will be more practical, making only tactical adjustments by shifting resources to public works and employment generating programs and slowing privatization. Another factor will be whether the new leadership can maintain ANC party unity, or whether the factionalization triggered by Mbeki's resignation will escalate, leading to governmental paralysis, widespread patronage, or creeping corruption in the public sector.

In foreign policy, the new leaders will be less seasoned and less familiar to the G-8 and other international circles. Any concerted push to make NEPAD more operational and influential would be one indication of their priorities. South Africa will remain concerned with Zimbabwe and the DRC—not least because of the mineral interests in both and the potential hydropower in the latter—and active in places where South African peacekeepers are present, like Burundi and Darfur. With an eye to strengthening the SADC, Zuma has already reached out to Angola to improve a relationship that was quite chilly under Mbeki. But it is questionable whether South Africa will take on many more peacekeeping burdens in other African conflicts, such as Somalia, Guinea, the DRC, or Chad. (See the section on Africa below.)

The changes confronting South Africa in the decade ahead will go beyond just this election. For South Africa to assume a larger role in responsible stakeholdership, it will have to deal with its deeper identity issues. In particular, it will have to absorb challenges to the entrenched one-party and one-generation domination of political leadership by allowing new forces to bubble up in society. It will have to respond to growing domestic pressure for more growth and poverty alleviation—relieving the pain of the "Third World" living conditions of the majority while maintaining the productivity of the "first world" economy of whites and an expanding black elite. At the same time, it will have to transcend ideology in addressing the future transnational issues, such as migration, climate change, unaccountable leaders, human rights violators, and weapons of mass destruction (WMD) proliferation that will, inevitably, affect South Africa along with others.

As noted earlier, the ANC is fragmenting into two or more parties. While this would disrupt the political status quo, thereby demanding development of a new order to replace it, a renewal of the political system could follow, allowing more debate and more leadership on both domestic and foreign policy issues. One prominent scenario anticipates a new centrist party with roots in the black community, leaving the rump of the ANC to carry the banner of the Left. Greater competition also holds the possibility of new alliances and coalitions, including across racial, ethnic, geographical, and demographic lines, with an end to one-party dominance and the potential for more accountability and transparency in government.

### The U.S. Response

Whatever the outcome of South Africa's leadership transition, the Obama administration can offer new ideas and areas of cooperation. Progress on world trade, closing the deep divide over agricultural policies and subsidies, could open the door to U.S.–South African collaboration to bring about a green revolution of agricultural productivity in Africa. Mutual concern over building African peacekeeping capacity, along with intensified U.S. involvement in conflict resolution across the continent, could also deepen ties and help overcome initial South African opposition to AFRICOM. South Africa already cooperates on counterterrorism, especially within southern Africa, and this arrangement could be enhanced. The United States should also engage South Africa on the role of emerging powers in Africa (e.g., China, India, Malaysia, and Brazil), including discussion of how to manage foreign competition, maximize benefits for Africa, and uphold standards for corporate responsibility, transparency, accountability, the rule of law, and open societies. Finally, the United States should consider working with South Africa as a potential model for how peaceful development of nuclear power can be achieved. This issue would respond to one of South Africa's critical needs—the supply of energy necessary for development—while making progress on one of the United States' top foreign policy priorities.

As part of a wider diplomatic frame to work with rising powers, the United States should also push to broaden international consultations beyond the G-8. In addition, the United States should perhaps find creative ways to expand the membership, or at least the outreach, of the UN Security Council to give middle-income countries like South Africa a greater voice and, thus, a greater stake, in the stability and effectiveness of the international system. The recent prominence given to the G-20, in light of the worldwide economic crisis, is a step in this direction—South Africa is the only African member. South Africa will continue to emphasize sovereign democracy as long as the international system is seen as discriminatory and working against the interests of the majority. These opportunities are discussed below in relation to the major issues and events that will face South Africa in the next decade.

## Africa

South Africa will continue to exert leadership in Africa even as it takes great care not to be seen as acting as a hegemon managing rivalries with other African aspiring leaders, such as Nigeria, Ethiopia, Angola, and Kenya. This will take several forms that have implications for South Africa's role in supporting a rules-based international system.

### Economic
South Africa's private sector is the largest financial investor in sub-Saharan Africa. Companies have moved beyond mining into banking, telecoms, retail, tourism, and other sectors. The South African government has facilitated this investment by reducing foreign exchange restrictions at home and through regional and bilateral agreements and public investments (e.g., in the Johannesburg-Maputo corridor). South Africa's prowess has attracted other investors. For example, China's largest investment in Africa is in South Africa's Standard Bank, which offers China a way to extend its economic position on the continent. However, China may soon outpace South African investors with its tendency to offer low-cost loans, fund major infrastructure

projects, and provide financial support for leaders' pet projects, such as sports stadiums and presidential mansions.

Along with this economic high profile go charges of a "neo-colonial" agenda, even for South Africa. South African companies have already been accused of being "predatory" and displacing local investment, reducing local employment, and impinging on local sovereignty.[20]

Yet even as South Africa faces greater economic problems at home, the trend of investment and commerce is likely to continue and give South Africa not just a stake in the continent but particularly in a rules-based structure for international business and finance. In this regard, the United States should work with South Africa and the economic players in the region (in addition to outside powers China, India, Brazil, Russia, and the European Union) to devise guidelines that build on Organization for Economic Cooperation and Development (OECD) standards, which the newer players and many Africans were not involved in crafting. Initiatives along these lines would also help the United States navigate the new "scramble for Africa" by outside actors, such as China, India, and Brazil.

**Conflict Resolution**
South Africa has played a major role in this area, in Burundi, Congo, Sudan, and elsewhere. It has been an important contributor to peacekeeping, both on its own and as part of UN peacekeeping operations. But South Africa is reaching the limits of its ability—the high level of HIV/AIDS being one major constraint, as noted earlier. South Africa has declined to contribute to Somalia and will unlikely be able to sustain further peacekeeping contributions to Darfur. It would also be constrained if such forces were needed in Zimbabwe, although the imperatives of reacting to the eruption of violence in such a close neighbor are difficult to ignore. South Africa's conflict resolution role is more likely to focus on the diplomatic realm. Economic problems at home and the change from Mbeki's personal focus on international matters, moreover, will limit the country's new leaders' appetite for international initiatives, with inevitable ramifications for their regional leadership role.

**African Union**
The pressure of domestic demands, along with African leadership transitions, not only in South Africa but also in Nigeria since Outgun Obasanjo left office, could undercut the African Union's response in addressing African conflicts and its stance on democracy. Smaller powers, such as Ghana, Tanzania, Uganda, or Rwanda may seek to fill the gap, but none has the weight of either South Africa or Nigeria, and not all are committed to democracy themselves.

Except for West Africa, Nigeria's future leadership role in peacekeeping and conflict resolution may not be politically sustainable. Any decline in AU readiness and willingness has serious implications for U.S. support of African and UN peacekeeping. As noted earlier, overcoming South African antipathy to AFRICOM will be necessary to build the type of cooperation that is essential for keeping African peacekeeping ability from regressing even further. Indeed, if AFRICOM were to focus more narrowly on goals in tune with African needs—peacekeeping training, military medical programs (especially regarding HIV/AIDS), maritime security, and humanitarian emergency and disaster relief—some of the suspicion generated by its earlier grandiose goals would be tempered.

## Trade Policy

During the Doha round, South Africa took the lead as the representative of fellow African nations. Above all, South Africa aligned itself ideologically with Brazil, India, China, and the ASEAN countries, even to the detriment of Africa's interests on some issues. Even though these countries' markets are as closed to African goods as they are to those from Europe and the United States, South Africa led the rest of the continent in joining an ideologically united resistance to liberalization of Asian and Latin American markets as part of an overall deal. But two wrongs do not make a right. Defending south-south solidarity against Europe and the United States may make a strong political point, but it is hardly good for Africa not to position itself to demand greater access to Asian and Latin American markets where its export potential may be substantial indeed. Of equal concern is the general perception that South African policy on these issues is purely ideological, rather than substantive or open to negotiation. It is unclear how long South Africa can sustain such positions, in the name of south-south solidarity, when they pose a sizable obstacle to Africa's global economic performance.

It should be stressed that moving South Africa away from its current positions will not be possible unless and until there is progress on other major issues in Doha, in particular EU and U.S. agricultural subsidies. But once there is the beginning of agreement on those issues that focus on the real interests of Africa, it should be a priority of U.S. diplomacy to encourage South Africa to see the potential benefits of working more closely together on trade. This will not be an easy sell because of South Africa's general approach to north-south issues, its suspicion of U.S. motives, and its desire to remain in step with its Asian and Latin American allies. These attitudes are so deeply entrenched that South Africa measures its leadership success, in part, by how well it stands up to the West. The gap can only be bridged by patiently working with a new generation of South African leaders and other African countries in a way that demonstrates the benefits of this cooperation, and of the U.S. positions, to the South African people and to Africa at large.

## Climate Change

Many studies of the effects of climate change predict severe impact on Africa. One consequence will be vastly increased migration, both within Africa and beyond. For a country already straining under the burden of sizable refugee and economic migrant populations, this creates tremendous challenges. South Africa could be expected to serve as a strong ally in any international program to address this issue. To gain its wholehearted cooperation, however, there must be, from South Africa's vantage point, real equity in any international agreement—which means a serious U.S. commitment to curb its own emissions and a system of considerable financial support to African countries that are experiencing the trauma of displacement and depletion of agricultural capacity.

The food crisis that squeezed poor countries in 2008 is a harbinger of what may come. And while South Africa's natural and technical resources give it great potential as a food exporter, any major disruptions to African agriculture could trigger an overwhelming flood of immigrants. Thus South Africa has a natural interest in international agreements regarding current and future food crises, and makes it a potentially valuable ally to the United States in spreading green revolution technologies.

## Nuclear Proliferation

The former apartheid government voluntarily dismantled the country's nuclear weapons arsenal before the 1994 transition and welcomed strict international inspection thereafter. South Africa remains solidly opposed to the spread of weapons of mass destruction—including any ambitions of Iran in this regard—and is foreswearing nuclear weapon capacity for itself. But South Africa is embittered by the failure of the nuclear powers to honor the compromises that it negotiated with the United States in the diplomatic deal for permanent renewal of the Nuclear Nonproliferation Treaty (NPT). The nuclear powers have moved no closer to nuclear disarmament; indeed, the United States has recently taken steps to improve its nuclear arsenal. The nonnuclear countries were also promised more consultation and a greater role in the implementation of the NPT, but there has not been any real change in how the treaty functions.

Furthermore, as noted earlier, South Africa is facing major power short-ages and is reviewing its nuclear options. In addressing the Iran issue, South Africa will staunchly defend the right of countries to develop and process nuclear fuel for peaceful purposes. Finally, after the Iraq war, South Africa will firmly resist any rush to judgment meant to hasten military action against Iran by the United States or Israel. South Africa will remain a key player on this issue as a member of the IAEA and with its moral authority for having relinquished its own nuclear weapons.

South Africa's ambitions for nuclear power pose an opportunity to fine-tune international safeguards to avoid any confrontation and establish a model for peaceful nuclear programs. If the United States were to take initiative along these lines with South Africa, it would not only respond to one of South Africa's major domestic needs, but reestablish a constructive leadership role and participate in setting the terms for responsible nuclear development.

## The United Nations and Other International Organizations

As long as South Africa sees itself as a prime candidate for a permanent seat on an expanded UN Security Council, Pretoria will continue to flaunt its independence from the West. This is another reason to expect votes such as those on Burma or Zimbabwe, or South African solidarity with other African countries on the Human Rights Commission, no matter how that undermines its own human rights credentials. Until there is some progress on UN Security Council reform—even a halfway measure such as creating a new advisory committee—South Africa will not be open to working closely with the United States and other major Western powers on many of the critical issues in the United Nations. However, a more determined respect for multilateralism by the United States would lay the foundation for more cooperation. Outside the United Nations, the United States' recent recognition of an enhanced role for the G-20 and talk of changes in the governorship and policies of the IMF and the International Bank for Reconstruction and Development (IBRD) are important steps in this direction.

## Bridging the North-South Divide

South Africa will be neither a fearless critic of human rights abusers nor a compliant member of any Western-dominated league or community of democracies. On the contrary, its strategy for extending influence and power emphasizes alliances with the global south's other industrialized powers and being a natural, even if somewhat off-putting, leader of Africa. But its mounting internal economic problems, domestic political splits, and social fissures will preoccupy the leadership—diminishing their international activism and prominence in the near-term, and prompting possible soul-searching and identity struggles about what South Africa stands for in today's world and what direction it should take as a leader.

The question is not whether South Africa should be a leader at all; that is a given. But the scope and direction of that leadership is not yet well defined, nor has it yet, even with the political changes under way, fully moved beyond the liberation mentality characteristic of newly independent states. What has emerged recently is a more populist lens that will shape perceptions on many issues. South Africa is not, technically speaking, a newly independent state, but it is a state reborn, newly legitimized, and empowered on the world stage after decades as a pariah.

Developments in the subregion, especially the trajectory of Zimbabwe, and elsewhere on the continent will have a major bearing on the direction of South African foreign policy. Persistent strains from migration (potentially intensified by the effects of climate change) and a lack of progress on African poverty, unemployment, and internal conflicts could prompt South African policy either to become confrontational, perhaps even militant, on the one hand, or more constrained and isolationist, on the other.

To enable a more positive scenario, the United States as a world leader must show that a rules-based international system will indeed respond to issues that speak to South Africa's political core, and that such a system will open doors to those countries that are most disadvantaged by the present global economic and trading arrangements. For their part, the new leaders emerging in South Africa must prove that they are ready to position their country as a unique and effective bridge between the rich and the poor, and the north and the south, both internally and internationally. No other country possesses the kind of credibility needed to span these widely disparate worlds. South Africa could reshape its influence on the world scene by building power as a "conciliator" rather than as a "combatant." It can be a "rainbow nation" in a much more profound sense, fulfilling many of the hopes of its inspirational rebirth on a global scale as a responsible democracy.

∽

## Khehla Shubane's Reaction

South Africa's foreign policy is indeed framed in noble terms and rooted in human rights. Respect for human rights was at the very core of the ANC government's policy soon after it assumed office in 1994. The constitution reflects the high standards the government set for itself. To this day, political leaders are fond of pointing to the lofty human rights ideals enshrined in the constitution.

As this chapter by Lyman and Baker points out, though, there has been a gap between the ideals and the practice of foreign policy. In its actions, the government has not always hewed to these declared ideals. The government has supported regimes with appalling human rights records. The Sudan government, with its shameful human rights record in Darfur, has received the South African government's support in resisting the International Criminal Court (ICC) arrest warrant against President Basheer. Mugabe has received rather mild criticism even as he orchestrated the systematic destruction of his country's economy and legal system and inflicted brutal violence upon his political opponents.

This failure to live up to ideals is not a matter of willful deceit by political leaders. Rather, it reflects the naiveté of the new South African policymakers regarding the workings of their own party and the wider world. The country's practice of foreign policy is more in line with the real world in which interests are a driving force in international relations, and countries orient policies around their interests.

It also reflects an expectation in South African policymaking circles for the industrialized global north to adopt more benevolent policies. Often government leaders appeal to the moral sense of their peers elsewhere in the hope that merely pointing out the shortcomings will persuade them to do the right thing. Thus, for example, President Mbeki is wont to highlight the precedent of the Marshall Plan as the model and standard for U.S. foreign aid. More recently, the European Union has transferred capital to the former Eastern Bloc to develop the economies of countries emerging from communist rule. The point is that the world should do the same to help Africa solve its economic problems.

### Foreign Policy's Domestic Roots

Foreign policy in South Africa is indeed shaped by a multiplicity of factors. The preferences of the ruling elite, the strength of the country, the economic resources that it has to underwrite its policy choices, and the public's appetite for engagement with the outside world are among the most important.

An immediate factor impinging on foreign policy in South Africa, however, is the very nature of the country's governing political party. The ruling ANC looks set to consolidate its dominant political position for the foreseeable future—a dominance stemming from its roots as a liberation movement, coupled with the association in many people's minds of opposition parties with apartheid. Historically, liberation movements have tended to be multiclass and multiethnic, with greater or lesser success over time. But in virtually every country with a strong liberation movement, that movement has produced a legendary personality who dominates politics in the country. Mandela in South Africa and Samora Machel in Mozambique, to take two examples, are immensely popular political leaders with almost messianic standing. It is very difficult to oppose the political legacy of such leaders.

Having taken the lead in ending apartheid, the ANC has cast itself as the only party capable of resolving persistent problems, such as the poverty that dogs the majority of the population. In doing this, the party regularly invokes its past as a premier champion of liberation. It also cites the apartheid-era role played by its current competitor parties to undermine claims that they can solve any of the problems they ostensibly helped create. Thus far these arguments have been sufficient to win the support of voters in steadily increasing numbers. Indeed, this political pattern is being repeated throughout most of southern Africa. The success of liberation movements in monopolizing power on the same basis has delegitimized the very notion of opposition parties and competitive politics. Consequently, an opposition party must compete not only against incumbent parties, but also with perceptions that have taken root in the population. In the few countries where opposition groups have gained power, their hold on power remains tenuous, as in Zambia.

This basic political power structure in the region explains the difficulties that political leaders have in criticizing their counterparts. When, for example, Mugabe became overtly undemocratic, other leaders with a background similar to his invoked ties of solidarity forged in their common struggles for national liberation.

Furthermore, back when they were liberation movements, these parties campaigned to be the sole legitimate representatives of their people. Thus, in closing ranks and fending off challenges from opposition parties, they are merely remaining true to their original political objective.

Until former liberation movements' firm grip on power is loosened and it becomes accepted that there is nothing unpatriotic in competing for political office, democracy will elude the region. For democracy to take root, it is critical for all citizens of a country to see themselves as free to join the parties of their choice and, through them, eligible to rise to the highest office in the land.

## South Africa's Global and Regional Roles

Back in its days of resistance to minority rule, and faced with a militarily strong government, international diplomacy was an important tool in the ANC's struggle—and one of its most effective, especially in mobilizing Western public opinion against apartheid. Arguably, it was the combination of political mobilization inside South Africa and the ANC's diplomatic success in casting apartheid as an affront to all people that finally convinced the South African government to negotiate the transfer of power. Up to that point, the apartheid government had presented itself as the bulwark against communism in southern Africa and consequently rallied Western powers against the ANC as a pawn of the Soviet Union in the Cold War competition. This was accompanied by the generally complacent posture of the world community as a whole. Quite soon after the end of the Cold War and the collapse of the Soviet Union, the race-based oppression in South Africa suddenly became a major issue against which people in Western countries united.

Once in power as the nation's president, longtime ANC leader Thabo Mbeki presided over a distinct shift in foreign policy vision—from a world governed by rules and the emergence of a global liberal international order emphasizing human rights to a realist framework in which South Africa refrains from trying to change the way countries govern themselves. After this shift, the ANC government's policy was to support its friends on all issues. The posture toward, say, China or Russia has little to do with respect for human rights, but friendship (i.e., the extent of the country's support to South Africa or other developing countries, especially in Africa).

Hence, in its dealings with Zimbabwe, South Africa has emphasized the importance of Zimbabweans themselves in breaking the impasse in their country. South Africa has even worked to keep the question of Zimbabwe off the agenda of the UN Security Council, arguing that the matter posed no threat to world peace. According to this view, sovereignty rests with the people of Zimbabwe and, when their nation confronts serious problems, the outside world should help them find their own solutions rather than invite itself to become more involved.

In an ironic twist for the notions of international leadership and responsible stakeholdership, South Africa's ambition to be added to the UN Security Council as a new permanent member is a major reason for its fulsome defense of sovereignty. Gaining a seat at the world's most influential intergovernmental table is a classically realist, self-interested objective. And as the country seeks to serve as the representative of African countries, South Africa's leaders have concluded there is little sense in alienating any of them.

Yet South Africa has certainly also played a positive role in Africa. The country has facilitated the negotiation of settlements in several countries around the continent. It has tackled the long-standing severe Hutu-Tutsi divide in Burundi, which is among Africa's most entrenched, polarized, and violent conflicts. The Democratic Republic of Congo, a profoundly dysfunctional country, also benefited from South African assistance, which has provided a basis for much-needed reform and reasonably credible elections. The DRC government is poised to make further improvements that would have been impossible without South Africa's critical initial participation.

### Neither Loyal nor Hostile to the West
President Mbeki is personally quite passionate about what he calls Africa's renaissance. A core premise of this reawakening is that Africans themselves should take a lead in rebuilding the continent. Mbeki has put his money where his mouth is by playing the role of peacemaker in several conflicts in Africa.

Undoubtedly there is a benefit to South Africa in an Africa that works. With sub-Saharan Africa's most advanced economy, South Africa is mindful of its links both to the regional and global economy, and to the connection between the two. The investments and technology transfer immanent in foreign investments are of considerable advantage to South Africa's economy. Thus, Mbeki's work in helping resolve problems in Africa is, in part, an effort to foster the kind of regional stability that will encourage more investment into South Africa.

Although South Africa has not always shown the support for U.S. initiatives that the U.S. foreign policy community might have expected, it can hardly be described as hostile to the United States. To cite one dramatic example, one of the suspects who was subsequently convicted and sentenced in the United States in connection with the attack on U.S. embassies in Kenya and Tanzania had been captured in South Africa, where he hoped to escape prosecution. On finding him in South Africa, the authorities immediately repatriated him, despite a law prohibiting the government from repatriating individuals to countries where they might face the death penalty without assurances that the suspect would not be sentenced to death. Pretoria did not even seek this assurance; it was only given retrospectively and after the constitutional court had issued a judgment that was highly unflattering to the government. The court in the United States took the judgment of the court in South Africa into account in passing sentence. In another instance, the government incurred the wrath of human rights groups by repatriating an illegal militant Islamist immigrant back to Pakistan where, it was argued, he was certain to be handed over to U.S. authorities.

And in an apt symbol of globalization and financial interdependence, the Johannesburg Securities Exchange (JSE) was recently shut down for almost the entire day because of a systems problem in London. The JSE is linked to an operating system in London that, if it crashes, makes it impossible for the market in South Africa to operate. This operational link renders the South African market completely dependent on a Western country for a critical function—not a link that would be countenanced by a government harboring deep anti-Western sentiment. But as with the rest of its foreign policy, there are political realities at work— in this case regional. Southern Africa is steeped in anti-U.S. and anti-Western sentiment; if South Africa seeks a leading role in the subregion and in Africa more widely, asserting a measure of independence from U.S. hegemony is important for its credibility.

## Notes

1. Chris Alden and Garth le Pere, *South Africa's Post-Apartheid Policy—From Reconciliation to Revival?* Adelphi Paper 32, Institute of Security Studies (Oxford: Oxford University Press, 2003), 12.

2. For example, during Mandela's triumphal visit to the United States in 1993 and his state visit in October 1994. Nevertheless, seeds of differences that would arise in later years emerged even in this period of high expectations; Princeton Lyman, *Partner to History: The U.S. Role in South Africa's Transition to Democracy* (Washington, DC: U.S. Institute of Peace, 2002), 225–61.

3. Michael Gerson, "The Despots' Democracy," *The Washington Post*, May 28, 2008.

4. Fred Hiatt, "In Burma, a U.N. Promise Not Kept," *The Washington Post*, May 12, 2008.

5. South Africa has 5.5 million people infected by the HIV virus, the highest number of any country in the world. Over 1.8 million South Africans have died from the epidemic since it began; UNAIDS 2008 Epidemic Update.

6. Colum Lynch, "U.N. Zimbabwe Measure Vetoed by Russia, China," *The Washington Post*, July 12, 2008.

7. Indeed, the forced resignation of President Thabo Mbeki in September 2008 (see below) was a reflection of the deepening splits within the ANC. Some top party leaders resigned from the ANC to form a new center-right party, the Congress of the People (COPE), led by Mosiuoa Lekota, the former defense minister and ANC chairman, and his deputy, Mbhazima Shilowa, the former premier of Gauteng Province, the richest in the country.

8. South Africa has expressed concern over the potential "neo-colonialism" of Chinese investment in Africa.

9. See Princeton N. Lyman, "South Africa in Retrospect," in Princeton N. Lyman and Patricia Dorff, eds., *Beyond Humanitarianism: What You Need to Know About Africa and Why It Matters* (New York: Council on Foreign Relations, 2007), 47–51.

10. *The Economist* (November 1–7, 2008), 56.

11. Wiseman Khuzwayo, "BEE comes of age with phase of two codes," Business Report, Johannesburg, December 22, 2007; "South Africa's booming black middle class," *People*, May 24, 2007, www.southafrica.info/about/people/blackdiamonds-230507.htm.

12. "Nelson Mandela Memorial Lecture by President Thabo Mbeki," University of Witswatersrand (July 29, 2006), 13.

13. "A Conversation with Jacob Zuma," presentation at the Council on Foreign Relations, Washington, DC, October 21, 2008.

14. The South African government was prepared to allow a trans-shipment of Chinese arms to Zimbabwe as that country was undergoing one of its worst and most violent instances of government crackdown on dissent. The refusal of dockworkers to unload the shipment, the outcry from churches and other representatives of civil society, and a court order prevented the ship from unloading.

15. Chris Alden and Garth le Pere, *South Africa's Post-Apartheid Foreign Policy—From Reconciliation to Revival?* (Oxford: Oxford University Press, 2003), 19–20. The ANC had in fact much earlier distinguished its struggle from that of universal human rights. The ANC rejected Jimmy Carter's associating the anti-apartheid struggle with that for human rights elsewhere. The ANC argued that their struggle was one against institutionalized racism, and against colonialism. They feared that their struggle would be "drowned" in the larger struggle; Padraig O'Malley, *Shades of Difference: Mac Maharaj and the Struggle for South Africa* (New York: Penguin Books, 2008), 193–94.

16. This section is drawn from the description of these setbacks in Alden and le Pere, op. cit., 21–24.

17. Amy S. Patterson, *The Politics of AIDS in Africa* (Boulder, CO: Lynne Reinner, 2006), 34–44.

18. Gerson, op. cit.

19. For a highly critical assessment of NEPAD, see Ian Taylor, *NEPAD: Toward Africa's Development or Another False Start?* (Boulder, CO: Lynne Reinner, 2005). For a more balanced assessment, see Gumede, *Thabo Mbeki and the Battle for the Soul of the ANC* (Capetown, South Africa: Zebra Press, 2005), 204–13.

20. Bridget Kenny and Charles Mather, "Milking the Region? South African Capital and Zambia's Dairy Industry," *ENZINE* 8 (May–September 2008), no. 2 (June 2008).

# Refashioning Iran's
# International Role

*Suzanne Maloney and Ray Takeyh*
*With a Reaction by Omid Memarian*

Since its explosive beginnings nearly three decades ago, the Islamic Republic of Iran has been the poster child for recalcitrance and misconduct in the international system—the archetype for a new category of rogue or outlaw state. Iran's postrevolutionary leadership has done much to earn this international reprobation, from the 1979 seizure of the U.S. Embassy and ensuing fourteen-month hostage crisis to Iran's embrace of terrorism as an instrument of statecraft, to its clandestine development of an extensive nuclear infrastructure. Dealing with Iran and its multiple challenges has become the quintessential policy "test case" for aspiring regional powers seeking to assert their influence and establish their bona fides as "responsible stakeholders."

For this reason, it may be tempting to consider any discussion of Iran's prospective evolution into a responsible stakeholder as a purely imaginative exercise. In reality, however, the possibility that Iran could transform itself from one of the world's foremost problem states into a respected problem-solver is not so far-fetched. With its long legacy of territorial integrity and relatively cohesive political heritage, Iranian influence has, over the millennia, dominated vast expanses of what is now the Middle East and Central Asia. During the Pahlavi period, Iran emerged as the dominant regional power broker, courting both superpowers and asserting itself extravagantly at home and abroad. Revolutionary Iran retained the messianic ambitions of its imperial predecessor, obviously with a distinctly religious flair. The vision of Iran as the heir to the ancient Persian empire, staking claims both to a history and a future as one of the "Great Civilizations" and regional powers, thus exerts a powerful hold on Iran's worldview.

Moreover, while the Islamic Republic has sowed considerable regional chaos since its inception, its foreign policy has undergone significant evolution, even if its durable status as the premier rogue failed to reflect those changes. Today, Iran is no longer a revisionist state challenging the prevailing international security system, nor a revolutionary regime seeking to forcibly impose its own model of governance on neighbors. While it would be imprudent to ignore the invective that emanates from Tehran, it is equally reckless to downplay the substantial gap between Iran's wild rhetoric and its wary approach to the world. In essence, the Islamic Republic is a medium-sized power seeking regional preeminence and asserting itself opportunistically against historic rivals, including Washington. The past two decades have shown that Iran can indeed play a constructive role in the resolution of regional crises. During the reformist period, Tehran—with apparent cross-factional consensus—established constructive relations with the GCC states, served as a relatively honest broker for the Azeri/Armenian conflict and the Tajik civil war, and even signaled potential new flexibility in its opposition to the Middle East peace process. Although more dogmatic and destabilizing than its predecessor, Iran's current leadership has indicated a continuing commitment to many of these policies, and even its regional troublemaking has been modulated by its interest in curbing regional insecurity.

Nonetheless, the general policies and specific actions of the Islamic Republic today represent the polar opposite of international responsibility—a posture that is both disturbing and destabilizing. Ultimately, a fundamental transformation of Iran's regional role and relationship to the international order will be critical for the Middle East and the broader Muslim world to become more stable, prosperous, and fully integrated into global norms and institutions.

Despite the ethnic, religious, and historical differences that distinguish Iran from its neighbors, its influence in the region is profound. Its strategic outlook and ideological posture are determining factors for the security environment in the Persian Gulf. Through its support for terrorism and pursuit of weapons of mass destruction, Tehran remains the foremost challenge to the regional status quo as well as to vital American security interests there. Economically, too, despite three decades of U.S. sanctions and its own leadership's disastrous economic management, Iran remains a latent power-house—thanks to its endowment of 11 percent of the world's petroleum and the second-largest deposit of natural gas, and its location at the crossroads of Asia's historic trading routes. As the center of gravity for the worldwide community of Shi'a Muslims and the heir to the ancient Persian empire, Iran exerts unique sway over a diverse and dynamic cultural sphere. If a durable rules-based global order is to emerge, and have meaningful impact in the perpetual zone of conflict that is the Middle East, Iran's constructive participation will be vitally important. Absent a genuine transformation in Iran's relationship to the broader world order, we can expect a perpetuation or even heightening of the exceptionalism and instability that has characterized the region for too long.

## Strategic Assumptions

In considering how Iran might transform itself over time from a rogue to a responsible state, four key assumptions frame the analysis below.

First, Iran will not be able to fully rationalize its approach to the world unless the international community—and in particular, the United States—recognizes the permanent changes wrought by Iran's Islamic Revolution and the authority of its current regime. For Washington, this recognition must be expressed in the abandonment of both the rhetoric and the implicit policies of regime change. Like all revolutionaries, Iran's leaders are trapped by their own insecurities, and thus especially eager for the international community's consideration of their interests and validation of their rule and their rightful prerogatives. Such gestures are not unique to Iran's theocrats; consider, for example, decades of Soviet demands that the United States officially acknowledge postwar demarcations of Eastern Europe. Any successful effort to persuade and/or pressure Tehran to use its influence as a stabilizing force must begin addressing Tehran's acute, abiding sense of insecurity, stemming from Iran's historical experience both before and after the revolution. Memories of the 1953 coup, in which a democratically elected prime minister was unseated with American assistance, remain powerful even in Islamic Iran. Those events helped to crystallize a "conspiratorial interpretation of politics" and an obsessive fear of internationally orchestrated instability.[1]

The events of the revolution's first decade only fed this persistent sense of vulnerability and mistrust. The formative experiences for Iran's were characterized by years of violence and challenges to the state's very survival. Consider the threats facing the Islamic Republic in its early years: tribal revolts in its provinces, social unrest in its cities, labor stoppages, economic sanctions, a war that brought a long-standing enemy right into its cities, and a vicious power struggle that devolved into an open terrorist campaign against its leadership. Just two 1981 bombings by the Mojahideen-e Khalq alone killed much of the Islamic Republic's senior leadership, including the president, the prime minister, the head of cleric's political party, and dozens of parliamentarians, cabinet members, and deputies. As a result of these ordeals, regime survival represents the highest priority for the Iranian leadership, accompanied by a deeply ingrained conviction that Washington, in collaboration with other world powers, is bent on its eradication. It is no mystery, then, that Tehran takes such a defensive approach to the international system. Part and parcel of accepting the revolution and its leadership must be a clear respect for Iran's territorial integrity.

The Bush administration's coy deployment of the rhetoric of regime change, together with persistent but unconfirmed reports of American and European efforts to exploit ethnic and sectarian tensions along Iran's borders, have only intensified Iranian leaders' paranoia. More disturbingly, the sense of siege has hardened Iran's determination to assert its influence across a region that is—thanks to U.S. policies toward Iraq and the Middle East peace process—coincidentally fortuitous. As Iranian leaders perceive the country's regional influence on the rise, they are correspondingly unwilling to settle for anything less than affirmation of and deference to the standing to which they see themselves as entitled.

A second overarching assumption regarding Iran's prospects as a responsible stakeholder also has roots in postrevolutionary history, the lessons from that period for Iran's attitude toward international law. This formative period instilled enduring doubts about the reliability and utility of international norms and institutions. In the official Iranian narrative, the 1980 Iraqi invasion represented a link in a larger plot, and Tehran's continued military campaign beyond its primary defensive aims was justified, by Ayatollah Ali Khamenei's account, as "not a war *between* two countries, two armies; it was a war between an unwritten, global coalition against one nation."[2] The international community's tepid response to such an egregious violation of Iran's sovereignty taught Tehran not to place faith in abstract principles or the world's willingness to defend them, and the world's failure to respond to Iraq's unprecedented use of chemical weapons effectively condoned Saddam's butchery.

This episode remains a prolonged and deeply problematic trauma, and a continuing rationale for Tehran's flouting of international law and norms. As a columnist in a hard-line newspaper declared last year, "our world is not a fair one and everyone gets as much power as he can, not for his power of reason or the adaptation of his request to the international laws, but by his bullying."[3] Gripped by their perception of an intractably hostile world and a conviction that the exigencies of regime survival justify its actions, Iranian leaders exploit every opening, pursue multiple or contradictory agendas, play various capitals against one another, and use pressure tactics—including the limited use of force—to advance their interests.

Ahmadinejad and many other second-generation Iranian conservatives on the rise interpret the experiences of the Iraq war as a cautionary tale against trust in the international community and are correspondingly averse to any kind of compromise on the grounds that conciliation only begets added pressure rather than reciprocal concessions. No effort to draw Tehran into a more constructive role within the region or beyond will succeed without altering these perceptions by steadily showing Iran's leaders, including its young firebrands, that they can have a more fruitful relationship with the broader world.

The third key predicate for any more responsible role for Iran in the international system is the reestablishment of a viable diplomatic relationship—though not necessarily harmonious or even amicable—between Tehran and Washington. So long as the Iranian leadership views the United States as a determinedly hostile strategic competitor, Tehran will be driven by perverse incentives to continue provoking, harassing, or constraining the United States, even where those policies contradict Iran's own interests. The perpetual estrangement and lack of direct communication fosters a vicious cycle of mistrust, antagonism, confrontation, and conflict that ultimately overrides the value of Iran's selective cooperation and baseline pragmatism. Iran cannot fully play by the rules—much less help to enforce and interpret them—so long as it is locked in a perceived existential struggle with the world's most powerful rule-maker.

Finally, meaningful internal change will be necessary to enable a more constructive posture toward the international order. This does not imply the necessity or the eventuality of regime change; indeed, as suggested above, Iran's foreign policy has already moderated in significant ways under its clerical leadership. Most notably, the reform movement of the late 1990s succeeded in reorienting Iran's approach to its neighborhood and even, to a lesser extent, with the world as a whole. It is not difficult to envision a future in which a different constellation of leaders of the Islamic Republic strikes a more accommodating stance toward the international system, whether spurred by generational shifts or the emergence of a new alignment of domestic political actors. Such a shift could build slowly but eventually manifest itself dramatically, particularly as game-changing external events intrude on Iran's political calculations—just as the Iraqi invasion of Kuwait and the tragic attacks of September 11 appear to have sparked past Iranian initiatives to repair frayed relations with the world. Still, the ultimate failure of the reformist experiment, along with their continuing marginalization in the Iranian political system, drives the real fact of the matter: the prerequisite for any durable commitment to the international order, one not dependent on particular individuals or factions, is systemic change in Iran, buttressed by legal and institutional protections.

The alternative scenario, that of revolutionary change, appears less likely but hardly impossible. Iran displays all of the risk factors for a revolutionary break: a disproportionately young population; restive ethnic minorities; an inefficient, distorted economy; and a regime mired in an obsolescent ideology, riven by factional feuds, and reliant on repression. But these signs of weakness are deceptive, outweighed by the Iranian regime's grip over society and apparent firm hold on power for the foreseeable future. Dissatisfaction with government policies is indeed high and has intensified as a result of Ahmadinejad's disastrous economic agenda. However, the components of successful prerevolutionary mobilization—such as a coherent organization, viable strategy, and the leadership of a core of committed activists who can rally followers, marshal resources, and develop and implement a specific program of change—do not seem to be in place. Moreover, a dramatic break with the ideology and power structure of the Islamic Republic would not necessarily move Iran toward the norms and parameters of global governance, in particular with respect to nonproliferation. In fact, Iran's nuclear ambitions did not begin with the onset of the Islamic Revolution, but rather date back to the early 1970s under the Shah. A set of strategic constants has sustained this program over the past four decades: status, prestige, and the appeal of the ultimate deterrent for a state in an unstable neighborhood. These considerations might well outweigh the nonproliferation norm, even under a different leadership.

## Internal Challenges

### Strengthening the Framework for Pluralistic Politics

Because of Iran's unique fusion of theocratic and democratic institutions and ideals, any process of internal transformation will likely begin with the ballot box. Elections have proven the only viable, if highly imperfect, pathway to political change within the Islamic Republic. They were central to the political strategy of the reformists during the late 1990s. And even though they failed to accomplish lasting change, the reformists' success in seizing elected institutions made the contests the focus of Iran's protracted power struggle.

Iranians have no illusions about the limited scope of their democracy, and yet organized boycotts have enjoyed little support, in part because voters understand the implications of choices even among lousy, limited options for their daily lives. Skeptics need only contemplate the contrast between Iran's current president, the wily demagogue Mahmoud Ahmadinejad, and his predecessor Mohammad Khatami, who ushered in a brief era of social and political liberalization and championed a dialogue among civilizations. While they are deeply problematic and ultimately frustrating for the true aspirations of its citizenry, Iranian elections do indeed matter.

Under the Iranian constitution, the country's elective institutions wield only modest authority, and are routinely constrained by legal and bureaucratic checks. Still, the presidency, the parliament, and more recently the local and city councils have been the focal point of more than twenty national elections in twenty-nine years, which has helped to engender a considerable popular commitment to their perpetuation and empowerment. The presidency has relatively limited specific powers, a continuing legacy of the mistrust of a powerful executive harbored by both the leftists and the Islamists in Iran's revolutionary coalition. Ultimately, "the real power he exercises depends on his unofficial relations with the other power holders around him."[4] Khatami tried, unsuccessfully, to expand the formal authority of the presidency, by inserting and asserting himself on all the vital affairs of state. His successor has de facto enhanced his own role in Iranian decision-making, although this recent aggrandizement of the position is purely a function of personality and circumstances and has not translated into permanent changes to the president's position within the power structure.

Beyond the presidency, the parliament is particularly prominent in the Iranian political imagination, thanks to its century-old roots, and wields some degree of authority through its oversight of the executive branch, approval of international agreements, and budgetary responsibilities. However, like the presidency, the parliament is routinely constrained by powerful checks on its authority and independence; the supreme leader has episodically intervened to block discussion of sensitive issues, such as liberalization of the press law, while in other cases the judiciary has attempted to prosecute MPs for remarks they have made during legislative debates.

Still, even with these constraints, the intense intra-elite politicking that surrounds electoral contests can have profound influence on the political and social environment over the long term. The consequences of the 1992 parliamentary elections, for example, were not evident to outside observers until five years later, with the emergence of the reform movement and election of Khatami. Similarly, the repercussions of the current divisions among Iran's conservatives and the dynamics of the 2009 presidential election will, in time, play out in ways that we simply cannot predict. In this way, even imperfect elections can lay a foundation for a nascent democracy more reliably than the sexy stuff of revolutionary upheaval.

We can sketch some of the markers of Iran's political evolution: the splintering of the revolution's true believers, the slow transition from factions to parties, the regrouping of regime opponents, and, most importantly, the commitment of Iran's citizenry to the ideal of representative rule, and Iran's elections, both in their implementation and in the accompanying framework for elective institutions. Improvements in the electoral rules and expansion of the political space allotted to elective institutions would boost prospects for more responsible Iranian policy more broadly. Bolstering the robustness and autonomy of Iran's elective institutions—in tandem with greater protections for nongovernmental checks on responsible governance, such as a vibrant civil society and independent media—would represent practical steps that could really enhance the power of the ballot box in shaping Iran's approach to the world.

Yet the link between democracy and a constructive international orientation is not a direct or simple one. The populist Ahmadinejad has, for instance, stirred enormous popular reaction, through regular tours around the country that elicited more than nine million letters to the president, who claims in return to have adjudicated thousands of individual grievances and provided 2.4 million Iranians with at least a token financial response. Under a different leadership, this sort of public engagement might suggest progress, but unfortunately, precisely the opposite is the case here—the lesson being that demagoguery and populism cannot substitute for genuine political competition and meaningful elective oversight.

## Enhancing Transparency and Accountability

In addition to its representative institutions, the Islamic Republic is governed via a powerful constellation of unelected institutions that are subject to limited oversight or accountability. At the apex sits the supreme leader, or *faqih*, the office that constitutes Iran's ultimate authority and is empowered to declare war, approve or dismiss the president, and supervise the general policies of the government. In the 1989 constitutional revisions in preparation for Iran's first and only leadership transition, the formal powers of this office were considerably expanded, giving the supreme leader an absolute mandate over all the affairs of state. The supreme leader is nominally subject to democratic accountability, since the council empowered, formally at least, to select and remove the *faqih* is itself chosen by national ballot, albeit in highly restrictive fashion.

A powerful adjunct to the office of the leadership is the Council of Guardians (*Shura-ye Negahban*), comprised of six religious jurists and six lay people. The council is charged with reviewing all parliamentary legislation for conformity with both Islam and the constitution, and with setting electoral procedures for the entire electoral process, which gives the body vast latitude to determine the relative freedom of that process. Protracted feuding between the Guardians' Council and the parliament during the 1980s gave rise to yet another oversight body, the Expediency Council (*Majma-ye Tashkhis-e Maslahat-e Nezam*), which is empowered to override both the constitution and sharia law in whatever it deems to be the best interests of the Islamic state.

Each of these institutions, and indeed every official organ of the Islamic Republic, remains effectively beyond any meaningful form of public oversight or accountability. Through these unchecked powers, Iranian hardliners have ensured that the prerogatives of the elected institutions and the demands of the public were effectively negated. They have used these state organs to assassinate critics and dissidents at home and abroad, intimidate a host of elected officials through spurious prosecutions, eliminate powerful rivals through violence or smears, and siphon off a vast bounty of oil revenues into Dubai. Repeated efforts by reformists to either capture these institutions through the electoral process or exert greater oversight through the legislative and/or investigatory powers of the parliament have fizzled.[5]

The result has been the further debilitation of Iran's weak elective institutions, the erosion of the country's traditionally vibrant political participation and civil society, and the ascendance of a hard-line agenda for which international tensions only help stoke revolutionary fervor and distract from domestic failures.

### Rebalancing the Civil-Military Relationship

Recent years have also seen a growth in the political influence of military institutions and some of their key leaders. In particular, the Revolutionary Guards (IRGC) have assumed a more prominent role in Iran's economy, securing key stakes in major projects, including in the energy sector, which until recent years was the sole province of the state oil company and its affiliates. Additionally, a number of current and former IRGC commanders have moved into the parliament and political posts widely through the Ahmadinejad government—most notably in the Interior Ministry, which not only commands Iran's internal security forces but also is charged with implementation of elections. The expanded role of the military leadership in Iran's politics and economy represents a significant shift from what had been distinctly separate civil and military spheres, although it is a somewhat predictable result of the eight-year war with Iraq, which was a formative experience for the postrevolutionary state and leadership.

The growing role of military commanders and organizations is accompanied by what one expert on Iranian politics has described as the "security outlook" of the current leadership—in other words, "a newly security-conscious state, bordering on paranoid, has indeed emerged."[6] This heightened sense of suspicion and defensiveness reflects both the innate predilections of Iran's new power brokers as well as intensifying American pressure. To see how the two factors reinforce one another, note Washington's move to single out the Revolutionary Guards for targeted sanctions and financial restrictions.

Conversely, any constructive international engagement by Iran will require a rebalancing of the scales to strengthen civilian authority over military institutions and leaders through legislation as well as through enhanced oversight by the executive branch.

## Protecting Basic Rights

Recent trends with respect to the rights and freedoms of the Iranian population have been particularly unfortunate. The era of Ahmadinejad has had a manifestly detrimental impact on Iran's political and social environment. Censorship of books and other media has intensified dramatically, Islamic dress codes and other social prohibitions are being enforced with renewed vigor, and, perhaps most significantly, the regime has targeted intellectuals, dissidents, student activists, lawyers, union leaders, and human rights advocates for repression and imprisonment.

Emblematic of Ahmadinejad's approach to human rights was his appointment to high office of two individuals with infamous track records on these issues. Interior Minister Mustafa Purmohammadi and Intelligence Minister Gholamhussein Mohseni Ezhei have been cited by Human Rights Watch and other organizations for their roles in several notorious episodes of human rights abuses in Iran, including the execution of political prisoners in the 1980s, the murders of dissidents and writers by Intelligence Ministry agents in the 1990s, and the prosecution of Shi'a clerics for espousing alternative theological viewpoints. Their records were so deeply problematic that even some members of the conservative parliament hesitated to confirm these individuals' appointments out of concern over how international sanctions might thwart their diplomatic travel and interactions.

Equally telling—and outrageous—was the decision to include the despicable Saeed Mortazavi, Tehran's prosecutor general, in its 2006 delegation to the United Nations' Human Rights Council in Geneva. Mortazavi is well known as the "butcher of the press" for his role in shuttering reformist publications and imprisoning journalists during the Khatami era. He is also alleged, credibly, to have participated directly in the 2003 interrogations of Canadian-Iranian photojournalist Zahra Kazemi. Those interrogations included physical abuse and torture and resulted in Kazemi's death while in custody. Her abusers have never been brought to justice, and the inclusion of Mortazavi in official Iranian human rights diplomacy has been cited by Human Rights Watch as proof of the leadership's utter contempt for the very concept and process. Like the inclusion of Mohseni Ezhei and Purmohammadi, the empowerment of Mortazavi speaks to an appalling brutality harbored within certain elements of the Iranian leadership, and tolerated by a wider range of officials.

A review of Iran's postrevolutionary history suggests a direct correlation between the domestic political environment and Iran's international orientation. During periods of internal liberalization—most notably, of course, the eight-year tenure of President Khatami—Tehran also was keen to engage responsibly with the rest of the world. The converse has also held true: as Iran has come under greater international pressure for its destabilizing policies, the very notion of domestic dissent becomes tainted as a "fifth column" subverting national cohesion in a time of crisis. For this reason, Iran's willingness to institutionalize greater protections for its own population is an important milestone for gauging its approach to the world.

## External Challenges

### Iraq

Iran has emerged as the chief beneficiary of the U.S.-effected change of power in Baghdad. Iranian officials harbored deeply seated and long-standing grievances with Saddam Hussein. Prior to the invasion, they publicly opposed Washington's decision to unseat him and then played a modest but generally constructive supporting role during the initial conflict itself. While Hussein was in power, Iran's leaders cultivated enduring ties with all the significant Iraqi opposition groups. None of these groups could have been considered wholly owned clients of the Islamic Republic, but their varying degrees of intimacy with and fealty toward Tehran were in all cases more significant than their tactical cooperation with Washington—even the Iraqi opposition's work with the United States in the run-up to the war and its aftermath. Moreover, as the only organized political forces in the postwar period, the Shi'a and Kurdish oppositionists were uniquely positioned to take advantage of the power vacuum, facilitated in no small part by retention of their militias.

Iran's strategic and financial investments in Iraq reflect the regime's deeply held conviction that Tehran has an existential interest in ensuring a friendly government in Baghdad, one no longer capable of threatening Iran directly or on behalf of the international community. The importance of the 1980–1988 war as a formative experience for Iran's postrevolutionary leaders and society has fostered a persistent sense of strategic vulnerability and a willingness to do whatever necessary to ensure the survival of both the Iranian nation and the Islamic state. This worldview underlies Tehran's assiduous and wide-ranging extension of influence in postwar Iraq.

Indeed, Iran's leadership is still involved in what amounts to an ongoing reinterpretation of the history of the war, with significant ramifications for Iran's political culture and international orientation. One particularly high-profile thread of this debate was the unprecedented questioning of the role of former president Akbar Hashemi Rafsanjani and other decision-makers during the 2005 presidential campaign. From its actions in post-Saddam Iraq, Tehran appears to have drawn several crucial lessons from the earlier war with Iraq. The first is the crucial importance of the relationship with Iraq's Shi'a community. Rather than seeking to impose its doctrine of *velayet-e faqih* upon its neighbors, Iran prudently opted to support a democratic framework advantageous to its coreligionists while simultaneously arming its local allies to put them in a strong position for any future competition for power. Secondly, Iranian leaders have sought to block any permanent American presence in Iraq that would once again leave a historic adversary with an open-ended presence on its borders. Finally, the legacy of the Iraq war has impressed upon Tehran the importance of ensuring a coherent, functional state in Baghdad.

In addition to Iran's political engagement, it has cultivated stronger economic ties, earmarking financial support and export credits for Iraq and engaging with Baghdad on specific assistance to key sectors, such as energy infrastructure and electrical power generation. As a result, Iran's wide-ranging economic relationship with the new Iraq includes billions of dollars in agreements for future investments in the power sector, two oil pipelines from Basra to Abadan, and other infrastructure projects.

Despite its general cooperation and coexistence with the U.S. presence in Iraq, as the occupation has dragged on Tehran has also sought to increase the cost of a continued American presence in Iraq—giving support to insurgents in order to maximize its own position within the country and leverage vis-à-vis Washington. And while the Bush administration's track record provides ample justification for skepticism of its allegations, the charges that Iran is providing arms and training to a range of Shi'a militias inside Iraq are supported by persuasive evidence.

Obviously, the perpetuation of an Iranian-American proxy war in Iraq would be entirely incompatible with a constructive Iranian role in the international order. And indeed, hopeful signs are discernable: Iran's copious assistance to Iraq's formal government and its efforts to moderate tensions among Iraqi groups as well as with Washington (most notably by brokering a truce that helped end recent fighting in Basra), as well as Tehran's apparent commitment to a durable central government. Iranian participation in regional and international initiatives to address the fallout from Iraq can build on its shared interest in a peaceful future for Iraq, and direct engagement with Washington could further wean Tehran from its tendency to view Iraq as a zero-sum competition with its primary adversary. Iran will wield enormous influence over the future of Iraq, and it is the international community's task to work with Tehran to channel that power in a constructive direction. Iraq may be the most appropriate starting place for cultivating a new Iranian approach to the world—particularly since Ayatollah Khamenei has publicly endorsed direct dialogue with Washington on issues related to Iraq, the first time since the revolution that the Supreme Leader has openly sanctioned such contact.

## Persian Gulf

How Iran's assertion of power in Iraq will play out on a broader Middle East stage is an issue of mounting attention and concern. Saudi Arabia and the smaller Gulf sheikhdoms view the close Iranian-Iraqi partnership with wariness and have spoken bluntly about the prospect of a "Shi'a arc" through the heart of the Middle East that will be inherently unstable and antagonistic toward its Sunni neighbors. They have played upon these fears to help win substantial new arms packages from Washington, which has prompted intensified debate on U.S. security commitments to its allies in the region.

Regional fears of a revived and coordinated Shi'a arc of influence are to some extent self-serving. By casting blame toward Iran for the chaos in Iraq, Iraq's Sunni neighbors deflect blame away from their own failure to do the utmost to stabilize the situation, and in one case—Saudi Arabia—the stream of citizens getting involved in the insurgency.[7] Moreover, the cultural and political revival of the Shi'a world need not represent an inherent threat to its Sunni neighbors.

And to the extent that these fears are connected to large Shi'a minorities in some states of the region—such as Bahrain, Saudi Arabia, Kuwait, and Pakistan—the dynamic will be driven much more by the overall tenor of these states' domestic politics, particularly on minority rights issues, than by Iran itself. Since the early years of the Iranian revolution, one focus of the Gulf states' internal evolution has been responsiveness to the concerns of historically marginalized communities, or at least to co-opt local Shi'a populations. Whatever their limitations, the Saudi "national dialogue," Bahrain's embrace of limited democracy, and Kuwait's dysfunctional parliament have had reasonable success in incorporating the Gulf Shi'a into their respective national polities. As a result, the prevailing relative quiescence of the region's minority Shi'a populations is not especially vulnerable to being shattered by either a demonstration effect or even direct intervention from Shi'a powerhouses such as Iran or Iraq.

In reality, it is the perception of—and the potential reaction to—a "Shi'a crescent" that represents the true threat to regional peace and stability. A disruption of the current uneasy balance of power along sectarian lines might be triggered not by the political dominance of Iraqi Shi'a, but by misguided policies on the part of Sunni-dominated governments directed toward some mythical Shi'a threat. Echoing from the dynamics unleashed after the birth of the Islamic Republic, other critical actors, such as Pakistan and Saudi Arabia, may respond to the new power alignment in the broader Middle East with heightened religious fervor and rhetoric or simply by trying to undermine post-Saddam Iraq simply because of its Shi'a leadership. Given the already-fertile environment for Sunni radicalism, such state support and provocation would be positively incendiary.

Yet there are also hopeful signs pointing toward reduced, rather than heightened, confrontation with Iran. Despite their fervent efforts to spur Washington to contain Iran, the Gulf states have made clear their own limited appetite for directly confronting Tehran themselves. In fact, many have undertaken important outreach to the current Iranian power structure—including several unprecedented visits for Ahmadinejad to participate in the December 2007 *hajj* as well as the 2007 Gulf Cooperation Council summit. For their part, Iran's leaders have also demonstrated some awareness of the need to maintain a constructive relationship with Riyadh and the Gulf states. Even so, Tehran has repeatedly felt compelled to dispatch envoys to Riyadh to assuage concerns over Ahmadinejad's rhetoric and Iran's escalating tensions with the West. The larger project of a new regional security framework that incorporates rather than isolates Iran will be an absolutely essential step to preserving and enhancing the fragile stability of the Gulf.

**Terrorism**

In the early years following the revolution, Iran explicitly embraced a universalist agenda of working to subvert its neighbors and promulgate its vision of an Islamic order. This enterprise included direct aid to terrorist organizations, subversion of Iran's neighbors through force as well as through propaganda, and threats (as well as active assassinations) of individuals abroad deemed enemies of the Islamic Republic. All this was sanctioned at the outset of the revolution by the messianic worldview that pervaded Iran's clerical leadership. In fact, the Islamic Republic's early provocative exploitation of indigenous Shi'a dissatisfaction in Kuwait, Bahrain, and Saudi Arabia ultimately solidified bureaucratically into a semi-official Iranian administration dedicated to toppling the status quo in the broader Islamic world.

Iran's involvement with terrorism is long-standing and widely diversified. During the 1980s, Iran helped to incite bombings, attempted coups and assassinations, and other subversive actions against its neighbors in the Gulf. During the same period, the Islamic Republic also provided substantial military and operational support to Shi'a resistance cells in Lebanon, helping establish and mold the paramilitary organization Hezbollah more than twenty years ago. In cooperation with Hezbollah, Iranian authorities helped coordinate an array of attacks in the region and beyond, including the 1994 bombing of a Jewish cultural center in Argentina that killed eighty-five people. With the assistance of Hezbollah, Iran has also forged intimate ties with the leading Palestinian militant groups such as Hamas and Islamic Jihad, despite sectarian differences; this support has been increased and magnified in response to the international community's attempt to isolate Hamas after the terrorist group's January 2006 electoral victory. Finally, in recent years there is evidence that Iran has cooperated opportunistically with both al-Qaeda, offering transit routes and safe harbor to operatives fleeing Afghanistan, as well as the reconstituted Taliban in Afghanistan.

Still, the historical record also strongly suggests that Iran's attachment to terrorism is not immutable. In the past fifteen years, Iran has largely abandoned its subversion of the Gulf states and pernicious practice of assassinating its own dissidents in Europe, spurred both by external pressure and an interest in rebuilding important relationships. For instance, the 1997 conviction of Iranian officials by a German court led not just to restrictions on trade but the departure of some European members of the Tehran diplomatic corps in protest. Given the costs, the Islamic Republic quickly abandoned the practice of targeting exiles. In a similar vein, the cessation of Iranian support for local radical elements was an essential *quid pro quo* in the normalization of Iran's relations with Saudi Arabia and the Gulf states in the 1990s. Once more, the strategic advantages of such a détente compelled Iran to pay the price.

A decisive break with terrorist groups and tactics and renunciation of the asymmetrical projection of power would constitute perhaps the most complex and significant component of an Iranian commitment to a rules-based global order. It will not prove simple or easy. In many cases, changes in Iranian behavior will require concomitant shifts in the regional order, international incentives and disincentives, and internal political rebalancing to achieve greater accountability over Iranian foreign policy. Still, such a pathway can be glimpsed in the prior calibrations of Iran's terror tactics as well as the ways that particular proxies' agendas and actions have become distinct from Iran's. For example, a viable Arab-Israeli peace process—including the integration of Hamas into any discussions—will inherently limit Iran's capacity for troublemaking in that arena and diminish its access to Palestinian proxies. Similarly, Hezbollah's self-interested efforts in pursuit of a prominent political role in Lebanon can propel a transformation in both the organization and Iran's involvement with it.

## Nonproliferation

Iran's nuclear ambitions are already on the international agenda as a top item, and it is here that Iran is frequently held out as a "test case" for responsible stakeholdership. Dealing with Iran's nuclear program is complicated by its leadership's long-standing commitment to such efforts—the earliest activities predate the Islamic Revolution—as well as the not-so-irrational strategic logic that underlies it. In fact the domestic politics of the nuclear temptation, in contrast with many other issues, appears to generate broad consensus across the Iranian political spectrum.

First and foremost, Iran's considerable investment in developing its nuclear options stems from the prodigious sense of insecurity wrought by the 1980 Iraqi invasion and subsequent eight years of war. Beyond the strategic rationale, the nuclear program stirs a distinct Iranian nationalism—one that has been astutely stoked by Ahmadinejad in recent years. In addition, for many in Tehran, maintaining some sort of viable nuclear program brings a benefit in the enhancement of the country's bargaining position with Washington. Notably, of course, there are greater divisions over the value of the associated confrontation with the international community. While moderates emphasize the benefits of Iran's regional détente and its commercial relations with Europe and Asia, hard-liners are not only undeterred by the prospect of international sanctions and isolation, but would in fact welcome a crisis in order to rekindle Iran's waning revolutionary fires and deflect attention from the domestic deficiencies of Islamic rule.

Since the May 2006 offer from the five permanent members of the UN Security Council plus Germany of discussions with Iran over the nature and scope of its nuclear program, the standoff between Tehran and the world community has focused on Iran's defiance of UNSC resolutions calling for suspension of its enrichment and reprocessing of uranium. There appears to be little prospect of a quick or easy resolution of this dispute. Even if the Obama administration showed new flexibility on the continuation of Iranian enrichment, which it did not during the campaign, the precondition precluding against enrichment in multiple UNSC resolutions poses a serious obstacle. Conversely, the Iranian government has repeatedly insisted that Tehran will never cede its right under the NPT to enrich uranium or otherwise eschew access to nuclear technology and activities.

Still, it is not difficult to envisage the contours of a durable bargain that meets both sides' basic requirements. The hard-liners associated with Ahmadinejad have long railed against both the process and the results of Iran's dealings with the IAEA and the EU-3. Yet a framework is conceivable—including twenty-four-hour monitoring, continuous environmental sampling, continuous access without prior notification, and limits on the amount of fissile material Iran can retain—that would effectively assure that Iran's nuclear material is not being diverted for military purposes. The greater challenge is to develop sufficient trust and credibility among both sides in a new negotiating process in the limited time available. A willingness to come to the table and work cooperatively toward sufficient confidence-building will represent a major step forward for Iran; given the extent to which the current leadership has staked its public mandate on the nuclear issue, such a shift will require a considerable amount of heavy lifting within the contested internal environment. Meanwhile, it is worth noting that while this issue represents such a thorny challenge for the development and defense of a global rules-based order, it can also serve as a valuable model for how to handle other would-be proliferators and for addressing the persistent ambiguities and inadequacies of the current global nonproliferation framework.

### Rhetoric

In recent years, President Ahmadinejad has galvanized considerable international outrage with his repeated calls for the elimination of the Israeli state and references to the Holocaust as a "myth." In fact, this sort of demagoguery has a long and shameful history in the Islamic Republic. Reprehensible anti-Israeli invective has been a basic component of Iranian political culture since the revolution, occasionally flaring up into especially flagrant excesses, such as the celebratory reaction of Iranian political figures to the 1996 assassination of Israeli Prime Minister Yitzhak Rabin. And while Iranians reacted to the September 11 attacks with an outpouring of popular sympathy and official pragmatism, neither has deterred various Iranian leaders, including Rafsajani, from perpetuating some of the most repugnant hoaxes about the September 11 attacks, hinting in Friday prayers that the attacks were committed to generate support for a war against Islam.[8] The same reports were repeated in at least one conservative newspaper, which compared the events of September 11 to seminal events in the American Revolution.[9] These far-fetched theories continue to have some currency among Iranian leaders, with Ahmadinejad recently speculating that "[a]n event was created in the name of the attack against the twin towers. We were all sad. It was said that 3,000 people were killed. . . . But the names of the 3,000 people were never published and nobody was able to respond to the main question, which is how is it possible that with the best radar systems and intelligence networks the planes could crash undetected into the towers."[10]

Being a cagey politician, Ahmadinejad appreciates that his callous denunciations of the United States and his contemptible denials of Holocaust actually enhance his popularity in a region where many people rely on conspiracies to explain their collective predicament. Through his use of Islamic discourse, identification with the popular Hezbollah, and invocation of local grievances, Ahmadinejad has managed to span the sectarian divide so that a Shiite, Persian country captures the imagination of Sunni Arabs. Still, an Iran that officially indulges in such vulgar demagoguery will only continue to find itself ostracized from the international order.

## The Legacy of Past Policies

Finally, any evolution of Iran's approach to the world will have to resolve the aftereffects of its prolonged antagonistic posture. Coming to terms with the legacy of the Islamic Republic's destructive policies, both externally and internally, will be painful for a country with a fulsome sense of pride and place in the world. Any thorough revision of Iran's interactions with the world, though, must bring the culpable to justice and acknowledge and redress past wrongdoings. In particular, just like Moammar Qaddafi's Libya, Iran will face a problematic legal legacy stemming from its involvement with terrorism. Meanwhile, a 1996 U.S. law permitting lawsuits against state sponsors of terrorism, for instance, has resulted in billions of dollars in damages against Iran awarded to families of Americans killed or wounded in terrorist bombings in Israel and kidnappings in Lebanon. At the same time, criminal investigations into some of Iran's other alleged attacks, such as the bombing of the Jewish community center in Argentina, have spurred legal actions against high-level Iranians, including former president Akbar Hashemi Rafsanjani, former foreign minister Ali Akbar Velayati, and former Revolutionary Guards commander Mohsen Rezai.

Accountability and expectations of restitution will remain a serious dilemma for Iran if it opts for full reintegration into the international community. This will be sensitive terrain for any future Iranian leadership to negotiate, particularly if change comes gradually and from within the current regime. An important part of any process to cultivate greater responsibility from Tehran will be viable mechanisms for to settle outstanding legal and financial obligations, while retaining some scope for face-saving.

### Difficult Stumbling Blocks

Unlike the other countries examined as part of this collection, Iran remains remote from even the most generous interpretation of responsible stakeholdership. Moreover, several of the traditional mechanisms of international integration—such as participation in international institutions and increasing penetration of the international economy—are less relevant to Iran's positive evolution than the internal domestic dynamics that determine the fundamental character of the country's governing regime and the trajectory of its political evolution. Since its Islamic revolution, Iran has been an active player in the international economy and especially since the end of the Iran-Iraq war, has engaged more vigorously in international organizations ranging from the World Bank to the Shanghai Cooperation Organization. There is little evidence that this web of multilateral ties has had a moderating impact on Iran's international agenda, in large part because the associated obligations and responsibilities that these interactions impose have been offset by the exigencies of regime survival, factional splits, and the steady influx of oil revenues.

The most difficult stumbling blocks for Iran and the world remain the repressive character of the regime and the tenor of its historical relationship with Washington and the wider international community. This reality is bound to complicate any potential transformation of Iran into merely a more responsible state, much less a contributing stakeholder in a new international order.

⌐

## Omid Memarian's Reaction

Mahmoud Ahmadinejad was the first leader among the "axis of evil" club countries to congratulate President-elect Barack Obama, on November 5, 2008. What's more, Ahmadinejad's letter was sent with the consent of Iran's Supreme Leader Ayatollah Khamenei. Thirty years ago, the founder of the Islamic Republic called the United States "Great Satan," and ever since then, rhetorical and political hostility between Tehran and Washington has been the centerpiece of both the Iranian revolutionary regime's agenda and the United States' Middle Eastern policy. So although Iranian leaders have tended to face more difficulties with Democrats in the White House than with Republicans, the current regime sees only a slim possibility of a U.S.-led military attack against Iran—prompting them to put the past behind them, act with respect, and seek reconciliation.

Fear of an American overthrow has been a constant concern for leaders of the Islamic Republic. The animosity between the two countries began the moment the United States decided to welcome the shah onto its soil in 1979. For Iranians, this meant having to ready themselves for another U.S.-orchestrated coup like the one in 1953, "preparations" that left fifty-three American diplomats as hostages for 444 days. Since then, the United States has persistently tried to undermine Iran's influence in the region by supporting Iraq in the bloody eight-year war between the two countries, imposing unilateral and multilateral sanctions and thus marginalizing the country from the global economy, and supporting Iranian opposition groups politically, financially, and morally.

## The Perverse Effects of Efforts to Isolate Iran

The urgency of a potentially imminent American threat has not only served as the centerpiece of the Islamic Republic's foreign and domestic policy, it has to a significant extent formed Iran's essential political characteristics. The demonstrable existence of external security threats has been the main factor in consolidating the power of political conservatives and radicals and allowing them to obliterate their opponents, suppress the civil society, and preserve their position after upheavals like the 1979 Revolution, the Iran-Iraq war, and Ahmadinejad's assumption of office.

From the perspective of many in the Iranian elite, it is hard to imagine how the regime could survive without a potential U.S. threat. Ironically, the United States' sanctions and refusal to recognize Iran as a sovereign nation and regional power are seen as the most influential factors in the rise of the Islamic fundamentalists. Consequently, the fundamentalists have had an iron grip on the political system since the revolution, marginalizing moderate elements politically, and weakening Iran's middle class—the very elements needed for the creation of democracy in Iran. The truth is that U.S. policy has not made the Iranian regime responsible, friendly, or accountable, but rather the opposite, causing the radical Islamists to consolidate power, sustaining Ayatollah Khomeini's idea of exporting the Iranian Islamic revolution, and feeding region-wide ideological polarization based on anti-

American rhetoric and policies in the region with the aim of enhancing the security of the regime.

Iran's influential propaganda machine, its opaque financial system, and sophisticated military structure, coupled with its connections to thousands of religious networks throughout the Middle East, have helped the government contain the risk of a confrontation between Washington and Iran. As some Iranian conservatives see it, Iran has deterred the United States by adopting a variety of aggressive policies. To put it another way, it is fair to say that the international community, the United States in particular, has fed the Iranian "regime survival" narrative for almost three decades.

## Internal Pressures for Reform

Yet contrary to the general perception in the West, the Islamic Republic of Iran encompasses a wide variety of political and social interests and views, making it confusing for foreign observers to understand the domestic political dynamics. It is neither a democracy nor a dictatorship, yet at the same time it shows characteristics of both. Iranian civil society is vibrant, journalists are relentless, women are well educated, and students are politically active—despite extreme pressure by the authorities that has sent thousands of them to prison. At multiple levels, the society is enthusiastically seeking changes, socially and politically. This dynamic has led to the emergence of moderate Islamists, even reforms to clergy systems, and pressures on the hardliners to be more responsible.

These were also the same conditions that laid the ground a decade ago for the election to the presidency of Mohammad Khatami, a moderate ayatollah who promised to bring reform to the political and social sphere and advocate for "dialogue among civilizations." He was among the rare leaders in the world, or at least the Middle East, to take the courageous step of exposing the killings of dissidents and intellectuals carried out by his nation's intelligence service, apologizing to the Iranian people and dramatically overhauling the intelligence apparatus. As a result, Khatami was widely respected among Iran's middle class, intellectuals, and even his opponents within the country and beyond. His government adopted numerous policies to develop civil society and empower social movements. In other words, the Khatami era gave a glimpse of how Iran's government could be more responsible and accountable, both domestically and globally.

Radical Islamists, however, knew that Khatami's path posed a threat to their power position as well as the financial and political operation of undemocratic institutions under the control of the Supreme Leader Ali Khamenei—the Guardian Councils, Islamic and economic foundations, the Revolutionary

Guard, parallel intelligence service, and Bazzare, the traditional financial and moral backbone of the Islamists conservatives in Iran. It was during Khatami's period that his allies in the government, parliament, and pro-reform media questioned all these institutions and demanded transparency and accountability, including for their past misdeeds. Khatami's agenda was based on the idea that democracy, even with a distinctly Iranian style, can enhance the regime's legitimacy and actually diminish foreign threats. It gave moderates, secular politicians, and activists more voice as a counterweight to the hard-liners.

But at the very moment when moderates and radicals were vying for the political upper hand, the United States adopted economic sanctions against Iran, showing that the international community had utterly misread the mounting domestic pressure for change. It was Khatami's government that cooperated with the United States in the 2002 invasion of Afghanistan, played a very responsible role in the 2003 invasion of Iraq, and, most importantly, suspended enriching uranium in hopes that negotiation with the Western countries would lead to a mutually agreeable solution. Tragically, it was not to be.

Indeed, the signals from Washington were quite the opposite. One of the playful slogans during the buildup to Operation Iraqi Freedom was "Real men go to Tehran."[11] Iranian leaders had never felt the U.S. threat more palpably than during that time. In the streets of Tehran, many people, frustrated by the policies of the regime, believed that Iran would be the next target. The Iranian leaders took the logical lesson from the cases of North Korea, where defiance led the international community to back off, and Iraq, where Saddam Hussein's cooperation with the United Nations and military cleanup failed to ward off a U.S. attack. They decided to follow North Korea's example. But the more the United States became bogged down in Iraq and Afghanistan, the more Iranian leaders understood the unlikelihood of a U.S. attack against Iran.

## Iran's Response to External Threats and Pressures

Regarding the consequences of these two wars, there is no doubt among Iranians that progress and societal change cannot be achieved through war. The U.S. threat, in this regard, has rallied a broad cross-section of people behind the flag and forged a strong consensus, even among the regime's opponents and dissidents, that a military attack will only bring misery and pain and endanger the prospects for democracy and freedom.

For that matter, it is hard to see how radical changes in Iran are even possible. Iranians have paid the price of a damaging revolution, which hurt hundreds of thousands of families. They have also experienced an eight-year war

(1980–1988) that killed a million people. After that, they faced devastating economic pressure during the reconstruction era (1988–1997). The Iranian society, while hungry for change in a number of different areas, is tired and suspicious toward any radical upheaval—a revolution or the overthrow of the ayatollahs by a foreign military invader like the United States.

Iranians believe that regime change,[12] or any radical changes, will lead to chaos and disintegration and a harsh reaction by the Islamic Republic's police state. In effect, such convulsion would establish a perverse geographic link between two tumultuous but separate centers of conflicts, Iraq and Afghanistan, and pave the way for region-wide anarchy.

Conversely, recognition of Iran not only will lift the security threat but also will help empower Iran's middle class and give more space for a dynamic civil society. Given the long-standing threat and hostility, though, we should note that recognition must entail "relinquishing both rhetoric and the implicit policies associated with regime change" respecting Iran's regional influence and integrating the country into the global economy.

Many among Iranian elites believe that the path toward a responsible Iran, regionally and globally, requires both systematic changes within the country as well as normalization of the relations with the United States. Iranian leaders have used foreign threats as an excuse for aggressive policies both inside and outside of the country. A lessened threat also will spur moderates within the Islamic Republic to push for reforms, ask for more transparency, and transform the military dominated administration into a civil one.

Contrary to the dominant international perception, the underlying strategy for Iran's nuclear program is less to threaten Israel than to deter Iran's nuclear neighbor Pakistan, Arab countries around the Persian Gulf, and, most importantly, the United States. No nuclear bomb can differentiate between Muslims and Jews, and the possibility of using such a destructive weapon against Israel is almost zero. There are powerful voices in Iran that believe participation in regional and international security arrangements, coupled with economic incentives, will make Tehran's current costly and Russian-Chinese–based nuclear program obsolete. They want to replace it with a program that is a modern, economically efficient, and a more peaceful system under the supervision of the international community, designed to build trust.

A review of the Islamic Republic's reactionary foreign policy indicates that most of the regime's problematic policies and actions have roots in its insecurity. These problems could be removed from their agenda via changes and compromises that allow Iran to play its natural role in the region and beyond. In this category are issues ranging from Iran's aggressive nuclear program to its support of groups like Hezbollah and Hamas, and its ambiguous role in Afghanistan and Iraq. Iran's nuclear program, for instance, is neither economically efficient nor environmentally safe, yet Iranians see it as a national security priority in order to preserve leverage for negotiations with the United States, an inevitability, sooner or later.

There is a faction among the hard-liners in Tehran, including Ahmadinejad and his allies, who believe Iran's persistence over its nuclear enrichment will deter the United States. Iran benefits from the stability of Iraq and Afghanistan, as long as a U.S. victory will not cause a shift of its focus to Iran. The Iranian government struggles with challenges on its eastern and western provinces from Sistan and Baluchistan to Kurdistan and Azerbaijan. These concerns are, at least in part, what has prompted Iranian leaders to agree to talk with Americans about the security conditions in Iraq four times in the past two years. The leaders' openness to discussions on a variety of issues, not just Iraq's situation, shows that they see the question of their role in the future of Iran and its key challenges as closely intertwined with the diplomatic agenda with the United States.

### The Potential Benefits of Peace and Stability

Iran's 2003 grand bargain proposal to the United States—asking for full-fledged talks about the main concerns of both countries, from the nuclear plan to Iran's support of groups like Hezbollah and Hamas—shows a significant break from the ideological agenda and an increasingly pragmatic path in foreign policy. There are many elements within the clergy establishment that support a two-state solution for Israel and Palestine and believe that the money that has been going to these groups should be spent for the Iranian people. However, as long as the threats against Tehran remain, these elements' voices will not be heard.

A close advisor to former President Khatami once told me that in terms of Iran's national security, Armenia and Israel are the country's natural allies in Central Asia and the Middle East. That is why Tehran sided with Armenia during its conflict with Muslim Azerbaijan. They know that historically and geopolitically, there is no historic rivalry between Tel Aviv and Tehran, but it seems almost impossible to overcome hundreds of years of hostility and animosity between Arabs and Persians. If the two sides of the Israeli-Palestinian conflict come to an agreement, Iran then has no reason to ignore the realities on the ground and continue to support the abovementioned groups.

The Iranian people have suffered as a result of actions supposedly taken on their behalf or in the cause of freedom in the Middle East—U.S. threats to overthrow Iran's government through a military attack, destabilizing its border provinces, and encouraging a sort of velvet revolution. The Islamic Republic's regime has justified its harsh repression of human rights activists, journalists, laborers, women, academics, and students as an effort to resist enemies, mainly the United States, which they accuse of using Iranian civil society, media, and academia to influence the country and attempt to overthrow the regime. Iran's marginalization from the global order and economy has also given the regime's intelligence service a free hand to suppress the dissidents without the fear of any international consequences.

The experience of Khatami shows that Iranian leaders actually care about their international image, but, on the other side of the scale, they will pay any price for the survival of the regime. If the pretext of external threats were removed, the Iranian government would feel enormous pressure from segments of the society that have been asking for change for the past two decades. Demographically, Iran is one of the youngest countries in the world, with 69 percent of its population younger than twenty-nine, and faces severe challenges associated with high unemployment and social inequalities between those with access to power and everyone else.

It might seem overly optimistic to think that any kind of economic and security incentives can guarantee a responsible Iran, given the Islamic Republic's ideological agenda. But the steep decline in the number of clerics holding elected office and the social pressures facing Iranian society from prostitution to drug usage, lack of trust, and social capital all highlight the regime's failure to fulfill its initial ideals of justice, equality, and freedom. In other words, men who promised their people to make life heavenly have made it hell instead—the usual narrative of bad governance in a highly corrupted country in which the state authorities have become alienated from the people.

The Iranian leaders cannot fulfill people's expectations without extensive changes domestically and internationally. The United States' bully policies, including calls for a "regime change" and $75 million to support democracy advocates in Iran, have only helped the government obscure its own failures and postpone reforms that could ultimately bring significant change to Iran's political system.

## Notes

1. Ervand Abrahamian, *Khomeinism: Essays on the Islamic Republic* (London: I.B. Tauris & Co. Ltd., 1993), 112.

2. "Supreme Leader Khamene'i emphasizes spiritual strength of Iranian army," Tehran Voice of the Islamic Republic of Iran Radio 1, April 16, 2003.

3. Mehdi Mohammadi, "The Meaning of Wisdom," *Keyhan* (February 18, 2007). Text accessed at www.kayhannews.ir/851118/14.HTM#other1409.

4. Asghar Schirazi, *The Constitution of Iran: Politics and the State in the Islamic Republic* (London and New York: I.B. Tauris, 1997), 299.

5. The reformist Majlis did endeavor to restrain the judiciary, and pursued a slate of legal reforms with less publicity but greater consistency than they had the vaunted press reforms. They did so largely through two mechanisms—deploying their investigatory power to expose and limit abuses in Iran's prison system, and crafting an omnibus bill to regulate "political crimes." A law to ban torture and physical pressure on prisoners received overwhelming approval in May 2002.

6. Farideh Farhi, "Iran's 'Security Outlook,'" *Middle East Report Online*, July 9, 2007. Text accessed at www.merip.org/mero/mero070907.html.

7. Susan Glasser, "'Martyrs' in Iraq Mostly Saudis," *Washington Post*, May 15, 2005.

8. "Rafsanjani condemns Israeli attacks against Palestinian refugee camps," *Voice of the Islamic Republic of Iran*, March 8, 2002, from BBC SWB.

9. "Daily draws a parallel between Sept 11 events and 1773 Boston Tea Party," *IRNA* (Internet edition), March 12, 2003. Fars News Agency, April 10, 2008.

10. David Dionisi, "America Held Hostage," December 30, 2007, www.teach-peace.com\americaheldhostage.htm.

11. Tony Karon, "What to do About Iran?" *Time*, July 22, 2004, www.time.com/time/world/article/0,8599,671919,00.html.

12. Reuel Marc Gerecht, "Regime Change in Iran? Applying George W. Bush's 'liberation theology' to the mullahs," August 5, 2002, www.weeklystandard.com/Content/Public/Articles/000/000/001/509udwne.asp.

~

# Laggards on Responsibility:
# The Oil Majors

*Susan Ariel Aaronson and David Deese*
*With a Reaction by Edward C. Chow*

For much of the twentieth century, large private oil companies roamed the earth in search of energy to fuel the world's development. Some eight years into the twenty-first century, these corporate behemoths (Exxon Mobil, Chevron-Texaco, and ConocoPhillips from the United States, and BP and Royal Dutch Shell from the European Union) still appear invincible. In recent years, their profits have grown to record levels.[1] However, the big five are not invincible. Although these firms remain among the world's most influential and most profitable companies, they are increasingly challenged by large well-managed national oil companies such as Sinopec (China) and Petrobras (Brazil). State-owned oil companies (hereafter the NOCs) are gaining market share and market clout. The five largest producing companies and seven of the top ten are state-owned. In contrast, the big five oil companies have fewer fields where they can exploit their economic efficiencies and technological prowess.[2]

Such state oil companies are in an increasingly dominant position because their abundant reserves translate into both production and pricing power. These state-run companies not only represent the top ten reserve holders internationally, but in total control some 77 percent of the world's oil reserves. Although prices are declining, many developing country oil exporters are using today's relatively high profits to control their reserves. For example, some oil-rich nations such as Saudi Arabia, Iraq, Iran, Kuwait, and Mexico do not allow the international oil companies to wholly own components of oil fields and infrastructure. Other countries such as Venezuela and Russia are restricting private sector access to their fields.

Moreover, many of these state-owned enterprises do not operate strictly on the basis of market principles. These state-owned firms are guided by multiple political as well as economic goals such as distributing wealth, maintaining energy security, achieving foreign policy aims, and creating jobs.[3] Some of these NOCs are not completely owned by the government—and many such firms operate mainly according to private sector decision rules. However, many such firms do not have to maximize stakeholder value on a quarterly basis, as do the big five. Finally, many (but not all) of the largest state-owned oil companies are members of OPEC, the global oil cartel. Taken in sum, these state-owned firms can frequently coordinate their activities and decisions to maximize profits and prices when it serves their interests, an option not available to private firms under national and international competition policies.[4] And many of these NOCs are affiliated with governments that at times ignore international norms for protecting the environment or respecting human rights.

In this chapter, we discuss how the big five international oil companies approach, incorporate, and interact with global norms for responsible behavior at the very time that they deal with the growing challenges of the NOCs. We examine whether or not these companies act as responsible stakeholders in the global economy. In particular, we focus on the areas of energy security, climate change and alternative energy, human rights, and transparency/accountability. However, we believe this topic should be handled with caution. Although corporations are often global market actors, international law generally applies to states, not to nonstate actors.

## Caveats on Firms as Stakeholders

We believe no company can consistently act as a responsible stakeholder because responsible stakeholdership is not defined under international law. Companies are very different from states, and cannot be held to the same standards as states. Where managers have control (e.g., when an issue affects their operations), companies can more easily conform to emerging international norms. But in other instances (as in climate change or national development policy), companies have limited leverage to shape emerging norms; they can only respond to market forces. In such cases, we discuss whether they use their influence appropriately or at all.

Although we can't firmly define "responsible stakeholdership" for the big five, we can delineate some broad parameters for such behavior. We believe that responsible private oil companies would provide affordable, plentiful access to various energy sources. They would also invest in alternative energies and do their best to plan for future energy sources when supply is limited and prices are high. In addition, these firms would strive to act responsibly in countries where governance (of the environment, markets, and human rights) is inadequate. They would develop policies to ensure that they were not complicit with human rights abuses and would work to ensure that their activities were not built on conflict or corruption.

In general, corporations do not have specific responsibilities under international law. Nonetheless, private firms do have some international responsibilities. As Georgetown law professor Carlos Manuel Vazquez has noted, corporations are artificial groups of natural persons. Just as individuals have some responsibilities under international law, so do corporations acting as conglomerations of individuals.[5] Corporations are not responding passively to this lack of clear standards; instead they are trying to shape such standards by active involvement in international organizations such as the ILO, UNEP, UNDP, and the OECD.[6] In other instances, firms have lobbied at both the national and international levels to clarify their responsibilities. Some oil companies, for example, have sponsored research or developed joint projects with international organizations, governments, and NGOs to address issues such as poverty, corruption, and sustainability.[7]

Although international law does not clearly delineate corporate norms, responsible stakeholdership interestingly is a term that comes from corporate governance scholarship. These scholars recognized that increasingly firms are expected not only to meet shareholder demands, but also to meet the needs of their many stakeholders: employees, suppliers, consumers, NGOs, and so on that can affect a firm's long-term success. But companies are not required by law to meet the needs of their stakeholders; instead, they are managed to enhance shareholder value. Thus, firms strive to meet quarterly earnings objectives.[8] Moreover, managers confront a world where these norms for corporate behavior are not only ill-defined but they can often be contradictory. For example, U.S. oil companies are forbidden by U.S. law to invest in nations such as Iran and Sudan, which are perceived by the United States (and many other governments) as rogue states. If these firms were to invest in such countries, policymakers from their home countries may have more economic leverage to change the behavior of these outlier states. Yet these firms could also be accused of propping up illicit or illegitimate regimes. In another example, the big five are under increasing public pressure to drill for more oil offshore. But that same drilling could undermine the environment and the health of the seas. How should companies respond to these cross-pressures? Managers have no road map to balance these multiple issues

Finally, all companies juggle to meet both their shareholder obligations and their stakeholder responsibilities. There is no one set model for responsible stakeholder practice in the oil industry or the business community in general (although there are overlapping or common responsible practices required in some areas). But it is particularly difficult for extractive industry firms.

Extractive industry firms must go where the extractive resources are located. As the supply of energy has declined in the West, managers of these firms have increasingly sourced from countries where governance is inadequate and where corruption is endemic.

Oil and gas production, like other extractive industries, is capital intensive. Extractive firms must make large investments long before they begin to produce oil or oil products. These firms are especially vulnerable to political, legal, and social risk and, in particular, corruption, given the huge sums involved.

Oil and gas producers are often the largest investors in such countries and therefore may hold substantial influence over the government. Although these firms are obligated to respect host government sovereignty, they are under mounting pressure to use their influence to change the behavior of host governments.[9] However, because of that same clout, oil and gas investors could crowd out the voice of other market and political actors. Yet these same oil and gas companies are increasingly under shareholder and stakeholder pressure to act in a responsible manner. Yet what is responsible is also "unclear."

## Energy and Security: Ensuring an Adequate and Sustainable Supply of Energy to Meet Societal Needs

Although energy security is a global and national public good, in general corporations and not governments provide the world's people with the energy they need. While some such corporations are arms of the state, as noted above, the big five are not. The big five therefore must meet state directives while juggling stakeholder and shareholder directives. Most states are determined to achieve energy security—a major foreign policy challenge for all governments.[10] Energy security can be defined as having an adequate and sustainable supply of energy to meet the needs of citizens, commercial interests, and public sector functions. But energy security in any one country is a function of global energy security.

The link between energy and security is a complex calculation of the "vulnerability" of any specific individual, country, or set of countries to serious social, economic, political, or military disruption stemming from change in one or more dimensions of energy—including its price, availability, or geopolitical effects. A country might be only moderately dependent on any one exporter, but low levels of available stockpiles or storage of that fuel and rigidity in the market might make that country quite vulnerable. Since oil and natural gas markets are generally international or at least regional in nature, national and international vulnerabilities often can only be reduced by sets of governments and firms working in collaboration. Given the constant barrage of events that can influence market conditions, corporate and government leaders share a collective interest in effectively monitoring and managing supply.

A wide range of public and private and national and international actors collaborate to provide the world with energy. As they drill, these actors must also protect the physical flow of oil or natural gas from the producing field to the consumer. Friendly and hostile governments as well as business competitors must work together. A wide range of political and market factors, including price volatility, threaten such collaboration.

The big five international oil companies sit in the middle of this quest to balance energy and security. They must find ways to profit between energy exporting states keen to maximize prices and limit supply, and importing countries determined to maximize supply and limit price volatility. The International Energy Agency has estimated that to develop and deliver energy to the world's people will require massive new investments.[11] Current supplies are not meeting the increases in demand. Thus, responsible stakeholders would invest heavily not only in new oil fields, but in energy efficiency and alternative energy sources as well.

But the big five energy companies have generally cut spending levels in real terms over the past ten years and reinvested in their own stock.[12] Moreover, the huge mergers in the industry have not channeled the resulting lower costs toward exploration efficiencies. As a result, Baker Institute scholars Amy Myers Jaffe and Ronald Soligo conclude that these firms are unable to respond flexibly to market conditions.[13] While buying back stock may well be in the short-term interest of shareholders, it is not in the long-term interest of energy consumers—i.e., global stakeholders. These firms have not acted as responsible stakeholders in regard to ensuring long-term energy security. Moreover, they are not even acting responsibly toward their shareholders. According to Jafee, "if a company is not replacing reserves, and they are spending their case to buy back shares, that is called liquidating the company."[14]

And by their failure to invest early and sufficiently, the world's people remain vulnerable to damaging price spikes, higher long-term prices, and possible supply disruptions from natural disasters, political upheaval, and/or terrorism. Many of the world largest suppliers—with the prominent exceptions of the United States, Canada, Britain, and Norway—have significant political instability and/or policy uncertainty. As outlined in table 11.1 below, almost 70 percent of U.S. imported oil comes from Saudi Arabia, Venezuela, Nigeria, Algeria, Angola, Iraq, and Russia.[15] Each of these countries has a low ranking in terms of democratic political institutions and a high risk of political, economic, and policy instability. The U.S. provides a good example of the repercussions of continued reliance on such states for oil and gas supplies. From 2002 to 2007, in fact, the United States has become

**Table 11.1.  U.S. Petroleum Imports, Political Stability, and State Efficacy**

| Country | 2002¹* | 2007* | Percent Change 2002– 2007 | Rank** | Political Stability 2006² (Percent) | Failed State Index 2008 (Higher Rank= More Stable)³ | Economist Democracy Index 2006⁴ (Lower Rank= More Democratic) |
|---|---|---|---|---|---|---|---|
| Canada | 1,864 | 2,243 | 20 | 1 | 80 | 167 of 177 | 9 |
| Mexico | 1,292 | 1,258 | -3 | 4 | 35 | 105 | 53 |
| Saudi Arabia | 1,551 | 1,487 | -4 | 2 | 26 | 84 | 159 |
| Venezuela | 1,387 | 1,336 | -4 | 3 | 12 | 79 | 93 |
| Nigeria | 620 | 1,131 | 82 | 5 | 4 | 18 | 124 |
| Angola | 332 | 507 | 53 | 7 | 27 | 56 | 151 |
| Algeria | 264 | 663 | 151 | 6 | 20 | 80 | 132 |
| Iraq | 459 | 485 | 6 | 8 | 1 | 5 | 112 |
| Russia | — | 412 | 412 | 9 | 23 | 72 | 102 |
| Ecuador | 102 | 182 | 78 | 10 | 19 | 68 | 92 |

1. Data from Net Crude Oil and Products Imports by Country of Origin in Thousands of Barrels, tonto.eia. doe.gov/dnav/pet/pet_move_neti_a ep00_IMN_mb.
2. Political Stability Indicators from Governance Matters 2007, the World Bank. Political stability indicators are expressed in percentile (0–100) rank. "Political Stability and Absence of Violence" measures the perceptions of the likelihood that the government will be destabilized or overthrown by unconstitutional or violent means. See info.worldbank.org/governance/wgi2007/mc_chart.asp and info.worldbank.org/ governance/wgi2007/faq.htm#2.
3. The Failed State Index was created by the Fund for Peace and provides snapshots of state vulnerability or risk of violence during a window in time. It relies on social, political, and economic indicators of possible violence such as mounting demographic pressures, criminalization or delegitimization of the state, and rise of factionalized elites. See www.fundforpeace.org/programs/fsi/fsindicators.php-.
4. Laza Kekic, "The Economist Intelligence Unit's Index of Democracy," from The World in 2007, www. fas.org/sgp/crs/misc/RL34137.pdf.

increasingly reliant on oil from fragile (relatively unstable) states such as Nigeria, Iraq, and Angola. The single largest absolute increase in exports to the United States over this period was from Nigeria, which is among the very least stable and transparent states in the world.

The table examines America's leading sources of petroleum, their political stability and their commitment to democratic accountable governance. (All of these suppliers except Canada are relatively unstable, and all except Canada and Mexico rank low on scales of democracy and good governance.)

As energy companies, both private and state-owned, pursue energy security by drilling for oil in developing countries, they have poured their investments into countries that are also extremely vulnerable to political risk. For example, among 177 states in 2008 Sudan ranked number two on the failed state index, Chad ranked four, Democratic Republic of Congo six, Kyrgyzstan thirty-nine, and Timor-Leste twenty-five.[16]

Many of these new energy suppliers have not effectively utilized the associated revenues to improve public welfare, diversify their economy, or develop sustainable democratic systems. While not all such countries are failed states, they are "fragile states" that are not well governed.[17] Many of these states suffer from the "resource curse": they are not able to use their abundant resources to achieve both sustainable development and equitable economic growth. When firms decide whether to invest in these countries, they must weigh the world's growing thirst for oil with concern that governments will misuse oil rents.[18]

## Climate Change

Oil and gas firms bear much of the responsibility for the world's environmental problems. The big five are not only are huge polluters, but are huge energy investors. They could use their profits to invest in both energy efficiency and alternative energy sources such as batteries and wind power. Moreover, these behemoths have significant political influence in both the developing and industrialized world. But until recently, they have not used their money or clout to foster a more environmentally sustainable future for the world's people. They have been laggards rather than leaders on energy efficiency and climate change. And the big five have been less responsible to the challenge of climate change than firms from other sectors. For example, a 2006 study by the Investor Responsibility Research Center (commissioned by Ceres) evaluated the performance of corporate executives and boards in establishing governance systems to address climate change. The results, given in table 11.2, compiled scores in the areas of board oversight, corporate management,

**Table 11.2. Average Industry Scores**

| Industry | Total Points (Maximum 100) |
|----------|---------------------------|
| Chemicals | 52 |
| Electricity | 49 |
| Autos | 48 |
| Equipment | 42 |
| Mining | 42 |
| Forests | 38 |
| Oil and Gas | 35 |
| Coal | 21 |
| Food | 18 |
| Airlines | 17 |

public disclosure, emissions accounting, and strategic planning. According to the study's criteria, then, the oil and gas sector has performed below most industrial sectors, including the chemical and electrical industries.[19]

While the sector has been relatively unresponsive, U.S. companies have been less responsive than their European counterparts. None of the American companies have distinguished themselves in their response to climate change. They were laggards. BP and Shell began to address climate change issues in the later 1990s. By 2001, BP achieved its initial goal to reduce its operational greenhouse emissions 10 percent below 1990 levels. Shell's long-term target is to hold emissions from its facilities to at least five percent below 1990 levels through 2010. In contrast, Chevron-Texaco did not begin to set goals for reducing its gas emissions and enhancing its energy efficiency until 2004. ConocoPhillips was the first U.S. oil company to join the U.S. Climate Action Partnership of large firms, and its CEO J. J. Mulva has consistently spoken out in favor of a strong, mandatory national program to reduce emissions. But the largest, most profitable firm among the U.S. big three, Exxon Mobil, was and remains the most intransigent. Exxon Mobil has resisted pressure to set targets for specific emission levels.[20]

With respect to energy efficiency, BP claims to have made $400 million in savings based on an investment of $100 million, which is certainly a benchmark for highly profitable and green strategy.[21] Exxon Mobil focuses on increased efficiencies at its refineries and chemical plants and reports a 35 percent reduction in energy and $CO_2$ intensity rates of production from 1973 to 2005. But neither Chevron-Texaco nor ConocoPhillips has reported any specific targets or achievements in energy efficiency.

The Europeans' IOCs not only moved earlier to address climate change, but they have invested more in alternative energy. BP tried to rebrand itself as an energy company, saying its initials stood for "beyond petroleum." The company took an early position in support of addressing climate change and in 1997 began to reduce its own greenhouse gas emissions.[22] In 2005, BP established an alternative energy business unit and announced it would invest $8 billion over ten years in alternative energy by solar, wind, natural gas, and hydrogen. By 2007 it was investing almost $1 billion per year in the development of renewable energy sources. In 2000 Shell committed to investing $1 billion on alternative energy. Today, it is the largest distributor of biofuels and it has hydrogen stations in five countries. The U.S. companies are now playing catch up. In 2004–2005 Chevron-Texaco and ConocoPhillips committed to invest at least $100 million a year in renewable and clean energy projects. However, committing to invest is not the same as investing. Chevron is spending about $800 million per year on what it calls alternative energy, but most of that supports their large-scale generation of geothermal power. Chevron is also investing in a large-scale biodiesel plant in Texas, and they have set up a subsidiary to invest in energy technologies, but have not delineated their support for "alternative energy." In 2006 ConocoPhillips spent $80 million on alternative energy research and development, including oil sands. It expects to spend $150 million for research on nonconventional oil and gas resources and new energy sources in 2008.[23]

Why were U.S. firms so slow to move on climate change? Managers at some of these firms not only rejected the concept of "climate change" but they also worked to block a policy response that would have facilitated both adjustment and investment in alternative energy. In addition, these firms collaborated with government officials to thwart both international initiatives such as the Kyoto Protocol and domestic movement. The Bush administration was sympathetic to this perspective; it rejected the Kyoto Protocol as too costly and based on unproven science. In fact, the Bush administration rejected any approach with mandates. Several senators put forward less stringent approaches, but none passed Congress from 2000–2006. Finally, in 2007, Congress passed and Bush signed the Energy Independence and Security Act of 2007. It raised fuel economy requirements, provided incentives for biofuel development and usage, enhanced efficiency standards for buildings, lighting, and appliances, and accelerated R&D of solar, geothermal, and marine energy. But this bill did not end tax breaks for oil and gas exploration in the United States.[24]

Perhaps the European companies have found it easier to respond to the challenge of climate change because the European Union has evolved a more supportive policy environment. The EU Emissions Trading Scheme established a cap and trade within which participants can trade emissions permits. This policy has encouraged all firms to reduce emissions as part of their regular business planning, while removing much of the concern about loss of competitive position to firms not participating. In addition, European governments have developed innovative strategies to encourage and stabilize investment flows into renewables. The feed-in tariffs (or set prices over time) for electricity produced from renewables implemented by Germany and Spain are crucial examples of leadership for sustainability. In the United States, a number of states have developed "renewable portfolio standards" in order to ensure that a specified percentage of electricity is produced with renewable energy. The U.S. federal government, however, has been ineffective in this vital area, thus leaving individual oil and gas firms to make their own decisions while responding to the U.S. state level requirements.

In sum, the European oil companies have been early actors on climate change and energy efficiency actors. But they have also benefited from a proactive and responsive regulatory environment. The big three American firms, in contrast, are late to the party.

## Promoting Human Rights

In recent years, many oil companies have struggled to ensure that their operations do not undermine the human rights of host country citizens, particularly in nations with inadequate governance. The connection between oil companies and human rights abuse first drew major international attention in 1995 when nine Nigerian activists, including the writer Ken Saro Wiwa, a leader of the Ogoni tribe, were executed by the authorities for protesting Shell's exploitation of their homeland. The Ogoni activists were calling for self-determination for their small ethnic group in the impoverished oil-producing region. They accused the oil company, Shell, of colluding with the military both to control the land and its people and the oil revenues. In response to the execution of the activists and the arrest and torture of hundreds of other Ogoni, some other states adopted sanctions against Nigeria, including suspension from the Commonwealth.

Shell and the other oil companies operating in the region (including Chevron, Mobil, Elf, and Agip) were widely criticized for their stance of noninterference, which some individuals interpreted as tacit support for the Nigerian regime. In the years since, these firms have dramatically changed how they operate in the region, but the local populace believes these firms perpetuate poverty by continued collusion with corrupt officials at the provincial and federal levels. Despite significant changes by the Nigerian government to achieve greater democratization and transparency, the companies are still subject to frequent protests, work stoppages, and animosity in the Niger Delta.[25]

Other companies have encountered similar problems in other resource rich developing countries such as: Chevron in Ecuador, Unocal (now Chevron) in Burma, and Exxon Mobil in Indonesia. Exxon Mobil and Unocal have actually been compelled to defend their international human rights practices in courts of law. Some activists have argued that in countries where human rights abuses are so egregious, the energy firm must withdraw (as the Canadian firm Talisman did from Sudan). But a withdrawal is not necessarily good for the local population in such countries. Many workers and associated businesses will lose jobs and income, and the energy company will relinquish financial and political leverage to influence the government to act responsibly. Clearly, then, there is no one right strategy for oil companies confronted with these dilemmas.

In response to this quandary, the U.S. and UK governments collaborated on a plan to help companies deal with some of the human rights issues related to their operations. The Voluntary Principles on Security and Human Rights is a set of guidelines adopted by governments, extractive companies, and human rights NGOs. The Voluntary Principles provide practical guidelines for how companies can protect the safety and security of their operations, while respecting human rights of people in surrounding communities. All of the big five international oil companies claim to follow the Voluntary Principles.[26]

Yet the Voluntary Principles do not cover other human rights issues such as corruption (a key obstacle the poor confront in trying to influence government and receive services), employment equity, resettlement of indigenous populations from mining areas, and the role that resource income plays in fomenting local conflict. A 2008 study prepared for the UN Special Representative on Business and Human Rights found that extractive industry firms are subject to more allegations of human rights abuse than other sectors—though it should be noted that allegations are not facts.[27] A 2006 study of the Fortune Global 500 firms found that the 69 percent of extractive industry respondents (this percentage was larger than other sectors) had experience dealing with a significant human rights abuse. Such experience had taught these firms to adopt "an explicit set of principles and/or management practices to address the human rights implications of its operations."[28]

Yet despite their efforts to adopt such codes and human rights strategies, oil company managers clearly struggle to incorporate human rights into their day to day activities at the local level.[29] Fundamentally, protecting human rights is not really a business problem; it is a problem of inadequate governance at the global and national level. But the human rights responsibilities of corporations are not clearly delineated in international law. The Universal Declaration of

Human Rights calls on all organs of society, whether civic groups, corporations, or governments, to protect and promote human rights. But executives are unsure which human rights they should recognize and how they must act to ensure respect for those rights. Moreover, some companies hold their suppliers to human rights standards but many do not. Finally, companies don't know how to monitor their human rights performance and have little incentive to do so—firms are rarely praised for positive steps, but consistently condemned for shortcomings.[30]

In recognition that global business (and the global community broadly) need greater clarification of the human rights responsibilities of business, former Secretary-General Kofi Annan in 2005 appointed Harvard professor John Ruggie as his special representative on the issue of human rights and transnational corporations. In April 2008, Ruggie put forward a framework to "anchor the business and human rights debate and guide all relevant actors." The framework, which was approved by the member states of the UN Human Rights Council, highlights the responsibilities of states to protect against human rights abuses by third parties, including business, the corporate responsibility to respect human rights, and the need for more effective access to remedies.[31] Many business groups have responded positively to the UN special representative's framework, but it remains to be seen whether they will make associated changes in behavior and whether the markets will reward such actions. And it is unclear whether oil companies can effectively meet these evolving human rights norms at the same time that they struggle to meet shareholder and stakeholder demands regarding profits, investment, and sustainability.

## The Resource Curse, Transparency, and Accountability

Oil companies may not be able to choose the countries where oil and gas are plentiful. But they can work with policymakers and the public in such countries to reduce corruption and, in particular, thwart the "resource curse." Many resource rich developing countries lack the governance expertise (or the dedicated honest officials) to translate energy income into sustainable development and economic diversification. Policymakers may allocate resources to the resource sector, and may pay little attention to other sectors of the economy. Without investment in sectors such as agriculture, manufacturing, or education, the economy will remain overly dependent on extractives for growth and development.[32]

This dependence on resources can undermine democracy. Although citizens "own" the natural resources of their county, policymakers often control natural resource wealth without the direct assent of citizens. In many cases, the citizens may not be aware of the sales or have political rights and expertise to challenge such sales in political and economic arenas.[33] In most cases where governments rely heavily on revenue generation from the energy sector, citizens are either not taxed or they are taxed unevenly or ineffectively. Citizens have less information about state activities, and this makes it difficult for them to press for public sector accountability. Finally, even as public expectations rise along with increased export revenues, citizens lack the mechanisms to hold their officials accountable and the information required for them to understand how increased revenues are allocated.

In addition, reliance on the energy sector for revenue may hinder the development of governance expertise and legitimacy. As rulers funnel oil and gas revenue to their families, tribes, sects, or political allies, these elites may make it harder for citizens and civil service officials to influence government.[34] Citizens' resentment and bitterness over the lack of social economic progress in the midst of sharply increased extractive revenues may lead citizens to use violence to achieve their goals. Rebel groups may oppose a government's policies and corruption, yet such groups may also fund their operations through illegal trade in extractive commodities such as oil, diamonds, gold, or coltan.[35] Meanwhile, governments may rely on repression to stay in power and spend significant amounts of their GNP on military expenditures.

## Extractive Industries Transparency Initiative

However, energy companies can help to end this negative cycle. The resource curse presents an opportunity for the public interest and the business interest to coalesce. Citizens in these countries and shareholders of extractive industry firms both benefit from governance that is transparent, accountable, equitable, and efficient. Both want to avoid corruption. Citizens want to avoid corruption because it makes it difficult for citizens to influence government; it can exacerbate poverty and inequality, and it can lead governments to ignore the needs of their citizens (a feedback loop is not created). Business wants to avoid corruption because it increases many types of risks to the firm's short- and long-term management. To meet their shared interests, many international energy and mining firms have "embraced" an initiative devised by the British government—the Extractive Industries Transparency Initiative (EITI). The EITI is a process put forth by the British government in 2003 to help developing countries effectively manage extractive industry revenues. If governments fully implement the EITI, they may, over time, create a feedback loop that allows citizens to monitor government revenues and expenditures and to hold governments accountable.[36]

The EITI does not ask very much of companies operating in countries that have chosen to implement the EITI (as of June 2008, twenty-three countries). They are simply required to disclose all material payments to the government, provide a clear endorsement of EITI on their website, and fill out an international level self-assessment (company form), which the EITI posts on its website. As of June 2008, some thirty-seven firms and many of the major extractive industry associations have agreed to support EITI. The supporters include firms from South Africa, Brazil, Mexico, and Argentina as well as all of the big five. But only eighteen of the thirty-seven supporting firms had filled out a company self-assessment form. All of the oil majors had completed this form except ConocoPhillips. That form affirmed whether the company has published a public statement endorsing EITI, whether it has provided links to any validations of its payments, whether someone at the company was responsible for EITI, whether the company had attended an EITI conference, and whether the company discussed EITI in its CSR or global sustainability reports.[37]

There is growing evidence that firms are not sufficiently supporting the EITI or disclosure as a means of preventing the resource curse in the countries where they operate. For example, in 2005, Save the Children UK examined corporate practice on disclosure of extractive industry royalty payments. (The NGO did not aim to assess their commitment to EITI more broadly.) The resulting study found that few companies were fully disclosing their upstream (exploration, development, and production) oil and gas operations. The researchers covered twenty-five companies with operations in Azerbaijan and Nigeria (among the first EITI countries) and then non-EITI nations Angola, Timor-Leste, Indonesia, and Venezuela during calendar year 2004. EITI does not require supporting companies to disclose payments globally or to specify on a country-by-country basis except in those EITI candidate countries. The researchers assessed whether firms were providing payments transparency, disclosing additional supportive information, and disclosing information about anti-corruption and whistle-blowing policies.[38]

The researchers found twenty-three of twenty-five companies provided little information at all. Two Canadian companies stood apart as exemplary: Talisman and TransAtlantic.[39] The biggest U.S. and European oil companies showed much worse results: of the big five, Shell was ranked highest, closely followed by Chevron-Texaco, BP, and Exxon Mobil. The worst performers were Total of France, Lukoil of Russia, and Petro China (partly state-owned), and state-owned energy companies China National Petroleum

Company (CNPC) and Petronas (Malaysia). These companies disclosed none of their revenue payments, provided little in supportive disclosure, and reported nothing on any anti-corruption and whistle-blowing activities.[40]

Some two years later companies were doing more to disclose their payments in resource rich countries, but such disclosure was still inadequate. In 2008, the NGO Transparency International examined some forty-two companies operating in twenty-one countries.[41] The group found more companies were reporting systemically on a country basis. The exemplars on payments to host governments, termed "proactive disclosers," included Nexen (Canada), Petro Canada, Shell (Netherlands), Statoil (Norway), Talisman (Canada), and Petrobras (Brazil). Thus, they included only one of the big five. The NGO, however, found wide differences among companies and even between different companies in the same countries. Disclosure was selective, depending on the country in question. Moreover, state-owned oil companies were less likely to report than international oil companies, unless they were listed on stock exchanges (i.e., with some degree of public ownership).

Clearly, EITI is helping to change the behavior of some oil industry firms some of the time. But these companies are not disclosing all such payments all of the time, and they are often not providing useful data for all countries.

However, some firms are taking steps to help EITI in some countries. For example, BP is widely credited as advancing EITI adherence in Azerbaijan. The company trained Azeri government representatives in financial reporting and economic modeling and is also funding NGOs. Likewise, Exxon claims it prodded Equatorial Guinea to join EITI, and the firm continues to encourage Angola to join the EITI.[42]

Yet the question remains: Given their economic interest in reducing corruption, why are companies not doing more? Executives offer several arguments. Some maintain that transparency demands placed upon them are unfair because many nationally owned oil companies (NOCs) such as China National Petroleum are not subject to similar expectations. But many other firms are partly state-owned and are publicly listed. These firms are also subject to pressure to act against corruption. Moreover, some state-owned firms are paragons of reporting, such as Brazil's Petrobras. Companies also complain that it is difficult to report these royalties because the accounting community has not yet agreed upon international accounting standards. However, the International Accounting Standards Board has developed such standards and is now soliciting public comments. These standards are also being reworked to align with the International Financial Reporting Standards and Generally Accepted Accounting Principles. Some companies have suggested that reporting on a country level is cost-prohibitive because of associated higher auditing fees. But this is all the more reason for these firms to be supportive of EITI. As noted above, EITI does not actually require its supporting firms to disclose all their operations everywhere.

Moreover, EITI alone is insufficient to help these countries prevent the resource curse. In several EITI implementing countries, civil society is often nonexistent, poorly organized, or ineffectual. The individuals staffing NGOs in the developing world may lack the education, organizational and dissemination skills, and political savvy to use the information provided under EITI to change their governments' behavior. But corporate supporters of EITI have been reluctant to support changes to EITI obligations.[43]

## Going the Way of the Dinosaurs?

This chapter examined the big five international oil companies as proxies to discuss how corporations respond to the challenges of "responsible stakeholdership." We began by noting how difficult it is for any firm to consistently act as responsible stakeholders; it is particularly challenging for oil and gas companies that are limited as to where they can drill for oil and gas. We described the oil companies as hugely profitable behemoths, confronted with dramatically changing market conditions. We also noted that the oil companies have unique operating conditions; they are often the largest and/or only investor in nations where they operate and bear extreme financial and political risk.

These firms also shoulder a range of different responsibilities, including providing energy, investing in alternative sources of supply, and not undermining global norms for the environment and human rights. If managed with sensitivity toward these responsibilities, their operations could help advance human rights, cap harmful emissions, and stimulate economic growth—yet the record often reveals the opposite. Oil companies have indeed earned their reputation as socially and environmentally irresponsible. These firms have at times justified their behavior by stating that they cannot compete with national oil companies that have fewer pressures for responsible stakeholdership. But such arguments don't eliminate their responsibility to help uphold international norms, especially in nations where governance is inadequate. Moreover, these companies have acted in an ad hoc manner, often responding only when faced with embarrassing stakeholder protests about their behavior. They have developed industry and firm specific codes of conduct or CSR strategies to guide their operations. However, because these ad hoc strategies are voluntary and limited, the more responsible companies indeed find it difficult to compete against state-owned firms that do not shoulder the same stakeholder and shareholder pressures.

In recent years, policymakers have developed initiatives such as the EITI and the Voluntary Principles to help these companies ensure that their operations do not prop up repressive regimes, undermine human rights, perpetuate corruption and poverty, and fuel conflict. But while BP and Shell have made significant progress in implementing these voluntary initiatives, the American oil and gas majors appear less committed. We do not attribute this difference between U.S. and EU firms strictly to better management; U.S. shareholders have retained a relentless pressure on maximizing profits and shareholder value. Moreover, the policy environment in the United States under the Bush administration was less supportive of efforts to develop global climate change or human rights norms compared to its European counterparts.[44] However, the three U.S. IOCs are likely to perceive greater pressure to address climate change and invest in alternative energies and to protect human rights from the Obama administration.

We conclude with the observation with which we began: the international oil companies are behemoths. They are huge, slow to move, and often perceived as irresponsible. As we all know, the dinosaurs had great difficulty evolving as the earth warmed. If they do not dramatically change their ways, the big five oil and gas behemoths may also go the way of the dinosaurs.

~

## Edward C. Chow's Reaction

The economic role of major international oil companies (IOCs) in the twenty-first century is an interesting topic and one that Aaronson and Deese tackle with vigor. The authors surmise that there is a tension, perhaps even contradiction, between IOCs' obligation to their shareholders and a wider responsibility to stakeholders. In common corporate parlance, "stakeholders" include shareholders, governments, customers, communities, and employees, so the concept explicitly accepts social responsibility on the part of companies. However, the authors go a good deal further when they judge IOC actions in the context of a supposed global commons and "stakeholdership" standard in the areas of diversity of energy supply including alternative energies and conservation, remediation of climate change, promotion of human rights, and elimination of resource curse and corruption. Let's examine whether these concepts are truly applicable.

## Shareholder Value and Social Responsibility

It is fashionable to claim that the modern American corporation's fixation on market expectations on quarterly financial performance is at odds with larger societal goals. Yet evidence is lacking. The essential function of petroleum companies is to deliver adequate and dependable oil and gas supply to customers in an efficient, safe, and healthful way. These companies are held accountable to do just that, as capital markets respond to their efficacy by either rewarding or punishing share price and creditworthiness. Quarterly earnings are an important but by no means the sole measure by which management's performance is judged.

More relevant to this chapter, it is hard to find any correlation between the supposedly narrow, short-sighted, and socially irresponsible approach of an IOC focused on shareholder value versus the necessity of an enlightened longer-term view in order to act responsibly. On the contrary, short-term market mechanisms have been quite effective stimuli for corporate responsibility. Take BP, the recent safety record of which in the United States was so poor that an outside commission chaired by former Secretary of State James Baker had to be brought in, and senior management was replaced in order to restore credibility. Once BP's share price had been punished for this poor performance, it was compelled to act.

The comparison between national oil companies (NOCs) and private firms only reinforces the point. State-run Pemex, PdVSA, and Gazprom— with their insulation from market forces—actually have miserable social responsibility records in their operations in Mexico, Venezuela, and Russia. In fact, the anecdotal evidence is that, as NOCs compete abroad and become partially publicly traded (such as Petrobras and Petronas), they develop more social and environmental responsibility precisely because they become subject to market discipline.

Admittedly no one's record is perfect. However, is the focus on shareholder value really the barrier or part of the answer? It can be argued that shareholders also have an interest in the sustained financial performance and brand value of companies, which are directly affected by their social performance. Is it possible, then, that shareholder value can actually be an ally in achieving the global "stakeholdership" that the chapter advocates?

## Oil Companies and Diversification of Energy Supply

Another common complaint is that oil companies do not invest enough in alternative energies and conservation. However, are IOCs truly the best candidates for this task? Major oil companies are notoriously bad at diversifying their business. In the 1970s and 1980s, they were also pushed to diversify their portfolios beyond oil and gas. They famously failed in mining (everybody), office technology (Exxon), department store (Mobil), and biotechnology (Chevron). Conversely, other major corporations diversified into oil and gas, such as Dupont's acquisition of Conoco and USX by buying Marathon; they ultimately abandoned the ventures as being too different from their core businesses.

Are there really inherent comparative advantages that make oil companies better investors in alternative energy and energy efficiency? There is no reason to assume that oil and gas companies will be effective or efficient in harnessing other forms of energy. In other words, society has valid reasons for wanting to invest in alternative energies and conservation, but is the oil industry the best vehicle for doing so? Indeed, the argument flies in the face of what we know about business innovation. Telephone companies with landline monopolies were not the first companies to popularize mobile phone services, even though Bell Labs may have invented the early technology. IBM did not create Microsoft, nor did Microsoft create Google, nor did Google create Facebook or YouTube, and nor did Kodak popularize digital photography. It is precisely because these major corporations were too deeply invested in their legacy systems that they have been so poor in promoting step changes in related businesses. Would oil companies fare better in the stated goals of diversifying energy supply away from oil and gas and in achieving efficiency gains in energy consumption?

Furthermore, the best estimates are that it would take at least twenty to thirty years before the world can shift decisively from a reliance on oil and gas as energy sources, given the vast scale involved. Therefore, IOCs have a big continuing responsibility to provide the oil and gas that will be needed during this period. Why not leave oil companies to do what they know best, which is to deploy technology, capital, and skilled manpower to extract oil and gas and to process and deliver them to market? What economic efficiency would be gained by asking oil companies to diversify? If the industry is underinvesting in this area, would society not be better served by oil companies passing along those profits through higher dividends or higher taxes so they are available for investment in alternative energy and conservation through either capital markets or government-sponsored research and development?

## American Oil Companies and Climate Change

This is an intriguing question: the relative responsibility of the government or the private sector in an area that directly impacts its business. Comparing European and American companies, the authors suggests that the more progressive behavior on the part of BP, Shell, and Statoil may be in response to home governments' and EU guidelines. So is the absence of such political consensus, until recently, in the United States the reason for American IOCs' hesitancy?

The argument about energy conservation has the same problem, with regard to the relationship between responsible behavior and shareholder value, as noted above. To the extent that energy savings are profitable, companies should already be practicing them and thus do not qualify as part of a program of global "stakeholdership." This behavior is certainly driven more by reducing higher energy costs than by any sense of social responsibility. Indeed, it is hard to see how first-generation biofuels and oil sands, also cited in this section of the chapter, contribute to diminishing greenhouse gas emissions and impact on climate change, since they actually worsen the problem.

In spite of best intentions, it is highly unlikely that the European Union will meet its Kyoto targets or its aspirational goals for reducing greenhouse gas emissions and increasing the use of renewable and bio fuels. It is also true that American oil companies are clamoring for national standards in order to counteract the proliferation of state and local climate change proposals and to avoid bearing the major burden in remediation, with the accompanying competitive concerns. Yet Aaronson and Deese may give oil companies too much credit for their influence over the political process. Do American politicians really respond more to this narrow constituency than to concerns in the wider public about the economic and social costs of limiting greenhouse gas emissions? It is hardly clear which set of concerns weighs most heavily on the public's mind; one need only look at consumer behavior for a start. For example, 70 percent of U.S. petroleum consumption is in the transportation sector, of which the vast majority is by the personal automobile. So is the greater political obstacle for policy consensus Exxon Mobil or the average American voter?

What seems clear is that meaningful steps to limit greenhouse gas emissions are contingent on a national consensus and internationally sanctioned rules of the game. It can be argued that IOCs should be leading the charge to arrive at a workable consensus and policy framework in an area so integral to their business. But again, there is a clear connection to shareholder value, leaving aside the question of global stakeholdership. Some IOCs are engaged exactly in this process, but not all, and it is not clear whether the variation in response, particularly between American and European companies, is due solely to a company's national origin or because of its home government's view of national interests.

## Oil Companies' Responsibility for Human Rights

This is another interesting case on whether oil companies have an obligation distinct from, and in excess of, compliance with home and host country laws and practices. Once again an argument can be made that it is in the enlightened self-interests of IOCs to do so, since it protects their long-term business interests. Indeed, human rights conditions are factored into companies' investment calculations—using a risked rate of return to weigh alternative investments. To the extent that one country is judged as riskier because of its human rights violations, companies will require an offsetting higher potential rate of return to compensate for assuming the risks associated with an unstable investment climate and operating conditions.

Should the international community demand a higher standard than this? And if so, what should the standard be? The Universal Declaration of Human Rights is probably not the right answer, since it is unevenly observed by its signatory states. Are there instead voluntary principles geared specifically toward corporations, just as the Sullivan Principles were during the days of apartheid South Africa, which can be used to advance human rights? Any such principles certainly would be beyond the scope and competence of an individual oil company, no matter how large and powerful. Can a mechanism be created to publicly expose bad oil company behavior and thereby prompt threats against corporate reputation and brand value? This approach could help harness competitive forces to discipline oil company performance on human rights concerns. The possibilities are ripe for further investigation.

## Oil Companies and the Resource Curse

It is certainly true that the resource curse frequently enables bad government behavior and inhibits the development of a more balanced economy, civil society, and representative government. It is less clear what individual oil companies are supposed to do about it, or whether the responsibility instead really lies with nation-states and the international system. The United States, Canada, Britain, and Norway are cited in the chapter as exception to the rule (Australia also belongs on this list). Yet IOCs were also the major developers of these countries' oil and gas resources, so it is clearly not their presence by itself that is the cause of the resource curse. Rather it is choices made by host governments and societies to which foreign oil companies are accountable, not the other way around. Governments are sovereign and companies are not, and this is the way it should be.

This raises a more profound question of whether there is a global commons and who is responsible for its well-being. It may be more important for governments to be signatories to the Extractive Industries Transparency Initiative than for companies to be. If host governments do not adhere to these principles, perhaps there should be some international recourse; the chapter would have been strengthened by added discussion about how EITI observance can be improved over time. It is worth recalling that the Sullivan Principles themselves went through many iterations and improvements before they were broadly embraced by multinational corporations operating in South Africa over the objections of the then apartheid government.

## Same Fate as the Dinosaurs?

This is perhaps the most provocative notion advanced by the authors and one that deserves more thorough exploration. It is true that governments have allowed IOCs to develop into the behemoths referred to in this chapter through major acquisitions (e.g., of Arco and Amoco by BP, of Mobil by Exxon, of Texaco and Unocal by Chevron, and of Phillips by Conoco). Has this been to the benefit of competition and market efficiency? The presumption was that growing to an even larger scale would allow IOCs to bear more risks in exploring and developing difficult fields in frontier areas—such as in deeper waters and more remote regions. Yet IOCs' exploration success since the mega-mergers has been minimal, and their performance in developments such as the super-giant Kashagan field in Kazakhstan (in which Exxon Mobil, Shell, Total, ENI, and ConocoPhillips are all partners) has been a major disappointment. Recent industry advances, such as developing nonconventional gas in the United States, have been led by small independent producers.

So does the future lie with smaller but still large companies, such as Marathon or Occidental, which can bear significant risks but are more nimble in the marketplace? Or is it with nonvertically integrated companies (like Valero, the largest U.S. refiner), which can better concentrate on competing in their segment of the market. It is hard to imagine that the state-owned companies, with their "home field" advantage, will achieve better efficiency, unless they are exposed to competitive forces. How successfully will emerging economy parastatals, such as oil companies from China, India, and Korea, compete as they invest internationally?

How would smaller international oil companies, NOCs, and parastatals perform on global "stakeholdership" as compared to traditional IOCs? If IOCs are doomed to extinction, will international governance rules become even more important to establish? Who will do this if IOCs are no longer around for us to assign the blame? These are serious issues for the twenty-first-century oil industry and the international system, which should be addressed in public policy discussions. This chapter has helped us make a promising start.

# Notes

1. Many global companies have huge revenues, bigger than the GDP of many governments. Thus, some observers presume that these companies have not only enormous influence, but also influence equal to governments of the same size. But this is not a fair comparison. Instead, we should look at a firm's profit and GDP, the value-added that an economy generates per year, so the proper comparison is between a firm's profits and GDP.

2. Baker Institute, "The Role of National Oil Companies in International Energy Markets," www.rice.edu/energy/research/nationaloil/index.html; Amy Jaffe and Ronald Soligo, "The International Oil Companies" (at press), November 2007, 2–3, available at www.policyarchive.org/bitstream/handle/10207/6801/NOC_IOCs_Jaffe-Soligo.pdf?sequence=1; and Robert Pirog, "Oil Industry Profits: Analysis of Recent Performance," CRS Report for Congress RL33021. On profits, Marianne Levelle, "Exxon's Profits: Measuring a Record Windfall," U.S. News and World Report, February 1, 2008, www.usnews.com/articles/business/economy/2008/02/01/exxons-profits-measuring-a-record-windfall.html. Put in context, Exxon's profits in 2007 were 80 percent higher than GE. Fortune reported that Exxon Mobil was the world's most profitable company; money.cnn.com/galleries/2007/fortune/0707/gallery.global500_profits.fortune/index.html.

3. In recent examples of how governments have used state run oil companies to achieve foreign policy goals, Russia has interrupted natural gas deliveries to Europe, Saudi Aramco decided to raise output in the wake of the Iraqi invasion of Kuwait, and Chavez has used favorable oil pricing to gain political influence in Latin America. China is using loans to gain access to oil and curry favor in Africa. See Matthew Green, "China Oils Nigeria Talks With Loan," Financial Times, April 21, 2008, www.ft.com/cms/s/0/c4f9e296-0fe8-11dd-8871-0000779fd2ac.html.

4. Robert Pirog, "The Role of National Oil Companies in the International Oil Market," CRS Report for Congress, RL 34137, August 21, 2007. Pirog notes five of the top ten oil companies are state-owned, including number one, Saudi Aramco. It is followed by Exxon Mobil, NIOC (state), PDV (state), BP, Shell, Petro China (90 percent state), Chevron, Total (French—private), and Pemex (state). The top ten reserve holders, with the exception of the Russian company Lukoil, were state-owned. Pirog stresses that national oil companies of more developed nations such as Statoil of Norway and Petronas of Malaysia tend to follow a more commercially oriented strategy than companies such as Petroleos de Venezuela or the Nigerian National Petroleum Company.

5. Some international agreements regulate the behavior of corporations but they do so by regulating states. For example, the Convention on Combating Bribery of Foreign Public Officials contemplates the criminalization of bribery by any legal person (including a corporation). However, rather than criminalizing bribery itself, the

convention requires states to criminalize such bribery when done on their territory. Carlos Manuel Vazquez, "The Four Doctrines of Self-Executing Treaties," *American Journal of International Law* 89 (October 1995): 695; Carlos Manuel Vazquez, "Direct vs. Indirect Obligations of Corporations Under International Law," *Columbia Journal of Transnational Law* 43 (2005): 927, at ssrn.com/abstract=844367.

6. International Association of Oil and Gas Producers (OGP), www.ogp.org.uk/.

7. In this regard, see John Browne, chief executive, BP, "BP Sustainability Report 2006," 1–2.

8. Henry Hansmann and Reinier Kraakman, "The End of History for Corporate Law," *Georgetown Law Journal* 89, no. 2 (January 2001): 439, 440–41; Milton Friedman, "The Social Responsibility of Business Is To Increase Its Profits," *New York Times*, September 13, 1970 ("[A] corporate executive is an employee of the owners of the business. He has [a] direct responsibility to his employers. That responsibility is to conduct the business in accordance with their desires, which generally will be to make as much money as possible while conforming to the basic rules of society").

9. Business Industry Advisory Committee to the OECD, "BIAC Statement on Conducting Business with Integrity in Weak Governance Zones: Issues for Discussion and a Case Study of the DRC," DAF/INV?WP (2004)1: 2–3.

10. See the detailed discussion of different threats and matching policy responses in Joseph S. Nye, David A. Deese, and Alvin L. Alm, "Conclusion: A U.S. Strategy for Energy Security," in Deese and Nye (eds.), *Energy and Security* (Cambridge, MA: Ballinger, 1981).

11. National Petroleum Council, Global Oil and Gas Study, "Facing the Hard Truth About Energy," July 18, 2007.

12. Robert Pirog, "The Use of Profit by the Five Major Oil Companies," CRS Report RI34044.

13. Jaffe and Soligo, "The International Oil Companies," 6–8.

14. Jad Mouawad, "At Exxon, Making the Case for Oil," *New York Times*, November 16, 2008, www.nytimes.com/2008/11/16/business/16exxon.html.

15. Energy Information Administration, Annual Energy Review, www.eia.doe.gov/oiaf/aeo/pdf/overview.pdf; see figures 12, 13, 25, and 63.

16. The 2007 index was just released in September 2007. See www.fundforpeace.org/web/index.php?option=com_ &ta.

17. UNESCAP, "What is governance?" www.unescap.org/pdd/prs/Project Activities/Ongoing/gg/governance.asp. Good governance is participatory, consensus-oriented, accountable, transparent, responsive, effective and efficient, equitable and inclusive, and follows the rule of law. It assures that corruption is minimized, and the views of minorities are taken into account.

18. In 2001, the Human Rights and Business Project developed a template delineating when a human rights situation is so volatile that the firm should withdraw. The template is now widely used by extractives; Margaret Jungk, Human Rights and Business Project, "Deciding Whether to Do Business in States with Bad Governments," 2001, www.humanrightsbusiness.org/pdf_files/decidingwhether.pdf.

19. Douglas G. Cogan, "Corporate Governance and Climate Change: Making the Connection" (Boston: Ceres, 2006), 22–23.

20. Ans Kolk and David Levy, "Winds of Change: Climate Change and Oil Multinationals," *European Management Journal* 19, no. 5 (2001): 501–9; Mouawad, "At Exxon."

21. See Miranda Anderson, David Gardiner, and Associates (for Ceres), "The Future of Oil: Energy Security, Climate Risks, and Market Opportunities" (Boston: Ceres, 2007), 14.

22. www.bp.com/sectiongenericarticle.do?categoryId=9021745&contentId=704 1006.

23. Cogan, "Corporate Governance and Climate Change," 233–35.

24. See John Vidal, "Revealed: How Giant Oil Influenced Bush White House Sought Advice from Exxon on Kyoto Stance," *The Guardian*, June 8, 2005; Fred Sissine, CRS Report for Congress, "Energy Independence and Security Act of 2007: A Summary of Major Points," RL34294, 2.

25. BBC News, "Nigeria Hears Ogoni Oppression," January 21, 2001, news.bbc.co.uk/2/hi/africa/1130555.stm; Human Rights Watch, "The Price of Oil: Corporate Responsibility and Human Rights Violations In Nigeria's Oil Producing Communities," www.hrw.org/reports/1999/nigeria/nigeria0199.pdf; and Reuters, "Shell Contains Oil Spill Caused by Sabotage," November 13, 2008, www.reuters.com/article/marketsNews/idUSLD69608820081113.

26. www.voluntaryprinciples.org/participants/companies.php.

27. For example, a report commissioned for the UN Special Representative on Business and Human Rights Michael Wright, "Corporations and Human Rights: A Survey of the Scope and Patterns of Alleged Corporate Related Human Rights Abuse," www.reports-and-materials.org/Ruggie-scope-patterns-of-alleged-abuse-Apr-2008.pdf.

28. John G. Ruggie, "Human Rights Policies and Management Practices of Fortune Global 500 Firms: Results of a Survey," September 1, 2006, www.reports-and-materials.org/Ruggie-survey-Fortune-Global-500.pdf, www.ipieca.org/activities/social/downloads/workshops/apr_08/p2_-_jflood_-_human_rights_tools_for_the_o&g_industry_1350.09375.pdf, and www.humanrightsbusiness.org.

29. Look up oil companies on the businesshumanrights.org website and follow the multiple articles/links: www.business-humanrights.org/Search/SearchResults?SearchableText=oil+companies&x=0&y=0.

30. Michael Wright and Amy Lehr, "Business Recognition of Human Rights: Global Patterns, Regional and Sectoral Variations: A Study Conducted under the Direction of John G. Ruggie, Harvard University," December 12, 2006, www.reports-and-materials.org/Business-Recognition-of-Human-Rights-12-Dec-2006.pdf.

31. Human Rights Council, "Protect, Respect and Remedy: a Framework for Business and Human Rights: Report of the Special Representative of the Secretary General on the Issue of Human Rights and Transnational Corporations and other business Enterprises, John Ruggie," A/HRC/8/5, April 7, 2008, www.reports-and-materials.org/Ruggie-report-7-Apr-2008.pdf.

32. Oil windfalls can push up the real exchange rate of a country's currency, rendering non-oil exports relatively uncompetitive. That can lead to "Dutch disease." As these sectors languish, the economy may become ever more dependent on oil.

33. Catholic Relief Services, "Bottom of the Barrel," Open Society Justice Initiative, "Legal Remedies for the Resource Curse," August 6, 2005, www.justiceinitiative.org/db/resource2?res_id=102966; Marcartan Humphreys, Jeffrey D. Sachs, and Joseph E. Stiglitz, eds., *Escaping the Resource Curse* (New York: Columbia University Press, 2007), 4. Kazakhstan provides a good example of this dilemma. On August 19, 2007, the ruling party of President Nursultan Nazarbayev said it had won 88 percent of the vote. Anton Troianovski, "Ruling Party Sweeps Kazakhstan Election, Official Count Shows," *Washington Post*, August 20, 2007.

34. Humphreys et al. *Escaping the Resource Curse*, 11–12; Terry Lynn Karl, *The Paradox of Plenty: Oil Booms and Petro-States* (Berkeley: University of California Press, 1997). She examined Venezuela, Iran, Nigeria, Algeria, and Indonesia. Also see Michael Ross, "Does Oil Hinder Democracy?" *World Politics* 53 (April 2001): 325–61; Richard M. Auty and Alan G. Gelb, "Political Economy of Resource Abundant States," in Richard M. Auty, ed., *Resource Abundance and Economic Development* (Oxford: Oxford University Press, 2001), 126–44.

35. Paul Collier and Anke Hoeffler, "Greed and Grievance in Civil War," Working Paper 2002-18, April 16, 2000; Macartan Humphreys, "National Resources, Conflict and Conflict Resolution: Uncovering the Mechanisms," *Journal of Conflict Resolution* 49, no. 4 (2005): 508–37; and James D. Fearon, "Primary Commodities Exports and Civil War," *Journal of Conflict Resolution* 49, no. 4 (2005): 483–507. For other papers on this topic, see econ.worldbank.org/WBSITE/EXTERNAL/EXTDEC/EXTRESEARCH/EXTPROGRAMS/EXTCONFLICT/contentMDK:20985555~menuPK:2729821~pagePK:64168182~piPK:64168060~theSitePK:477960,00.html and econ.worldbank.org/WBSITE/EXTERNAL/EXTDEC/EXTRESEARCH/EXTPROGRAMS/EXTCONFLICT/0contentMDK:21315494~pagePK:64168182~piPK:64168060~theSitePK:477960,00.html.

36. Susan Ariel Aaronson, "Is EITI an Answer to the Resource Curse," revised for *Ethics and International Affairs* (copy in possession of author); Susan Ariel Aaronson, "Oil in the Public Interest," Vox/EU, www.voxeu.org/index.php?q=node/1395.

37. eitransparency.org/node/218, last searched January 7, 2008.

38. Save the Children UK, "Beyond the Rhetoric: Measuring Revenue Transparency-Company Performance in the Oil and Gas Industries," and "Beyond the Rhetoric: Measuring Revenue Transparency-Home Government Requirements for Disclosure in the Oil and Gas Industries," March 2005, www.publishwhatyoupay.org/measuring_transparency/pdf/homegovts.pdf.

39. Canadian companies had the best results because in 2005 Canada was the only country that required country level disclosure. As of June 2008, Norway also requires such disclosure. In May 2008, U.S. Congressman Barney Frank put forward H.R. 6066, the Extractive Industries Transparency Disclosure (EITD) Act, which would require publicly listed companies to report any payments made to governments to ex-

tract resources; www.publishwhatyoupay.org/english/pdf/releases/pwyp_usa_release_frank.pdf. The European Parliament also called for country-by-country disclosure of revenue payments.

40. Save the Children UK, "Beyond the Rhetoric," www.publishwhatyoupay.org/measuring_transparency/pdf/homegovts.pdf.

41. Transparency International, "Frequently Asked Questions: Promoting Revenue Transparency Project," www.Transparency.org/revenue_transparenc; Transparency International 2008, "Promoting Revenue Transparency: 2008 Report on Revenue Transparency of Oil and Gas Companies," April 2008, www.transparency.org/revenue_transparency.

42. Interview with Sheldon Daniel, director of corporate responsibility, BP, April 23, 2008, www.bp.com/sectiongenericarticle.do?categoryId=430&contentId=2000578. On Statoil, Ameilia Shepherd-Smith, "Investing for Security," *Ethical Corporation*, October 2007, 21.

43. Susan Ariel Aaronson, "For the People, but not By the People: The EITI, Investors and Signaling," under review, *Foreign Policy Analysis*.

44. In this regard, see Susan Ariel Aaronson, "Minding Our Business: What the U.S. Government Has Done and Can Do to Ensure That U.S. Multinationals Act Responsibly in Foreign Markets," *Journal of Business Ethics* 59 (2004): 175–98.

# Index

Note to index: An *n* following a page number denotes a note on that page. A *t* following a page number denotes a table on that page.

123 Agreement, 173–74

Aaronson, Susan A., 340
Abe, Shinzo, 49, 54
Afghanistan: attacks on al-Qaeda after 9/11, 12; European commitment to war in, 79; Japan disarmament efforts in, 64; narcotics trafficking in, 180
Africa Command (AFRICOM), 278, 284
African Growth and Opportunity Act (AGOA), 278, 281
African Union (AU), 95, 260, 274
Ahmadinejad, Mamoud, 299, 300–301, 302, 303, 304, 308, 310, 311–12, 313, 318
AIDS. *See* HIV/AIDS
Alliance of Civilizations, 203
American exceptionalism, 11–12
Annan, Kofi, 332
Anti-Secession Law (China), 112
Armenia, 205, 208

arms control: China, 109–10, 112; Russia, 170–72, 191–92; United States, 12, 170–72. *See also* arms sales
arms sales: Japan, 64; Russia, 169; South Africa, 271. *See also* arms control
ASEAN+3, 110
ASEAN Regional Forum (ARF), 61, 68
Ashton, John, 239
Asia-Pacific Economic Cooperation (APEC) group, 105
Aso, Taro, 49
Association of Southeast Asian Nations (ASEAN), 95, 272, 284
Azerbaijan, 208

Babacan, Ali, 215, 217
Bağci, Hüseyin, 217–22
Bali conference on climate change, 115, 126
ballistic missile defense (BMD), 172, 191
Bangladesh, 159

Beijing Consensus, 118, 185
Bharatiya Janata Party (BJP), 129–30, 140
birthrates, in the European Union, 81–82
Black Economic Empowerment, 268
Black Sea Economic Cooperation (BSEC), 208
BP, 328–29, 334, 335, 337, 338, 339–40
Brazil, 225–56; 2010 elections, 244–45; Amazon, historical phobia about, 250, 254–55; and Cardoso, 232–33, 236, 251–52; climate change, 235, 238–40; corruption, 247–48; crime, 246–47; deforestation in, 7–8, 239, 254–55; democracy in, 232–33; diplomacy by, 233–35, 248–49; domestic consensus-building, 249–50; economic milestones, 246; economic stabilization, 229–32; energy sector in, 239, 252, 256; Fome Zero anti-hunger initiative, 230, 240, 252; foreign investment in, 231–32; future of, 251; globalization and, 231; human rights and, 255; indifference by global powers, 225–26; international leadership, 253–55; Itamaraty, 233–34, 255; Latin America, leadership role in, 236–38; leadership record, 235–43; liberalization in, 231; and Lula, 231, 233, 236–37, 239–40, 245, 251–53; as multicultural, 228; and multilateralism, 243, 254; and narcotics trafficking, 235; nationalism in, 252; nation-building, 241–42; natural resources of, 228–29; new prominence of, 226–27; peacekeeping by, 235, 240–41; physical size of, 228; political culture of, 253; and poverty, 230, 231; Public-Private Partnerships in, 255–56; reaction of Landau, 251–56; reform agenda, unfulfilled,

255–56; rules-based order, past/future commitment to, 243–51; stability, political and economic, 244; support network need for presidents, 245–46; Worker's Party in, 252; and world trade, 242–43
Brazilian Association of International Relations (ABRI), 246
BRICs (Brazil, Russia, India, and China), 94–95, 166, 234
Brzezinski, Zbigniew, 32
BSEC. See Black Sea Economic Cooperation
Burma: and China, 111–12, 150; and India, 150; and South Africa, 272
Bush administration (G. W. Bush): aid to South Africa, 278; arms control, 170; exemption of India from nonproliferation constraints, 131–32; missile defense policy, 172–73; Proliferation Security Initiative, 26; unilateralism, 12

Cambodia, 64
Cardoso, Fernando H., 232–33, 236, 251–52
Carothers, Thomas, 184–85
Cartagena Protocol for Biosafety, 239
Central Intelligence Agency (CIA), 12
Chavez, Hugo, 237, 238, 241
Chevron, 331, 339
Chevron-Texaco, 328, 329, 334
child soldiers, UN ban on use of, 20
China: arms control, 109–10, 112; assumptions/understandings about, 101–2; and Burma, 111–12; challenges to becoming responsible stakeholder, 102–16; climate change, 34, 35, 114–15; constructive framework for, 118; core concerns of, 118; currency undervaluation, 105; domestic instability, 102; domestic political evolution, 103; energy

consumption and conservation, 115–16; and the European Union, 94–95, 104; facilitating rise of, 117–18; global finance role, 105–6; health issues, 107, 112; humanitarian assistance/developmental aid, 107–8; and human rights, 150; and India, 104, 111, 139, 158; international economics/trade/investment, 119–20; international institutions/public goods, 106–10; in international political councils, 101–2; and international property rights, 105; and international trade, 104–5; and Iran, 113; and Japan, 110–11; and Korean peninsula, 110; military affairs, 113–14, 120–21; multilateral exemplary behavior, 121–22; nationalism issues, 102; nonproliferation, 109–10, 113; and oil market, 119–20; one-party political system, 101; peacekeeping by, 108–9; political evolution, 119; projected GDP, 99; reaction of Wu Xinbo, 117–22; regional hotspots, 110–13, 120; regional security mechanisms, 110; self-image, 101; self-perception of role in world, 100–101; sensitiveness to slights/hostility, 102; and South Africa, 282–83; and Sudan, 112–13; and Taiwan, 112; territorial/sovereignty issues, 103–4; territorial unity and integrity, 101; and the United States, 41

China-Africa Development Fund, 107–8
China-ASEAN summit, 104
China National Offshore Oil Corporation (CNOOC), 120
China National Petroleum Company (CNPC), 334–35
Chow, Edward C., 337–43
Churkin, Vitaly, 178
CIA. See Central Intelligence Agency
Climate Action Partnership, 328

climate change: average industry scores, 328t; Bali conference on, 115, 126; and Brazil, 235, 238–40; challenges to the United States, 34–35; and India, 34, 35; and oil industry, 327–30, 339–40; and South Africa, 285
CNOOC. See China National Offshore Oil Corporation
Collective Security Treaty Organization (CSTO), 180
color revolutions, 209–10
Comprehensive Nuclear-Test-Ban Treaty (CTBT), 63, 130, 136
concert of powers approach, 42
ConocoPhilips, 328, 329, 334
Conventional Armed Forces in Europe Treaty, 179
Cooper, Robert, 76–77, 91–96
Council of Guardians, 302–3
CTBT. See Comprehensive Nuclear-Test-Ban Treaty)
CTR. See U.S.-Russian Cooperative Threat Reduction
Customs Union agreement, 214–15
Cyprus, 202, 204–5, 213

Darfur, 112–13
Davutoglu, Ahmet, 212
Deese, David, 340
deforestation, 7–8, 239, 254–55
Deng Xiaoping, 68, 162
Department of Energy (DOE), 27, 28
Dervis, Kemel, 200
Doha Round, 33, 145, 242, 254, 277, 284
"dollar diplomacy," 46–47
"Dutch disease," 346n32

earthquake diplomacy, 204
East Asian Summit, 110
East China Sea, 104
East Timor, 254
EITI. See Extractive Industry Transparency Initiative

Erdogan, Recep T., 200
EU-3, 311
EU-China summit, 103
EU Emissions Trading Scheme, 329–30
European Security and Defense Policy
  (ESDP), 213
European Union (EU), 73–96; Africa
  strategy, 88; birthrate, 81–82;
  and China, 94–95, 104; coal/steel
  community, 74; death penalty ban,
  80; demographics, 81–83; domestic
  challenges, 80; economic/social
  prosperity in, 83–86; external
  challenges, 86–90; external
  effectiveness of, 87–88; foreign
  policy, 86–87; and geopolitical
  competition, 94; identity issues, 84–
  86, 95–96; immigration issues, 82; as
  indispensable stakeholder, 90–91, 96;
  Islam effect on, 82–83; legitimacy of,
  85–86; marginalization of minorities
  in, 85; need for compromise,
  93–94; path to unification, 74–80;
  postmodern identity of, 76–77,
  78; reaction of Cooper, 91–96;
  regulatory/legal overreach by, 80;
  Russia as threat to, 89–90; security
  issues, 79; soft power of, 88–89;
  Turkey membership debate, 86, 197,
  200, 202, 209, 210–11, 218, 220; and
  the United States, 74, 77–78, 89,
  92, 93; as Wilsonian project, 89, 93;
  Wilson's European heirs, 93–94; and
  world of law, 75–78, 79–80, 90, 92
exceptionalism, American, 11–12
Expediency Council, 303
Extractive Industry Transparency
  Initiative (EITI), 333–36, 342
Exxon Mobil, 328, 331, 334, 339

failed/fragile states, and oil industry, 327
failing and weak states, and American
  leadership, 18–19

Forum on China-Africa Cooperation,
  107
free rider, China as, 107
Fukuda, Yasuo, 54, 57–58

G-7, 234
G-8, 190, 234, 254, 274, 276–77, 280
G-13, 234, 254
G-20, 234, 242–43, 249, 282, 286
Gandhi, Indira, 127, 149, 154
Gandhi, Mohandas, 126
Gaulle, Charles de, 226
Gazprom, 181, 182
geothermal power, 329
Getulio Vargas Foundation, 230
Gill, Bates, 118, 119–22
global fisheries, 65
Global Initiative to Combat Nuclear
  Terrorism (GI), 175
Gorbachev, Mikhail, 189
Greece, 204, 207, 213
Greek Orthodox community, in Turkey,
  202
greenhouse gases, 34–35, 65, 115, 126
Group of 77, 126
Group of Eight, 21, 144
Guantanamo Bay, 12, 15, 38
Gul, Abdullah, 201
Gulf Corporation Council, 308
Gvosdev, Nikolas, 38–42

Haiti, 109, 237, 254
Hamas, 310
HIV/AIDS: Brazil and, 234; in India,
  146; the United States and fight
  against, 35
Hu Jintao, 104, 116
human rights: and Brazil, 255; and
  China, 150; and India, 149–50, 151;
  and Iran, 304–5, 319; and Iraq, 12;
  and oil industry, 341; and Russia,
  185–86; and South Africa, 259, 264,
  271; and the United States, 15, 22–23

Human Rights Commission, 286
Human Rights Council (UN), 304–5
Human Rights Watch, 304

IAEA. *See* International Atomic Energy Agency
IBRD. *See* International Bank for Reconstruction and Development
ICRC. *See* International Committee of the Red Cross
IEA. *See* International Energy Agency
IMF. *See* International Monetary Fund
India, 125–64; agriculture in, 127, 148, 161; Bharatiya Janata Party in, 129–30, 140; and China, 104, 111, 139, 158; and climate change, 34, 35; and consensus-building, 144; domestic economic policy, 127; domestic industry, 144; economic growth of, 143–44, 145, 148; family planning need, 146; foreign policy, 152, 162; future of, difference from past, 152–53; future role of, 162–63; global economy role of, 160–62; as global growth engine, 143–47; global security role of, 138–43, 157–60; and global trade, 145, 161–62; green revolution in, 161; health sector, 146; Hindus in, 151; human rights in, 149–50, 151; and intellectual exchange, 151; internal security, 160; international nuclear order and, 128–38; and Iran, 136–38, 156–57; liberalism and realism, 153–55; literacy rates, 146; military expenditure, 139–40, 141t; and multiculturalism, 151; multinational companies in, 144; Muslims in, 140–41, 150, 157; nationalism in, 152–53; new nuclear order, 132–35; NGOs in, 150; Non-Aligned Movement, 127; noninterference principle in, 142; nuclear deal, separate, 131–32; and nuclear power, 24–25, 28; nuclear testing interest, 129–31; and nuclear weapons, 135–36, 155–57; outsourcing to, 143–44; and Pakistan, 138, 139, 155; peacekeeping by, 143, 158–60; peer-to-peer development, 147; Persian Gulf policy, 157; population of, 126; post-independence, 126–28; prosperity/poverty in, 147–49; protectionism in, 127–28; reaction of Mohan, 152–63; refusal to sign nonproliferation treaty, 129; religious minority protection in, 150; Sino-Indian clash, 138–39; terrorism and, 140–41; tourism in, 151; "two nations" problem, 162; unskilled work force in, 144–45; urbanization in, 161; U.S. relationship with, 139
India-Brazil-South Africa Dialogue Forum, 42
Intermediate-Range Nuclear Forces (INF) Treaty, 171–72
International Accounting Standards Board, 335
International Atomic Energy Agency (IAEA), 29, 133, 137, 138, 156, 286, 311
International Bank for Reconstruction and Development (IBRD), 286
International Committee of the Red Cross (ICRC), 150
International Convention for the Suppression of Acts of Nuclear Terrorism, 175
International Criminal Court, 39; U.S. need to participation in, 15–16; U.S. refusal to participate in, 12, 14
International Energy Agency (IEA), 325
International Monetary Fund (IMF), 42; and Brazil, 232; and China, 105; legitimacy crisis of, 183–84
international oil companies (IOCs), 337, 338–39, 340, 342

Iran, 295–320; anti-Israeli invective, 311–12; attitude toward international law, 298–99; barriers against responsible stakeholdership, 313; basic right protection, 304–5; censorship in, 304; and China, 113; civil-military relationship in, 303–4; defensive approach to international system, 297–98; diplomatic relations with the United States, 299; external challenges, 305–13; external threat/pressure response, 316–18; foreign policy, 296; human rights in, 304–5, 319; and India, 136–38, 156–57; internal challenges, 299–300, 300–305; internal pressures for reform, 315–16; legacy of past policies, 312–13; nonproliferation, 136–37, 310–11; nuclear power program, 24–25, 28–31, 44nn23–24, 318; parliament of, 301; peacekeeping by, 296; peace/stability benefits, 318–19; perverse effects of efforts to isolate, 314–15; pluralistic politics framework, 300–302; political evolution of, 302; and power balance in Persian Gulf, 307–8; presidency of, 301; radical Islam in, 315–16; reaction of Memarian, 313–19; regional influence of, 296–97, 298; relations with Iraq, 305–7; Revolutionary Guards, 303, 304; sharia law in, 303; strategic assumptions, 297–300; terrorism involvement, 308–10, 312, 318; and Turkey, 203, 207, 213; unelected institutions, 302–3

Iraq: human rights abuse by the United States in, 12; U.S. imposition of American-style democracy, 23; U.S. troop withdrawal, 23–24

Iraq war: Japan role in, 48, 59; preventative war doctrine, 12; Turkey role in, 206–7

Islam, 199, 200–202, 211, 219, 221

Israel: and Iran, 311–12; and nuclear weapons, 28

Israeli-Palestinian conflict, 16–17

Itamaraty, 233–34, 242, 255

Jaffe, Amy Myers, 325–26

Jahangir, Asma, 142

Japan, 45–72; arms sales, 64; collective self-defense, 55; demographic challenges, 51–52; diplomatic priorities, 53–58; dollar diplomacy approach of, 46–47; domestic impediments, 50–53; economic reform, 51; and environment, 65–66; foreign policy strategy, 54–55, 70; historical grievances resolution, 53–54; and humanitarian relief, 60–61; influence of America, 69–71; international leadership/foreign policy style, 46–48; and international security, 58–67; leading by example, 66–67; Miyazawa plan, 61; nationalism in, 47, 52–53, 66–67, 68; nature of leadership, 68–69; and nonproliferation, 63–64; "normal" nation proponents in, 48–49; Official Development Assistance levels, 56–57; peacekeeping by, 60; political reform, 50–51; postwar political culture, 46; reaction of Tamamoto, 67–72; regional prosperity, 61–62; regional security, 61; region in balance, 71–72; and rise of China, 57–58, 71; as soft power, 69; split Diet in, 50–51; trade with China, 104; UNSC status, 55–56; U.S.-Japan alliance, article 9 of, 48–49, 55, 56, 57, 58–60

Johannesburg Securities Exchange (JSE), 292

Justice and Development Party (AKP), 199–202, 214–15, 219

Kabila, Joseph, 273
Karasin, Grigory, 177
Kashmir, 139, 141, 150
Kato, Shuichi, 68
Kazemi, Zahra, 305
Kennan, George, 91
Khamenei (Ayatollah), 313, 315
Khatami, Mohammad, 301, 315, 316, 319
Khodorkovsky, Mikhail, 181
Kissinger, Henry, 26, 63
Koizumi, Junichiro, 47–48, 49, 57–58, 62
Krastev, Ivan, 89
Kurdish Democratic Society Party (DTP), 200
Kurdistan Workers' Party (PKK), 200, 201, 205–6, 207, 213, 214, 219, 220
Kyoto Protocol: Chinese refusal to sign, 66, 114; expiration of, 126; Japan and, 65, 66; U.S. refusal to sign, 12, 14, 34, 66, 329

Landau, Georges D., 251–56
Latin America, 95. See also Brazil
Lavrov, Sergey, 167, 178, 180
leadership, American, 11–44; climate change challenges, 34–35; credibility, crisis of, 12–13; credibility, restoring, 15; dealing with Iran, 28–31; development assistance by, 35–36; and exceptionalism, 11–12; and globalization/trade, 31–34; human rights, 15, 22–23; in institutions, 20–22; international law and norms, 19–20; and international order, 15–23; Middle East peace, 16–17; minimal nuclear deterrents, 27–28; need for multilateral approaches, 13–15; obsolete nuclear policies/weapons, 24–27; reaction of Gvosdev, 38–42; security in global order, 23–31; terrorism, 17–18; view of others on, 36–37; weak and failing states, 18–19
Lee Kuan Yew, 68
Leonard, Mark, 87
Leverett, Flynt, 38
Losyukov, Alexander, 177
Luers, William, 30
Lukoil (Russia), 334
Lula da Silva, Luis I., 231, 233, 236–37, 239–40, 245

Machel, Samora, 289
Majlis, 320n5
Mandela, Nelson, 259, 264, 271–72, 273, 289
Manuel, Trevor, 269–70
MAP (Action Plan for NATO Membership), 191
Marshall Plan, 91
Ma Ying-jeou, 112
Mbeki, Thabo, 261, 264, 265, 267–68, 269, 273–75, 278, 280, 281, 290, 291
McCain, John, 13
Medvedev, Dmitri, 178; financial reform under, 184; on sovereign democracy, 193n19; on trade-offs, 193–94n4
"The Medvedev Doctrine," 168
Memarian, Omid, 313–19
Mendelson, Sarah, 185
Mercosur, 242
military stability operations, 19
Millennium Challenge Account, 35–36, 229–30
MINUSTAH. See Stabilization Mission in Haiti
Mobil, 339
Mobutu, Sese S., 273
Mohamad, Mahathir, 68
Mohan, C. Raja, 152–63
Moscow Treaty on Strategic Offensive Reductions, 26
Motlanthe, Kgalema, 270

Movement for Democratic Change (MDC), 275–76
Mugabe, Robert, 261, 273, 276, 288
Mulva, J. J., 328

Nabucco pipeline project, 208
NAFTA. *See* North American Free Trade Agreement
Nakane, Chie, 54
NAM. *See* Non-Aligned Movement
narcotics trafficking, 235
National Intelligence Council, 226
National Intelligence Estimate (U.S.), 29
nationally owned oil companies (NOCs), 335, 336, 338
nation-rebuilding, 19
NATO. *See* North Atlantic Treaty Organization
NEAPSM. *See* Northeast Asia Peace and Security Mechanism
Nehru, Jawaharlal, 126–27, 152–53
neo-Ottomanism, 212, 218, 221
New Partnership for Africa's Development (NEPAD), 275, 276–79, 280
Nexen (Canada), 335
Nigeria, 272, 284–85, 330
NOCs. *See* nationally owned oil companies
Non-Aligned Movement (NAM), 127, 148–49, 274
nonproliferation, 25–26; and China, 109–10, 113; and India, 129, 131–32; and Japan, 63–64; and Russia, 173–75; and the United States, 128–28; and Soviet Union, 128–28
North American Free Trade Agreement (NAFTA), 32
North Atlantic Treaty Organization (NATO), 14, 91, 178, 179, 198, 206–7, 208, 209, 210, 212–13, 220–21
Northeast Asia Peace and Security Mechanism (NEAPSM), 106

North Korea: and Iran, 176–77; and Japan, 62; and nuclear power, 24–25; and Russia, 176–77
NPT. *See* Treaty on the Nonproliferation of Nuclear Weapons
Nuclear Nonproliferation Treaty (NPT), 25, 27, 63, 109–10, 171, 260, 285
nuclear weapon fuel production moratorium, 135
Nunn, Sam, 26

OAU. *See* Organization for African Unity
Obama, Barack: and arms control, 171
Ocalan, Abdullah, 200
oceanic ecosystem, 65
OECD. *See* Organization for Economic Cooperation and Development
OIC. *See* Organization of the Islamic Conference
oil industry, 321–47; BP, 328–29, 334, 335, 337, 338, 339–40; Chevron, 331, 339; Chevron-Texaco, 328, 329, 334; China National Petroleum Company (CNPC), 334–35; and climate change, 327–30, 339–40; ConocoPhilips, 328, 329, 334; energy-security link, 324–27; and energy supply diversification, 338–39; Extractive Industry Transparency Initiative (EITI), 333–36, 342; Exxon Mobil, 328, 331, 334, 339; failed/fragile states and, 327; firms as stakeholders, 322–24; and human rights, 330–32, 341; and international oil companies, 337, 338–39, 340, 342; Lukoil (Russia), 334; Mobil, 339; nationally owned oil companies, 335, 336, 338; need for change, 336–37, 342–43; Nexen (Canada), 335; and NGOs, 323; and OPEC, 322; Petrobras

(Brazil), 256, 335; Petro Canada, 335; Petro China, 334; Petronas (Malaysia), 335; proactive disclosers, 335; reaction of Chow, 337–43; and resource curse, 332, 341–42; shareholder value/responsibility, 338; Shell, 328, 330, 334, 337, 339–40; Shell Netherlands, 335; state-owned companies, 321–22; Statoil (Norway), 335, 339–40; Talisman (Canada), 334, 335; Total (France), 334; TransAtlantic (Canada), 334; transparency/accountability, 332–33; Unocal, 331; U.S. petroleum imports, 326t–27

"One China" policy, 101
Operation Active Endeavor, 208
Organization for African Unity (OAU), 260, 272, 274
Organization for Economic Cooperation and Development (OECD), 111, 231, 254, 283
Organization for Security and Cooperation in Europe (OSCE), 186
Organization of the Islamic Conference (OIC), 199, 211, 215
OSCE. See Organization for Security and Cooperation in Europe
Özal, Turgut, 199, 218–19

Pachauri, Rajendra, 147
Pakistan: and India, 138, 139, 155; and nuclear power, 25, 28; peacekeeping by, 159
Patriota, Antonio de Aguiar, 40
peacekeeping: Brazil, 235, 240–41; China, 108–9; India, 143, 158–60; Iran, 296; Japan, 60; Pakistan, 159; South Africa, 283
People's Liberation Army (PLA), 121
Perry, William, 26
Petrobras (Brazil), 256, 335
Petro Canada, 335
Petro China, 334

Petronas (Malaysia), 335
Pew Global Attitudes survey, 12
Pickering, Thomas, 30
PKK. See Kurdistan Workers' Party
PKO (UN Peacekeeping Operations), 60, 158, 159
PLA. See People's Liberation Army
Polaski, Sandra, 145
President's Emergency Plan for AIDS Relief (PEPFAR), 278
preventative war doctrine, 12
Proliferation Security Initiative (PSI), 63, 70, 173
protectionism, 118, 127–28
Public-Private Partnerships (PPP), 255–56
Putin, Vladimir, 166, 170, 171, 177–78, 185, 186

Rabin, Yitzhak, 311
Rafsanjani, Akbar H., 306, 312
reformers, division between Western states/conservatives, 43n17, 44n18
"responsible stakeholder," coining of, 1
responsible stakeholder, defining, 50
Rice, Condoleezza, 181, 226
Rome Statute, 12
Roosevelt, Franklin D., 42
Ruggie, John, 332
rule-based international system: Beijing model, 39, 40; Brussels model, 39, 40
Russia, 165–94; arms sales, 169; and democracy, 184–85, 184–86; demographic issues, 190; economic goals, 169; economic recovery of, 165–67; energy security, 180–83; foreign policy, 167–69, 189; future of, 186–88; and Georgia, 167, 173, 174, 177, 178–80; global economic stewardship, 183–84; and human rights, 185–86; and Iran, 176–77, 191, 192; and Kosovo, 177–78; limitations of, 192; military spending, 169; missile defense,

172–73, 191; and North Korea, 176–77; nuclear arms reduction, 26, 27–28; nuclear technology/ nonproliferation, 173–75; oil production, 181; as oligarchy, 190; per capita income, 169; reaction of Trenin, 188–92; regional security issues, 177–80; resurgent Russia asserts itself, 167–69; strategic arms control, 170–72, 191–92; as threat to the European Union, 89–90; and Turkey, 198, 208–10; turnaround of, 165–70; and Ukrainian gas dispute, 181–82; and the United States, 188–89; and U.S. view on Ukraine, 191; and Yukos affair, 181, 182. *See also* Soviet Union

Saakashvili, Mikheil, 178
Sachar Report, 140
SADC (Southern Africa Development Community), 260, 272, 273, 274, 280–81
Sarney, Jose, 236
SARS. *See* Severe Acute Respiratory Syndrome
Schiffer, Michael, 118, 119–22
SCO. *See* Shanghai Cooperation Organization
Severe Acute Respiratory Syndrome (SARS), 107
Shanghai Cooperation Organization (SCO), 42, 110, 179–80, 209, 220
Sharma, Anand, 148–49
Shell, 328, 330, 334, 337, 339–40
Shell Netherlands, 335
Shubane, Khehla, 288–92
Shukla, Jagadish, 147
Shultz, George, 26
Silva, Marina, 239
Singh, Manmohan, 126, 128, 135, 149, 154
Six-Party Talks, 62
Soligo, Ronald, 325

SORT. *See* Strategic Offensive Reductions Treaty
South Africa, 259–93; African Union, role in, 283–84; ANC in, 259–60, 266–67, 289, 290; ANC leadership transition in, 269–71; and Angola, 280–81; anti-Americanism in, 278; arms sales, 271; and Burma, 274; climate change, 285; crime in, 267; and Democratic Republic of Congo, 280, 291; economic challenges, 266–69; economic growth, 265; economic policy, 259–60, 265–66; election, U.S. response, 281–82; election 2009, 280–81; foreign investment in, 265, 282–83; foreign policy, 271–72; foreign policy, domestic roots of, 288–90; foreign policy, pillars of, 279; foreign policy, redefining, 273–76; foreign policy, setbacks in, 272–73; future of, 280–82; global and regional roles, 290–91; HIV/AIDS in, 261, 267–68, 274–75, 283, 284; human rights and, 259, 264, 271; identity crisis in, 262–64; immigrants in, 267, 269; internal strengths, 264–66; and international organizations, 286; judicial system, 264–65; leadership role in Africa, 282–84; medical facilities, 265; military intervention in Lesotho, 273; and NEPAD, 275, 276–79, 280; and Nigeria, 272, 284–85; north-south divide, bridging, 286–87; nuclear proliferation, 285–86; peacekeeping by, 283; power shortages in, 268, 286; private sector, 282–83; reaction of Shubane, 288–92; relationship with West, 291–92; as rogue democracy, 261, 263; social class issues, 267; social services, 265; sovereign rights, 278–79; trade policy, 277, 284–85; and the United Nations, 286, 290–91;

unemployment in, 267, 268–69; and
the United States, 260, 278, 284;
and Zaire, 273; and Zimbabwe, 261,
276, 278, 283, 290
South American Regional Integration
Initiative (IIRSA), 236
South Korea, trade with China, 104
sovereign democracy, 185, 193n19
Soviet Union (U.S.S.R.): military
spending, 169; nonproliferation and,
128–28
Stabilization Mission in Haiti
(MINUSTAH), 237
state-owned companies (NOCs),
321–22
Statoil (Norway), 335, 339–40
Strategic Arms Reduction Treaty
(START), 26, 170, 192
Strategic Framework Declaration,
Russian-American, 171, 173, 175
Strategic Offensive Reductions Treaty
(SORT), 170–71
Strauss-Kahn, Dominique, 183, 184
Sudan, and China, 112–13
Sullivan Principles, 341
Surkov, Vladislav, 194n19
Suslov, Mikhail, 194n19
Syria, 205–6, 212, 213

TAFTA. See trans-Atlantic free trade
agreement
Taiwan, 103–4, 109
Talisman (Canada), 334, 335
Tamamoto, Masaru, 67–72
technology: Japan as leader in, 65;
terrorist use of, 77
terrorism: and India, 140–41; and Iran,
308–10, 312, 318; and Turkey,
213–14, 219, 220; and the United
States, 17–18
Tibet, 111
Tokyo International Conference on
African Development (TICAD), 57
torture, 12

Tosovsky, Josef, 183, 184
Total (France), 334
TransAtlantic (Canada), 334
trans-Atlantic free trade agreement
(TAFTA), 215
Transparency International, 247
Treaty on the Nonproliferation of
Nuclear Weapons (NPT), 128–29,
130, 134, 136
Trenin, Dmitri, 188–92
tuberculosis, in China, 107
Turkey, 197–223; and African Union,
215; and Armenia, 205, 208; and
Azerbaijan, 208; and Brazil, 215; and
Cyprus, 202, 204–5, 213; domestic
reforms in, 218–19; economic
growth in, 215–16; economic
recovery in, 199–200; economic
reforms in, 218–19; energy security,
207–10; EU candidacy, 86, 197, 200,
202, 209, 210–11, 218, 220; foreign
policy, 198–99, 218, 219–21; future
of, 216–17; gas pipeline project,
206–7, 215; geostrategy of, 202–17;
and globalization, 214–16; as global
player, 221–22; and Greece, 204,
207, 213; and Greek Orthodox
community, 202; and India, 215; and
Iran, 203, 207, 213; and Iraq war,
206–7; and Islam, 199, 200–202,
211, 219, 221; and Israel, 212, 213;
Justice and Development Party in,
199–202, 203; Kurdish separation
and, 199, 200, 205, 206, 214;
nationalism in, 198, 202, 204–5,
209, 211; and NATO, 198, 206–7,
208, 209, 210, 212–13, 220–21;
neo-Ottomanism, 212, 218, 221;
and Palestine, 203; pressures for
change, 199–202; reaction of Bağci,
217–22; and Russia, 198, 208–10,
220; soft power of, 221; sovereignty-
consciousness in, 198; strategic
location of, 218; and Syria, 205–6,

212, 213; terrorism and, 213–14, 219, 220; threat assessment, 212–14; and the United States, 211

Tutu, Desmond, 259, 261

Ukraine: gas dispute with Russia, 181–82; NATO membership and, 191

UN Convention on the Elimination of All Forms of Discrimination Against Women, 20

UN Human Rights Commission, 16, 271

UN Human Rights Council, 15, 16, 332

Union of South American Nations (UNASUR), 237

United Nations (UN): ban on child soldiers, 20; Congress refusal to fund U.S. dues, 20; counterterrorism activities, 18; Human Rights Council, 304–5; and South Africa, 286, 290–91; and U.S. opposition to curbing small arms, 12

United Nations Peacekeeping Operations (UNPKO), 60, 158

United States (U.S.): and China, 41, 104; and the European Union, 74, 77–78, 89, 92, 93; and India, 139; and Iran, 299; migration to, 33–34; nonproliferation and, 128–28; oil companies and climate change, 339–40; opposition to curbing small arms, 12; and Pakistan, 18; and South Africa, 260, 278, 284; and Turkey, 211

Universal Declaration of Human Rights, 331–32, 341

Unocal, 331

UN Peacebuilding Commission, 19

UN Preventative Deployment Force (UNPREDEF), 109

UN Security Council (UNSC): and China, 106; and India, 111, 136; and Iran, 310–11; and Japan, 55–56; reform of, 20–21; and South Africa, 263; and Turkey, 199

UN Security Council Resolution 1540, 133

UN Special Representative on Business and Human Rights, 331

UN Stabilization Mission in Haiti (MINUSTAH), 109

UN Standby Arrangements System, 108

Uruguay Round, 33

U.S.-Indian security ties, 120

U.S.-Japan alliance, 48–49, 55, 56, 57, 58–60, 120

U.S.-Russia Agreement for Peaceful Nuclear Cooperation, 173–74

U.S.-Russian Cooperative Threat Reduction (CTR), 175

U.S.S.R. See Russia; Soviet Union

values diplomacy, of Japan, 54–55

Vazquez, Carlos M., 323

Voluntary Principles on Security and Human Rights, 331

Walsh, Jim, 30

Washington Consensus, 118, 149

weak and failing states, and the United States, 18–19

weapons of mass destruction (WMD), 172

Wiwa, Ken S., 330

The World Bank, 42, 148

World Economic Forum, 147

World Food Programme, 36

WorldPublicOpinion.org, 12–13

World Trade Organization (WTO), 234

Wu Xinbo, 117–22

Yilmaz, Mesut, 200

Yukos affair, 181, 182

Zaire, 273

ZANU government, 276

Zimbabwe, 261, 276, 278, 283, 290

Zoellick, Robert, 100, 184

Zuma, Jacob, 269, 270, 277–78, 280–81

~

# About the Contributors

**Susan Ariel Aaronson** is associate research professor at the George Washington University Graduate School of Business and the Elliott School of International Affairs. She is also affiliated with the Institute for International Economic Policy at GWU. She is the author of six books and numerous articles on trade, investment, human rights, global corporate social responsibility, and other globalization issues. Her most recent book is *Trade Imbalance: The Struggle to Weigh Human Rights in Trade Policymaking* (2007).

**Paulo Roberto de Almeida** holds a Ph.D. in social sciences and an M.A. in international economy. He has been a career diplomat since 1977. In addition to his professional duties, he has engaged in academic activities in Brazil and abroad, dealing with Brazil's economic history and international economic relations. He is currently professor of international political economy at UniCEUB-Brasilia and associate professor at Instituto Rio Branco, the Brazilian diplomatic academy.

**Ronald D. Asmus** is executive director of the Brussels-based Transatlantic Center and responsible for strategic planning at the German Marshall Fund of the United States. He served as deputy assistant secretary of state for European affairs from 1997–2000 and has been a senior analyst and fellow at Radio Free Europe, RAND, and the Council on Foreign Relations. He has published widely and is the author of *Opening NATO's Door*.

**Hüseyin Bağci** is professor of international relations at Middle East Technical Universtiy in Ankara. He was previously a guest researcher at the German Society for Foreign Affairs and senior fellow at the Center for European Integration Studies in Bonn. He has published several books and a large number of articles on Turkish Foreign Policy and Turkish-German relations. Bagci was a visiting professor at Bonn University, at La Sapienza University in Rome in 2007, and Lublin University (Poland) in 2008.

**Pauline H. Baker** is president of the Fund for Peace, a leading educational and research organization, with innovative programs such as "The Failed States Index," a global ranking of conflict risk that is published annually in *Foreign Policy* magazine. She was previously a professional staff member of the Senate Foreign Relations Committee (serving as staff director of the Africa Subcommittee), deputy director of the Aspen Institute's Congressional Program, research scientist at the Battelle Memorial Institute, and senior associate at the Carnegie Endowment for International Peace. Dr. Baker is also adjunct professor at Georgetown University's School of Foreign Service.

**Zeyno Baran** is director of the Center for Eurasian Policy (CEP) and senior fellow with Hudson Institute's Center on Islam, Democracy, and the Future of the Muslim World. Baran previously directed the International Security and Energy Program at the Nixon Center, and before that, the Georgia Forum and the Caucasus Project at the Center for Strategic and International Studies (CSIS). She has published numerous studies, articles, and book chapters on issues ranging from European and Eurasian energy security and stability to Muslim integration in the West.

**Edward C. Chow** is senior fellow at the Center for Strategic and International Studies in Washington, DC. An international energy expert with thirty years of industry experience around the world, he specializes in oil and gas activities in emerging economies. He has developed government policy and business strategy, and successfully negotiated complex, multibillion dollar investment ventures. He previously spent twenty years with Chevron Corporation in U.S. and overseas assignments.

**Steven Clemons** directs the American Strategy Program at the New America Foundation, where he is also a senior fellow and previously served as executive vice president. Publisher of the popular political blog *The Washington Note*, Clemons is a long-term policy practitioner and entrepreneur in Washington, DC. He has served as executive vice president of the Economic

Strategy Institute, senior policy advisor on economic and international affairs to Senator Jeff Bingaman (D-NM) and was the first executive director of the Nixon Center.

**Robert Cooper** has since 2002 been director-general for external and politico-military affairs at the General Secretariat of the Council of the European Union, where he has aided in the development and implementation of European security and defense policy. He previously served as special adviser on foreign affairs to British Prime Minister Tony Blair. He is author of *The Breaking of Nations* (2004). The views expressed in his comment are purely personal.

**Barbara Crossette** is the UN correspondent of *The Nation*. She previously served as *The New York Times* chief correspondent in Southeast Asia and South Asia in 1984–1991 and later as a diplomatic reporter in Washington and UN bureau chief. She is the author of *So Close to Heaven: The Vanishing Buddhist Kingdoms of the Himalayas* and *The Great Hill Stations of Asia*. She won a George Polk award for her coverage of the assassination in 1991 of Rajiv Gandhi.

**David Deese**, professor in the Department of Political Science at Boston College, researches the politics and institutions of international economic relations, particularly international trade, energy and security, world oil markets, and U.S. foreign economic policy. He is the author of *World Trade Politics: Power, Principles, and Leadership* (2008) and editor of the series *The Library of Essays in International Relations* for Ashgate Publishing. He is currently writing on international political leadership theory.

**Miguel Diaz** has followed Latin American affairs in numerous capacities, including as the director of the South America Project at Center for Strategic International Studies (CSIS), as the senior Latin America economist for Nikko Securities, and as a CIA analyst. He has an M.A. in international affairs from the Johns Hopkins University School of Advanced International Studies. Diaz is married to a foreign service officer and currently resides in Tokyo.

**Bates Gill** is director of the Stockholm International Peace Research Institute (SIPRI). Prior to joining SIPRI, he held the Freeman Chair in China Studies at the Center for Strategic and International Studies and previously held positions at the Brookings Institution and the Center for Nonproliferation Studies of the Monterey Institute of International Studies. His most recent book is *Rising Star: China's New Security Diplomacy*.

**Nikolas Gvosdev** was editor of *The National Interest* and a senior fellow in strategic studies at the Nixon Center prior to joining the faculty of the Naval War College as a professor of national security studies. He is the author or editor of six books and coauthor of *The Receding Shadow of the Prophet: The Rise and Fall of Radical Political Islam.*

**Weston S. Konishi** is adjunct fellow at the Maureen and Mike Mansfield Foundation and recently completed the Council on Foreign Relations/Hitachi International Affairs Fellowship in Japan. As an IAFJ, he conducted research on Japanese diplomacy at the Institute for International Policy Studies and the National Institute for Defense Studies. From 2004 to 2007, Konishi was director of programs at the Mansfield Foundation. He has been a contributing columnist for *The Daily Yomiuri* and has taught U.S.-Japan relations at the George Washington University.

**Andrew Kuchins** is a senior fellow and director of the Center for Strategic and International Studies Russia and Eurasia Program. From 2000 to 2006, he was a senior associate at the Carnegie Endowment for International Peace, and for a while was director of its Moscow Center. He is codirector of the Russia Balance Sheet Project, a collaboration among the CSIS, the Peterson Institute for International Economics, and the U.S.-Russia Business Council; it will lead to a book in early 2009 of the same name coauthored by Kuchins with fellow project codirector Anders Aslund.

**Georges D. Landau** is a Brazilian lawyer and administrator who has been an adviser to several cabinet ministers, including the minister for external relations. He spent twenty-seven years as an international civil servant with the Organization of American States and Inter-American Development Bank, and more recently as a consultant with the World Bank and the United Nations. Landau returned to Brazil in 1992 as president of Hill & Knowlton Brazil and, in 1994, started his own firm, Prismax Consulting, specializing in government relations for foreign companies operating in Brazil.

**Ian O. Lesser** is senior transatlantic fellow at the German Marshall Fund of the United States in Washington, where he focuses on Mediterranean affairs and international security issues. Dr. Lesser has been vice president and director of studies at the Pacific Council on International Policy, and a senior analyst and research manager at the RAND Corporation. From 1994–1995, he was a member of the State Department's Policy Planning Staff.

**Tod Lindberg** is a research fellow at the Hoover Institution, Stanford University, and editor of *Policy Review*. He is the author of *The Political Teachings of Jesus*, a philosophical analysis of Jesus' teaching about worldly affairs. He is the editor of *Beyond Paradise and Power: Europe, America and the Future of a Troubled Partnership* and coeditor of a recent Stanley Foundation book, *Bridging the Foreign Policy Divide* (2007). He is a contributing editor to *The Weekly Standard*.

**Princeton N. Lyman** is adjunct senior fellow at the Council on Foreign Relations. He is also adjunct professor at Georgetown University and professorial lecturer at the Johns Hopkins School of Advanced International Studies. Lyman's career in government included assignments as deputy assistant secretary of state for Africa, ambassador to Nigeria, director of refugee programs, ambassador to South Africa, and assistant secretary of state for International Organization Affairs. He has published works on foreign policy, African affairs, economic development, HIV/AIDS, UN reform, and peacekeeping.

**Suzanne Maloney** is a senior fellow at the Saban Center for Middle East Policy at the Brookings Institution. Previously, she served on the State Department's Policy Planning Staff and as Middle East advisor for Exxon Mobil Corporation. Dr. Maloney directed the 2004 Council on Foreign Relations Task Force on U.S. Policy toward Iran and is the author of *Iran's Long Reach: Iran as a Pivotal State in the Muslim World* (2008).

**Omid Memarian** is a journalist and blogger known for his news analysis, regular columns, and blog. He was chief researcher for Reese Erlich's book titled *Iran Agenda: The Real Story of U.S. Policy and The Middle East Crisis*. Memarian is currently a World Peace Fellow at the UC Berkeley Graduate School of Journalism. In 2005, he received the Human Rights Defender Award, Human Rights Watch's highest honor.

**C. Raja Mohan** is professor of South Asian studies at the S. Rajaratnam School of International Studies, Nanyang Technical University, Singapore. He writes a column for the *Indian Express*, where he previously was strategic affairs editor, and served on India's National Security Advisory Board in 1998–2000.

**Suzanne Nossel** is a scholar affiliated with the Center for American Progress. From 1999 to 2001 she served in the U.S. Mission to the United Nations under Ambassador Richard Holbrooke and led negotiations to settle the United States' arrears to the world body. After her government service, Nossel was a vice president at the media companies Bertelsmann Media Worldwide and Dow Jones and is currently a senior executive at a large international organization.

**George Perkovich** is vice president for studies and director of the nonproliferation program at the Carnegie Endowment for International Peace. He is the author of *India's Nuclear Bomb*, which received the Herbert Feis Award from the American Historical Association and the A. K. Coomaraswamy Prize from the Association for Asian Studies. He is coauthor of the September 2008 *Adelphi Paper*, "Abolishing Nuclear Weapons."

**Michael Schiffer** is a program officer at the Stanley Foundation, responsible particularly for programs on Asia. He is also a Center for Asia and Pacific Studies Fellow at the University of Iowa. Before joining the foundation, he was a Council on Foreign Relations International Affairs Fellow at the National Institute of Defense Studies in Japan. From 1995 to 2004, Schiffer worked for U.S. Senator Dianne Feinstein (D-CA) as her senior national security adviser and legislative director.

**David Shorr** is a program officer at the Stanley Foundation, currently focused on the U.S. role in the world. A recent project resulted in a coedited volume of bipartisan essays, *Bridging the Foreign Policy Divide* (2007). Shorr spent many years in Washington, DC, with foreign policy advocacy groups including Human Rights First, Refugees International, Search for Common Ground, British American Security Information Council, and Arms Control Association.

**Khehla Shubane** worked as a researcher for the Centre for Policy Studies for ten years. He then helped Nelson Mandela establish the Nelson Mandela Foundation as an institutional base from which the former president of South Africa could continue his work. Shubane's most recent position was with the BusinessMap Foundation, a small research and monitoring organization dedicated to black economic empowerment and tracking foreign direct investment. Shubane currently works as a development consultant with a focus on low-income housing and local government issues.

**Ray Takeyh** is a senior fellow for Middle Eastern studies at the Council on Foreign Relations. His areas of specialization are Iran, the Persian Gulf, and U.S. foreign policy. He is also a contributing editor of the *National Interest*.

Dr. Takeyh has published several books on the Middle East and is currently working on the forthcoming *The Guardians of the Revolution: Iran's Approach to the World.*

**Masaru Tamamoto** is a senior fellow of the World Policy Institute, New York, and adjunct lecturer at Meiji Gakuin University. He resides in Yokohama, Japan. He is a graduate of Brown University and has been a visiting scholar at Cambridge University.

**Dmitri Trenin** is senior associate of the Carnegie Endowment for International Peace and deputy director of its Moscow Center. From 1972 to 1993, he served in the Soviet and Russian Armed Forces. His recent books include *Getting Russia Right* (2007), *Russia's Restless Frontier: The Chechnya Factor in Post-Soviet Russia* (2004), and *The End of Eurasia: Russia on the Border Between Geopolitics and Globalization* (2002). In 2005, he edited, with Steven Miller, *The Russian Military: Power and Policy.*

**Richard Weitz** is senior fellow and director of the Center for Political-Military Analysis at Hudson Institute. He also serves as head of the Case Studies Working Group of the Project on National Security Reform. His recent books and monographs include *China-Russia Security Relations: Strategic Parallelism Without Partnership or Passion* (2008), *Kazakhstan and the New International Politics of Eurasia* (2008), *Mismanaging Mayhem: How Washington Responds to Crisis* (2008), *The Reserve Policies of Nations: A Comparative Analysis* (2007), and *Revitalising US-Russian Security Cooperation: Practical Measures* (2005).

**Wu Xinbo** is professor and deputy director at the Center for American Studies and associate dean at the School of International Relations and Public Affairs, Fudan University. Dr. Wu has written two books: *Dollar Diplomacy and Major Powers in China, 1909–1913* and *Turbulent Water: US Asia-Pacific Security Strategy in the Post–Cold War Era.* He serves on the editorial board of *The Washington Quarterly* and the International Board of the East-West Center's *Studies in Asian Security* book series.